ICEBERG

Exposing Psychopathic Behavior
and Restoring Our Humanity

JON MYERS

Copyright © 2019 Jon Myers.

All rights reserved. No part of this book may be reproduced, stored, or transmitted by any means—whether auditory, graphic, mechanical, or electronic—without written permission of both publisher and author, except in the case of brief excerpts used in critical articles and reviews. Unauthorized reproduction of any part of this work is illegal and is punishable by law.

CONTENTS

Forward ix

Chapter 1	Why me, why not?	1
Chapter 2	Two Tracks; Headed for an Iceberg Collision: All that glitters is not gold.	13
Chapter 3	The Iceberg begins to emerge	23
Chapter 4	The roots of hatred	29
Chapter 5	The nature of personality disorders	37
Chapter 6	The courts of America	44
Chapter 7	The characteristics of the Deviant Personality Type	50
Chapter 8	Reclaiming our Integrity	59
Chapter 9	The Science of Inner Strength (part II)	71
Chapter 10	Establishing Societal Parameters around goodness and decency	79
Chapter 11	The adversity I encountered and how it formed me, if not forged me	86
Chapter 12	How you begin to find your true inner strength	95
Chapter 13	The impediment: The Iceberg	107
Chapter 14	Equal and opposite reactions, and goodness itself	127
Chapter 15	Forgiveness	142

Chapter 16	Forgiveness Part II 157
Chapter 17	Letting Go and allowing our inner goodness to arise..165
Chapter 18	Defining The World's Best Mediator 176
Chapter 19	The impact of my story 188
Chapter 20	The Core of Oneself......................................199
Chapter 21	My story and the rest of the world 221
Chapter 22	Our Precious Planet......................................232
Chapter 23	The way forward, how to become a Champion these days....................................238
Chapter 24	How emotional abuse relates to everything else.. 246
Chapter 25	The keys to finding your inner strength in this world...................................258
Chapter 26	What is really going here? 276
Chapter 27	Compassionate Genius: My Gift to the world 310

Prescriptions for Greatness...354
Melting The Iceberg..390
April 21, 2018: From caterpillar to Butterfly:
Lessons for the world 507
The American challenge : Why my story will change the world for the better 512
The germ of narcissism and psychopathic behavior 519
October 30, 2018: Reclaiming our humanity.....................521
Epilogue (Part 2)...523
The new psychology..529
Jon Myers ten lessons of this journey 538

Statement of Intent:
"There are two thing you never want to see being made: Laws and sausage."

A couple of things dawn on me, in the enormous undertaking of putting together this work. One is, that is not, nor will it ever be perfect. There will be typos and the like. For the loving perfectionists that exist, this may not be the work for you. I understand and respect that. This is a work of spirit; for those who are concerned with their own spiritual growth and/or the positive development of our planet.

Second, I will reiterate, this entire work is a process and for that matter, will continue to be. I am in entirely different place, than I was in 1996, when this really broke out; and even from 2015, when I began writing again. At least in part, what you are seeing, is the making of sausage or truth, or a philosophy, with a sense of the inside view, which again is not for everyone. Over the last four years, last year, even last day, lol; my work and how I present things grows and changes.

What began on some part as a way of calling some folks, which is not irrelevant, has shifted over the years to more about teaching, perhaps even in the wildest sense healing. If my mindset could spiritually shift so substantially, then others can as well. I have taken it as some sense of a calling to bring this message out to society. In the final analysis I do so with love and respect, and today would only make the statements I do, in a mainly gentle sense. Although perhaps, this is a hidden third point; that those who have saw my inherent kindness as a weakness, are ultimately mistaken. Thank you.

Prayer for peace, with love:

There is no question that I ended up in a different place when I ended this book, then when I began it, which in some ways is the biggest story of all. Challenge provides us with the opportunity to grow and change immeasurably as a person. Because, I was faced with such monumental challenge, if not adversity for over twenty-three years, gave me the opportunity to grow and change so much.

In that spirit it is with a sense of love that I conclude this Memoir for now. There is not a person that I mention in here, that I do not PRAY for and desire the best. The extreme narcissistic, even psychopathic way of thought that in some ways has gripped our country/world must be challenged and can be overcome with our humanity. None of us is truly "privileged" to use a word of the time, to be able to sit back. The world is at too challenged a place.

We must assert our goodness, our care, our determination. The agenda that grew out of my life and work is to steer us away from condescension and hatred, and towards decency and our humanity. It is a shift in mindset that I seek to invoke. Like a doctor, I say: "This will not hurt much." We can do it. Our goodness, our cooperation, our care is our strength, and by applying those qualities we will be more economically successful and better able to overcome challenges.

I PRAY for the best for ALL; and even thank those who challenged me so greatly. It is my fervent desire that if, possible you take the lessons contained in my memoir and if possible, apply them to your lives. I came through unfathomable adversity and challenge. In that regard, it seems my sacred responsibility to share with others. I do not wish anyone to go through the challenges that I did; better to learn from them. I write with love, Jon

FORWARD

MAY 22, 2019

I consider this to be a once in a millennium story, given the intensity of the spiritual and emotional assault that was launched on me. On the other hand; that assault is what gave me the opportunity to grow my inner strength. So, I am thankful for everything.

I need to make clear this memoir was written over a four-year period. Over the course of those four years, my life grew and changed greatly, as it has for the past twenty-three years. So, while in the beginning (gee that *is* a tad Biblical, is it not 😊) there is a tad more of a rant to my presentation; over time, qualities such as forgiveness, and perhaps ultimately education grew within me.

I choose to interpret this situation that I was given this unfathomably intense spiritual situation over the course of thirty years in some ways, to strengthen myself immeasurably, and to develop a message to teach the world. That message among other things, takes the form of the Science of Inner Strength. What you see, in my presentation is the inside, (like Jonah and the Whale) of a person put inside this horrific emotionally abusive situation from my own family, American divorce law, and more.

Unlike other presentations of self-help and the like, I am not telling you what to do. I am showing you what I did. All of those expressions, like "everything happens for a reason;" and "challenge is opportunity" are credos that I lived by; sometimes in the starkest of emotional and financial situations. All along, my love for Sophie and Sam, my children; my life, and the world in general propelled me forward, and would not let me quit.

To those, who I may have offended in this true tale. Well for those who truly abused me, take it as justice and a learning lesson. To one or two more minor characters; well I tempered things greatly, and the truth is the truth. If I have my dream world, it will be about healing anyway. If not, these are appropriate stands I have chosen to take.

All of which has come under the umbrella of helping and restoring humanity and decency in our world. I thank you for reading this. I thank the world for the opportunity.

It never in my wildest dreams dawned on me that I would discover the world of psychopathic behavior. I was talented, as a kid growing up in Scranton, PA, athletically and academically, but nothing in that small city environment, beginning in 1958 could have prepared me for understanding the world of the psychopath. Like Jonah, who survived, in the whale; to learn great lessons, I am convinced that this entire experience was meant to happen; and the understandings, I was to develop were meant to be shared with the world at large.

My professional life since 1980, has predominantly

been about helping others, in the Greater Boston area, from running a residential program for emotionally disturbed youth, to developing a nationally recognized youth program; to directing housing programs in three cities for low and moderate income residents; to serving as a Cambridge City Councillor, to developing and directing a non-profit to serve urban youth; to finally, in 2002 forming Calm Interventions Inc., what I describe as my third child, with an aim to spread mediation around the world.

What I have discovered is that there is essentially an underworld to American, if not world life. There is a world that many of us, of baby boomer, and post baby boomer generation were raised in. In that world, our parents were relatively heroic, everything would be provided and taken care of; that was their implicit promise to us. The generation that Tom Brokaw called "The greatest generation" surely would deliver on all they promised.

This is not merely a generational thesis; that those of my generation were betrayed by our parents generation; instead, the thesis has to do with exposing a realm of American life that is predicated on corruption and deceit; and in all likelihood is at the root cause for so many of the challenges in the world today. The discoveries I have made beg for authenticity and the renewal of true American values that have become sadly tarnished; those of liberty and democracy, and truly equality.

I have developed a science; something that I call The Science of Inner Strength, and one of its fundamental tenets is that most people are good. Yet, the messages and caliber of our discourse of today does not overly resonate with goodness. Further the sense that if good people sit back, and do nothing, then it will not take much for negative, and even evil influences to take a much greater hold on our potentially fragile planet.[1]

Crucial to understand; is that at this very moment there is a great tension in the struggle between forward truly progressive movement, and backward repressive thinking. New ideas, in the realm of spiritual understanding, an openness of thought, acceptance of others have doggedly plunged forward; and yet at the same time, not only do we face obvious threats such as terrorism, but there is a part of our basic societal spirit that is punctured by corruption, and a lack of adhering to our principles and ideals.

It is seems quite plausible that certain things will be exposed in what follows. Yet, at the same time, it must remain abundantly clear that my intention is solely for improvement, for human progress. All but the vilest, must be afforded forgiveness and understanding, with at times appropriate penalties. Those who must suffer our true disgust and most severe sanctions are those who would deceive, as well as profoundly harm others.

A central thesis presented here is that it is not only foreign threats, with masks and advanced weaponry, who are our threats. There is a corruption in our midst as well, that emanates from psychological disjuncture. That psychological disjuncture is not well understood at this point in society. Indeed, that disjuncture takes the form of an iceberg, where we can see 10% of the real problem, and

---

[1] It is worth noting that the actual age of Planet Earth is estimated at well over 5 billion years; yes billion, but as for humans that is a whole other story.

the other 90 percent, that really threatening part resides below the surface.

The psychological disjuncture that jars our understanding of our world, and is wildly contrary to the world in which we grew up is the world of the psychopath, and other Cluster B type Personality Disorders. It is the world of the psychopath that so dramatically jars our understanding of reality, and distorts the promise that many perceive America to have and most of us deserve.. Without a proper understanding of this personality type, we are threatened, if not destined to not just spin our wheels on endlessly, but suffer far more damage and harm in our daily lives.

It is my sense that what I will describe as psychopaths, are everywhere; often disguised in positions of prominence and power. The psychopath I am describing is not our familiar reference of a serial killer type of personality; the psychopath I am describing permeates our political, judicial, corporate and cultures taking a vast toll on the majority of us, who are in the main good people, striving for our sense of the common good.

The psychopath I am describing is parts controller, manipulator, abuser and more, but perhaps most fundamentally a person, whose interest is not the public good. The psychopath I am referencing has a bloodthirsty tenor to them, who not only solely operates in their own interest, but actually enjoys causing harm to others. Indeed, in its most desperate sense the psychopath, to whom I reference, at times, sinks to a level of acting in a way to cause harm to others, AND enjoying it. The latter notion, BTW, comes preciously close to a precise definition of sadistic behavior;

in its most simple sense as Webster would say: "Deriving pleasure from the pain of others."

This is why, the concept of Iceberg is so crucial to our understanding. Because, it is the vast part of what we don't see, underneath the surface, that can be so harmful and so devastating to our souls and psyche. When I use the word psyche, there is an added layer of hurt and pain caused, because the meaning and inference of psyche here, is something that runs contrary to our common expectation, doubling or tripling the amount of pain we feel. When we expect an interaction to go a certain way; even a customer service type of thing, and we are met with this unexpected and unwarranted antipathy, we are not just hurt, if we are not attuned, we can be shocked as well, by someone who so perverts our expectation of a reasonable transaction.

It is not totally clear what is driving the emergence of this distortion of our good nature, in terms of our common culture today. Surely the internet gives a vast proportion of the world's population a platform to hurl and otherwise bring forth their perspectives in highly charged manners. Yet, it is not just the technology, it is the personality types themselves emerging, in the way and form on some level of extremely hurt and wounded individuals, who see fit to fling their hurt and pain forward unto the world, posing as intelligence. A sure error in this judgment is that true intelligence must contain elements of kindness, or at least our notions of the common good, to ultimately be construed as intelligence, as no one is that smart unto themselves; as to hate others.

What I am setting forth is just the tip of the iceberg,

Iceberg

so to speak, in terms of understanding, coming to terms with, and ultimately appropriately responding to these personality types. A plausible question might be, well where did you, Jon Myers yourself; gain such insight into these personality types? In a general sense that is a plausible place to begin.

CHAPTER 1

WHY ME, WHY NOT?

There is an iceberg world, in the United States, probably most of the world, surely relative to the world in which we were raised. Most people, perhaps until very recently went along with their business, reasonably anticipating relatively normal interactions, when they went into a store, or that kind of thing for everyday interactions, and surely on a more profound level, when interacting with our institutions, political, judicial and economic in this country. I know that I surely came forth with such an innocence, and I do not know everything, but I know that that innocence would be typical of those of us, who were born in the 1950's and 60's and slightly beyond.

Superficially, our world, and surely our country is founded on principles of liberty and justice for all. Yet, there is a violent and vile world below the surface that has serpent life iceberg qualities, where the very values we purport are not just discarded, but blended like mincemeat, in a blender. Welcome to the world of the psychopath.

It is not my perspective that I have, in an academic sense studied psychology more than trained psychologists and psychiatrists; it is my perspective that the sense of psychology that I am bringing forward is a more accurate, substantive, humane and surely morally honest rendition than much of what passes a psychiatry or therapy today. At a minimum, what I bring forward, I believe is a profound advancement on the state of modern psychology, and psychiatry, and surely ultimately more helpful and useful to humankind.

So, if I was not trained formally as a psychologist or psychiatrist, how then did I come to such profound understandings? These understandings too, are due to The Science of Inner Strength, because, at its core, my belief is that whatever quantity of adversity we encounter, affords us with the avenue for an equal and/or greater amount of opportunity.

So, being confronted with unfathomable adversity was, then in essence, over the course of more than twenty-three years through today, and virtually twenty-four/seven is an opportunity to develop human understandings, and indeed advancements in human psychology, understanding, and communication themselves.

I lived to tell the story. My aim is societal improvement; advancement for most of us, who truly value, appreciate, if not deserve a wonderful life. Most of us, are not totally being afforded that sense of opportunity in the way of our lives, due to political, legal, and/or economic realities, and it is the iceberg in our midst that functions on so many levels that deceives us, and stands in our way.

With regard to how, was I the one, or at least a one, who developed these understandings with the depth and breadth that I have; on some "odd" [2] level, the story for

---

[2] "odd" was a word used by my daughter, to begin to describe our familial situation, and unknowingly at the time, an iceberg.

lack of a better date begins around March 22, 1996. First of all, if even lightly sharing my story, it is solely to depict and reveal my understanding, to display at least some of my credentials; it is has less to do with exposing others solely and more with helping society. My role is to speak to central truths that I have gained that have overriding value to society, which is where my heart is. Indeed, a good part of what I offer is a dire warning to society, in terms of the understanding the iceberg that lies below our surface.

Suffice it to say that the beginning of my learning about the iceberg nature of human relationships began in March, 1996. There were precursors, and habits that began to evidence themselves as early as 1980, if not before, but my journey to understanding the phenomenon began in March, 1996. That was the time, when essentially my parents, brother, and his wife, entire extended family, my then wife, and her extended family teamed up to begin a rather savage dynamic, initiating separation and divorce things, which played themselves out over a matter of years, if not decades.

The point that I am making is not that we began separation and divorce things; it is the dynamic that sided with my ex-wife was a total frenzy of virtual hatred and animosity to me. There is an extremely fine line I am walking, in terms of not wanting to pinpoint peoples' behavior, or unduly call attention to it; it is more about bringing forth the psychological understandings of the issues that confronted me, and what society needs to know about these issues.

This process for lack of a better date, was the beginning of my collision with my own personal humongous iceberg; AND my developing a science of understanding around these issues. You see at this point, I still had been indoctrinated in the sense that my family of origin was in the main supportive of me as a human being. I had grown up in what is known as the Hill Section of Scranton, PA. Being born in 1958, there were many facets of what we would truly call "old school." Patently for instance, in my grade school James Madison, we would be paddled with wooden bat-like paddles, and the rows of chairs were screwed to the floor.

Within a six or so square block area, resided two sets of Jewish Grandparents, our home, the grade school, and the Temple we attended, with Hebrew School and Temple four days a week. In retrospect, it now seems like an extremely orchestrated life, but at the time we were kids, and it all seemed relatively safe, from what we could tell. My father would walk us to school in the morning, although after school, as early as first grade, I was kind of thrown out there to walk the five or so blocks home, on my own. At lunch time, we would walk the five or so relatively long blocks home for lunch; and then return for the afternoon.

The overriding air, as I interpreted it was essentially to do well, and be of service to the world; as my father was becoming a prominent attorney, who had travelled to the Deep South in the 50's and 60's to be involved in civil rights causes. My mother Sondra, had a developing interest in arts and humanities, although a lot of our early years, she seemed a rather full time mother. For the most part, I tend to see my early years as positive; although there is possibly cause for revision of that perspective, and there were fault lines, that could prospectively have served as predictors of things that would happen years and decades later.

For instance, even though there was some fun, and I ended up playing a lot of sports, there was essentially an extremely rigid aura of strictness in our home. Bed time was 7 p.m. well into six or seventh grade. There was no soda or virtually pasta allowed. Television was especially taboo, although eventually David's and my natural energy did push the boundaries to at least get some Friday and Saturday night viewing, and eventually the floodgates came down on that one, but not until High School.

Indeed, in high school there was a rather seminal event around age fifteen. To put it in perspective, I was relatively forced to play what turned out to be eight years of Northeastern Pennsylvania organized football. At age eight I was taken to a group called the Central City Indians for sign-up. Don't get me wrong on the playground I was a very good player, especially I suppose for a Jewish kid; how and where I got my athletic ability, I will never know. Still there is an enormous world of difference between essentially sandlot football and organized football. My indoctrination to organized football began at age eight, when on my very first play, a youngster R.Z. who would later become a star, and was then five years old, gave me a cheap shot on my first ball carry.

The Central City Indians, were virtually identical on their level to the Green Bay Packers of their time. The Indians, pardon the lack of political correctness of their time, had a record of about 105-5 over a ten period; due in no small part because it was the only team in our area for the most part, who welcomed African American players. The oldest kids at age thirteen, when I first joined, were a rather legendary group of names and players, in Scranton football lore; virtually all who went onto play well in High School, as well as several being part of football playing families.

Even though our grade school James Madison was one of the first to also welcome African American students, which greatly enlivened our playground for our lunchtime sporting games; it really was the Central City Indians that began to rip aside the cocoon sense of our little world in the Hill Section, along with our Temple activity. When I say Temple activity, I must add that I, along with others virtually always saw Hebrew School and the like as pure torture, after school for two hours. In addition, our home had virtually no spiritual sense at home, so there was not only no reinforcement, but in essence no continuity between being forced to attend religious indoctrination, and any sense of religious practice at home.

In retrospect, I can only wonder at Morey Myers' motivation for essentially forcing me into what turned out to be eight years of Northeastern Pennsylvania organized football.

Oddly at the end of my Senior year, for instance, he let slip to me: "You should have just stuck with basketball." What? It wasn't like I was the one to choose football, but anyone. Football, for those interested, is a phenomenally wonderful game, in its essence; the ball itself, a fall day, the mathematics of it; but in an organized sense, it becomes like Gladiators from ancient Roman times; not something, we universally need to carry forth.

Anyway, at age fifteen, my sophomore year, after starting at quarterback for the freshman team over ten other fellows, my life seemed to take a dramatic change one night. It was the first time, I went out with three other guys, who became the core of my high school social scene. This guys, two Irish and one Italian were from another part of town, on the football team, and began to introduce me to that amazing Northeastern Pennsylvania staple: Beer. Yes, that was the side that I suppose Morey Myers did not anticipate. Again in retrospect, I believe he kind of pushed me out there for senses of his own image.

Yes, beer was an integral part of Northeastern Pennsylvania and as I was to learn high school football. So one night, on one of my first indoctrinations to beer, I was with these three other compatriots, along with many others, as a local hamburger joint and its parking lot, became an accepted locale for the considerable high school hangout and beer drinking scene. Acceptable, as in those days, the police would drive through, we would put our beer behind our backs, and wave, and the police would wave back; surely a different genre than today.

Anyway, this one Friday evening, it was getting later. I sincerely do not believe I had ever been out later than 9:30 p.m. before if that, and these three pals asked me if I wanted to go to the midnight showing of "Blazing Saddles." Even as recent as today, I saw a poll rating "Blazing Saddles" as the funniest movie of all time. This Mel Brooks Western satire, in the right frame of mind, being fifteen with a ton of beer in him for instance, was downright hysterical. Being able to bond with these three other guys and watch that movie was one of the basically revelatory experiences of that era of my life.

In rather stunning fashion, after waltzing in around

2:00 a.m., the next morning Morey Myers and I had an eye-to-eye. Morey asked me several times where I was. In rather typical teen-age, although with a bit more tenacity I would only respond: "Out." On some level, the battle for my soul was starting to be waged in earnest, at least with some pushback from me. It was as if the horse was out of the barn door; and I somehow in my heart and, I knew I would not be turning back. Indeed, the next night or so, Sondra Myers joined me, in going to see "Blazing Saddles" for a second time for me, and even she laughed rather hysterically.

For one, Morey Myers really pushed me onto the high school football field. While my emotional development was not extremely progressed at the moment, something in me was rather intuitively fighting back, in my own. The football culture at that time, was very much carousing and drinking beer; on some level Morey Myers pushed me into it. Second, as dependent, and this is a key concept as Morey and Sondra Myers emotionally tied me into them; while I would certainly not at this stage of my life condone adolescence drinking; at those times, it was rather virtually appropriate, and in an "odd" way, albeit thanks be to God that I made it; drinking provided an escape route from that emotional control they sought to "impose."[3]

Indeed after pursuing a path of strong independence throughout my high school years; it was with pressure from Morey and Sondra Myers that I made my college choice to attend Oberlin College, rather than finally being accepted at the University of Pennsylvania. It seems rather

---

[3] Impose was a notion that an Attorney for Morey Myers brought up to me, as late as 2013.

Iceberg

remarkable to me, after running into my personal iceberg that the choice often for Sondra and Morey Myers was to send me to the most emotionally isolating place. For instance, I was the only ten year old Pennsylvanian, at a ski camp, with twelve to fourteen year old New Englanders. We were sent to summer camps against our desires, for two months from age seven onward; I was pushed into chess tournaments in New York, where I would board the bus as a twelve year old, and walk the eight or so blocks to the Hotel McAlpin; I was the only Jewish kid on the football team, and so on and so forth. This is not a criticism per se; solely an effort at factual recitation, and and being "objective"[4] One of the unfathomable points I am making about this entire recitation is that there is such thing as truth and facts; even if it is one person standing as a majority in a sea of a thousand.

While on some level, I am inferring that the subliminally at least the intention of Sondra, perhaps in particular and Morey Myers was to emotionally isolate me; I seemed to virtually always find a way to keep myself entertained, and chart some kind of course, even, if not especially in the midst of these extremely challenging circumstances. Arriving at Oberlin College, in 1976; it seemed that the sixties were just dying down, in terms of wild flower dresses; and yes how shall I say, liberal experimentation with those fun substances of the day.

While on some level, football brought me to Oberlin,

---

[4] When I went to Morey and Sondra Myers's home around 1998 to seek emotional support in the midst of an extremely challenging separation, indeed orchestrated by them on some level Morey Myers's response to me was that we need to be: "objective."

as they somewhat desperately recruited for their meager football team; I really was not looking forward to four more years of organized football, and chose not to play. Curiously I did play four years of rugby, and even ended up as captain of the team; rugby was marked by no coaches, as well as something called the third half, which brought both teams together in hilarious renditions of rugby songs, beer chugging and the like.

Virtually miraculously it was in the summer between my junior and senior years that I began to find my life purpose. The central career decision in my life, seemed to be whether I would be a lawyer or not. Somewhere in the midst of letting things go, in my junior year or so, I decided that I would not become a lawyer. That summer, I along with a friend Frank S. set out for the West Coast. Initially, we secured jobs at a hotel owned by my uncle in San Francisco; yet it really did not provide us ultimately with the stimulus we desired. In a miraculous last second thing; we finally got these jobs that a mentor of mine, at the time, a late Brian McDonnell from Scranton, PA, was able to hook us up with in Los Angeles.

Brian McDonnell had quite a storied life of his own; among the highlights fasting on the White House lawn for thirty-eight days, and then becoming extremely friendly with Secretary of State Henry Kissinger, along with President Richard Nixon.[5] Among Brian's fortes were a human touch, and running off and on in his career, a

---

[5] Indeed, I had an out of body experience upon hearing Kissinger's eulogy of the President, when he referenced hearing from Brian, in a wonderful phrase: "across the chasms of the decades." One of many miracles that seems to have touched my life.

range of social service enterprises, geared towards those most in need. In the summer of 1979, Brian headed up a series of drug and alcohol rehabilitation services in some of the rougher parts of Los Angeles. It turned out that my pal Frank ended up working at a support place for alcoholics called The Way Back Inn. I ended up working in a slightly rougher setting at a place called Pacifica House near Hawthorne, California that had street level heroin and PCP users. The program was also one of these extremely intense shock therapy kind of programs, where clients wore signs around their necks, saying: "I am an asshole," were waken out of bed at three in the morning to clean and stuff like that; when they acted out.

In the heart of that situation I discovered my true calling, which was be interested in, and to provide help and service to other people. That was it; in the summer of 1979, I began to find my true calling. I suppose this was the first inkling of the natural sort of embedded compassion I had; discovered as it turned out, a long way from home. It was that sense of helping others that was to carry with me through my undergraduate graduation at Oberlin College.

As I readied to leave Oberlin College, I was looking to continue my aim to help and provide service to others. Indeed, Brian McDonnell had promised me a job in Los Angeles; and it was my sense, it was there I would head. Probably in the last week, before my graduation, I made a call to Brian's office; and they told me that he was no longer there; he had gone to London, to work with his friend Marc Knopfler of the band Dire Straits. I had met Marc too, through Brian, and while it seemed wondrous for him; there I was, needing to make a decision about my future.

I had a girlfriend at the time, who had a sister in Boston; we also had another family friend in Boston, with some possibilities of a job; and instead of Los Angeles; it was Boston here we come. There was another notable situation, pertaining to the entire Iceberg concept that occurred on the eve of my graduation from Oberlin College. My younger brother David showed up; and in what I really see as the first fault line, in the eventual iceberg within our family; David out of the blue announced that he: "Wanted to fight Dad." Both the look in his eye, and the utterly random nature of this pronouncement were both emotionally eerie and outright shocking to me, although the moment passed.

In that, I had relatively always seen our growing experience, as a cocoon, with a rather consistent level of support, at least financially with a good home, and solid meals, the thought for me, of "fighting Dad" just seemed so unfathomably farfetched. Yet, something, either internal to David, or external circumstances indeed brought David to this point. In retrospect, while I can, in hindsight, see other instances from our growing years, involving Sondra and Morey; this was the first introduction of a vast irrationality into our familial system; and the first emergence of the iceberg phenomenon that I was beginning to face.

CHAPTER 2

TWO TRACKS; HEADED FOR AN ICEBERG COLLISION: ALL THAT GLITTERS IS NOT GOLD.

From that moment onward, there were two tracks in my life, headed for a rather inevitable collision. On one hand was my actual life; the life that I began in Boston in June 1980; and the life was to begin to blossom shortly thereafter in Cambridge, MA going forward. The other track was the formation of the iceberg, which in my unattuned state, I had not the slightest inkling was forming, due in no small measure that the iceberg was being created by the very people, who seemed to provide a sense of security and standing to me in the world. Boy was I mistaken; and a major purpose of this work, is to indicate that perhaps, many other good people are mistaken, in the same way I was emotionally hijacked. There is indeed, an emerging iceberg of psychopathic behavior in our world that must be understood.

My work in Cambridge followed a relatively intensive and inventive path. Once the position in Los Angeles fell through; I was still pursuing a sense of social service and counseling in the Greater Boston area. The first apartment I had with my girlfriend, was shared with another couple; and we paid $100 each per month in Brighton, MA, near Cleveland Circle. I must say that given the relatively insulated emotional cocoon in which I was raised, with my parents as relatively strict taskmasters, combined with my escape through high school and college, with their support, I brought this overly optimistic, not yet tested perspective into the world at the time. My sense was that everything would work out, and life was one big party; not so out of touch, with the times of which I grew up in; yet my optimism of today, is a much more steel-focused tried and proven philosophy.

My first job, procured through my own auspices, not through any connections or that kind of thing was at a school called the Charles River Academy. The Charles River Academy on Clinton Street in Cambridge was an alternative high school for kids with learning and emotional challenges. Unbelievably for me, I ended up as a residential counselor in the dorm. The dorm was a place where, initially seven to nine students lived for five days a week. I was hired at $8500 a year, with three overnights per week, in my regular schedule.

Talk about the beginning of an education onto itself. I was twenty-two years old, and the students were anywhere from thirteen or fourteen to eighteen years of age. Mind you, these were students, who, in essence, could not live at home. Boy, did I begin to learn the ropes. The young people challenged me, and yet I was good enough in basketball, even dare I say at the time, wrestling, and had enough smarts and heart in the right place to be a successful counselor. After the first year there, I worked with my supervisor, a gentleman by the name of Dennis McGuire to expand our realm of service. We began to move towards being a seven day a week program, with more staff, and perhaps students. I became the head residential counselor and got my first hiring and supervisory of experiences. In retrospect, it was quite an indoctrination into the realm of New England; and adult responsibility. There were nights where these kids, well actually teens acted out, whistling, getting out of bed, and all kinds of things. In addition meals were provided; with the ideal being the students would cook the meal with supervision. Talk about a deep education in life training; and somehow I held it together there. When I left after three years, I do recall Dennis McGuire's written reference ended with the line and I paraphrase: "If you are fortunate to be in a position to hire Jon Myers, please do, you will find none better."

At the same time, because I enjoyed it, and I really wanted to improve my writing skills, I pursued a Masters Degree at Harvard University through their part-time program in literature; although as I will mention later my diploma was actually from Harvard itself. The entrepreneurial side of me, also began to emerge and develop during this time period. Chess, is a game I had learned at an early age around six or seven years old, and I was barely twelve years old, before my parents put me on a bus from Scranton, PA, and would send me to New York City for tournaments.

When I arrived in Cambridge in 1980, there was a fledgling chess scene that I helped substantially grow through organizing tournaments. I began organizing outdoor tournaments in the Plaza area of Au Bon Pain ride in the midst of Harvard Square around 1982/83. Serendipity struck in July 1983, when I met Margaret Carney while I was organizing a chess tournament, who several years later was to become my wife and I, her husband. When Au Bon Pain was just getting started, we connected, as I founded the Cambridge Run for Peace, affiliating, also with a group called Educators for Social Responsibility for a 10k road race that attracted quite an outpouring for its first year; while raising money and advancing the notion of global harmony. There was even an honorary committee, with names like Sen. Ted Kennedy, Governor. John Kenneth Galbraith, Saundra Graham, Michael Dukakis and Harvard negotiator Roger Fischer on board. At our fundraiser, I even uttered the line: "We are the world:" a year before the song came out.

The event reflected both my entrepreneurial spirit and commitment to helping the world; two facets alive and kicking thirty-seven years later. In chess, my organizing was as promising putting together Massachusetts first international Round Robin event; with a celebrity match with then Boston Celtic Bill Walton and Cambridge Mayor Francis H. Duehay that received a nearly full front page coverage in the Boston Globe Sports Section, as well as working to bring the 1988 U.S. Open Chess tournament to Boston.

My professional work remained engrossed in providing service to others. In 1984, I was hired by the Cambridge Housing Authority to develop and direct a teen pre-employment program for youth living in public housing. My winning pitch to them, in obtaining this job was the combination of my youth work with the Charles River Academy; as well as the entrepreneurial spirit I was developing, in terms of the capacity to go out and outreach to employers, to help provide pre-employment slots for youth living in public housing. On this one, I did receive a welcome nod from a friendship that I developed with the then Mayor of Cambridge, the late Leonard J. Russell, who kind of directed me towards this job, even though I had originally applied on my own. The results in short order were relatively spectacular. The program, which became known as the Work Force program, became an extremely attractive program to the youth. At the time there were essentially two of us in running the program me, as the program developer, eventually director, and a young man from Jefferson Park, our primary housing development, named Ron O'Connor, whose title I believe was youth worker. Ron, who has since passed away, brought wonderful connections with local youth.

What is not known so prominently is particularly then, Cambridge was an extremely diverse city, with a very high percentage of low and moderate income residents. [6] The housing developments, in which I worked were extremely challenging sites, with very hard-nosed putting it politely New England teens. For older kids, I even set up a street hockey league; which with support from Mayor Russell, also spun off the Mayor's Cup street hockey tournament, bringing youth from around Cambridge to-

---

[6] I can recall statistics from the Greater Boston area, had Cambridge as the ninety first out of ninety nine communities in terms of median income.

gether. Bob Goodwin from the City of Cambridge played a wonderful leadership role.

The Work Force, grew somewhat exponentially. My office was right in then-Jefferson Park, over the years its name changed to Jackson Place as well. Wen the woman upstairs flushed her toilet, it would leak into my office, if you know what I mean. I would do home visits on-site to bring young people in; also aided by two assistant youth workers, in addition to Ron O'Connor, Patricia "Trish" Avakian and Tim O'Connor Ron's younger brother. Young people if not flocked; came to the program in a steady stream. I was able to go out to the employers of Cambridge, the Harvard's, MIT's, Cambridge Hospital, Draper Labs and many more, who willingly agreed to take on these youth; as I believe in the main, we were paying the stipends.

The funds came from the Commonwealth of Massachusetts, through what was then known as EOCD. At the time I was hired; my boss Steve Swanger was having such difficulty in finding the right person; he alluded to me, they almost thought about giving the money back to the Commonwealth. Steve Swanger is the one who comprised the original proposal, and basically conceived of the program. Instead, of giving the money back to the state in the first year we created such a buzz and interest among youth and employers that funding for the program was actually doubled in the second year, and we were allowed to develop the Work Force at other housing developments in Cambridge. In particular Newtowne Court, one of the country's very first public housing developments were selected as was Roosevelt Towers, along with additional staff

Iceberg

and youth enrollment. The program has been functioning more than thirty-seven years later.

On one level I was running on virtually all energy and enthusiasm. It was virtually all get up and do it, along with my inspiration to help others. A lot of it was really clicking. I had arrived in New England in 1980, and here just few short year later, right after graduation I was getting a lot of things going, meeting with successes, but I don't really think I really understood the New England culture underneath; nor would there be any reason that I really could, because I, had not been there before.

Both due to the friendship I had developed with Mayor Leonard Russell, the relationship that began to be developed with Margaret Carney, and I suppose mainly, just my own interest, I was beginning to gain an interest in politics. I remember in the early days of meeting Margaret Carney, even in 1983 that I discussed with her my interest in running for political office; and she shared with me a story about her citizen activism from her native Oklahoma. I recall when I was named to the inaugural Cambridge Human Rights Commission in 1985, I perhaps naively acknowledged and then it became known that I was interested in running for Cambridge City Council.

In mid-1986 I decided to leave the Cambridge Housing Authority position. The decision was based on my growing political interest, as the Housing Authority was a quasipolitical body in Cambridge, and I could not do both; also the feeling of having my office in a setting where the water from above would fall on my head, was starting to wear on me. The Work Force continued to grow; in 1990 the Ford Foundation awarded it a national innovations award, as one of ten in America; and the program continues today.

To hold some time, before fully beginning to launch my political career for the 1987 Cambridge City Council election, I first did some consulting work for ERI, the local employment agency, and then taking a one year position as Housing Director at Tri-CAP. Tri-CAP served Malden, Medford and Everett; providing housing, energy and food assistance to low and moderate income residents of those three cities. As Housing Director I oversaw a staff of about seventeen and a budget in excess of a million dollars; actually this position was from 1987-1988 for reasons that will become clear.

In March 1987, I launched my first run for Cambridge City Council, with a thoroughly wide-eyed totally public service approach. The Cambridge City Council was a rather entrenched body with a long held, believe it or not conservative majority; headed by icons Walter J. Sullivan and Alfred E. Vellucci, with an average length of service of about seventeen years or so. There were nine incumbents and about eleven or so nonincumbents vying for the nine seats.

I raised the bar, in terms of Cambridge City Council elections, somehow or other raising nearly $40,000 far exceeding the typical council race of the time. I ran a flashy campaign with materials, yet relied on a very intensive door-to-door campaign, accompanied by my then amazing campaign manager, the now late Brian Murphy, who was resilient, and with back-up from my soon-to-be wife Margaret Carney. As elections go, it was relatively sophisticated with the virtual dawn of computers at that time, and the use of data systems and follow up letters and the whole nine yards.

I had no clue how I would do on the first go round; and it was truly the morning after the election that I received a phone call from a Vince Dixon, who told me I better get down to the count, as I was doing better than expected. The count is reflective of Cambridge's unique voting system proportional representation, where people vote for as many candidates as they like and rank them in order. In those times, and until the last decade or so, the counting process would be done by hand, with many elderly women and some men, counting each ballot individually over the course of several days. It was almost like Chinese water torture, in general; working so hard on an election and then seeing your fate being conducted over this hand counting over the course of three or four days.

In fact, I had received 1338 #1 votes, enough to put me in ninth place in the counting, just ahead of one of the incumbents, Saundra Graham, who ironically had served as the Honorary Chair of the Cambridge Run for Peace I had organized, with the good auspices of Au Bon Pain and the Educators for Social Responsibility just a few years earlier. Well, in the proportional representation system there is something called the transfer of votes, which continues until nine candidates have reached what is known as the quota. Frankly, it kind of reminded me of the Shirley Jackson short story "The lottery." In any event, being an incumbent Saundra Graham was much more likely to get more transfer votes, and she did, and I ended up missing election by 132 votes; very much seen as a virtual victory of sorts.

So it was that intermittent period between the 1987 election and the 1989 election that I applied for and was hired for the position at Tri-CAP by a gentleman by the name of Ron Cournier or something of the like, as my memory fades, just a tad on that one. It was also during those two intervening years that the other more significant events to this story occurred or began to occur.

CHAPTER 3

THE ICEBERG BEGINS TO EMERGE

It was clear enough from the election of 1987 that I would in all likelihood run again for Cambridge City Council and plausibly stand a chance of getting elected. My year with Tri-CAP; given all else that began to happen in my life thankfully was relatively nondescript. For the first time, I was not developing nationally recognized things or being recognized as being the "best;" I was relatively speaking just doing a job, mainly due to election prospects and events that began to happen my beyond my control.

1988 was a seminal year in terms of both the personal iceberg that began to come into my life, and on some level the understanding of this concept as a whole. Three massive events occurred in 1988, with regard to my personal and familial history. One is that on just about the one year anniversary of our marriage, Margaret Carney and I separated for what turned out to be a five month period. The separation itself was relatively flabbergasting in terms of me and my families' understanding. There really had been virtually no divorce in my family; certainly not among my grandparents, parents, and even immediate aunts and uncles. Everything was posed as just right; perhaps that was in itself a precursor of iceberg like things; on the surface everything appeared to be okay.

Margaret and my separation, was what it was. We were both thirty or so year olds who had met in the middle of Harvard Square; from extremely different backgrounds: Me this intensive Jewish upbringing in Scranton, PA: and she this Christian childhood, wreaked by the death of her Mom, by a drunken driver, and she being the youngest of seven children. Our marriage, while it produced two wonderful children, was virtually a happenstance unto itself. Suffice it to say, like virtually all young people of our time, there were not the requisite emotional intelligence and knowledge of relationships, and marriage that would bode well for our future.

One net result of our separation, was that it was as if the emotional floor of my family was kicked out in some way; an emotional vacuum was created. In the psychological/emotional make-up of our family that I was familiar with, never before had such confusion taken hold. I will slightly interject for a moment that the word

"confusion" is just one potentially key word; as I do believe there are chances that my exwife Margaret Carney is at least slightly touched by borderline personality disorder; and confusion is a key element of what people with borderline personality disorder seek to create. With this virtual smoke bomb, if not more set off in the middle of the family; against the backdrop of a family, whose general framework heretofore, was essentially:

Iceberg

"Everything's fine;" there was the potential[7] for enormous chaos.

Into that potential calamity/opportunity, entered one anti-hero David Nathan Myers. It will become increasingly clear whether David Nathan Myers was, and is more the tip of the iceberg, or a relatively substantial part of the body underneath the water. Much has to do with whether David Nathan Myers was, in essence an instrument of Morey and Sondra Myers, or whether the degree of hatefulness that he brought forward was of his own inspiration, along with his wife Nomi Maya Stolzenberg. This question will be explored throughout this work.

In any event, one early September Saturday in 1988, I received a phone call from my younger biological brother David Nathan Myers. David called "randomly" and asked said he was in town from LA, and asked if I wanted to watch some college football that afternoon. I was on some level delighted. David had purposefully put distance between for in my view, not good reasons, and we had originally watched sports together as young boys. So I said sure come on over; as my separation was still ongoing as well.

Little did I know, but the agenda of David Nathan Myers was not a clear and clean one. I straightened up the good sized apartment in North Cambridge; purposefully putting a small stack of about six bills aside; noticing that one was a day or two late, and another a little longer.

---

[7] Potential is a funny word in this scenario, as the reason Margaret Carney ended up in the middle of Harvard Square in 1983 was that she was promoting a board game, called Pente created in Stillwater, Oklahoma that had the word "potential" as a key element.

Nothing's perfect; it was post college not the end of the world; surely something I would take care on Monday. I did have a funny feeling about those bills, as the one imperfection David would see.

Sure enough, David showed up, and his interest was not at all watching college football. He stepped away, presumably to conduct an illicit and false search of my home. I suppose the only thing he found was those bills, and within seconds he began verbally accosting me. Factually, it was a stunning event; David had called me, come over to my home under false pretenses, did an illegal search, and essentially began berating me for next to nothing, if not nothing itself. He ended up screaming: "Look at you;" here I was in one of the first comfortable moments of the entire separation process lying on my couch, looking forward to watching college football, with my only question being whether we would watch one or two games; and I was on some level being mercilessly berated, by my younger brother, who lived on the West Coast of all things. It was a shocking turn of events, and yet this was literally, and figuratively the beginning of the Iceberg that I would encounter.

David was just getting started. David's next move was to get on the phone to call Scranton, PA, where Morey and Sondra Myers were; along with a family "guru" a Brian McDonnell. David was so alarmist, and/or this had been previously planned, to the point where the folks in Scranton jumped in a car, almost immediately and drove the five hours from Scranton to Cambridge. I was kind of looking forward to seeing my folks, I thought; although this entire thing seemed utterly shocking in a way.

Indeed, when the folks arrived, the late Brian McDonnell said, something like: "You seem okay; we thought you were going to have a revolver in your mouth." I am still trying to make sense out of this, as the only thing I was looking to do was watch a college football game or two. What I am beginning to pose here, are the outlines and tenors of psychopathic behavior. The psychopath, is creating a false world, and then beginning to attack you, for not comporting to that extremely false narrative. Your world is beginning to be turned upside down.

David's narrative, foaming from the mouth, was flimsy. There is a grain of truth in everything, and still we must learn about facts and truth. The psychological tomahawk that David began to wield as a function of family dynamics entailed a savage attack on my mental health. David, lived 3000 miles away; had not seen me in a while, generally by his choice, and now was attempting to form extremely pejorative opinions and definitions about me, based on his psychological distortions.

It turned out that I was seeing a therapist briefly at the times, due to my marital separations, and the "family" insisted on going to see him the next day. I did not mind; I had nothing to hide. The therapist laid out for the family that he saw nothing wrong in any underlying sense with me; it was mainly that I was experiencing some challenges due to the separation, which virtually anybody in their right mind would as well. Still, at that moment, it became clear that some dynamic was in place, particularly, it related to David, who, was not going to change his perspective no matter what. Indeed, as we were leaving the therapist's office, I debated whether to verbally chew him out, or merely say: "I think you overreacted a tad." I chose the latter, somehow not worrying about it too much, although with a lingering sense that I would be dealing with it, down the road.

This interaction was akin to a ship's first contact with an iceberg on the surface. There is some contact, yet; it is just not clear, what the depth of the interaction maybe. Little did I know that that first contact with the iceberg was to play itself out over a thirty-year period in my life.

CHAPTER 4

THE ROOTS OF HATRED

"The human spirit is greater than any obstacle" -George C. Scott

One of the things that the iceberg revealed, was what amounted to be the hatred, jealousy, and rage of others. While I still have not addressed the question as to whether my younger brother at that time, really initiated those activities on his own, or whether he was the tip of a family dynamic; twenty seven years was to evidence those lesser qualities, and surely psychological disorientation of those parties.

That a brother who lived 3000 miles away, who had chosen to go a separate way from me, would make such a "vigorous"[8] out of control foray into my life became abundantly clear that the true motivations were things such as rage, jealousy and hatred, rather than the laughable

---

[8] Years later, my biological father Morey Mayer Myers used this word in the midst of such legal battles we were beginning to have at the time.

assertions they were trying to make, about any genuine concern for me. Through the then twenty-seven year period, in increasing sense over the years, resulting in the development of a science on my part; I have become interested with how humankind can understand and defeat hatred, and these lesser qualities.

In a myriad of ways, we are seeing hatred, animosity, rage and jealousy arise in our society. My work, in reaching for the sky, would like to a stemming of the tide, if not reversal of hatred. When I reference hatred, I mean not only extremist groups, at home and abroad; but the tone of discourse in on-line and social media websites; as well as challenges we see in our political, judicial and even economic systems. Hatred is often based on a false sense of superiority, which is the source of a lot of cruelty today, and the iceberg effect in society today.

What is most important for me to articulate, is that hatred, and irrational jealousy are weaknesses; not strengths. Those who act unnecesarily tough, and compare themselves to others online, are really not acting with strength or intelligence. People who function in such negative ways are not acting in strong or intelligent manners; as I am a believer as the Science of Inner Strength indicates, most people are indeed strong and intelligent at root; we have not been taught what true strength and intelligence are.

I am not saying that we will get rid of all hatred on earth. What I am suggesting, is that we can shift a vast proportion of mindsets from acting meanly to becoming more kind. The shift really depends on two things: One is to come to an understanding, of how stressed, or even confused, with little fault of their own, a lot of people are. I am a grounded optimist with hard work of course; extremely grateful to our ancestors and what has come before us, but there are information and understandings available to us in the twenty first century which were not apparent in earlier centuries.

Respectfully, I would say that the parenting, and general tenor of the parent-child relationship prior to the last generation or so, was not a child centered, emotionally healthy and well-being model. Think about it, America in the late nineteenth century was an industrialized society with factories that had children working long hours. These dynamics were not so many generations ago, mainly our great-grandparents in some ways. We are where we are; we cannot go back and change the past, only learn from it.

The opportunity in 2015 and beyond, is phenomenally different than the psyche and attitudes of nineteenth and even twentieth century America. Even as one, who would be considered slightly-post baby boomer; the world in which I was raised was not an emotionally intelligent; nurturing the child, kind of place. Many good things were given to us, in terms of basic values and for that I am very grateful, and not with respect to emotional intelligence.

A crucial element of The Science of Inner Strength, which I have developed, is predicated on the premise that most of us are good at heart; and in the main deserve to be nurtured and encouraged, rather corrected. The problem, arose not as much with our grandparents, but in terms of today, with our parents, who seemingly have had difficulty grasping that the world is fundamentally changing, more than the internet and even climate change; it is our psyches and spirits that are being challenged and must adapt.

Like the industrial society and even a giant freight train, it is virtually as if our parents had a hard time putting on the breaks to the banging of human pegs into holes, and moving people forward in a calm and appropriate ways. Something shifted, as much as people today, would want to deny the sixties, and clearly we needed adjustments from that, but there became a point in time, where peoples' souls and spirits began to really matter in society.

The freight train that our parents were driving was going too fast at the time; perhaps tragically like the recent Amtrak derailment in Philadelphia, and people began to get squeezed. The promise and sense of a future of the post-World War II era did not begin to materialize. There are greater and lesser extremes, from parents who actively were working more in their interest, than the values they espoused; to parents mostly, who were probably innocent victims of larger economic and social systems.

Suddenly those round human pegs, stopped wanting to be put into square holes, and simply put, our parent's generation was not equipped to handle it. Suddenly human beings were human beings, and not merely items or ornaments to put on display. It is not so much about blame, although there are those who will seek to make it that way. It is much more about our understanding our shared and current reality so that we can now work together to make it better.

The problem is, our parent's generation implicitly, if not explicitly had a promise to us; and that promise was that things were, on some level, being taken care of. There was a direction and a sense of a future for all of us: The American Dream, even, if you will. The challenge is that simply put, the true infrastructure was not there to sustain the promise, our parents offered us; as well as in a more innocent sense, society dramatically began to change in the late twentieth/early twenty-first century. Again, this change had more to do with technology and an obsession with money, and not a broader movement towards the understanding of the human soul and psyche. When we look at the levels of hatred and dysfunction in America society, at least some of the responsibility, as I am not ultimately big on blame whatsoever, resides at the feet of our parents, no matter how well-intentioned many of them were. In a compassionate sense though too, they were products of the hard-driving, if not brutal industrial era. Indeed, I am not a blamer at all; what is, is what is, and we must respond to the challenges of today; I am pointing out how it happened. I do appreciate what came before; we need adapt and improvise.

The economic and social systems necessary for us to grow, change and thrive are simply not in place now. Instead we are faced with vast systems, that like the recent FIFA scandal are really based on their own corruption and dramatic self-interest. Witness as well outbreaks of unfathomable protest within the African-American communities that exist, as the tip of the iceberg with community-police issues, but on a much greater level, the shocking disparity in jobs, education and economic opportunity for communities of color. I recall some years ago, driving through a section of Philadelphia that, just raised connotations of a

Vietnam war zone, with block after block of burned out buildings.

While I do not see such obvious devastation in my home area Boston; I do not know everything, but I know Philadelphia is not alone in facing senses of despair; witness the murder rate in Chicago; violent protests in Baltimore and Ferguson, MO, and so on and so forth. We are not just seeing isolated instances of police and community issues; we are seeing fractures in the infrastructure of the American dream. These fractures and fissures, will not be addressed by our parents' generation; and the ideologies and philosophies that got us here, must be built upon and adapted, without throwing out the baby for the bathwater.

Don't get me wrong; on some level we must have gratitude to our parents and grandparents for having gotten us here, on so many levels; yet the issues and challenges of today need a much different approach. To understand the surge in outright animosity and hatred in our culture today, surfacing often on on-line comment boards and the like, is to understand the psychological confusion and sense of challenge felt by people of my generation and younger.

Any nurturing that does not ultimately nurture the spirit and the soul of a human being is doomed for failure. Failing to respect and nurture the human soul and human spirit, were clearly the underpinnings of slaveries, tyrannies, discriminations and corrupt systems aimed to keep one class or group in power, at the expense of others. Anything that does not treat the human being in a nurturing and egalitarian way, is doomed to failure; because the human soul at root yearns for, needs, and is constantly moving towards equality, liberty and true democracy, no matter how painful the struggle.

So there is a bit of potential collision between the old industrial world, on which our social structure is built and the opening of the human spirit. Importantly though, is the notion of people feeling left behind, or not truly being provided the opportunities of which our parent's generation and America promised. The hatred and animus in society that arises is a function of essentially trapped souls that have not been nurtured, and encouraged to the point of emotional maturity, and understanding the importance of our emotional worthiness. For the early part of our childhood, our parents did well; the direction they set was a reasonable and a viable one; yet something changed. Now admittedly, as I will evidence as necessary, I am drawing vast examples from my own personal story, but I do not know everything, but I know that my story is one of divine destiny. There really is a reason for all of this. I see it as a once a millennium story, with respect to its lessons.

My life is living proof of not only the need, but for the necessity of spiritual change in the world. Of course, I will be attacked for making grandiose statements, but the depth of what I went through provides me back-up.. In its underlying sense, my story is one of biblical proportions, not because I want it to be, but because as Dr. Seuss wrote at the end of Bartholomew Cubbins: "It just happened to happen." That Seuss story, along with the Lorax, is my favorite of favorites, of which, I used to read not only to my own sacred children, but to kindergartens in Cambridge, MA. Ironic a couple of short years later, Seuss is repudiated by a kindergarten teacher in Cambridge, with a tad of overreaction. I feel like Bartholomew Cubbins, sometimes, this innocent unsuspecting knave, who was swept up into a much greater story.

Albeit the analogy only goes so far, if I am not so serious as a person; my message ultimately is. Something happened. There was an intense disillusionment on the part of our parents. Maybe it was that the world they were promised by their parents, was beginning to fall dramatically short of what they were promised. Why did they have to work so hard, go through World War II, the Great Depression, and other traumas? Our children today, will not ask these questions; perhaps it is up to me, again like the Lorax, to keep these ideals alive.

Yet, I am more than a storyteller; the point of the moment is that dramatic hatred, irrational and disturbed psychological disorders emerged; like an iceberg catching society nearly totally off-guard.

CHAPTER 5

THE NATURE OF PERSONALITY DISORDERS

With an iceberg, there is the part we see, and as we were raised in school; ninety percent of the iceberg itself lies below water, hidden. The entire realm of what are psychologically described as Cluster B Personality Disorders, is one of the two or three greatest phenomenon in our society; and perhaps, beyond climate change, economic disparity, the one most determinant and least understood.

Where did this hatred, where do emotional vampires come from, and why are there such impediments to a humane and just society. Perhaps the greatest disjuncture, if not failing of previous generations, or perhaps better said, in terms of the opportunity of our generation is to understand the phenomenon of what a personality disorder is.

I have a rule of seventy-five percent, which means that I believe that at least seventy five percent of people want to do well, and believe in the goodness, and positive direction of society. Most public discussions, be they political, economic, judicial must be geared to the seventy-five percent of society, who affirm a good, decent and just society. Other categorizations such as Democrat, Republican, black, white, gay, straight, must fit under the umbrella of fairness and goodness. The room for luxury is over. We have squandered our capability to not address our true challenges. There are real perils in this world, economic, racial, ISIS, corruption, you name it. The divides can no longer be sustained among good and decent people. The challenge of Congress for instance is to govern; holding onto ideological extremes can no longer be tolerated.

We have lost our basic common sense, with regard to understanding, that the political job is to do right and do well for the American people; not to pontificate perspectives that clearly serve serve a narrow base. Missing from the radar screen is for one, our sense of collective purpose, as a nation, as a world. Other than here, who is truly calling out to discuss, let alone define our common purpose?

Missing from discussions of purpose, are for starters a sense of gratitude and appreciation. Entitlement, narcissism and worse afflict us and drive us to extremely low level discussions, when we need and deserve better. The problem is not merely our parents' generation; it is our children as well, who risk, taking the façade, of opportunity that exists in the way of the internet and cell phones, and misplacing these technological advancements with values themselves.

Therein lies the great societal question and contradiction. In between our parents and our children how and where did we lose our values and purpose, and what role does the deviant personality type have to do with all of this? My sense is that as our parents began to see the illusion of their world view; they began to get desperate. Rather than truly being about their children; in a desperate sense they began to be about themselves. The system worked well through the sixties, when people somewhat older than me, and then our generation were encouraged, or at least found a way, to party and be happy.

Merriment was not just allowed, but encouraged. The order, the near tyranny that our parents experienced in their growing years was slipping away; as drugs and rock music and "Dancing in the street" became the modes of the day. There was a collapse in America's psyche that occurred somewhere between two wars I suppose. Contrast the difference with the heroism of America's role in World War II in defeating the obscene Adolph Hitler and then the Vietnam War ending around 1971; a mere twenty six years later. Suddenly the overwhelming superiority of America's moral authority was in question. Richard Nixon's collapse as US President, also was a jarring example of the difference between American ideals, and our actual conduct, along surely with the horrific assassinations of John, Bobby and Martin.

A deviance was entering our culture that dramatically had more to do with greed and "success" than life, liberty and the pursuit of happiness. I am drawing major parallels between what happened in my life, and current trends in society, because my story in some ways embodied all of that; in terms of the American dream. Raised by two parents, who stood as symbolic pillars of a community, exemplifying the American dream; I dramatically had the rug pulled out from under me; and in some ways, it mirrors the great moral challenge facing America today.

In my life, in the most extreme of senses, as far as the parties around me are concerned; a depraved attitude was created, due to an unfathomable mix of what I refer to as deviant personality types that run the range from Borderline Personality Disorder, Extreme Narcissism, even Psychopathic behavior, as well as some sadistic and parasitic personality traits, which I will get into. You see, an entire village was created around my life that had to do with the worst of human behavior. Perhaps unintentionally, a perfect storm that even reached evil was created around my life. The pefect storm was comprised, in part by peoples' sadistic desires to do me harm; as well as our judicial and divorce court system, which is wretchedly out of control, with respect to true care for children and families.

One heinous tool used by abusers, entails a to the core defamation. Falsely defining is an atrocious tool of true evil doers: That interest and capacity to try to label good people in false and derisive terms, is a malicious tool functioning in today's society. Defining one's enemy or creating a false enemy at that, is a notable and wicked tool of evil: For instance, Hitler sought to create a sense of a "Master Race;" and attempt to define Jews and others heinously as genetically inferior.

The deviant personality type needs an enemy, because their own psyche is so shriveled up; so puny perhaps literally and surely in their own mind that the only way they can create a sense of well-being, is by attempting to attack and destroy others. If such people really felt well, and healthy then, there would be little, if any need for enemies. So the need for enemies, often comes from an underdeveloped sense of self.

It is similar the amount of hatred that arises in on-line communities, Twitter and the internet with regard to the vitriol and disdain displayed. While most human beings are smart; many do not know it, and instead use unfathomably rash opinions as a method of showing intelligence, which in the end is not intelligence; People do not need to outdo one another in order to be smart. If a person is smart, it will evidence itself; it does not uniformly need competition, and surely does not need an enemy.

Needing an enemy, when one is not necessary, is a reflection of a psychological state of desperation on some level; one that comes from a sense of lack, and an underdeveloped or undeveloped sense of self. In unearthing what transpired in my familial situation, I somehow stumbled upon the notion of my biological father Morey Mayer Myers and/or younger brother David Nathan Myers having a personality disorder. A personality disorder is, an iceberg unto itself.

We see a surface or superficial view of a person; that facet which they want us to see. Ninety percent of the true person, is kept underwater, and hidden, as much as is possible to the outer world. Indeed, an overriding component of their personality is to deceive the world at large. So much energy goes into creating this superficial image above the surface; while the true personality and all of its deficits are kept below, in iceberg form.

It may be that the person victimized by the person with the personality disorder is just one person, if the victimizer can draw enough psychic blood from the person they are victimizing. This is where we have also come across the term "emotional vampires; "people, who for their very own subsistence draw some emotional blood from other people. If one person becomes stuck or victimized enough, one person, may be sufficient for the victimizer; otherwise more than one or a group of people may be targeted.

In my instance, due to the heinous capacity to draw in my ex-wife as a collaborator in this deranged emotional crucible, thereby ensuring that my children would be used as pawns, Morey Myers was able to focus virtually all of his emotionally parasitic tendencies on me. Although, it is worthy noting my biological mother Sondra Myers could be more controlling even in helping to set up a psychological prison for me, they considered "permanent.". What Morey Myers or maybe more David Nathan Myers did not count on, was my capacity to breakthrough his sense of prison, by developing a deep spiritual understanding of these issues, and ultimately seeing their sophisticated abuse for what it way/. A crucial element to understand here, is that there are people who have no real emotional development or capacity to stand on their own two feet; they really depend for their psychic sustenance on others, which includes my Mom, Sondra.

This lack of emotional well-being, translating into an internal emptiness for some, can comprise the beginning of, and the essence of, evil. It is fascinating that my definition of evil, follows a definition that only afterwards I learned was generated by Albert Einstein, in his book, "God and Science;" where Einstein defines evil as an absence of light, or something to that effect. That is along the lines of my understanding as well; evil in a person arises because there is really no internal caliber or substance to a person; they are in some spiritual sense, empty inside.

When I reference spiritual; I surely do not mean tied to organized religion, or necessarily a conscious choice to accept God. When I reference spiritually empty or not; I am at a minimum level referencing the capacity for a person to have some true benevolence, buffer or goodness inside that prevents them from carrying out destructive behavior. Destructive behavior can take the form of maliciousness, manipulation, causing harm, essentially without any relent, or capacity to show remorse.

The deviant personality type is, an extremely confused and deprived individual. The emptiness inside, emanates from an extreme sense of lack. The lack of faith in anything positive gives this person an tunnel vision view of survival, where thereby manipulating and/or outdoing their fellow human being is the only mode they know how to get what they want. Somewhere along the line, society lost its buffer or at least its perceived buffer, with the sense that we are a good society, with the aim of helping others.

The deviant personality type is this unforeseen iceberg phenomenon in society that taints our capacity to relate to society in a good and caring manner. The iceberg effect of this deviant personality is that if society is not what it seems, or surely not what it is supposed to be, then many unsuspecting people are being manipulated by the basic betrayal of the person with the personality disorder.

CHAPTER 6

THE COURTS OF AMERICA

"In heaven there is no beer; that's why we drink it here." The beer barrel polka.

While I cannot speak with absolute certainty how much the iceberg effect exists in American society across economic, political and other areas, one area where I have seen first-hand the drastic iceberg effect of the confused state of American values, is our court system itself. Naively we grew up with the sense that American was the land of the free and the home of the brave; the place where "life, liberty and the pursuit of happiness" are guaranteed by our very own US Constitution. Like Alice in Wonderland, up has become down, and down has become up.

In horrific sense, the place where such values are virtually obliterated, is within the US court system. On some level, we are seeing vast protests from members of the African American communities, as it pertains to Ferguson, MO; Baltimore, Cleveland, New York and more; yet there

Iceberg

is a much more quiet assault on the life and dignity of the American people in other areas, perhaps most pronounced in our family court system. There is at times an incendiary mindset within parts of our governmental structures that assaults the mindset of its constituents.

The degree to which America strays from our stated ideals, and the actual practice can be astonishing. Mind you, my perspective is guided by someone who stood toe-to-toe with the divorce system and more, for twenty years running, for the life and emotional wellbeing of my two children. Indeed, I consider it a facet of divine intervention that I was called to fight the battles of the horrors of the American family court system on behalf of the average person and me. It was the phenomenally deep family values that I inherited in Scranton, PA, that were historically destined to collide with the tragic nature of today's modern divorce system.

The divorce industry evidently exists to fold, spindle and mutilate American families, especially men, who have the displeasure of walking into a court room to face this figurative monstrosity. Within five minutes an astute person will understand that the entire sense of Justice we learned in school, no longer applies, when entering an American divorce court room. Just picture your entire life has been grabbed by the throat, by someone vicious and not concerned at all, with a factual representation; and your case is being heard in front of forty other parties awaiting their turn.

Welcome to Middlesex County Probate and Family Court for one; and in all likelihood many other courtrooms across America. The devastation done in the name of divorce is unfathomable. My own sense is that many couples, at least initially are at the emotional maturity of a high school break-up or something, and all of a sudden, restraining orders, freezing of assets, possibly losing one's home, not to mention children are all in play.

Sorry to say, it is an almost insect like mindset, and not a friendly one that comprises some of those in the divorce industry from lawyers, to yes, Judges, to psychiatrists, to court workers. Today, a major part of the system is predicated on child support laws.

Many peoples' jobs and livelihood depend on a certain slant within the court system, to uphold jobs and maintain their industry.

It is truly ghastly is to see divorce related personnel who will worse than lie about your children and your family; to promulgate jobs and an economic system. I am talking about people in positions of power over your children, in an "odd"[9] way who project little or no genuine interest in your children.

Entering the family court system is running into a substantial piece of an iceberg in America. Our expectation, in America, at least until recently, is that liberty and justice would rule. Instead innocent people walk in, and it is like running into an iron bar; in terms of the contorted world of some of the lawyers and the family court culture. It is unfathomable to think that America can operate with such disjuncture from its stated and understood values, and still have a healthy society. Particularly when the areas in question have do with the very building block of American society, our children and the American family.

---

[9] A word my sacred daughter used to describe our family dynamics.

Iceberg

This was but one facet of the massive iceberg that I ran into in my life. You see, my story is not a lament; it is a cautionary tale, an effort at illuminating deep societal issues so that we can overcome them. I am not beating my chest when I say that the combination of issues that came at me, were not only a perfect storm of circumstances beyond my control; but to me, something reminiscent of a 500 year storm or something; even a once in a millennium kind of thing.

You see the truly odd thing in my situation was not just facing a borderline personality ex-wife, or the deep challenges of a modern day court system; the true kerosene on some level that was tossed on the figurative fire was, what I believe amounted the psychopathic behavior of someone in my family of origin. Therein lies the most iceberg like characteristic of my story, and what I bring to the surface. I do not know everything, but I know that if I experienced issues thrust upon me so massively; that similar issues exist for other people.

Indeed there are on-line communities and many articles having to do with psychopathic, narcissistic and borderline personality individuals. The recognition of the deviant personality type is the most jarring facet of the iceberg that threatens at the core American society, and our civilized world. Underneath not just ISIS, the Boston Marathon bomber, the racist depraved killer in Charleston, South Carolina, but also people who push greed way too far; people who act totally without compassion or empathy in legal, economic, or political settings lies the deviant personality type; often enough associated with psychopathic behavior.

While we have not much problem naming heinous killers as deviants and psychopaths; what is not yet understood by society is that true deviants function in emotional and psychological ways, without leaving a trace of blood on their victims or their hands. The psychopath or deviant personality type runs at the undercurrent of American life in many heretofore unknown ways; even or especially taking the form of people who appear "successful." Why can systems be so indifferent and bombastic? Because at their root may well be a few truly deviant personality types craving and holding power.

Issues like income inequality, racial divisiveness, massive political divisions, unjust civil and criminal court systems don't just happen naturally. . Such massive inequities happen because underneath it, are deviant personality types, who as I will describe see nothing in the world, but for their own extremely narrow, "vile,"[10] self-absorbed, intensely greedy points of views. Therein lies an enormous perversion in the American way, because most people until now, reasonably anticipate reason and normality when dealing with American authorities, and the culture in general.

The reason problems are so hard to solve, is because there is a relatively small, and yet extremely influential group of people, who want nothing in the world to do with the resolution of human issues. In fact, for some, there is a sadistic element, where the infliction of pain on others, not just brings them joy, but is a motivating

---

[10] At one point, I received a letter from a family member saying to me something along the lines: "Even if, we are the 'vile' creatures you think we are…"

influence for them. It is easy to see Hitler in that light; but how many are acting much more silently, in a bloodless manner to inflict their own brands of cruelty on the ordinary citizen, or not yet legal immigrant for that matter.

It is essential for the growth and health, not just of America, but of the world at large to understand the characteristics of the psychopath; the one with this deviant personality type. When we continue to run into things that are grotesquely unfair, we are running into this personality either as an individual, or embedded into our systems themselves. Yes, the American legal system has facets of this in operation, as but one glaring example.

The key is of course, knowledge and shining a light on this situation, and these situations because I come from the premise that most people are good, and desire to see good things for themselves and the community as a whole. The deviant personality type is surely a minority, perhaps truly in its most severe form 2-5%; and yet its influence and toll on the culture is staggering.

CHAPTER 7

THE CHARACTERISTICS OF THE DEVIANT PERSONALITY TYPE

"Roxanne, you don't have to turn on the redlight..." Sting and the Police

First let's talk about how we get here. How does a person develop psychopathic, narcissistic, borderline or other personality types that on some level are deviant? In the most odd sense, in some ways we really are talking about a lack of love and nurturing, in the most empathic caring sense. This is not a knock categorically against the parenting of yesteryear. Along the lines of a main premise, most people are good; essentially trying their best. Yet, the emergence of the hate, the psychopathic deviant personality in the main, emanates from basically a lack of love and nurturing in childhood.

Most human beings want and basically need the same things. Food, clothing, shelter, surely throw in oxygen; there are extremely basic physical requirements for the human species. Yet, on another level of need, not so far below those basic needs; are things such as affection, caring, affirmation for who we are as people. In the main, society as a whole has not necessarily prioritized those basic requisites of human existence. When we think back of major events in world history, the Industrial Revolution, the Civil War, World War II, we do not necessarily see the qualities of love, care and compassion emphasized.

It is kind of silly to think as human beings that we all do not need, and thrive upon basic levels of care, unconditional love, and encouragement to be who we really are as people. Yet, the emotional needs have been left behind on some level; and even with the advent of emotional intelligence, as put forth by Daniel Golman, we really have not discussed, much less conceptualized the notion of what a truly caring society would be; or even putting a value on the development of healthy, happy, productive members of society. In no small part this lack of emphasis stems from the notion that many of those in control in society do not put a premium on the development of the whole person, rather the image of the person, and the "bottom line" itself.

Many parents for instance, in all likelihood faced real, if not severe economic pressure in raising children, and understandably did not uniformly prioritize the true emotional and spiritual development of the child. The result of children being raised without a deep sense of nurturing and affirmation, rather than punishment for instance, at home is that many children grow up with senses of longing, loss and emotional need that as they morph into adults starts to take on elements of bitterness, anger, and even vindictiveness. Our opiod crisis tells us something.

A complete or at least very deep lack of emotional well-being itself causes this sense of bitterness to harden, like an iceberg. Rather than facing a human being, with a true range of emotions, in an extremely unsuspecting sense, an innocent person may well find themselves confronting a person, who has virtually zero range of human emotions, and perhaps even less capacity to see the world in anything other than the most deprived manner. By now, most, if not all of us have confronted this type of antagonism in greater and lesser ways; the store clerk, who is suddenly and needlessly vicious in their interaction; online commentary that goes straight for the jugular, and can virtually toss human bodies aside; people in positions of power, who use human souls like staples to slam down and threaten to callously throw away the broken ones.

It goes well beyond recognizing that our very systems from judicial to political to surely economic can rear their ugly heads with this type of abusive behavior. I am talking more than occasional rudeness, but institutionalized senses of entitlement that turn the entire expectation of a rational human interaction on its head. At the core of these types of behaviors are those with essentially deviant personality disorders. So deep is their sense of deprivation and entitlement that they have virtually every interaction enters into a sharp-edged one, where a reasoned person, can virtually never win, never do enough; even the very best of efforts are met with a rather indifferent shrug at best. Hello, by the people and for the people…

Reasoned and basically good people must essentially recognize that it is not them causing this great deviation and disparity in the relationship. They have run into an iceberg, a person with a personality disorder. As long as, society as a whole emphasized the "bottom line" solely and not an emphasis on the raising of the healthy child; we will produce more and more of people with these extremely sharp-edged virtually immovable mindsets and patterns of behavior, replete of respect, and empty of empathy.

What we need to understand is that like a factory itself, we are producing these very type of personalities and mindsets that ultimately cause human and societal burnout; like driving a car without pads on the breaks. The psychopathic behavior in some ways is learned behavior in some cases, AND can be unlearned. The psychopath, narcissist, borderline personality type essentially devours relationships and people, for those who are not aware, as many are not. Basically good people follow corporate lines of deceit, thinking that is the only means of survival, or "the way it is;" without really realizing their basic integrity, if not humanity, is being vacuumed up, by somebody else's mindset.

The character of the personality disordered, is such, that it values other human beings not in the least; and sees life as some mere competition to plunder and virtually suck the life from others.. On an individual level, when one runs into a person with a personality disorder, there is virtually no negotiation, and for that matter, no upside. The best that one can obtain is a minutely human interaction on a limited basis; contrasted withe the basic human being desire to work together and/or share some joy; there is no joy whatsoever in any interaction with the personality disordered.

The perverse evil of the personality disordered is that

they have uncanny capacities to find the weak spots of kind people; and then come up with horrific psychological and emotional tactics to cause as much pain, and disruption in the life of their target as possible. In my case situation; it is unfathomable that so many people coalesced in this "vile" blood-sucking dynamic around my life; showing the weakness of group thought..

I write about it now, not to get back at anyone, only to forewarn others; as well as feel on some level an appropriate sense of heroic pride that I was able to figure this out, and ultimately detach myself from this dynamic, and pose a better way. The process occurred over a period of twenty-seven plus years; demarcated with an unfathomable alliance involving my deep-rooted Jewish family of origin and my ex-wife of Christian faith. I include the religions, solely as an indication of just one more layer of the psychological manipulation that took place in forming this alliance, in crossing blood lines, or as a prominent and flawed psychiatrist said to me: "Jewish families don't do this to one another." Strike three Gruenbaum. The alliance that included parents, brother, sister-in law, aunts, uncles cousins and more; had one focal point and one focal point only: The infliction of severe emotional pain, if not more on me.

I must confess I am smiling just a tad in writing these words, because I survived and even thrived through it all. The psychopathic personality is such that it works in serpent like, extremely devious ways; it strikes in a time and a manner least expected. That is why when my brother knocked at my door in September, 1988, he had falsely assured me, with his unexpected call that he was there to watch a football game; before embarking on, an illegal search of my home, which was destined to find nothing, because there was nothing to find. Mine is, the quintessential story of adversity making you stronger, to me, of even Biblical dimensions, as those in the Bible were people too!

Having no grounds or rationale to attack and make a false case against another human being, deters the psychopath none the least, if fact they live for it. You see, it is not a rational thing they are seeking. The psychopath, extreme narcissist or borderline, as the term "emotional vampire" alludes, essentially want the psychic blood of the other human being, no more, no less. Most people are good; and most people are thereby unsuspecting of the possibility of such an assault occurring. We can see little pieces of it from the rude store clerk, on-line hate chat; even t.v. news with biased slants; yet in the main, these are relatively limited interactions, where we as a consumer have the opportunity on some level to walk away; less so in a familial or even work type of situation.

Put these psychopathic kinds of energies into a more enduring situation, and a person can become virtually trapped in a nightmare world. A workplace situation can be horrific, and yet even that cannot compare on some level, with a familial situation. And virtually nothing in the world can compare to a familial situation that involves one's parents and ex-wife teaming up, in a psychopathic type of bond against you, bringing in ALL kinds of extended family on their side. You see, when you have two beautiful children whom you love a great deal; and those parties are willing to use the children as pawns on some level; you can fall into a deeply nightmarish kind of trap. Few, if any situations in the world would involve one's very own parents, brother maliciously and viciously siding with an ex-wife against you, for "decades" on end.

This type of alliance entails deviance of the highest order, or better said lowest order. This is the message of the deviant personality type; they solely seek psychic blood, and it can come from anybody. Indeed one's own family because a most susceptible place because the a psychopath, extreme narcissist, or borderline personality type, in essence knows the weak spots emotionally, or perceived weak spots of the person they are preying upon. Because of its deceptive qualities, and its capacity to prey upon essentially good people; emotional and psychological abuse of this order is going to be one of, if not the biggest issue of the rest of the twenty-first century.

As an after effect of my parents' and ex-wife's alliance against me, which they virtually gleefully dragged on for more than ten years in Probate and Family Court and beyond; I discovered and brought forth significant understandings about the Tort for the Intentional Infliction of Emotional Distress into our court system; addressing severe issues of emotional and psychological abuse. As a Pro Se or self-represented litigant, I was extremely proud on several occasions to make it as far as the Pennsylvania Supreme Court, and the Massachusetts Supreme Judicial Court; in fact the last time I was before the Massachusetts SJC, two of the Justices recused themselves because they had had previous involvement in the cases I brought forward. I very much considered that last detail a victory.

Like people who railed at the overturn of slavery long

before its abominable activities were turned over; while I was not totally successful within the courts, I very much consider my work a major victory, if not a major success, because I was not only doing the right thing for my sacred children and me; but I was advancing an understanding of an area of society that must be much more fully understood. Understanding the ways of the psychopathic deviant personality, and the unfathomable impacts of emotional and psychological abuse are a growing piece of work that society must do at this point.

The central issue for American society is really; do we have a true commitment to being an honest and fair society, as the ideals of the U.S. Constitution for starters indicate that we must? It is relatively clear that certain facets of American institutions such as our legal system, our political and economic systems have substantial facets that are not based on fairness, liberty and equality to all. The philosophy I espouse embedded in The Science of Inner Strength is something readily accessible to most human beings. Therein lies the solution, as it is really the great commonwealth, the great mass of humanity that must wake up and demand change in the way of fairness and equality for all. I am shining my own light here.

Changes in the right direction will not occur readily from those in leadership today. Those in leadership have too much vested in the current world order. It falls on those who live and work by the standards of fairness and hard work on an every day basis to collectively stand up and demand that these kinds of changes take place. The mass of humanity has "squandered" its true influence because on a collective basis so many people have been lulled and misdirected by certain areas of leadership that on some level exhibit psychopathic characteristics because of their fundamental commitments to control and lack of fairness for society.

CHAPTER 8

RECLAIMING OUR INTEGRITY

The Science of Inner Strength: "He (or she) who has a why, can endure almost any how." –Neitzsche

My work has led me to a point, where on the most large and simple level; I am advocating and enunciating a seemingly small and yet massive shift for human kind. Maybe it is a little like the quote made, when humans landed on the moon: "one small step for man; one giant step for humankind." The fundamental shift in human understanding, human psychology, and even human spirituality that I am leading is as simple as starting from the notion that human beings are good at heart. This tiny shift can and will take massive energy on the part of society to recognize.

When you really think about it; so much of human history, as well as our societal conditioning teeters massively on the premise that we are essentially flawed creatures that need to be corrected. So much of society is based on control, from schools, to places of worship, to government, just as a sense of the prevailing human practice can be geared on many levels to dumb us down, and not acknowledge our true intelligence in the first place. Again, I begin from the notion that most of us are intelligent in our relative human sense; and deserve to be treated as intelligent beings. Even our needs for "security" cannot be allowed to dampen our true human spirit.

Imagine the change in society that would start to come about based on relatively simple notions that we are good creatures who must be encouraged, rather than flawed beings that must be corrected. So many of us have accepted this discouraging way of looking at the human condition; to see us as animalistic, which technically we are, but still negating our higher and spiritual sense of selves that we are indeed wondrous and mainly intelligent beings that need love and support to reach our highest and best potential.

The Science of Inner Strength begins with the notion that most of us are good; AND on some level many of us are on some level not acting in alignment with our goodness on a regular basis. It is virtually like we must reorient, if not retrain society to start from the point of recognizing our goodness. Think about it, how many people in American prisons, as but one example, are probably somewhere in there good people; who either were not given full economic and other opportunities, or who had so much junk and garbage put on their heads that they had no chance but to behave and think otherwise: Even people who were bad, or parents who parented in a less than exemplary manner; this is not in the main about blaming the past; it is about reorienting the future.

Virtually intuitively by starting from the notion that we are basically good and intelligent, and extending to the individual, we create a much more benign and compassionate, not to mention fair sense of a society as a whole. Corollary elements to the notion that we are basically good as people, have then to do with the sense that we must begin to assess and judge people predicated on their entire persona, not on some narrow element, that virtually any narrow interest group or hateful entity can use to attack or bring down another. There are a percentage of what we would universally declare as

"bad actors" in society; I would argue that most of these are those with outright AND subtle deviant personality types; yet we must reserve our disdain for those who fall into that category, and even then most of us, must in the main be channeling our energies into worthy and health products and projects these days.

The world is simply at a point where we cannot sustain the vitriol and needless exhibition of hatred that permeates parts of society; Good and noble actions are what must carry forth the vast majority of us, who are good at root. To effect a societal change on a relatively major level, we virtually need a time-out; a time to pause, take our breath, and really assess where we are. A significant part of my persona is valuing the deep and abiding message of adversity; yet, it would be great to see fundamental world change come about, without a major catastrophe on this planet, which is why I write.

Money is an important and valued part of society;

and yet it cannot remain an obsession, or something we worship. Money must increasingly become a reflection of good and noble acts, and not a mere reflection of dog eat dog mindsets, which will continue our harmful, if not hateful dynamic. My life and story are on one level such a call for a timeout for the world.

You see, I would have developed nary a notion of the depth of the world, and the vital need for change, if I had not run into my personal iceberg itself; which was ultimately a catalyst for discovering my innate goodness. I have little or no reason to believe that my goodness, is any different than the basic goodness that resides within most of us as people; and can be realized by most!

There are two parts to the goodness within me that I have found. First was the discovery or affirmation of that goodness, and then there became the work of bringing that goodness out to reveal and share with the world. I must confess I thought the latter part would be an easier route, and yet, it the unfathomably arduous nature of it, makes it seem all the more worthy and worthwhile. It is also worth mentioning that other relatively spiritual people at times, reference goodness, as Godness meaning that our basic goodness is a reflection of the divine itself; as I came to that sense in my own way.

The beginning of my discovery, or rediscovery or affirmation of my goodness came about primarily with my running into my personal iceberg in March, 1996. It was that moment when I was somewhat rudely introduced to a marital separation. I say rudely because my ex-wife was not piece of cake in the matter, and the entire scenario was doubly or trebly intensified by the fact that, my own family of origin, was deeply entrenched with working viciously on the side of my ex-wife; talk about a horror.

Within a few days after the jarring separation, where I was rather unceremoniously told to leave the home I alone had purchased, without any physical violence or anything like that, I made my way to my former hometown of Scranton, PA. Even though things were not declared at that moment, I did not initially feel safe in going to my parents, Morey and Sondra Myers's home, the home I grew up in as a child. I spent a couple of nights with my then Grandmother Mae Gelb.

Finally, I did go to Morey and Sondra Myers' home for a night or two. Not really feeling emotionally safe in that environment, I did reach out to some mental health professionals, as my entire safety net seemed to have evaporated. It was at that time, with some support that I had a middle of the night revelation. It was in the middle of the night that I felt a sense of peace and calm enter me, in a way that I could only describe as the divine, or even God entering me.

In short order two or three central truths descended upon me that at this extremely vulnerable moment were to provide a basis of my new work and new philosophy from that moment onward. First and foremost was the remembrance or affirmation that the four year old within me was really a great person. I remembered back to that four year old and affirmed that he was a really good; and that whatever craziness was going on around me, had no real relation to that four year-old, which was the true me.

That recognition became a formative piece of who I became then, and who I was to become over a matter of years. The matter of my goodness came over me like a divine light. It was common sense; looking back to that four year child; it was clear I was a good and innocent child, like most of us are.

It is that four-year old within us that must be protected, and all kinds of appropriate and loving actions must be developed to protect that child. When we come in touch with our goodness as a human being, it is life transforming because not only are we developing confidence; but we are developing an implicit and deep trust in ourselves. The opinions of others become less meaningful, in terms of our true selves.

Those with personality disorders are functioning without this basic sense of goodness; it is not on some level that they are not good. It is more that their goodness has been so covered over, with a variety of bad teachings, and self-inflicted doubts and fears. The less the sense of goodness is nourished within us; the greater the prospects for deviant or evil behavior to take hold. It all goes back to the sense of goodness that we either have discovered or can discover within us.

As I indicate, it was virtually an accident with me or divine intervention or running head-on into adversity or a sense of iceberg that patently helped me discover or rediscover my own goodness. Once that goodness was identified, I felt like a tiny Bambi in the woods; and it became my work over the years to build the support around that Bambi into a mighty buck. My premise is that most people at the age of a four year-old have that goodness within them.

That goodness is the true us; that self that wants to

do well, and have success in this world. We may not know all about success at that point, but most of us want to do well in the world, and be good people, whether we know it or not. Harsh economic circumstances, unstable personalities, systems themselves, all kind of things can begin to dramatically affect the psyche of the individual that starts to dull, if not pound down their basic sense of goodness over the years. Before you know it, that sense of goodness, can be flattened like a pancake over the course of circumstances and years.

This is where a societal adjustment must begin to steadily recognize our goodness, and begin to open the doors so that such intelligence can enter in our psyche. The pace of modern society, complicates matters, because virtually everyone can justify not having the time to stop and make a mid-course adjustment. Yet, that mid-course adjustment is precisely what the world needs right now.

Involving ourselves in win-lose, rather than win-win dynamics; creating systems and discussions that do not recognize our intelligence and need for respect of one another, ultimately is a system that can wear us all down into smithereens. While the word "sustainable" has entered our lexicon in matters pertaining to the environment, and related matters; we must first and foremost create an emotionally sustainable culture. A hallmark of an emotionally sustainable culture is beginning from a place of for one, our own goodness, and for two, a need for respect and decency towards others.

Because our own sense of inner strength, has on a societal level been so beaten down, we need a great deal of work, and societal adjustment to discover, and make strong that sense of inner strength, within most of us. For me, the journey to discovering inner strength, was a rather unfathomable journey; due to circumstances beyond my control, I was put in a state of rather constant legal conflict; and had to develop my own sense of inner strength; and The Science of Inner Strength, as a means of surviving and thriving.

The basic cauldron that I was put in, entailed an extremely unusual situation where my deep-rooted family of origin actively and one could argue viciously sided with my ex-wife in a twenty plus year campaign aimed to defame, ostracize me, and speciously cut off relations among my two sacred children and me. I reference this, not because I want to discuss it all, as I continually work on forgiving all that; I merely seek to present to you the reader the backdrop from which, I was pressured to develop my own foundation of inner strength.

To me, adversity is the wonderful teacher of our lives. Solely under the most challenging of situations can we learn the really deep and significant lessons of life; akin to the notion that diamonds were coal under extreme pressure. Adversity is a wake-up call to learn, and/or change course. My story is part wake-up call to the world.

My situation was, or at least I interpreted it as such a calling from above. I do not know everything, but I know that the level of emotional distress, and emotional tension posed around my life, by circumstances beyond my control, was of unfathomable proportions. Emotions are so much of human existence, and formulate a significant portion of our responses to situations; such as "I feel this way; or I feel that way." What I did was interpret the entire emotional situation formulated around me, as not just a divine intervention, but an emotional cauldron, in which I was dumped to forge, like an anvil, some incredibly deep understandings of human beings and our earth.

While the situation unfolded over the course of decades; and I surely wanted it to end, at some point, I also accepted it as my destiny, and said this was the figurative fire, the training ground, in which I was to learn unfathomable lessons about humanity, beginning with myself. So, while in some ways, I wanted it to end; often I realized that the timing was not in my control and further that there were amazing lessons to be learned by standing in the cauldron, standing in the pain, if you will.

While I am surely not a masochist; by not running from the pain, I was able to absorb unbelievable lessons. If you are simultaneously fighting a bizarre and hurtful court system, an out of control ex-wife, and most of all, and most viciously an extremely deep-rooted and deep-pocketed family of origin, then you are experiencing emotional pain and hurt at legendary levels. Sometimes, I say the perfect storm that was created around my life, was in an emotional sense, a once in a millennium event.

The question, then becomes how did I withstand, if not overcome it? I walked the walk. The answer resides in having discovered my inner strength, for my own purposes, and developing this Science as well. I became an incredibly different person then when this entire journey began, and that is putting it mildly. I found my own inner strength, and I will for the first time share my secret, of it ALL.

The secret resides in divine purpose, or our true

purpose. I did not know my initial purpose when this ordeal began in 1996, but over the course of years, in addition to my own work, I was to discover it. The secret of developing your inner strength is to have a divine purpose, a divine anchor even; something that inspires you and motivates you and grounds you virtually every single day of your life. The work itself was extremely hard, but the mathematics in substantial part of finding my divine purpose were relatively easy.

Given the vast array of influences and forces arrayed against me, and without getting into great detail, it really was enormous, the purpose that arose within me, in "nearly"11[1] divine fashion was protecting the emotional health and well-being of my two sacred children. It is crucial to have an anchor in life; a real one, and an appropriate one. We can set goals, and move towards successes, but if what is inspiring us, is not appropriately ours, at some point we are doomed to failure.

For instance, when it came to the parenting of my children, I was not the one who initiated the divorce, it was virtually ALL spelled out for me. We co-parented for years, but it seemed that my ex-wife and the influences rather wantonly backing her, including my parents, brother and sister-in-law were just chomping at the bit, to go at me again. That they did, in initiating a rather horrendous custody dispute in 2002. I was clear that given the background I have come from; even for starters; I was a very good parent.

In my growing years, I was raised by a strong mother and father, and I had two Jewish grandmothers, within a few block area, who lived to 105 and 100. My mother's sister was close by. These women, all ran their homes, and surely their kitchens with strong elements of organization and attitude. It could not help but rub off on me, a somewhat nurturing side, also as an older brother, and even a dexterity in the kitchen to some minor degree. My two grandfathers were turn of the century immigrants, who became a doctor and a lawyer; so the elements of societal success were well ingrained as well.

My ex-wife, was a rather direct contrast, in terms of her history with parenting. Margaret was the youngest of seven children; who tragically lost their mother, in a car accident with a drunken driver. Margaret was about four years old. My ex-wife's father worked essentially two jobs, and the household was overseen by the eldest sister, Patty, when she was about twelve or thirteen. The family also had bouts of alcoholism and evidently manic depression as well.

So the basic structure of our approach to parenting, was like night and day. It was a background, and a heritage on my part that was every bit worth appropriately fighting for, in the raising and parenting of our two sacred children. The fact that the divorce was taking place in Middlesex County, perhaps the most challenging and slanted towards women county in the United States was another hurdle, and part of my destiny.

The fact that my entire deep-rooted family of origin sided with my ex-wife was essentially the wild card from hell; AND the challenge that allowed me to find my inner strength at an extraordinary level. What I am getting at, is that to me, I was sincerely fighting for the lives and well-being of my two sacred children, so there was not a lot of doubt, or lack of appropriateness in my fight; as I sincerely considered myself to be the better, at least more directly caring parent, under these most extraordinary of circumstances. In addition, I was working directly to buffer, if not remove my children from this dynamic that seemed much more about taking me down; then the other side participating for the appropriate and genuine interests of Sophie and Sam.

Rather than get into the entire dynamics of the "fight;" but as needed, what I am illuminating is first, I had a divine light, a purpose that was entirely substantial and appropriate to me, with respect to the lives of my children. Second, the enormity of the struggle itself, gave me "ample"[11] opportunity to develop my inner strength. This is one of the basic notions of The Science of Inner Strength: However large the obstacle that you or anyone is facing; we basically have the opportunity to develop an equal or greater amount of strength to overcome the obstacle, as we are willing.

---

[11] "ample" was a word used by the Honorable Bonnie McLeod to dismiss, a fledgling lawsuit that I voluntarily withdrew. The Judge cited ample reason to dismiss it, with which I respectfully disagreed; yet, in reading my novice level complaitn at the time, she also called the story "palpable."

CHAPTER 9

THE SCIENCE OF INNER STRENGTH (PART II)

Finding our divine light.

Once we understand that we have a divine light within us; a sense of a divine purpose, our whole world can and will change. I see this as the fundamental distinction in the world: Those who have in some form or another discovered their divine light; and those who have not yet come to that discovery. Let us be clear; history has not emphasized the notion of spiritual development in a true sense to this point, so most people as of yet, have not fully discovered or surely realized that divine light within them. Yet, it is my considered view that most people do indeed have this divine light; and however painful but for those with personality disorders society is moving in that direction.

Divine light, or inner strength if you prefer, is perhaps the deepest concept I will share with you, and constitutes what I consider to be the jumping off point, if not the fundamental fault line in society as a whole. From this point forward, I do not know everything but I know that human beings must get to know, embrace, trust, respect and relish their divine light. Divine light to me, has little to do with organized religion.

The essence of divine light is understanding, that life, in its most general sense is precious; that we did not truly invent ourselves, that we came from a place, in spiritual form that is greater than we are. Whether you call it God or not, is up to you: I have seen it called as goodness, spirit, source, essence, presence, the universe and more. The opposite of this greater influence is that it seems many people today, have this sense of expectation, if not entitlement that the only thing that matters about life, is whether they have an iphone 6 or iphone 5, or now 10.

We collectively, are not stopping and saying; "wait; this is amazing technology that puts us in touch in one another in ways we never thought possible." Where is this collective genius coming from and for starters don't we owe it to somebody to have enormous appreciation for what we have? Where we came from, is surely not my question to answer; and yet we, owe it to ourselves to have a basic appreciation for the sense that we are even here, and alive today.

Think of it, if we began from a place of appreciation, how much lesser ours' and the world's problems might be. Nobody is entitled to success. We did not create the earth; some higher energy is at work in how we got here. Square one, is not just to learn our ABC's, but to me, it is also collectively as a society to enunciate some basic appreciation for our life here on earth, in the first place;

joy is not far behind. Even through human tragedy, the human spirit has persevered and prevailed.

From there, it is not a huge step to begin to build an understanding of the basic goodness of us as individuals. There is where I depart with some major characteristics of some major organized religions. A good portion of religion teaches that we have sinned and are flawed. While, there is little or no question that each of us as individuals can and does "sin" or have flaws, we can consider reversing or at least substantially massaging this basic bit of the human paradigm.

I begin from the presumption and understanding that most of us are good from our start. In this regard we must begin with the essence of a child. Putting aside our challenges parents, and how would do well, to evolve in our parenting; most of us would agree that children in their most vulnerable and innocent stages are good. I have done substantial work around the issue of the inner child; and it seems that a crucial marking point for understanding the basic innocence and goodness of a child, pertains to age four. I did some great work around the inner child, with a book from Dr. Margaret Paul, and her associate Dr. Erika.

At age four a child is developed enough, and in the main, is not overly exposed to the ways of the world. Age four is a wonderful point to understand the goodness of a child. If and when most of us can reflect back to our lives as a four year old; then it is my confidence that most of us will see ourselves as innocent and good. Just this morning, September 9, 2015, I was watching a great movie by the recently passed away Wayne Dyer, called "The Shift." I have not even finished the movie at this point, and yet, it seems like a wonderful movie. One of the similar points made by Wayne Dyer also related back to our basic goodness, or perfection as a child or for him, even in the womb.

It really gets to the notion of how we perceive life. Do we perceive life as some entitlement notion; that we like dinosaurs are just here to stomp and walk the earth, before our departure; or are we more graced with the beauty and essence of the gift of life itself, and recognize and appreciate that gift fully? Clearly for me, and in the philosophy that I espouse, it is the latter that we must more uniformly begin to approach life from the essence of appreciation, and hold sacred, in a general sense, the child itself.

When we stop to think about it, the child is our most basic extension of the gift of life; it is literally our renewing and extending life forward. In that regard, it becomes a moral calling, if not responsibility of ours to treat that child not just as ours to mold, but as a precious extension of the most basic premise of life itself, our sustenance and furtherance of the species. On this level, we can then begin to treat the child in a more precious fashion. Once we ourselves begin to treat the child in a loving and gentle fashion, automatically we are imbuing in the child, a sense of his or her basic goodness.

This becomes our fundamental calling, to affirm and support the goodness of life, through our role as parents and community members. Society operates today, as if the only, or at least the main bottom line is economic success. We get that, I get that, you get that; money matters a great deal in life. Yet, what I am proposing is that money cannot be our sole bottom line; it can be a piece of our bottom line, no issue there. Yet alongside money, as a twin engine, must be our basic goodness, and benevolence for ourselves and others. There is no longer the luxury of operating solely for the "bottom line." Smart businesses must also function with a true sense of the well-being of the planet, in a way that I call purpose. Sustainability must become part of our human psyche, as well as the environment, and other societal areas.

We must begin from the point of the well-being and basic goodness of the individual. We must influence, if not change the basic premise of society that the individual is some flawed being to be fixed and corrected, or a round peg to bang into a square hole, and come much more from the sense that the individual, the child is good, if not a gift in the first place; AND with our encouragement and proper development will become great.

How do I know this? Well because I have done this in my own life, through The Science of Inner Strength, I have developed skills of greatness, and it is my basic sense that if I can do it, most other people can do it too. How did I go about it? Well it has to do with the sense that a diamond, was once a piece of coal under unfathomable pressure. Ironic, in a sense that I originally came from an old coal mining town Scranton, Pennsylvania, with regard to my transformation.

The extreme pressure in my life as I have alluded took the form of this unfathomable cauldron of emotional and psychological abuse that flowed from a combination of my family of origin, and an ex-wife, and a relatively cruel divorce system. Rather than complain overly about all those things; I took those circumstances as my training ground or forming ground, unknowingly initially, like a diamond from coal. This training ground has persisted for more than twenty-two years unbelievably.

It was as if I was inside this giant cauldron, and my response was that I used this cauldron, as an incubator to learn many things and develop a science. A person who wants to slay dragons figuratively speaking might learn best about it, from actually being in the belly of the beast of the dragon, or at least attempted to be kept captive by it for decades. The levels and degrees of lessons that I learned are off the charts.

It is like a quote that I enjoy of Nietzsche: "He who has a why, can bear almost any how." The "why" in my life was several things, but based in the emotional health and well-being of my two sacred children, for a long period of time, even on some level until today; yet other commitments and priorities also enter the picture. One of those is a spiritual sense of self, and eventually elements of justice and fairness for society.

I suppose all of the journeys, struggles and challenges in life have prepared me to enter into that spiritual place. It really is our sense of joy that matters. When I say that, some may retreat to a sense of, well we cannot be merely about our joy. In that regard, I respectfully say it depends how we define joy.

If by joy, we mean the use of drugs and alcohol and other addiction like things in a hedonistic fashion; then that what I would describe as false joy would be inappropriate. However, if by joy we mean the move and even entrance into our true self; then we are talking about existing at a higher level, and higher than society encourages at this point in time. Another suitable word for the type of joy, I am describing is authenticity, also deeply aligned with purpose, and appropriateness for that matter. Appropriateness is a wonderful word; contrasted with political correctness, which relies on outside sources to impose things, authenticity stems from our own sense of decency.

If and when we reach these kinds of parameters in our own personal interactions then we start to experience a kind of joy on another level. It is not totally important to me, whether you attach this kind of joy with God, the divine, presence, the universe or whatever higher sense of consciousness floats your boat. On a human level, the point is more to move into these higher level qualities such as joy, authenticity, purpose, appropriateness and respect for our basic existence.

These qualities then become part of our inner strength and divine light. I am not suggesting anyone sacrifice their sense of economic well-being; expect perhaps the richest of the rich. Instead I am commending that most of us, will be more financially successful by finding our purpose, as well as happier. Society must recognize the necessity of goodness in our present and future actions.

I seek to moderate only slightly and redirect the obsession with money that is both blatant and implicit in today's society. I am all for making money. My requisite is that we earn money by doing things that are benefit to society. Clearly teachers and others jump off the page, in terms of people underpaid, although perhaps American education must be substantially revamped as well. I am also talking about major corporations, in that we develop corporations as I am doing with Calm Interventions Inc.

fully committed to the public good. It is not enough just to make money these days; it must occur with purpose.

In a word, The Science of Inner Strength can also be boiled down to "goodness," along with determination and values. It is about affirming and developing the basic goodness of the individual, while establishing societal parameters that convey and lead to goodness and well-being, for the greater good. It is an integral imperative, establishing the societal parameters of goodness. Establishing our decency and appropriate parameters are, more than any other area, where society is falling short. Many will say it is impossible; I say that it is not only possible, but necessary for the health and well-being of our planet.

CHAPTER 10

ESTABLISHING SOCIETAL PARAMETERS AROUND GOODNESS AND DECENCY

Doing the "impossible." "Some people see things the way that they are and say why; I see things the way that they can be, and say why?" Robert F. Kennedy Jr.

To me, the great challenge in society today, is a fundamental "nearly" corruptness, a lack of honesty that we have allowed to ensue. The notion of America is founded upon liberty, and justice for all. How in the world can we function without a basic sense of honesty in our interactions? Problems on so many levels such as political dysfunction, legal injustices, police-community relationships, environmental issues, our national debt emanate from or are exacerbated by a lack of respect and honesty in our society as a whole and/or our collective inability to positively and rationally discuss these things.

It is less important obsessing on who to blame, as it is

to getting a broom and cleaning up the mess. The absurd notion that society cannot set moral tones and mores for ourselves cannot be true. The obsession on the part of those at the top, in positions of influence, be they political, be they the media, be they our legal process is with money itself. This is where the true horror can come in: Money without purpose can lead to disaster.

I am a great believer in an economically healthy society; an American where people can get rich, and our middle class and lower economic sectors dramatically improve their economic standing. Yet, there is a glaring error in the current values and outlook in the corporate view in society itself. Economic success cannot exist as single-pronged end in itself. Economic success must be accompanied by a sense of our public good; as well as an appreciation for the very system, which allowed that creation of wealth.

I noticed a speech recently by a Professor David Orr of Oberlin College, noting that today we exist at a critical point. The choices we make going forward as a society will directly affect our well-being; the days of fooling around are essentially over. Professor Orr was making his comments mainly in reference to the environment; yet I make a similar statement with respect to our social society as a whole, economic, political, judicial and beyond. I reference our national psyche.

When people tell you that it is "impossible" to change and influence society for the better; on many levels they are telling you that their economic bottom line, is about meeting their own end, and nothing more. Let's ring the bell, saying "Time out" people; we did not sit down and make this earth with a hammer and a nail as human beings. Something greater than us created the earth, whether you believe in God or not; it would be ludicrous to say that we as human beings were creators of our own universe; surely on its most minimal level something bigger is at work.

Meaning: Compete hard, yes; I am all for it, and yet compete with a sense of appreciation for something larger than ourselves. The NBA for instance, is very popular these days, but in an NBA game, people cannot just run onto the court and do whatever they want. There are rules of participation, and if people thought about it; an appreciation for something that induces such a large economic impact. Similarly in our society, we must be attuned to the notion that there is something greater than us, and we all benefit on some level by being part of an organized group and/or civilized community.

Yes, there are those who would argue for differing political agendas or models; yet like an NBA player almost, their very participation is ensured by a greater good, a system that provides a basic playing field to live, breathe and work on. We owe something to the greater good; so at the end of the day, we must be bounded by appreciation

Political conversations must end with a handshake and a realization that first and foremost we participate in a "civilized community.". Not all will buy into this model, but most can. The point is, society must set parameters, a moral code; not of coercive rules, but of accepted appropriate boundaries. Everybody throws up their hands and says well how do you do that? We build a basic decency, if not morality into our society.

The media might say that is impossible, but then again

the media is responsible in good and not as good ways, among others. The media is at also a profit driven entity with a bottom line; so it too must participate in a sense of a greater good. We must create an umbrella of the greater good that encapsulates virtually all discussions, with parameters of engagement Everything political, legal/judicial, corporate, media must pay its dues and encourage AND be mindful of the greater good.

Instilling the greater good, into our basic parameters requires a shift in our paradigm; and yet such a shift is positive, economically stronger, healthier and more sustainable.. Society is stuck at a point of a conflict in our approach and our philosophy. The shift is not a huge one, conceptually; yet the pace of our modern society makes it difficult to enact a newer and better philosophy. Because my philosophy was reached through such pain and trauma even; I would rather others reach it through gentle persuasion.

Yet, on some level such a philosophy is inevitable, as society as a whole is continually, often painfully progressing towards a greater good. Martin Luther King Jr.'s words were:

"The moral arc of the universe bends towards justice." My aim is to take spiritual principles and go out on the playing field of life; to change society with my approach.

I don't know everything, but I know I have done my homework. I sincerely believe my life was touched by the divine, in March 1996. My work is understanding the sense of the divine or at least positive possibilities, and then bringing those forward to my fellow human beings. I know if the divine exists within me; it exists within everyone else. I am not special in being blessed in that way; as that would be a crazy, lol, thought.

I am blessed, because unfathomable adversity pealed back the layers of the onion of the divine within me, stripping away my lesser parts. When my ex-wife and I separated, and my biological parents were not emotionally there for me, in 1996; I was figuratively and virtually literally between a rock and a hard place. In the darkness of the night, a presence entered me; a calmness appeared, and I could only ascribe as God entering my life. I remember that moment; it really seemed like the divine to me.

One of the first tenets of discovering the goodness within me, within the next twenty-four hours of that seeming divine influence entering my life, was a remembrance of myself as a four-year old boy. As I travelled back in my mind to that four-year old boy; I resonated to the sense that that four year old within me, as a good and innocent person.. The second divine moment, came well before I had read any books on the inner child or knew of the concept. Like a fair number of things in my life, I stumbled upon these concepts by myself. Although there has been much reading, writing and work sense then.

Virtually intuitively I knew that that four-year old boy was still within me; that I as a human being deserved good in my life; and indeed was good as a person. It took this harsh "crisis" in my life, true adversity for me to come to the realization at age thirtyseven that the four year old within me, was a crucial part of my being, and was intrinsically good. I virtually felt like a little Bambi in the forest, and knew that one of my main tasks from there was to grow that young Bambi into a full-grown buck.

A third wonderful concept I learned at that turning point moment in my life was the relative futility of anger. Temper and associated moderate non-physical rages were an inherited part of my familial culture. I had carried these forth mainly into a marital relationship that thank God never reached the point of physical violence or the like. Still, at this turning point moment, I learned two unfathomable things about anger that made me drop it like a bad habit.

Deepest, was the sense that anger was not a real emotion. The true emotion was something like sadness, disappointment, fear, loss, and those kinds of things. Anger was the reaction, rather than a response that was used as a cover-up for those truer emotions. I learned to start working with, and understanding, and then feeling the true emotions. As I would tell my children, being sad is okay; being mad is not.

The second point was even more flabbergasting and instantly effective. I was doing some written work that asked me to visualize the times that I got angry, and I did. The worksheet in rather beautiful fashion, then asked: "Did you get what you wanted at those times?" When I looked at those instances, I was shocked to see that virtually never did I get what I wanted, in terms of a relationship, from another person. I would want a person to come closer, and most human beings will retreat from anger.

In that instant I dropped anger, almost completely for good. I mean, I am a rational human being. I want to get the things I want. If and when I saw so dramatically that anger would not get me what I wanted; it became a part of life that I wanted to drop that instant, and did, in excellent and surely not perfect fashion.

On some level the mere dropping of anger itself alone, was an amazing contribution to the emotional conduct of my family of origin. In that instant, seeing anger's utter futility; it was dead to me. I won't say that I am perfect with that concept for goodness sakes, but it is an abiding concept in my life. For me there is virtually always a better way than being angry to get the things that I want. I suppose it dovetails with my commitment and interest to being honest, and when one desires to achieve great results, honesty is the first path to greatness; otherwise things become tainted and non-enduring

CHAPTER 11

THE ADVERSITY I ENCOUNTERED AND HOW IT FORMED ME, IF NOT FORGED ME

At the core of everything I discuss, is the notion that adversity can be the great, if not ultimate teacher in our lives. Thereby the notion that the greater the level of adversity we experience, the greater the opportunity for true learning. In that regard I sincerely believe that I have been taught some of the great, true redeeming lessons in life, and it is my responsibility to bring those forth into the world.

One of the vast areas of understanding that I bring forward begins with understanding psychopathic/personality disordered behavior. As the title of this book indicates, currently society is experiencing an iceberg like phenomenon with these kinds of things, because the degree of knowledge and insight about such personality disorders is not yet on society's radar screen.

Thus, I want to bring forward an added understanding of the realm of dealing with people with what in a psychological sense is known as Cluster B personality disorders. Most present in my figurative tsunami of challenge, was the entrance of my younger brother David Nathan Myers onto the emotional and psychological landscape of my family and extended family. Beginning in 1988, well into 2015, I have become increasingly convinced that what I am dealing with, in my younger brother, is someone, who has a very deep level of pain and trauma from his early childhood, or at least has chosen to worship or build a mountain of a minor amount of legitimate discontent.

Well, actually today, October 16, 2015, I have reached a level of forgiveness in my sense of my familial situation so I am not certain what I wish to focus upon. I suppose I can tell you the degree of emotional pain and pressure I experienced due to circumstances mainly beyond my control; and what their collective effect was on me, in an overriding sense. In that regard I will focus more on what I have described as the "miracle angle;" by a yoga teacher by the name of Rod Stryker. The miracle angle which is really the core base of my philosophy of "Turning hard times into better times;" is the notion that whatever adversity is occurring near you, to you or around you; there is a miracle angle of positive growth that you can make out of the situation.

The miracle angle of the positive growth is an astonishing one, at least for me; perhaps for God, it is just a matter of everyday work, lol. You see, adversity the most untoward circumstances changed me in a way that I can solely ascribe to God; or at least tapping into the divine that must exist within all of us, not just me. To describe the "indescribable"[12] part of the emotional intensity that I encountered, and to be clear the intensity was indeed that, emotional and psychological, which in some ways to me, is the most intense of all, was the perfect storm of circumstances that arrayed as challenges for me to overcome. I mean, I had perhaps the roughest and harshest Probate and Family Court County in America, in Middlesex County, Massachusetts to address; I had an ex-wife, who perhaps through limited fault of her own was willing to be a virtual and figurative bullet in a figurative gun, in terms of aligning against me in the Probate and Family Court system; and then the most crazy, and the harshest of the harsh was that my own previously supportive family of origin, in rather merciless fashion put their full and deep-pocketed throttle against me

I am laughing out loud, because significant parts of this dynamic began to happen around 1988, and continue on some level until today, in October 2015 and beyond for a course of twenty-seven years. The dynamic itself was an excruciatingly unfathomable dynamic of emotional abuse and psychological persecution, and I am not kidding. In fact, in all sincerity, without undue bragging in nature; I sincerely believe it, perhaps is the worst case of emotional and psychological abuse in human history.

Yet, again the miracle angle was that because I had a central and underlying purpose; I took the entire situation virtually in its entirety as this massive training ground for my life, and ultimate spiritual development. The image I

---

[12] Indescribable is a word my glorious daughter used to describe our familial situation in part, in a marvelous college essay of hers around 2008.

wish to depict is that it was like this giant training ground, or massive figurative fire, you know the kind used by the blacksmith, in using his anvil to bang out tools and weapons and other metal objects forged under the most unrelenting of heat. That is the imagery of which I ascribe to my life, for twenty seven years, in greater and lesser parts, I was under this figurative fire of life; having my life banged and shaped by the great blacksmith, if you will in the sky.

That is where purpose really comes from; that heat, that figurative fire; banged and shaped by the larger forces of our universe. The financial, emotional psychological, legal and social situation that formulated around my life was that gigantic fire; of which if I wanted to reach the goals of a good home, time with my children, financial success, and a successful altruistic business, a great marriage for that matter, then I was just going to have to go through that fire, and/or sit with it, whatever was offered to me on any given day, unless and until I reached the point of actualization that the divine had in store.

So two things, one is that I know that degree of emotional and psychological fanaticism and intensity that was attached to my life, while I do not know everything, I know that it is a once in a millennium type of event. You could not possibly have such a thing, of such a perfect storm of the most brutal Family Court in America; my ex-wife with some confusion, and my family of origin in "assault"[13] in fanatic format aligned against you for twenty

---

[13] I heard my father Morey Myers recently reference that he would be "assaulted" for forming a political PAC; I can see now where he got the word, lol.

seven years. The second thing is then in a relatively "miracle" fashion the words that come out of my mouth, or pen, or computer for that matter are words of not just deep authenticity, but words of profound accuracy.

I did not go through the unfathomable challenges that I went through, not to come out of it with an agenda to profoundly help and better the world. If I do not ascribe to the notion that everything happens for a reason, which perhaps it does; I at least trust the sense that we have an opportunity in most situations to create a miracle angle or something deeply profound. Such is the essence of my work as The World's Best Mediator with Calm Interventions Inc. and how I work with my clients to create something truly great out of the challenges/opportunities that face them.

In more specific mode, when I reference that figurative fire, and what its net effect was on me, as a human being, I would speak to positive impacts on both an intrapersonal level, as well as it pertains to a professional agenda to substantially influence the world for the better. Well, to digress even further, I believe that the events that surrounded my life were so unfathomable as to not only be a once in a millennium type of event; but a happenstance so stark and so unusual that I irrevocably had a purpose and responsibility to bring my story and its accompanying lessons out to the world at large.

On an intrapersonal basis the things not only I learned, but that became deeply ensconced in the fabric of my being were things such as determination, as compared to stubbornness; gentleness, understanding of my fellow human being, respect and all kinds of related virtues. It takes a clear and subtle mind to distinguish between determination and stubbornness in our actions; but then again I lean to the side that most people are good, and want to learn, if not do the great things in life. One major difference between determination and stubbornness is that determination implies a sense of direction and purpose, a real goal; not merely holding on for the sake of the ego. Determination in my world views means that we are going somewhere; there is a positive direction or aim associated with the effort.

Stubbornness, while occasionally positive has more to do with our refusal to do something or our pursuing goals that really are reckless, and blind to the public interest. It is an extremely fine line that I have had to and chosen to walk in the pursuit of The World's Best Mediator, because a plausible reaction would be that I am pursuing goals that are way beyond my surface level capability. In more specificity my story speaks to my general principle of how adversity is the great training ground of our lives; and perhaps solely the only path towards true greatness, if not genius.

Recently, I have done some work, and for better or worse, a ton of my testing ground; my laboratory, is my own life, around the concept of doing all the work you can do, yes; however also taking time, when you have done as much as you can do, to just sit within the adversity, and trust that lessons are being transferred to you. This notion of sitting with the adversity, is a measure or even test of divine faith, as in adhering to the adage that this too will pass; and allowing the full range of the intended lessons to seep into the fabric of your being. The iceberg that began to appear in my life in 1988, was in my considered view, nothing short of remarkable in terms of its historical and emotional/psychological intensity, if not savagery AND irrational nature. Although, I am still learning a lot more about my families' capacity to isolate and scapegoat as time goes by, as a fuller extent of the iceberg emerges.

Still, it is the ferocity, the unexpected nature of the circumstances, along with the intensity and duration that makes my story stand on its own. A psychological crucible, if not prison like structure was created around my life. As I say, it really was the perfect storm of events, in terms of encountering all at once, the challenging Massachusetts Probate and Family Court system, an emotionally challenged ex-wife, whom I believe was a borderline personality type, and a family so concerned on some level with its image that it lost its bearings as far as decency and morality. Any of those three factors would be an unbelievable challenge to take on, in its own right. I do not know everything, but I know, to take on those three factors combined, with "outstanding"[14] intensity and duration was simply an act of divine blessing, if not divine strength. God, the divine and/or the universe were testing and preparing me.

Here again, resides a principle of The Science of Inner Strength, as I had an endearing, principle within me that could pull me through and guide me during this

---

[14] "Outstanding" was a word employed by Richard S. Bishop, Esquire of Scranton, PA an attorney for my biological parents Morey and Sondra Myers, to describe my ex-wife's parenting; albeit more so as I see it, to cover up things done in Scranton, and work to keep my two sacred children from me.

outrageous ordeal, in the form of the love and care for Sophie and Sam, for one. In an emotional and psychological sense I was somewhat imprisoned; as the landscape of the courts was so biased towards women, that I was not going to get fair and equal treatment as far as my sacred children and my ex-wife seemed to terrifically enjoy the game aspect and the manipulation involved in being as vengeful and hurtful to me, including the use of our children. To top if off the normal and anticipated place I would turn to: My family of origin, was viciously orchestrating and commandeering the whole thing against me.

Given those kind of odds, I had to turn to divine and/or spiritual types of resources; as all the things you would expect to be fair and reasonable were no longer there. For instance, I would have anticipated an American court system to be fair and reasonable, my experience at least initially was anything but; I thought an ex-wife with whom I was imperfect with, but still done lots of good, would ultimately smile in my favor, nothing doing there. I thought my family who had raised me to be an excellent person and do good in the world, would terrifically have my back; and in most outrageous tenor, I struck out on that one too. With nothing else left, it fell upon my shoulders, and for me, it required a spiritual sense and/or sense of the divine.

I suppose that speaks to a crucial issue, right there, although it did not happen all at once. What do you do, when every human resource you have been raised to depend and rely upon is not only missing, but attacking you as well? Well that is where The Science of Inner Strength, and in my view a sense of the divine or at least some form of a higher power must enter the picture.

It is precisely that kind of rock and a hard place scenario that we can find ourselves in, in life that lends itself to the possibility of finding the divine. I did not ask for the divine per se. The divine found me. It was only in the dark of night, when there seemed nowhere to turn, that the divine entered my life, in a calm, quiet, and gentle way.

CHAPTER 12

HOW YOU BEGIN TO FIND YOUR TRUE INNER STRENGTH

> *"Nothing in the world will take the place of persistence…talent will not… genius will not…education will not… Persistence and determination are omnipotent."* Calvin Coolidge.

That moment when the divine entered my life subtly changed everything in terms of who I was, and who I was to become,; and what my work turned out to be. When the divine entered my life, it was an extremely quiet moment in the middle of the night and I just recall that calm presence entering my life, in the way of an understanding. Since that understanding entered my life; I have no reason to believe that such presence is not readily also accessible to more and more people.

Two or three major understandings about myself and my life began to flow forward at that moment, including, but not limited to: Recalling my four year old self, and knowing that that child was good; learning to let go of anger and that kind of tension, and along the lines of that inner child, developing a more trusting, respectful attitude about myself, others, and the world. While I do wish to discuss these in more detail, at the moment, I believe it is incredibly important for people who are at least somewhat open-minded, to learn and discover about how to make that important shift and psychological transition without enduring the pain that I did.

In the time of Caitlyn Jenner; the word "transition" has taken on a whole new meaning and sense of relevancy. Not in terms of necessarily sexual or gender identity, but in terms of spirit, or just being ourselves; I do believe there is a "transition" that most of us or society as a whole can make to take on a greater sense of our own identity. While I will reemphasize, the transition I am referencing, has nothing in my case to do with sexual identity; the notion of a societal shift and a spiritual change is beneficial, in finding our true selves

The shift or "transition" that I am referencing applies to any person, family or organization that is open-minded, and/or pressed through adversity, into a situation where either change feels necessary, or rather magically occurs. Inner strength is, about authenticity, and finding our inner goodness; the real us. That real us, has on many, many layers been covered over, and lies dormant as a pipe dream in most of our lives. The basic "reality" of life experience beats down that true self and can leave people feeling like a shirt on an ironing board.

I for one, no longer live my life like a shirt on an ironing board. Like the Wizard of Oz, I have my heart, and brain, and courage, and use them on a regular basis. So the principles I espouse are not necessarily brand new; it is that I have walked the walk and bring them to life, in a new way. That is the value of my story; in that I have formulated and walked the walked with these things for twenty-two years; they are thoroughly tested.

So the question I pose to you and me, was in essence how do you the reader begin to make that transition to finding your inner strength; the good or great you, and how do you begin to manifest that strength in your life, work and actions? Once again, before I get fully to that answer, since I used the word "manifest;" and that is a word closely identified with the Law of Attraction; I might take moment to reference how my work dovetails and/or not with the Law of Attraction.

I admire the Law of Attraction; I see it as a useful tool, among others to accompany a person on their spiritual journey; yet my Science of Inner Strength pre-dates the Law of Attraction in this way. While I agree that maintaining a positive upbeat attitude is a crucial ingredient to reaching one's goals; I say predate, because I believe that one must connect to the divine first; and have developed a sense of a purpose first; and not solely rely on the Law of Attraction. I also believe in the notion of work itself, both in terms of our own internal work, as well as work in the world as key ingredients in terms of manifesting results, not relying solely on being in the right place at the right time, although that could work; and I am not one to tell believe another what to believe.

Now, we get to the notion of how you as an individual, a couple or an organization can start to access

The Science of Inner Strength, and tap into your own inner goodness. One of the great things about adversity, in general, is that it is basically a crying wake up call for change. More often than not, what adversity is telling us is that something is not working in our lives, or at least our current trajectory is putting us on a collision course with something. So, adversity is one of the major ways that people can begin a process of finding their inner strength; as something is calling to people to make changes, and find something within them. For me, I find that adversity is virtually, the only way, or at least, the main way that people can begin to find their inner strength. On an overall societal level, we are wired too much at this moment, into the land of pretense, and doing what you have to do; to begin to discover our inner strength, at least without some sense of dissatisfaction and/or desire for something deeper and more meaningful.

The first light that must hit, us has to do with determination, although I am tempted to say first we must discover and affirm our goodness. Yes, in a slightly subtle way I believe our goodness must be our first realization. Our goodness is our worthiness, our sense of desire for success and fairness even; the sense that we are good, and as good as the next person. By goodness I must affirm that I truly mean goodness, not selfishness. The desire to want success, what we believe is due to us; inherently means that we will work to achieve said goals by fair and meritorious methods. The first step in the process is recognizing and affirming our goodness.

In addition to adversity, we can also discover this innate goodness by really great parenting, or coaching, teaching/mentoring, especially as these things get better understood.. One reason that adversity is particularly valuable in this regard; is that it helps us often enough, determine what we don't want, and emphatically state what we do want. So the first step is to recognize this unique inner goodness within us; this shining light that we were brought into this world for a reason. For me, it was particularly illuminating to remember myself as a four year old child, and to recognize that this child, could not be much of anything but good; as I basically believe most four year olds are.

It is a really hard lesson for people to see and understand that little four-year old, that lies within them, as a prospectively great person. Right now, in the main, society does not raise us to function from a place of our goodness; so much of society is predicted on this dire sense of economic need that we are essentially programmed into these rather narrow channels of "success" and "failure", and what we should and should not do.

Yet, that is one of the challenges in today's world, our systems are not really working in fair and meritorious ways; and there may come a point where the world reaches a crisis point, or a degree of adversity that prospectively provides that fundamental wake-up call that is needed; indeed this is it. Fault lines in our systems include intense economic pressure within American society, where a great portion of people struggle to make ends meet, let alone enjoy a life of comfortable living; American inner cities are vast areas of underperforming achievement based on lack of equitable economic development and schools; world terrorism at least emotionally beckons at our door;

corporations are lands of huge profits; our legal system is greatly challenged, our political process seems inappropriate and unsatisfactory; it is less than clear that our media seeks honest and beneficial answers to human challenges, before even getting into the issue of climate change and those kinds of things. Most of all to me, is our dramatic difficulty in even having intelligent and constructive discourse on these matters.

In essence, the notion of divine light requires a wakeup call on an individual and societal level. The other way, other than adversity is to teach the notion of goodness, and inner strength, as well as societal goodness on much broader levels, at much earlier points. It is the macro picture that guides the micro at times, even though it is the individual who begins to waken up prior to society as a whole. The duality is such that more and more people will reach a point of their inner strength and goodness, as society starts to value these things; and yet society will only value these things as individuals wake up and strongly influence society to make these changes.

The point on a societal level is that the planet simply cannot withstand our current trajectory, without a fundamental shift towards cooperation, and working together. The first step in individuals starting to find their inner strength, other than adversity itself has to do with recognizing and appreciating their own inner voice, and getting in the habit of not discounting that inner voice. We cannot continue to produce over-stressed people, who see their lives as a function of a large economic machine. By developing a more trusting attitude towards ourselves and people in general, we can gradually encourage peoples' innovation and problem-solving skills as healthy and well-intended people, rather than as square pegs to attempt to bang into round holes.

Societally we must learn and work to teach people that their own lives, their spirit, their inner voices really matter; and that those qualities will be appreciated and applauded in this lifetime. The kind of shift I allude to, while massive, is doable in a twenty first century society. Who will be those first corporations not just to value its people, as good souls but to step out from there, and encourage their basic goodness, and creative skills?

The shift towards goodness, will naturally tame a somewhat out of control American media. As we look at the current 2016 presidential campaign, we see again that the basic tenor can be one of destroying people, under the guise of "vetting" and the like. Let me begin at the endpoint; unless people are really hardcore criminals, which most of us are not; or who aim to do destruction to individuals and society as a whole, or are utterly devious, we need to recalibrate[15] our standards for participation in the game of life.

Rather than wielding vicious tools of evisceration and mob mentality, with regard to peoples' flaws, we must begin from a standpoint of acknowledging and honoring our basic humanness, with an understanding that anybody worth their salt has probably encountered some adversity in their lives. Anyone who has grown up through the sixties and seventies, in the best sense is not a perfect creature, or is anyone else for that matter, lol. We cannot

---

[15] To use a word used by President Barack Obama pertaining to one of his policies.

use standards of finding one relatively minute flaw within a person, and using that to drill and drill and drill until we have brought that person down.

Instead we must all calibrate ourselves to a basic standard of decency and goodness. Such a standard is predicated on being able to understand the whole human being, including a sense of a person's intentions. Most people are well-intended. Society is at too critical a point to waste virtually any time and energy spending time and money attempting to bring down otherwise good people. We have real and abiding challenges, in the vein of terrorism, financial, education, environmental to not get real and focus virtually all of our energy on solving problems, and preserving and promoting our common good.

The shift that can and must occur at the individual and societal level is about learning and making changes. We are almost due a massive time-out for society, prior to facing some truly unwanted catastrophe that forces us to change. The media is a valuable and protected group that must play a more responsible role with the advent of cable news and all of that. Looming over that discussion is that there is no articulated sense of societal purpose right now, from those in positions of leadership.

We have almost subliminally shifted into a world, when in an unarticulated sense the only thing that matters is money. Money is not the root of all evil to me; the irresponsible use, and as I once read the worship of money is the root of evil. Money is an excellent tool in society; the hard part is, when money does not stand for anything with respect to our values; instead it stands as an end unto itself.

Money is not the sole end. The pursuit of positive and constructive actions that will better the human race is a better reasonable end, if there is such a thing, or at least a guidepost. The media as one instance is also so consumed with the "bottom line" of money and ratings that it does not play a needed role in identifying appropriate societal standards, as of yet. In terms of societal standards, I am referencing the notion that most of us are in the same boat. Major issues such as economics, climate, education, terrorism, and so on and so forth must be addressed by a collective of society as a whole; and creating reasonable standards and parameters of discussion.

The problems among us are great and we cannot follow a path of simply allowing the rich to get richer, and keep their head in the sand, as well as other leaders in terms of truly addressing America's and the world's problems. We are at that point. I recall the words of Professor David Orr of my undergraduate alma mater Oberlin College, along the lines that we are a crucial point in terms of society, in terms of the environment and other issues. My work in seeing the challenges within our American judicial system has underscored that notion of being at a crucial moment in our human history, in other areas.

There can be a point where we deviate so far from our stated ideals, such as liberty, equality, and fairness that we cease to exist as a noble and just society. Mine, is not solely a message of dire warning, as it is an assertive call to discover and illuminate our true strengths. In order for people to address their inner strength, we must get rid of the overlay of corruption in society. You can only fool people so long; A lack of basic, not perfect honesty permeates our political, economic and legal systems, along how the media is representing it. Part of the iceberg is the basic dishonesty that we are allowing to occur in society today.

The Science of Inner Strength is not much more in its lighter moments than affirming and bolstering our recognized senses of justice, liberty and common sense that resides deeply within our population. We must inspire, encourage and support our citizenry and appropriate non-citizenry to take their own heroic stands, and importantly, for society to reward these stands. We stumble due to losing sight of our values.

The issue of reward is imperative. The money exists in this country; some surely have it. The issue has to do,not with a matter of re-distribution, but with true opportunity for all, as well as in vital fashion actually rewarding those who are contributing the benefit of society including, but not limited to: police, teachers, nurses, entrepreneurs and more. Money must reflect our values; which brings us to the critical issue of today; our failure to live up to and substantially articulate America's values that unite us.

Our pursuit of money, has in a subliminal sense reached a frenzied level in America; steadily eroding the walls of our values and what we actually believe. In haphazard sense we have allowed the pursuit of money, to be our highest value; rather than our true, at least stated American values of liberty, equality and justice for all. Capitalism can coexist with purpose.

When our court system gets eroded, if not temporarily corrupted, then the core of America, like an apple core gets weak and soggy. The prospective moral weakness, with all due respect not only makes our society weaker within, but makes us more prone to external, i.e. terroristic attacks, because we on some level are not assertively standing for what we say we are standing for; and hypocrisy is one of the least desirable human characteristics. A quote resonated recently that said: People are not evil, systems are."

How can America possibly improve, if not regain our standing in the world, if we refuse to be honest about what is going on? Yes, let's deal with external threats but also let us not be distracted from the things we must do internally, including but not limited to improving our schools, our economy, our roads and bridges, our immigration policy, the environment, economic opportunity, and so on and so forth. It is our pursuit of money functioning without appreciation and awareness of our humanity that confuses us.

Tthese issues become impossible to deal with, under the current climate, without a fundamental adjustment of our political perspective, a certain amount of relinquishing being right, and a fervent embracing of the notion of working together .Working together is reflective of our inner strength, because working together virtually is about our goodness, and implies a common you know what: purpose.

Purpose is virtually totally aligned with inner strength, because it brings forth our inner strength. This is the critical element; let's take Democrats and Republicans as examples; if each group does not in some way subsume itself to the overall good of the country then, we cannot thrive and prosper; without a third party or some other massive new type of movement. Purpose defines why political parties actually exist, at least in theory.

We live in such challenging times, because on some level we are exaggerating and amplifying our differences, and losing sight of our common purpose and common good. True to the Calm Interventions philosophy of "Turning hard times into better times" and The Science of Inner Strength, it may well take adversity, for people to stop their current course, and regain a better sense of the big picture. I write BTW, with the sense that perhaps waking up now, can offset, if not prevent the larger hardship.

On an individual basis we gain our inner strength, by learning to speak up in relatively calm and assertive ways. It is a multi-step process that I am describing, because on one level when people realize that their voices have been squelched or perhaps manipulated on some level; the first tendency might be to throw off the sense of repression in a bitter and angry way. While such a tendency might be understandable and just for a slip second might be almost necessary, one of my basic tenets is that anger is a counter-productive reaction, a cover-up emotion that ultimately will obscure the otherwise worthy cause that the proponent is advocating. There are more constructive ways then anger to express oneself, as the Science of Inner Strength delineates.

So it is multi-dimensional and demanding a lot of people to recognize: A) on some level we are temporarily not on the right path and; B) we must define our true path and then; C) learn to communicate this new path in calm, appropriate and assertive ways.

CHAPTER 13

THE IMPEDIMENT: THE ICEBERG

"Every action has an equal and opposite reaction." The third law of Sir Isaac Newton

In the most simple sense, along with emerging extreme narcissism and psychopathic behavior. malicious dishonesty is the iceberg. Corruption; not living up to American ideals of liberty, equality and justice for all; on some level there is significant corrosion in the American system that no amount of military might can pull us out of. We are even starting to see the drawbacks of substituting military force for true global morality, as the American military seems challenged to solve the problem of global terrorism unto itself. The answer is perhaps far more complicated and mandates a new global conversation. The new global conversation must be geared towards positive communication and building bridges of understanding and mutual recognition, along with the defeat of ISIS and other terroristic threats, while developing an American ideal.

Underlying the corruption that makes us vulnerable in this country is still what I acknowledge as the Iceberg effect; that hidden element of psychopathic, narcissistic, borderline and other deviant personality types that are virtually perverting the sense of fairness in America and the American dream. You see, heretofore, people have not been aware of the iceberg effect; and the vast disturbance in personality types that resides underneath the surface of American life. Previously it was seen that people achieving a certain level of societal status was enough; and that was a barometer of their goodness or societal contribution. Clearly now, we are seeing that mere achievement and/or money does not equate to morality. .

Indeed facets of the opposite effect may true; in that people with deviant personality types may be more likely to attain higher levels of success in society. People with challenged personality types can be more likely to achieve outer world success, because they both embrace deceit as a tactic; and they are utterly ruthless in achieving their goals, irrespective of who they climb over, or what tactics they use to get there. What needs to be understood, is that it is not mere meanness in evidence, but personality types that are only superficially and remotely rational; and who will essentially stop at nothing to achieve what they have their eyes set upon.

I do draw heartily on my own experience, as a virtual divine tutorial that was deposited into my life. I say this for the purposes of illumination and societal advancement, not revenge or anything of the like; more in accord with the famous third law of Sir Isaac Newton: "Every action has an equal and opposite reaction." Someone or something induced a psychopathic attack against me, within my family of origin. It is hard to absolutely pin down the exact source. I attribute at least the tip of that iceberg to my younger brother David Nathan Myers; although at present it is how clear how much he has been pushed to that point by his wife Nomi Maya Stolzenberg or even his mother-in-law Judy Levine of Cambridge, MA; or whether Morey and Sondra Myers, my biological parents are the galvanizing energy, in the long run.

However the energy came about, it manifested in my life, like an extremely sharp spear pointed and prodding at my life, over a period to date, of more than twenty nine years. Surely the most virulent part took the form of David Nathan Myers himself, in terms of the vigor and frenzy of a virtually totally berserk message. It may be that David's taking this, with all due respect form of psychopathic behavior emanated from his lack of sense of self, and/or was induced by Sondra Myers, or even his wife Nomi Stolzenberg.

In fact, that is a major component of deviant personality types and deviant behavior; they have no enduring spiritual sense of self, or fully developed emotional sense of self. This type of emptiness is the opposite of The Science of Inner Strength, which is all about finding our inner strength, our inner light, our true decency, a sense of compassion within us. People who developed these extreme and enraged personality types are extremely hurt and devoid people inside, which although we can understand this, we must also protect ourselves from this vile and deviant behavior. There is also a sense that people with this true emptiness inside cloak themselves with notions of religious supremacy and singular understanding of God, such as ISIS and other extreme entities.

While it is clear that America is being threatened by entities as outrageous as ISIS; it is less clear to most, what our internal threat is as well. The deviant personality type is an unfathomable threat to our inner peace. The threat of the deviant personality type is that for one, most people are remarkably unaware of these personality types, and the capacity for those with those characteristics to insinuate themselves into positions of authority in our society as a whole. Clearly, I have personally seen, witnessed, and indeed contested the horrific skew within our American legal system.

The legal system is the place where American values are supposed to be most fervently embraced; those values of equality, liberty and justice. Instead there is, with all due respect, a rather grotesque permutation of American values. The area pertaining to divorce and family law is an egregious example. While the tendency may well be for people to roll their eyes and tune out, when they hear the topic of divorce; the reality is that a great proportion of marriages do end up in divorce; and the lack of care, attention and compassion is, with all due respect harmful in this area of American justice that relates directly to the health and well-being of our families and children.

I literally had my first divorce attorney, a J. White of a then prominent law firm of White, Inker Aaronson tell me they were going to "carve me up;" and he was *my* attorney for goodness sakes. While the attorney was referencing my financial assets, which was bad enough, and not my body; he was after all representing me. Families are emotionally, psychologically, and financially being carved up within our Probate and Family Court system. The levels of harshness and unfairness are astounding; at times based on what attorney can be most malicious and most conniving towards a family, whose children, he or she, has virtually zero care about. Attorney Honora Kaplan to me, exhibited these reckless qualities on behalf of my ex-wife in our situation.

The lack of justice in our Probate and Family Court area is an incendiary snake that interweaves its way in and out of society; in ways that are both different and similar to issues that African Americans and people of color have within our criminal justice system. BTW, for any prospective critics from Black Lives Matter please be illuminated that I worked directly with and set up nationally recognized employment related programs for youth of wonderful diversity dating back to 1980 in Cambridge, MA; and that commitment to equality and human dignity is deeply imbued in my fabric.

Still, it goes beyond individuals; the iceberg effect: This psychopathic, emotionally abusive behavior is alive and well in American systems. The iceberg, be it pertaining to individuals or systems often plays itself out, with regard to emotional and psychological abuse. That is, its vast hidden quality is the fact that the abuse is occurring in emotional and psychological ways; rather than outright physical or sexual abuse makes it so incendiary. Also, the damage is being done, below the surface, and unknown to many people. The person being victimized is often then made out to be "crazy" or something.

Deceit and its older cousin emotional and psychological abuse are the humongous internal enemies of our country. There is a fundamental dishonesty, with all due respect functioning in America, and it is blossoming in our judicial, political, and economic systems; as well as in the media. It is as if, the American people do not know everything, but know that something is off; and yet cannot, as of yet, put their finger on it. This state of confusion is the golden tool of the narcissist/psychopath, and the emotional abuser. The one with the deviant personality will set up something that is almost right, or seems right, and yet people feel they are not treated fairly, and feel powerless to stop it.

This is one of the two or three great truths of my story: Coming to terms with and understanding a fundamental dishonesty within our culture, AND the role of the psychopathic behavior and/or deviant personality type in terms of bringing about this dishonesty. The person functioning with the psychopathic personality is like a grand grotesque jester, just slightly behind the curtain, in American society. I will reiterate again that I do not know everything, but I know that most people are good. There is however, a disproportionate degree of influence that those with deviant personality types can play, due to their ruthlessness, along with their seeming almost right. A key point is, that this type of behavior is often learned behavior.

By almost right, I mean these folks are so slippery that people do not challenge them, or they find a way to virtually slither their way out of every conversation and situation. Those days of such escape are coming to an end; by the shining the light of honesty upon those people and situations. The deviant personality type functions in such a way, as to slant and deceive virtually every circumstance.

America becomes much the weaker, if we do not hold up to American ideals as most people deserve emotional well-being, as well as, our economy ultimately demands this truth and fairness. I am convinced that my story occurred for me not just to develop The Science of Inner Strength but related understandings for society as a whole. The iceberg is this fundamental dishonesty; the iceberg is this slippery snake of the personality type posing as a person who cares, or who is doing right, when their fundamental intention is to deceive, often for them, in a sadistic manner.

It is not clear to me, as to whether I truly have adequately conveyed the depth of the experience that confronted me. The unfathomable part was to have an entire family system so horrifically and heinously aligned against me for so long. Without provocation or substantive reason, my family turned against me twenty-nine years ago, and has not stopped. Those who have not had some degree of experience in dealing with a psychopathic or extreme narcissistic personality type, may have some challenge in initially understanding my story. It just seems unfathomable that so many people for so long, would maintain an utter wall of hateful behavior towards me, beginning with my own family of origin; yet it happens, and this story is living proof.

Yes, on some level a substantial portion of the hatred,

did seem to begin with my younger brother David Nathan Myers and his wife Nomi Maya Stolzenberg; and yet the notion that the entire program was endorsed and vigorously accepted by my biological parents Morey and Sondra Myers of Scranton, PA is both ghastly and astonishing. Who, in the world ever anticipates that their biological parents will turn against them with such ferocity and sheer hatred? Indeed, my parents seem to thrive at the wheel of this animus.

Ironic to the core, in that I mainly perceived my biological parents, as being basically good to me, in our childhood, surely it was so, on a superficial level, although now surely in retrospect the seeds of the discord were at least somewhat apparent, no pun intended, lol. You see it was 1988, when the tide irrevocably changed against me. Then my grandfather Morris B. Gelb passed away in Scranton, PA, and left an estate of approximately $10 million. My parents Morey and Sondra Myers as part of the controlling group of these funds, along with an aunt and uncle and my grandmother in a figure head role, reported approximately $2.1 million to the IRS. With no proof on my part; the turn in temperament was severe that I even have questions as to how exactly my grandfather died; as my mother at point said to me that he had: "a very unusual illness."

That timeframe brought a stunning turn in the attitudes and actions towards me. My younger brother began outrageously assaulting my mental health, with absurd validity. I was experiencing a marital separation at the time: The combination of these two backdrop scenarios and the handling of my Grandfather Morris B. Gelb's estate all in catalyzed in 1988, AND created a perfect storm dynamic that had one and only one binding point: An outrageous and totally irrational hatred of me.

These types of matters escalated terrifically in 1990, when the first of my two children was born, Sophia Rose Myers on March 17. Sophie, like her younger brother Sam, who was born in 1993 seemed a rather exceptional child, in terms of personality and appeal. It is like the group of extended family from in-laws to cousins, to aunts and uncles, developed an obsession with my children, and sought endless ways to ingratiate and flaunt their favor at my children, geared often to tear down my fatherhood. I recall, when Sophie was less than three years old, and my biological mother Sondra Gelb Myers sneaking around and whispering in her ear: "Be independent." I mean, who in the world, would do that to a two year old, and independent from what and whom? Wowsie.

The entire matter was terrifically exacerbated, like a match to kerosene by the fact that my wife, later to be ex-wife, was a Zelig like character, who would, with all due respect, in an emotional sense contort herself into virtually any position, particularly if after a certain point in time, it was going to cause emotional hurt and pain to me. My own sense is that my ex-wife Margaret Carney in addition to familial illnesses pertaining to manic depression and alcoholism; had something resembling a Borderline Personality Disorder. Yes, unfathomable circumstances, and yet as I say. this truly was a perfect storm of events; leading ultimately in response to my divine calling.

A salient point that I am making is not only did such an unfathomable alliance cause such ongoing and severe emotional distress but that those same set of circumstances while, somewhat prison-like provided the most intense learning ground and training ground that a person could imagine. It was akin to when Nelson Mandela was asked. what did twenty- seven years in prison provide you; he replied in one word: "Maturity." Although differing even from Mandela, I was accused of no crime. The most crazy and insane, and most arduous of circumstances have that capability to provide the deepest and most profound of sacred lessons.

Those lessons come about especially if and when the person develops a purpose to all of this; which is what these circumstances did to, and for, me. These circumstances became the incubating grounds for my own inner strength. It is "odd" for sure that my own commitment to children and family came from my parents and my grandparents; the former who were the people who attacked and abused me for having such a commitment.

Indeed, just this week, on of all days, Pearl Harbor Day, December 7, 2015, I brought to my father Morey Myers what I learned to be was a gratitude letter thanking him for his role in raising me, and the degree of support he provided me. Rather than on any level return the gesture in kind; he not only began verbally assaulting me, but he exhibited this unfathomable narcissistic lack of self-awareness where he started telling me my kids were "coming along" well; totally in denial of the fact that he and others were working round the clock to brainwash my sacred children and keep them from me.

The point was that no matter how confusing a set of circumstances were concocted around my life, I was relatively blessed with having a mind of my own, and even rudimentary skills of making up my own mind at an early age. Thus, when my younger brother and his wife; my parents, and my ex-wife all joined up to "mob" against me, lie about me; and all of that, I paid precious little attention to the substance of their lies; as I had a deeper purpose to attend to, then the relatively heinous actions of those folks.

Namely I had my own sense of self, and for large parts of the discussion the emotional health and well-being of my two sacred children to preserve and protect. This is what I am getting at, in terms of having a sense of purpose, which is closely related to our inner strength. I was raised to care for my children, on some level by my grandparents and parents. "Odd" though it seems, the grandparent, who died first in 1971 at the age of seventy eight, who was probably seen as the most challenging and temper-prone, in his actions; towards me was the most humane and gentle. Samuel Z. Myers would make paper hats out of newspaper for me, and had a kind and gentle touch; although I heard stories from previous generations about his temper, which I did not see.

This caring touch, no matter how clouded over, and used and misused by others, was probably all a part of my nature. It is probably one of the characteristics, along with my authenticity that most enrages and scares my family, along with my empathy and compassion. Empathy and compassion two true strengths in the world are the opposite of narcissism and psychopathic behavior. It is not at all that I want to convey a sense of victimhood around my life, actually quite the opposite. What I am illuminating is both the depth of the psychological asteroid that hit my life; along with using my life to make the general principle that as Sir Isaac Newton scientifically laid out centuries before me: "Every action has an equal and opposite reaction." This is such an integral part of my story; I was hit with such an asteroid of emotional hatred that it propelled me towards decency and my own sense of greatness.

The depth of the emotional torture that I was put through; as long as I have a sense of purpose and figure out ways to survive it, would ultimately in equal and opposite fashion produce something beautiful. I am a tad stunned myself at the simplicity of that concept of beauty, but that is really the nature of things. To firmly establish my credentials, it becomes necessary to understand the process that created those credentials; namely the severe psychological and emotional torture chamber that was created around my life.

I am working to establish a deep understanding of emotional abuse, and both its direct as well as subtle reverberations in society as a whole, through a culture, which can be dishonest. Emotional/psychological abuse is a fascinating subject to understand, as it becomes more in play in our contemporary society. The realm of emotional abuse in my life, as it would in most peoples' lives, begins by essentially deviant personality types assaulting a weak point, or at least a perceived weak point of the person they are seeking to often destroy, in the guise of "care;" like a wolf in sheep's clothing.

It is hard for me to determine whether this unfathomably vicious assault began from my younger brother solely; my parents, even my sister-in-law Nomi Stolzenberg or a combination thereof. In any event, pertinent to emotional/

psychological abuse, is the notion of a disturbed or deviant personality type seeking to essentially hurt or harm another human being for no rational reason. Many people in this world, are genuine, and primarily seeking to just go about their business; as life is tough enough, without having deviant and unneeded enemies. Crucial to understanding emotional/psychological abuse is that it essentially is constructed upon a sadistic, if not parasitic mindset.

The perpetrator by and large has some form of woefully developed personality that continually keeps them locked into repressed pain, and without appropriate checkpoints allows them to antagonize and seek to harm another human being. In my situation this mindset seemed largely to have formed, somehow in the embodiment of my younger brother David Nathan Myers; and yet, it is hard to tell as to how much influence in total his wife Nomi Maya Stolzenberg, along with his mother-in-law Judy Levine; along with Morey and Sondra Myers brought upon him.

The astonishing thing truly, is that this mindset of hatred and rage towards me, which I submit is of Biblical proportions has gone on for over twenty nine years; and was able to lock in so many other members of extended family upon extended family. I mean, my ex-wife and her several siblings bought into it; my four extremely well-heeled first cousins and their spouses bought into it to a greater or lesser extent; aunts and uncles; the whole nine yards. The entire group was in a frenzy-like fashion virtually totally aligned in defaming, hating and pointlessly ostracizing me from my own family. The pointless and irrational aspect to thist is stunning.

Given that I was raised in an extremely deep-rooted Jewish sense with four grandparents, beginning in 1958 in Scranton; the grandfathers were a doctor and a lawyer, and the two grandmothers lived near one another and lived over 100 years each; the betrayal on the part of my parents, in and of itself is astounding. How many parents after raising their kids in a certain way, find money or something, and then totally turn against their first born? Such are the ways of malignant narcissism.

What I am seeking to convey is that particularly in this case, and generally as well, there are extremely deep ties that bind us to family; and thereby cause such potential emotional hurt and pain. There are movements and discussions of things like No Contact and other prospective remedies in dealing with narcissistic and psychopathic individuals and even families, and yet to fully separate emotionally from one's family is the most intricate and painful journey that one can fathom. This separation is all the harder, due to the emotional sabotage and savagely unexpected nature to all this.

My biological father Morey Myers developed a drill like obsession with my life; having me followed and orchestrating along with my biological mother Sondra Myers all kinds of harassing, and essentially emotional/psychological stalking types of events for decades. To recognize adequately the degree of emotional abuse that I withstood, I am laughing out loud a little because it really is like a cosmic earthquake of some kind hit my life; and that is why I have virtually no choice but to take it, if not accept it as an act of God; even further to use it for my good!

There is a real danger in people misinterpreting what I am saying; particularly in this day of internet heroes and palpable hatred that is flung around society. One of the key points I am making is that there is such a thing as truth; not absolute truth, but a societal standard for reality and decency that most of us would accept, when we get ourselves into a reasonable discussion. This reasonable discussion is part of my goal.

Specifically, most of us want to live peacefully in our homes and neighborhoods, most of us want homes for that matter, and reasonable employment fitting of our skills and interests; most of us would want quality schools and bridges, and the like. In order to have most of those things we must realize there is a common and shared interest on all our parts, to get to a better functioning society. An astonishing skewing factor is the amount emphasis on finances and with all due respect, greed that is occurring.

This is a subtle point of the societal implications of The Science of Inner Strength; we from richest to poorest must think in terms of our common and shared interests. It is one thing to go out on the playing field of life and be extremely successful; it is quite another not to realize there us, a game and a playing field set up for us; by something greater than us. I am all for fair and open competition, and it must be with the human spirit of fairness and gratitude, and not dog eat dog, which is a philosophy that was advocated by businessman Trump in a book, of his I read. Ah President Trump, more later perhaps.

So, the notion that there are basic and shared truths in society is not so far away. It is just that we as a society have not yet come to a point of identifying and articulating those points of fairness and decency, along with shared interests and truths that could unite us. Again, in this day of ISIS and terroristic threats and financial difficulties and on and on, the days of our not working together must come to a close.

How then does this relate to me generally, or the facets pertaining to my biological father Morey Myers in particular? Again, I am getting at, the notion of truth; and in this regard we must become much better and for that matter, more sensitive in recognizing what truth is. As I say, the entire ideal of truth is within us for starters, and not far out of our reach, it is just that we have been so beaten down and bamboozled by the iceberg facets of society that most people are not fully aware that truth is available or needs to be furthered, or that goodness can prevail.

What I am saying is that there will be a tendency to blame or muckrake some of the things I am saying; due at least in part to our societal tendency for everybody to be a genius when it is not earned, along with the virtual tsunami of negativity that we have allowed to take hold in society. One of the reasons for those erros is the misunderstanding of emotional/psychological abuse itself. In making everybody a keyboard king or queen, we have lost sight of what is really accurate, and who is really qualified in what ways to speak on certain things. Not to mention that we have dropped like a hot potato, our sense of societal purpose, and believe we somehow or other have right to eviscerate one another.

Time out! Who invented computers anyway, who brought us to society with so many advantages and technological advances? Countless humans before, and to function without appreciation is like driving a car without brake pads at best; if not without brakes. What I am getting at is that there is such a thing as emotional/psychological abuse and it can be as "vile" and harmful as razor sharp swords. For those who doubt the existence of emotional/psychological abuse; perhaps some of your ancestors, I say, slightly tongue in cheek also vigorously disputed the existence of oxygen, because they could not see it. How about living in a world without oxygen? If you catch my drift. Just because, we cannot see it, does not mean, it does exist.

We must develop a capacity to listen to one another; to recognize that a portion of society functions in mean and unfair ways, and others in society actually happen to get a sadistic enjoyment out of harming other human beings. Meaning that when a person states that she or he has been treated unfairly or harmfully, we must listen, and more generally stop blaming the victim. The emotional/psychological abuser banks on the idea that they will be able to isolate and otherwise neutralize the person they are attacking, be it through social, financial, emotional and/or psychological factors. This goes beyond merely men's and women's issues; not only must we stop all of men's abuse of women in all forms, we must be aware in family courts, it is men who are getting pulverized.

As Martin Luther King said: "Injustice anywhere is injustice everywhere;" and it goes beyond discrimination based on race, gender, sexual preference and those kind of things; it gets to the basic rights and dignity of every human being. What I am getting at is that there is such a thing as accuracy in society. In my story, to a great number of people it will appear "ludicrous"[16] that I would say that a group of people would act so hatefully, so maliciously, so irrationally for so long, and yet that is precisely what I am saying, and happened. Abuse can happen to anyone, not limited to gender, race, sexual preference or any specific category. We are all human, and deserve a basic human dignity.

In this culture, where not only does everyone have an opinion, but many feel utterly entitled to express it as seemingly viciously as they want; we must put a brake on things, and learn to express things appropriately and for that matter with accuracy, or at least to understand that there is such a thing as accuracy and it matters. Society is at too vulnerable a place, to lurch in uncaring and reckless directions.

So, I will tell my story, and the first reaction may be; that that cannot be so, he is being weak, or poor pitiful him. Indeed. I am being the opposite; I am being extremely strong, and I am identifying a vast iceberg in American society, that of emotional/psychological abuse, brought on by the emergence, if not proliferation of, the deviant personality type and our age of entitlement.

In other words it matters not, if 100 people are on one side, and one on the other; the only thing that matters is a careful and caring recitation and understanding of what the truth really is. We cannot rely upon sheer politics or numbers in terms of accuracy; we must use our true intelligence, with a realm of compassion to discover the

---

[16] Again a word, my younger brother, with all due respect in psychopathic sense threw against me.

truth of situations. Many of those who have been treated unfairly or even mobbed, are seen as lesser than, doubling or tripling the amount of emotional pain and anguish they feel.

In determining my own inner strength; I see it as a divine purpose to have been put in a psychological/emotional purgatory for more than twenty years, for me to develop this strength, and these societal understandings. It is this psychological abuse, this false sense of superiority of some, that is the most challenging thing to society.

To face down the hatred of my deep-rooted and deep-pocketed family of origin, with me as one person, facing tens of others, became my destiny and my calling to develop my inner strength. It must be reiterated that people must be riveted on the fact that my parents and ex-wife were linked psychologically at the hip in hatred and viciousness towards me. People must really appreciate this; my biological parents, extended family joined with my ex-wife to create this cauldron of unfathomable hatred, and action, using a knife-edged court system, and the use of my children, to stop at virtually nothing to attempt to defeat, if not destroy me. The mere writing of these words, speaks volumes to my victory already.

Part of the intelligence of society, that we must develop is the listening ear, if and when any person comes forward we listen at the deepest levels; because there is, this iceberg of deviant personality types operative in society. By deviant personality types, I am referencing people whose fundamental purpose is to cause pain to others, and/or accomplish their own advancement, in as ruthless and cruel capacity as possible, based profoundly on their lack of emotional development.

I lived to tell this story and to develop these understandings. While there could well be fifty or a hundred, perhaps 999 people on the other side of my perspective; I am telling the truth, and on that basis alone, society must hear, see and recognize my story; in the same way, we must hear the stories of many, such as women being violated and others; and develop our accuracy as a culture. People have a right to their opinion yes, and we have a responsibility to discern the inaccurate from the accurate!

CHAPTER 14

EQUAL AND OPPOSITE REACTIONS, AND GOODNESS ITSELF

People still may have a hard time deciphering the psychological prison, if not torture chamber that I was put in, by family and ex-wife. When a group of people develop a mindset and get vicious enough, they can act in a ghastly fashion towards another human being. Emotional abuse is a horrific dynamic. Having tens and tens of people aligned against me, and willing to attack me, at my perceived most vulnerable points, such as my own sense of self, my marriage and then my children was extraordinary. That my own parents, brother, extended family and ex-wife cold maintain this tightly stretched wire of hatred towards me for more than twenty some years and counting is extraordinary.

Yet, I more than offset these things, but having deeper beliefs that guide me and carry me forward. These types of beliefs formulate the basis of The Science of Inner Strength and the basic goodness of human beings. My beliefs were my own innate goodness which I discovered more and more as time went by along with, my commitment to my two sacred children, and just the well-being of the world in general. The psychological and emotional, along with legal and financial torture chamber they were able to construct against me, formed the deepest crucible imaginable, in which I was to grow and change as a human being, and develop profound understandings about myself, as well as the capacity to influence, if not change the world. A human diamond was being formulated from coal, as once again, my hometown Scranton, was old coal country.

That is the nature of adversity, regarding its learning potential. Psychologically a prison of sorts was set up around my life. For one, the group attacked me for a solid eleven years or so, in Middlesex County Courts, with my family of origin, using my ex-wife as the bitter tool. They put me and my sacred children through separation, and divorce, and then custody proceedings, and then post-custody, over a period of ten years, before I even began to pro-actively fight back. They defamed me to my core, trying to create and attack non-existent mental health issues, although the ferocity and intensity of their hatred, could well have broken a human being, but for the commitments that I had. They ostracized me severely from my deep-rooted family of origin, going to the lengths of actually replacing me, in my own family of origin with my ex-wife; something I liken to putting one's nose on somebody else's body. Further, because I was ganged up upon by so many people and facing a court system that was tragically unfair, I lost virtually every penny that I had, and faced near homelessness, and extended periods of virtually no money. As my old hero Maxwell Smart from the "Get Smart" 60's television show would say: "And loving it."

The point I make, is that because I had underlying commitments, and beliefs and visions, I was able to endure and withstand the hatred and insanity they perpetrated against me. Indeed, I was able to learn and develop the construct of how adversity can teach us, also while developing my sense of the divine. Once we have goals that are appropriate and fitting to us, we can withstand almost anything, in the pursuit of goodness, which leads to greatness. Like a slow drip, the twenty nine or so years of psychological and emotional abuse formed this prison like attitude, which became a laboratory for growth and change.

I was a mainly regular career-oriented successful person, like our common world indicates these days, and then it was like whoosh, I was pulled into this deeply spiritual world; where I learned about God, and the existence of evil. Now, I am not saying that I saw a physical devil, and yet, I am saying that I fought enemies and situations that were devilish in their intensity, as part of a perfect storm. Along with the wins and losses, I am pointing to, a whole other ramification of all this; the effect of all of this, on us as a person, and the level to which we grow and change as a person through adversity.

As Mandela learned "maturity" during his twenty-seven years in prison; I learned perhaps not just "accuracy;" but goodness and compassion as a person. All of the levels of exuberance and boorishness and outer world rowdiness were worn down, at times beaten away spiritually, and the innate goodness was pushed and nurtured to come into place. Most of us. know that we are good people at heart, or in some way, and yet, most of us are not fully given license to act in good and compassionate ways; instead we are often taught that this roguish toughness is the right way or represents strength itself.

Ultimately, I am saying that this superficial societally supported toughness is not true toughness or strength. Calmness and gentleness can be much greater strengths, when they are indeed coming from a place of determination. The important point is, that I had goals and visions. You see I had no real opportunity to be with my children in the manner in which I truly desired unless, I went through ALL of this. This was the terrain that I was given AND I was not willing to be a secondary parent; I did not believe my messages were meant to be partially bestowed upon them. So I was willing to go through extended periods without seeing Sophie and Sam, to keep alive the true nature of who I am both as a person and a father.

Unbelievably today even December 16, 2015, and of recent, the evidence is flowing in that my children, now twenty five and twenty two have grasped onto my basic messages of God and love; and that all of those years of pain and separation even, will be undoubtedly worth it. What more inspiring can there be then passing on a positive ideology or philosophy even, in this world. Yet, it is not dependent even on them; the philosophy exists on its own right, as I learn more and more all the time.

It is said, and evidently true that a diamond was coal under pressure. Again, I am grateful to have been born originally in anthracite coal country, Scranton, PA;

a significant hub in its day of coal and enterprise. The unfathomable, in some ways relatively torturous psychological and emotional chamber that was I was thrust into; was that exact pressure that was needed for me to make that transition figuratively from coal to diamond; not that most people in Scranton are of coal, I am merely alluding to my history and journey.

It was that unfathomable pressure that methodically scraped away all of the "mishigas"[17] that resides within me, and most of us for that matter. The only difference with me is that I was subjected to more than twenty-nine years of emotional/psychological abuse. Given that I had an appropriate inner goal: that of caring for my children, developing myself, and an agenda to better the world; I was able to sustain ALL of the pressure. In the process what was happening was that great portion of animosities, the weaknesses, even the adolescent alcohol interests were chipped and chiseled away; like a Rodin statue..

This must be why I consider this all, my historical or even divine destiny. I was taught these values on these levels for a reason. People know the expression of today: "Everything happens for a reason;" well I have profoundly chosen to adopt that notion. How else am I supposed to

---

[17] Not only a wonderful Yiddish word that described our foibles and that kind of thing, but a word a Judge in Middlesex Superior Court used to say that it if I filed another court action, it would be the height of "mishigas" actually I believe she said "chutzpah, a related word; yet I filed a two or three actions after that anyway, not out of defiance but of love and care for my children.

describe[18] what happened? Even more so, it became the intricate part of developing the philosophy and Science of Inner Strength. It was the direct result of the occurrence of the intense emotional trauma that directly led to my finding my inner strength, and The Science of Inner Strength.

The crucial thing is having that sense of purpose. Purpose is the thing that can pull us through virtually anything, or similarly said: Divine light. It is fascinating over the New Year's weekend, 2016 I reacquainted myself with some of the work of Eckhart Tolle. In some ways it was like an icing on the cake moment for me; as messages that I peripherally had acknowledged, previously kicked in at a deeper level. Tolle's main message is focused upon being in the "Now" or the present moment. Surely Tolle is not the only person to have advocated such a philosophy, and yet being able to make a transition from some of the issues from my past to the present moment much more fully, was enormously liberating this weekend.

I raise the work of Tolle, because on a deeper, more subliminal level his concept of the

Now, is related to my notion of divine light, or Abraham Hicks notion of "being in the vortex;" or the late Wayne Dyer's notion of being connected to "Source." My interpretation of these various approaches is that essentially they all infer, if not state a connection to God, or a sense of the divine.

---

[18] In a famous familial college entrance essay, my daughter Sophia described the events happening in our family as "indescribable." Well it may have taken decades, but I am starting to describe it Sophia.

The image I use for simplicity purposes only; it is as if we are plugged into the central energy of the universe, or for lack of a better word the "purpose" we are here in the first place. Admittedly the decision to grasp that we are here for a purpose is a choice, or even a leap of faith, or even perhaps a human-made creation; yet it is surely the one that I prefer. Pardon the pun, but it is just too animalistic to view that we are only here to eat, sleep, fight and destroy. Life itself, grasping onto a notion of appreciation connotes a divine connection, as the air, the water, the blood, the life itself are such wonders, if not miracles unto themselves.

Then as well, the sense that the human trajectory is basically towards progress of some kind; some type of improvement of ourselves and the planet, even with such pain underscores our commitment to purpose, in some way. Then again, it is not an absolute science on my or anyone's part, to proclaim the divine; it is ultimately a belief system. We can believe as we wish; to me, having a belief system enhances our experience.

Before I digress too much, the point I am getting at, is the wonder of Eckhart Tolle's perspective of being in the moment, and on some level its correlation to what I am saying regarding divine light or our sense of purpose. It is not so different. What Tolle argues is the reason for those, who are not yet at the point of being in the present moment; rather than challenged or personality disordered, Tolle would attribute such characteristics to people who are so shut off from their true selves or sense of alignment, which is a perspective I respect and applaud as well.

Using my brother David as an example if only in the

most general sense; he is, a person who is so cut off from his true emotional life, and to the opposite extreme, uses his intellectual side to understand, conceptualize and ultimately rationalize virtually everything, remiss of meaningful senses of empathy, remorse, compassion or those types of attributes. Tolle does not delve into a great deal of psychological analysis as to how and why people either reach or do not reach such states; rather he states such realities as he sees them. Although Tolle also attributes challenge as a great learning tool.

I also question without knowing definitively, where Tolle stands on issues of emotional pain and grieving for instance; and on some level the process that people must traverse to reach points of being in the present moment. As much as I do feel a boost of enlightenment in connecting with his ideas this weekend; I also sense at times, a kind of giggling, sniffling tiny bit of condescension on his part for facets of the human condition; and perhaps therein the process by which human beings make changes; yet his perspective is a good one, if taken at a deep level, and no one is perfect that is for sure.

My point of emphasis is different from Tolle's with regard to focusing on what one does with this sense of enlightenment. Where I believe Tolle's perspective is extremely useful is as a way and reminder that to really act for a better world, we must in essence be that change itself; not much different at all then Gandhi's notion of "Be the change you wish to see in the world."

Tolle himself acknowledges the role that adversity can play in affecting or bringing about our desire for change. I am not sure that he goes as deep as I go on one level, regarding indicating that adversity itself has a divine purpose. Esther Hicks of Abraham-Hicks espouses virtually the opposite, by essentially stating using the Law of Attraction as her basis that essentially when adversity comes, we have in essence attracted it; which can be a substantially onerous burden to put on a victims of child sexual abuse, cancer and those type of tragedies.

Even my notion of discovering the divine purpose within adversity, must be gently approached with those who have suffered at the deepest levels. So, while I would not insist absolutely that adversity has a divine purpose; I would make the point of distinction to say, that in most cases, that purpose is there to be discovered; when a person is open and works to discover that point of the divine, during adversity.

What the adversity can do, is clear away the layers and layers of societal gunk that is laid upon us, from birth onward. Again, this is not a blame game, per se; except for those who really should know better. Most parents of my day, were, in the main following the habits and dictates of the generations before them. In addition, the religious institutions, the schools, a fair amount of society, works to correct people rather than to lift them.

Adversity hit me in a way; so as to dramatically cleanse or at least amend a lot of the learning that was passed onto me. Of course, some of the stuff, I received from my parents and grandparents, was well-intentioned, if not good itself. Having a great home, a college education and all of that were wonderful things. Yet, my story unveils that a lot of previous methods and attitudes of my family, were, even in their most tame elements neurotic, and at times extremely fear-based. Although I surely respect the upbringing that I was given; and that was not the problem, it was the frenzy that began in 1988.

In short, I was not taught, to have, what can be termed emotional intelligence. My grandfather Samuel emigrated from Poland, and arrived in this country as a two year old, and rose in short order to be what seemed to be a modestly successfully doctor in downtown Scranton. My grandfather Morris Gelb emigrated from Hungary without a penny virtually, and rose to be a very successful lawyer and banker in the Scranton area. According to stories Morris was mocked in boyhood years, for not knowing any English.

One can hardly blame people of that time and that generation to focus virtually solely on economic success, with the dedicated and narrow paths that they worked to achieve. There was probably a great deal of pressure on my grandfathers, and grandmothers for that matter to be successful, and really for the most part keep their noses to the grindstone. The times of the early twentieth century were hardly times of emotional intelligence, following the Industrial Revolution, a coal boom in and near Scranton, and then the Great Depression and World War II.

So there can be little or no fault laid at the feet of those who raised me, in the main, with not teaching children about empathy and respect for others I suppose. On many levels, I sense that the home I grew up in, was surely calmer than the home Morey Myers grew up in, with his older brother and father being renowned for tempers and in the former's case voracious fistfights. Sondra Myers, my biological mother, would virtually never talk about her growing years; and I sense her home was not really an overly emotionally warm place; given the financial pressures of her time. My late grandmother Mae Gelb showed me the Passbook Savings account book from her early married years, which reflected about $27 one week, and then $28 or so the next and so on and so forth.

So there cannot be overriding blame for the generations and times of my grandparents, and for the most part, with respect to my parents, for not having a sense of emotional intelligence; a book and concept made famous by Daniel Goleman. The conditioning of society is towards "success" and "achievement" and to some extents a win at all cost mindset. What we have forgotten or "missing"[19] is our basic humanity and perhaps even more important our valuing of that humanity. We teach and train ourselves in ways that devalue or at least do not appropriately recognize the goodness, and basic humanity that resides within us.

The point is, much of this is learned behavior. We are learning these things and teaching these things; and they then become the norm in society. We cannot ever fully expect human culture to head in the right direction unless and until we are in the main healthy and whole as individuals. This is a very subtle point; as, I am not condemning the past. Whatever it took for us to get to this

---

[19] It was December 9, 2015, when I made a voyage to Scranton, PA to hand to my biological father Morey Myers a gratitude letter, for his work with me, in my early childhood. We ended up getting into a discussion of what was "missing" what from the conversation. With all due respect, when I saw he was not really willing to extend love to me; I garnered my own sense of what was "missing"

point; this is where we are. We surely cannot change the past. Still, we are at a juncture when we need a different psychological framework; for the success for one, of the individual, along with the success of society.

It is a subtle shift, from repudiating the past, which many people will not want to do, to say, we must live an improved future. From an individual standpoint the shift entails coming from a standpoint of our goodness, rather than our condemned or conditioned selves. If we start to believe that we are good at heart, rather than pegs to banged into some hole; than we can generally proceed forward on the basis of confidence and enthusiasm, rather than fear and avoidance. So, while most of us would not want to condemn the lives that our parents gave us; most of us spiritually would accept that good, and desire to improve spiritually on our future growth and direction. It is almost a shift in a way, from our head to our heart; our head containing more of the opinions that others have shared, and our heart and soul reflecting more of the reality and essence of who we are. Continually it can be stated that such goals are not a harm or a threat to existing society, and; rather they are necessary improvements that must take place for the benefit of our planet and species.

There is a wonderful calming effect that would occur, if and when society as a whole began to function from its goodness; no longer would we have to scurry and duck about so much. There is so much occurring in society today, that reveals that society is missing the boat, individuals are being misled. The culture of hate and false intelligence that pops up on the internet and online forums and the like, reveal these lesser qualities. Many of these people are no doubt actually intelligent. It is just that the manner in which people have learned to express their intelligence is flawed.

People basically have learned to express their intelligence from a perspective of, for one comparing themselves to others. People feel on some level that they are not intelligent, unless they are comparing themselves to another person. When in fact, intelligence is something that exists on its own; it needs no comparison to anything else. Second, the meanness emanates in the main, from a sense of lack and deprivation, if not fear, and people fear somehow if they are not cruel in their delivery that they will not be heard.

Really the opposite of such meanness is true. Think about it, you, me, most people desire to be talked to, in calm and respectful manners. What else can be true? Nobody really desires meanness or disrespect being aimed at them.

These lesser qualities are often learned behaviors. Society is telling us; that being mean or strident is an effective mode of communication. Such a direction is anything but true. The Trump phenomenon is an interesting one, because his message on some level of fixing a broken system is very much needed and yet, his delivery has been so antithetical to fixing something that his role as a messenger may well be bound to fail.

Meanness is by definition is weakness. I am not saying Trump is weak, that is just a point of reference, I am saying in general, meanness as a human quality is ultimately weakness. Society is, in many ways teaching us false lessons, including that meanness is a strength, which we must reverse. Partially it pertains to the pace of society; in that society is moving so fast in a technological sense that people feel a pull to catch up, and on some level not even think. Groupthink to me, is a great evil.

The saturation levels of climate change, economic challenge, faulty schools, not to mention terroristic threats and opiate crises, and the like; seems to be running at a level that will ultimately be unsustainable. The planet needs a realignment in some ways. If we don't start thinking about our purpose in being here, we surely risk negative outcomes.

I am not even talking about answering our sense of purpose in the largest cosmic sense. I mean how we really got here; what are deepest purpose is; are questions perhaps beyond our human comprehension, at least mine at the moment, lol.. Still, we can and must respond in a relative sense to our sense of purpose for the human species. The issue of what direction human behavior goes in; is a necessary to consider. For me, the basic civility of our culture is a paramount, if not the paramount issue.

First and foremost, we must learn to talk with one another as human beings. Virtually every issue and challenge that we can name is relatively meaningless, unless and until we can develop a terminology and a way to have inclusive and comprehensive discussions on these issues. We cannot solve problems, unless we can talk to one another, and in that regard, we must connect on the basis of our humanity and common purpose.

Our commonness is our very humanity. If we cannot live and express our humanity with one another, we seem to be headed to harmful places.. Ultimately our greatest point of commonality is our goodness, our shared humanity; our relatively speaking common purpose. The survival of America and our planet are in play, based on our behavior.

CHAPTER 15

FORGIVENESS

"Perhaps the butterfly is proof that you can go through a great deal of darkness and become something beautiful." Anon.

Forgiveness is a most unfathomably complicated subject in today's day and age. Let me begin with the sense that most of the abuse that occurs in society is abuse of emotional and psychological nature, and will become increasingly so, as other more obvious forms of abuse, such as sexual and physical become better understood; and less tolerated by society in general. Emotional and psychological abuse will eventually be understood in the same way perhaps, but the road there is longer and more arduous.

Emotional and psychological abuse is so incendiary because it is like an iceberg, and the person being victimized is continually made to look like a unstable or crazy, or something. There is more I can say about this, but I choosing to focus this chapter on forgiveness. Suffice it to say that I do not know everything, but I know that I was subjected to one of the more emotionally abusive situations in the history of this earth. I mainly am writing about where I am today, as a matter of choice with respect to potential forgiveness. I dovetail into the realm of emotional/psychological as a pathway towards forgiveness, from deep pain: Like the butterfly finding beauty through its darkness.

Much of made of forgiveness in this day and age, with common "progressive" type perspectives being that forgiveness is a rather necessary thing for one who has been abused. I can only say that the walk to such a place is unfathomable; and that no one can or should be pressured into considering forgiveness at all. Common perspectives tout that forgiveness is not for the other person, but really for oneself. On some level that is true; and yet the walk to get there can be excruciating, and not for everyone.

Christian perspectives delve into Biblical senses of forgiveness and in some ways commend, if not command forgiveness, and in other ways insist that forgiveness is solely for those who apologize and take responsibility for their actions. I suppose I want to interject a third type of element, which has to do with forgiveness as an emotional release from the person(s) who has victimized us. At a deep point in my journey I somehow discovered that my biological mother Sondra Gelb Myers was at the root of some of the psychological/emotional abuse directed towards me.

I must walk very slowly at this moment, and respectfully request the reader to walk equally slowly at this point, to profoundly understand what I am saying. In the nature of things all of us have emotional attachments to someone or something. I am not saying that I am the only one to say this, but I do believe that my experience has brought me a new type of understanding of the nature of the emotional/psychological bond among humans, particularly those of biological family members

What I am getting at, is that no matter how painful, like lemons into lemonade, I used virtually my entire experience as an opportunity, a scientific like laboratory to observe, contemplate and appropriately study the entire realm of the emotional/psychological bond among individuals and their families; this in an "odd" way is a facet of my divine purpose through ALL of this. One discovery that I have come to is that emotional tenors and the emotional fabrics of those who influenced us in childhood, parents for sure are somehow embedded within us. It is virtually like our heads and hearts,s are in some part influenced and/or affected by those significant relationships.

How we feel, when, we are unaware of that deep emotional impression that others, particularly parents make upon us is at least in part related, if not dependent on how those others treat us; especially if they are not functioning in honest or caring manners. Most of us do not grow up thinking that our parents have agendas against us, and most parents do not; yet those with personality type disorders can and do act against us. The most precarious part is that is an extremely unsuspecting manner, in which they undercut us.

So the very first emotion, in addition to pain that a person, who is being undercut by their own mother or father might feel, beyond pain, which is significant; is that of confusion. It is a type of emotional sabotage. On many, many levels we cannot for the life of us, wrap our brains around the fact that our very parents could act against us; even once we begin to understand this on an intellectual level, the emotional facet, can take a much longer time, if ever to truly adjust to these circumstances. Expanding exponentially the level of pain, and the iceberg effect; is the sense that those parents basically acted in positive ways, in your youth.

In addition, the emotional dynamics of a family can be unfathomably complex. A person, in a position of influence, if not control can subliminally entrap many other members of a family system into types and patterns of behavior that confuse not just the person being isolated, but even those who perhaps unwittingly are carrying out these rather merciless defaming, ostracizing and otherwise hateful behaviors.

In good conscience I can interject that part of the emotional buffer on the road to forgiveness and other things that I, for one, have built in, is surely the understanding that those who attempt such seemingly hateful behaviors are at root are very hurt and injured people themselves; which does on occasion allow for some compassion, irrespective of the pain they may be inflicting upon you.

In my case at least, I must believe I am like most people in this regard the emotional bond between my mother and me, was very deep; if not always recognized. Like many things that can reside dormant, it only became most obvious, when the tenor of the bond, switched from positive or at worst neutral, to what I can solely describe from my perspective as an all out assault on my very psyche as a human being.

These are things we perhaps deep down intuitively recognize, but have not in the main articulated as a culture. In the same way, as an aside, I will say after all kinds of resistance and relatively violent opposition to my ideas; at some point psychiatrists and psychologists will say that they knew them all along. The bond is extremely deep between people, especially members of families; even if it is not positive, there are all kinds of relatively unknown ways that family members influence our emotional state. All of which is to say that when a family member becomes confused, or even unhinged they can inflict a ton of pain and hurt on other family members.

Given that I was an am a basically compassionate person; although through my high school and college days, I was not so aware of that myself; my mother for one, would know my vulnerabilities. The only way I can begin to broach the subject now is by laughing a bit, because, if I just jumped into a straightforward recitation of it; virtually no one would believe me, because unless and until you have dealt with someone with truly deviant personality characteristics the entire thing makes no rational sense whatsoever. It is not part of our emotional lexicon, at least the one we grew up with, to anticipate that a person(s) would begin acting in a ruthlessly harmful and vengeful way towards for no significant rational reason.

Such is the world of a person with borderline personality disorder, narcissistic personality disorder or even psychopathic behaviors. People with those kinds of characteristics can develop a parasitic, sadistic pipeline into your emotional psyche, aiming to dog you and bring you down. In order to come to even a tad of psychological understanding of this kind of dynamic, one must first recognize the profoundly deep emotional bond that can exist between two people; and then further through ALL of the haze and confusion sort through the type of personality characteristic that one is confronted with, before even remotely moving onto notions of psychological safety, then healing; well before any notions of forgiveness.

It is on some level, as if you were attacked by 1000 bees or hornets, and yet in this case, they do not want to go away. The only way to release the pressure is follow all of the steps of understanding your emotional/psychological bond, realize what you are dealing with, find some emotional distance, build some more permanent emotionally safe space, find ways to heal, and then sky is the limit. I liken dealing with an extreme narcissist or psychopath, as if having a spiked metal ball, inside one's very head.

In my case, the pattern of abuse dramatically escalated over a more than twenty seven year period, with twenty or so years in unfathomably outrageous fashion. It was a good many years in, before I even remotely knew what I was dealing with. I did know that I was being emotionally abused. I raised my first legal complaint addressing emotional abuse back around 2007 or so; and it was a Judge in Scranton, PA of all places who turned me onto the Tort for the Intentional Infliction of Emotional Distress around 2009; so I found there actually was a law to support my claims, albeit the courts were not in any way prepared to address the type of Complaint I was making, as a Pro Se Plaintiff, on territory that was extremely challenging and unfamiliar; even though I do not know everything, but I know that I was right on the merits.

There is a fair amount of discussion and forum on line with recognition of extreme narcissistic and even psychopathic behavior; and yet, I dare say that no one I read about, ever brought up a situation as complicated and vindictive as mine, with parents, brother, ex-wife, extended family all aligned against me, with such intensity to inflict emotional hurt. I say all this not to be a victim; as per, The Science of Inner Strength, virtually every lemon or hurtful behavior directed at me, was turned into figurative lemonade or some wonderful learning experience, and yet those pains, lol are considerable.

I put these experiences once again under the rubric of forgiveness precisely because The Science of Inner Strength and that kind of thinking is pointed towards and geared towards our victory. So many, if not most of my efforts, were not only to overcome the challenges posed at me, but also to find relief from the emotional pain and trauma that was directed at me. Suffice it to say that if your own outwardly supportive parents turned against you, and joined with your ex-wife over a more than twenty year period to defame and ostracize you; let alone used your children against you there would be enormous amounts of emotional pain and trauma involved.

Still my journey was not, nor virtually ever to live as victim and so my journey, thankfully in that I had the emotional health and well-being of my children to protect, was virtually always about overcoming, about getting to the right and best place. For those who consider forgiveness, and feel as if they are getting forced into it; you might console yourself with the sense that for ten years or so; I initiated legal actions in response to the emotional hurt and pain. While I did not achieve massive victories at every juncture; I did achieve significant legal settlements, which at a bare minimum allowed my personal growth, as well as work to grow and thrive.

At some point, so far and deep into the process II came to terms with the fact that my biological parents were who they were; or at least that they were not going to change, in a manner that most people would. For people who are not in a rational state, such as with all due respect I see my family of origin, or even further in deep narcissistic or psychopathic states; they in fact thrive on your fighting back, and their sense of being able to attempt to deny your very existence.

This, becomes one of the defining elements of life; the capacity to establish and work for our own emotional satisfaction. Along as our emotional satisfaction is, in any way. in the hands of others, particularly those who are acting with manipulative, rather than caring qualities, we are destined for a ton of pain and emotional hardship. Therein lies the great challenge; to establish our own emotional sanity and sense of well-being. To the degree *our emotional well-being becomes codependent with a familial situation, particularly an* unhealthy familial situation we are susceptible to the whims, and craven desires of others.

This is where the notion of forgiveness can begin to come in. Because the notion of establishing our own emotional health and well-being, is perhaps a paramount, if not the paramount issue above all, as far as our life. A rational person will respond positively for the most part, with your efforts to establish boundaries and be self-protective. A person with a personality disorder will not understand, or even worse feign a lack of comprehension, in order to inflict even more emotional hurt and pain on you.

One of the many versions of forgiveness I studied articulated by a Christian Pastor Joyce Meyer is that forgiveness is necessary, and that it needs be replaced by a sense of vision. After countless notions of studying forgiveness; this particular notion hit home, to an extent, because it essentially infers that no matter how deep the hurt and pain one has gone through; we have the seeds and the ways to develop something stronger than the perceived obstacle. So, if the challenges directed at me were so deep then the opportunity was there to develop the strength to overcome those obstacles.

I just did not know that in my case the obstacles were in the words of one serious former Air Force Colonel from here to the moon; nonetheless, the seeds were there for me to develop the strength to be that much better, than even those monumental obstacles. Again, fathom your parents, brother, extending family joining with your ex-wife AND using your children to see how much emotional pain, trauma and even mayhem can be established, in your life.

So what then, is forgiveness? Defining forgiveness is on some level an age old question, and on some "odd" level, what I will ultimately attempt to put forth is my definition. Perhaps one of the first concepts along the way that I encountered on my spiritual journey that began in March, 1996 is the sense that forgiveness is not the same as reconciliation. In and of itself, distinguishing forgiveness from reconciliation may alleviate a great deal of pain from those who have been deeply aggrieved, and hurt mercilessly by psychopathic, borderline and narcissistic types of behavior.

On some level the definition of forgiveness that I came to, entailed a level of emotional disconnection; which, when such circumstances pertain to one's family of origin, it can be quite a massive piece of work unto itself. This is why I went to some length to describe the degree of emotional connection that existed between my mother and me; and I would readily suppose applies to many, if not most people is to recognize the emotional *connection that exists between ourselves and familial members, irrespective of whether* that connection is good, bad or indifferent.

We are pulled and we are connected together; which is why the first emotion for a child, or even an adult child who is being emotionally abused is that of shock, and a sense of sabotage, and intense confusion. Abuse of a loved one; is perhaps the ultimate betrayal. Because the child, even as an adult becomes emotionally shocked by an assault from one someone they naturally crave love and affection from; and who instead violates that relationship to such a degree by misusing their child to vent and perpetrate their own emotional anxieties onto. So like black widow spiders or other animals stun their prey with a poison; the first assault of the emotional abuser, is to stun their prey.

One key concept as to why the first assault can be so rash and so stunning is that the emotional abuser lives with such ingrained anger and dismay that it builds up to the point where they just snap and/or lash out. The person being targeted is stunned, because prior to that point that have essentially depended upon, or at least trusted that the relationship was of a certain tenor, and suddenly the bottom has dropped out.

This shock is another great weapon of the emotional abuser, because inherent in their assault they seek, and know the very most vulnerable emotional point of the person they are targeting. Again, this is where the analogy of a black widow may be apt, because in an emotional sense the abuser is going for serious destabilization, if not psychologically at least, the kill. Once the element of shock is introduced, a hierarchical structure is put into place, because the person victimized, on one level, cannot believe that the basic trust was violated so deeply; and more painfully spends so much energy thereafter trying to get the relationship back to that perceived trusting place.

The sad reality is that without some profound intervention, the emotional abuser has little, if any desire in reestablishing the previously trustful relationship. Instead in a perverse sense the emotional abuser may be deriving a sadistic like satisfaction in continually keeping their target off guard; and enjoying that superiority that perversely begins in their mind. Albeit the suddenness of the emotional assault, may well end up causing circumstances for which the person victimized develops a dependency on the abuser, be it financial, emotional, social or otherwise.

Such can be the starting place for someone sabotaged on an emotional basis; the very relationship that was supposed to be caring and enduring has provided the most savagely pointed assault. That is the backdrop of which the survivor, let alone the one who thrives from emotional abuse must begin. There are different theories as to how one might overcome such abuse. Some theorists such as Eckhart Tolle and Esther Hicks might counsel one to be in the moment, and focus all of our energy in the here and now. Another like Melanie Tonia Evans has a complicated quantum healing process.

My work begins from the notion of understanding that we have been attacked at essentially our most vulnerable point. That is the way of the psychopath and extreme narcissist; cultivate closeness and a sense of trust; and then strike with a vengeance at that most vulnerable place. The recovery process for such an assault can be indescribable unto itself. Most people would never anticipate such an emotional assault; and further efforts to describe it and talk with others, can fall on deaf ears, due to the unprecedented and uncomfortable nature of some of these stories.

As the founder of The Science of Inner Strength, I would say that no matter how painful,, the opportunity for growth and success is even greater than the horrid impact. The first opportunity that is on the table is to get to know oneself on a much deeper basis. Unfortunately with our culture as it is today; it may solely be that the true champions and true winners, may first have to be violated; to learn what they like, what they do not like, and that they are worthy creatures, who can conquer the world..

When we are struck at our core; through the pain, we begin to define a sense of ourselves and our values. Some have trusted their parents so much, it is only when they violate us that we truly begin to separate and define who we are. This is the nature of how adversity can educate us and serve as an opportunity. None of us early pioneers, would have sought this intense psychopathic assault, and yet it does provide the pathway to the true leaders and heroes in our culture. The deeper the abuse; the greater the opportunity to define who we are, in a new and expanded way.

That is why I write, so that others can benefit from my experience and do not have to go through the true horror of this type of experience on their own; or at least that it can be ameliorated, by virtue of my work. The first step is recognizing that something is totally off and not right; our sense of values are violated, when experiencing this type of assault. Next must come, a commitment to overcome it, as well as our own personal healing.

February 3, 2016; what a day or two in an "odd" way. Yesterday morning, my sacred daughter Sophia called me at 9:50 a.m. and asked if I had a minute to hear some "very bad news." I said sure. With a profound sense of sorrow, Sophia shared with me the news of the passing of her mother. Life is the greatest teacher, when we are attuned. I found myself with a deeply "odd" set of emotions. For one, I could not for the life of me, take back or even critique in a major way the custody wars we shared; and how I believed in and still do believe in my cause on behalf of my two sacred children.

Yet, I would be remiss if I did not honor and acknowledge the sense of loss, and on some level the profound impact Margaret had on my life. It is a great teacher to show us that even when we disagree profoundly with someone to the point of a total and appropriate breakdown of communication, they are still a part of us. For better or worse, Margaret's work like virtually like a huge body blow to me that was inculcated as a part of my psyche and experience.

While there is an intellectual part of me that knew Margaret had extremely challenging issues; as much or more in the moment I am honoring a woman who brought an unfathomable fight to me and my life, with regard to her energy. I find myself, in an "odd" sense wanting to honor the positive contributions that she has made; while still simultaneously needing to move my life, business and vision for my family forward. It is a wonderful lesson that even those who cause us the most pain are impacting us in unforeseen ways. It is such an awe-inspiring process in some ways to work through this situation now with my children; although they will do so in their own way first.

I am looking for the fascinating lesson in the midst; namely to perhaps be even more mindful of our collective position as human beings; even when we disagree with people. None of us can turn back the clock; I am proud of my previous stands, which will in ALL likelihood distress those who sought to bring me down; and yet going forward I find that I am learning or assimilating an even deeper mode of human interaction.

That deeper mode incorporates the sense of how much we mean to each other, or at least affect each other, even in, the midst of conflict. While I would not wish Margaret's passing on anyone per se at a relatively early age of fifty eight; I cannot argue with God's world for one, and find these remarkable lessons of humanity embedded in learning about her passing, with regard to have this remarkable opportunity to assess the impact of both having had such an active relationship, then conflict with someone, and then their sudden and unexpected departure; it provides a remarkable opportunity to fully gauge and assess a complete pantheon of emotions, in this very chapter on forgiveness.

The lesson in going forward must be versed in understanding on a human scale how people who challenge us, are an extremely important part of our lives, and we are learning from them in the process if and when we ever have the opportunity to end the conflict or perhaps equally as importantly to approach situations in general, with a bit more care and caution in the future. This entails an unfathomable balancing act on the part of humanity; as often we are responding to, if not reacting to the unfathomable pain that the other person is causing us. I virtually feel in some "odd" way, even though she lived a heartfelt fifty eight years, Margaret's life is being donated to science; kind of like old football players and their brains being used for concussion research.

CHAPTER 16

FORGIVENESS PART II

This entire detour does dovetail with the discussion of forgiveness. One of the notions of forgiveness has to do with letting go, and letting God to use a popular expression. In other words, when we feel that a person has really wronged us, and perhaps the pursuit of justice will appear to turn us into something as bad, or nearly as bad as the one who has wronged us; a crucial element of forgiveness is, and can be to turn a problem over to God, or a at least a higher sense of order in the universe. Look on some "basic"[20] level, I understood that Margaret was acting so harmfully to me, and prospectively our children. Yet, with the Courts as clouded as they are, and with my own family of origin siding against me, it seemed like the more I sought to make the case, the more that I potentially could be seeming like the problem.

This can be the most exasperating of feelings for

---

[20] One of our last marital discussions ended with Margaret telling me that I did not know the "basics." [22] Sam's text message to me around January 1, 2015 indicated that his love for me was "nearly" infinite; a most amazing expression.

one, who is relating to, and being affected by a person with fundamental personality disorder issues, or who has stealth like manipulative qualities; the relatively innocent one, and I do not know everything, but I know that many people can related to this, could be driven crazy, because things are continually turned against them. I cannot say at any given moment that I felt like I totally forgave Margaret; surely; not while I still saw her actively carrying out things to hurt Sophie and Sam; yet I did work on and build elements of forgiveness into my approach; even writing her notes of forgiveness and pointing out her positive qualities.

It is most scary to put things that you care the most about, into the hands of God, or whatever you may consider as a larger influence, if not force in the universe. So while I was not completely there, the news of Margaret's passing, as challenging as it might be to say this; with all due respect seemed to confirm facets of my basic approach. The web that Margaret spun, putting aside emotionally malicious, was just so plain irrational, even "ludicrous" that the logic of the universe virtually dictates that it cannot sustain itself. Karma, maybe; gravity for sure; as nothing can really spin in completely irrational circles for an "infinite"[22] period of time.

As I say, I have a ton of gratitude towards Margaret; and yet the whole development of The Science of Inner Strength, is predicated upon developing an understanding of people who we believe might have personality disorders. Consistent with The Science of Inner Strength, the amount of adversity or even pain we go through provides the opportunity for an equal and/or greater positive experience. Still in fairness to myself I must on some level acknowledge the pain that Margaret put me through, and I mainly sought to

"protect"[21] the children from being direct recipients of this pain.

When you take the things that mean the very most to me from my children, to my family of origin, to my own standing in my community, and have a person either by negligence or intention, or ignorance attempt to cut them down and shred them, the pain can be unfathomable. In addition to my own efforts replete with patience and perseverance; there always was some type of faith in God that even though in its most severe forms the situation lasted nearly twenty years; it could not last forever. Margaret's passing was the end of an era.

There are a couple of things I am getting at: One, is the notion of allowing the natural order and God to take its course. I cannot even predict how the future will go; and yet as much as I am grateful to Margaret for some of the things she contributed to me, the level of deceit and manipulation simply could not continue, and in that regard certain things were well above my pay grade to resolve; it was for God. Second, I do want to profoundly affirm the notion that I believe there is a natural order to things, geared towards goodness, logic and ultimately truth..

People must develop patience to see their biggest of dreams and goals come to pass. I suppose in an appropriate sense I am also patting myself on the shoulder

---

[21] Margaret would claim on occasion that she was "protecting" the children. Wow.

and realizing how much pain Margaret really did put me through; no pain, no gain as they say, as she stretched my persona virtually from California to Massachusetts and New England to Florida. All along, I am affirming the Science of Inner Strength, with regard to saying that by having a purpose of my children, my life and my business I was able to outlast, if barely at that, lol; this unfathomable siege.

In the last day or so, I had occasion to talk with a lawyer friend of mine, PT, who knew of this situation. It helped a lot to have a person, who has excellent elements of compassion and understanding, because as we recounted, with touches of humor interspersed here and there, the last twenty years have been truly unfathomably painful at times for me, along with the growth. What I have come to is that with all due respect Margaret was The World's Best Manipulator, leading to my becoming The World's Best Mediator; with respect to an equal and opposite reaction and then some. Margaret for one, I am not certain it is totally on her, but perhaps with some substantial part, was able to turn virtually every single person in the world falsely against me from parents, to brother and sister-in-law, to extended family, to neighbors to courts. Although perhaps, my mother Sondra, as I have grown to learn could exceed Margaret as a manipulator.

It truly is beyond remarkable how many people played into this incredibly false dynamic [22]of me, and sought to bury me and cover me with mud. As I say, it was having that commitment to something tangible in my sacred children that could somehow allow myself to see

---

[22] Surely is a Margaret word

my way through. So where does this leave me with this considerable topic of forgiveness?

In most situations we should and by should I mean, this is my opinion, I am not imposing this on anyone; but to strive for forgiveness in most normal human interactions is worthy and plausible, and ultimately does just free us up to be ourselves more and embrace ourselves and our normal human interactions. With regard to people with personality disorders, be they borderline, psychopathic, or narcissistic; the topic of forgiveness becomes a much more complicated process. The infringement on our personal space, the violation of our very being becomes so intense that often times forgiveness is only a possible by-product of our basic journey to survive and eventually grow.

I must say for accuracy say; again, normally, one who births children, serves in some ways as a great mother requires a virtual lifetime pass with regard to love and understanding. The wonders and beauties of childbirth do exalt a woman to a terrific status in society. In my mother's case and perhaps a tad \with Margaret's, there is pretty much, like the adage: "an exception to every rule." At this moment, in the way of my own judgment formulated over a twenty year or so period, I can with as little rancor as possible say, that in an extreme rarity for a woman and a mother, Margaret's negatives actually outweighed her positives; "surely" with all due respect to her effect on our familial environment. Such is the case in dealing with a person, with a personality disorder. At least Margaret had an excuse of sorts, that is all she knew; my own mother on the other hand promulgated benevolence and interdependence and the like.

I get no great joy out of saying what I said. Tto me it is a sense of objective reality that is relevant in this particular instance as well as for the world at large. So as I say forgiveness for me, in this situation is perhaps not my responsibility. If forgiveness is some kind of moral responsibility or at least higher aspiration; and evil pertains to approximately 2% of the population, I suppose I would all due respect be at least afforded the sense that in 2% of the cases, we are truly not required to forgive.

Instead it may well be in those most extreme type of cases that forgiveness means cutting our emotional ties, and yes somehow, someway leaving things up to God and the karmic justice if you will of the universe: Reaching such a point is unfathomably hard work; traditional "fighting" with such people, beyond just your basic human needs; entails enormous peril of being continually and falsely seen as the one causing the problem. People can appreciate and take in for their behalf the countless hours of work and sweat that went into these thoughts on these type of things; often borne out by wild dreams at night, to process the trauma of emotional abuse and work towards forgiveness..

Nightmares, while initially phenomenally painful, also became a resource and a way for me to comprehend my deepest thought and feelings, which do not necessarily fully surface in our waking hours. The thoughts and images that would come into my nighttime sleep provided fertile ground to work on and understand these entire sets of issues. As we used to say in Scranton PA, or at least our teachers would: "Believe you me;" I would much prefer that you take the fruits of my rather unfathomable work, and not have to go through these senses of nightmares, literal and figurative themselves.

So forgiveness for me, in Margaret's scenario at some point entailed allowing enough room for God to come to the rescue. It is illuminating and educating to reassure yourself that not ALL problems are ours to solve on our own. One of the incredible things about life is adopting a much more trusting attitude that things will work; which on some level runs contrary to the way we were raised. Fear was a predominant element in our collective psyche's prior to this, and we cannot blame our historical ancestors so much for this, as they were doing the very best that they could presumably.

One of the unfathomable points that my experience offers as well the notion of when to let go, and when to proceed forward. It is an unbelievable balancing act to know and to have the courage at times to let go. Being honest with my feelings; I did surely have some feelings upon hearing of Margaret's passing. As I said this person for better or worse was a substantial part of my life for some significant period of time, and literally birthed our two sacred children into this world.

I am not acting absolutely in saying however, that I must move forward, and see the perspective that I have developed in the "nearly" twenty year period of our separation as a time when I was profoundly right about my life, our situation, our children and beyond.

Yesterday I heard apart of my children's testimonials on her behalf, and it ended up with the sense that she was living her life dream by raising chickens in Oklahoma, whereby my commitment is to raise children and potentially grandchildren in Massachusetts; we ended up in two different places for sure; she sooner than me evidently, Rest in peace.

In any event part of the notion of iceberg is that we must be much more accurate with our human behavior and understanding of it. There is such a thing as evil in the world, and we would do well to understand it, as it is so important for most of us, who are good. In order for people and culture at large to act in the most judicious, accurate and positive manners, we must come to an understanding of people with deviant personality types in the way of borderline, narcissistic and psychopathic personality disorders..

CHAPTER 17

LETTING GO AND ALLOWING OUR INNER GOODNESS TO ARISE

One of my favorite topics and tools these days, has to do with working on letting go; not making every fight our own, even at times when it should be, or at least could be. As I mentioned how do we know when to press forward and when to let go. First of all, there are certain times, when adversity hits when there can be little if any choice. I went through many years of this, when I was so pushed to the edge by the emotional and financial conditions created by my ex-wife and family of origin that it seemed that I little or no choice in a lot of things. The key element in circumstances such as this, was that I found my inner strength, and because the pathway for success was so narrow, almost everything on some odd level was mapped out for me, because I was not going to quit..

We can however, get beyond this bare survival point, once we establish our bottom line commitment, in the situation. Then our choices can get more confusing. Do we consider forgiveness, to we push unfathomably ahead, or find ways to honor ourselves as well? While confusing these are ultimately more liberating choices than purely fighting for our survival. Joy at this point must be a parameter and consideration of our lives. I suppose I am living testament that God or faith or logic does eventually enter the equation, no matter how challenging it can be.

Recently I read a fascinating depiction of the word "Amen." It was kind of like Amen had a meaning of its own. We say our part with our actions or prayers or some combination thereof, and then we must release certain things as they are beyond our scope. It is not to say that someone cannot develop a mastery of things to make the prospects all that much better. Yet, ultimately the fulfillment of things entails things beyond our control, and Amen is the kind of release.

One thing to judge is truly how are we feeling. Do you feel that we have done enough in a particular situation? On some level I surely do on mine, at least in the immediate, if not short-term or longer horizon. Although on some level I did not begin the fight with those folks; they did with me, and I am working for my children's sakes, so I will for the most part take it one day at a time. Today is a relatively wonderful Sunday, where I have found a great cup of tea, and writing space at a local French Press café, and it seems delightful.

Which as I say, does bring me to an important element in all of this, finding your joy. Again, The Science of Inner Strength does proscribe that most of us have a genius, a wonderful talent inside of us that must be developed and joy in some ways is the fuel that can get us there. It takes courage to throw away the fear-mongering of the past; and point towards our future, with a more blissful outlook. Sometimes I wonder if I must fight with my family for one more round, or whether much of the battle is done, and it is just time to move on with the rest of my life.

Sometimes it takes more strength to walk away; the letting go. Letting go is such a wonderful feeling. I do enjoy working hard, and yet when I was at Oberlin College, I realized how much I enjoy lying on the grass. I enjoy nature. My talent is helping people resolve complex situations, as well as find their inner strength. Perhaps it is a moment just to pursue that; and once again allow God and/or the universe to take care of the rest: It would be a happier route in some ways, and fitting with my sense of genius. It is this notion of leaving to God what is God's, along with the sense that I have a vision of spreading the orange dove of my company around the world.

Can you fathom the possibility of connecting people of different countries around the world, in positive and creative, not to mention cooperative communication? Although I must digress a tad; you see part of my work in establishing myself as The World's Best Mediator is not just developing the understanding of the iceberg; that depiction of the psychopathic personality, but also penetrating the entire façade of my familial situation. In the regard the latter two are interrelated.

Related particularly with respect to the discovery of a true psychopathic personality within my own family of origin. That behavior is displayed by my younger brother David Nathan Myers. The psychopathic personality is either David Nathan Myers in his entirety or David

Nathan Myers as a composite of other peoples' energies. Sometimes these folks are so ludicrous I wonder as to whether I should just "forgive" them and move on; albeit at least for the moment I seem to be following a path of calling the question on this situation, as my children are involved.

A psychopath is essentially able to turn your entire life upside down, creating this life of deceit, and then working to ingratiate him or herself in with everyone else. This is why on some level, it is better to disconnect from such folks. Yet, my children's lives are at stake and I enjoy the genius of working for a proper and decent outcome.

On some level that was the degree of true evil in this situation; the connection of those two personality types Margaret Carney and David Nathan Myers. Margaret, surely in her passing is the more sympathetic figure. David Nathan has this sadistic delight with regard to virtually running a pick-up truck back over and over my life. Except for today, I sent his attorney a lengthy possible complaint, notable for the essence of declaring David Nathan Myers a psychopath.

I am chuckling, as this has been just the most unfathomable ride, and the normal response to a psychopath, ought to on some level be to disconnect from his or her energy and go No Contact; and yet in this case with my own children's lives at stake there seems to be almost zero possibility of doing so. Speaking in the first hand for the moment; it is surely "indescribable" to be psychologically stalked by a person with a personality disorder such as David Nathan Myers. The entire family system he seeks to set up, is my elimination from my rightful place; and then his mocking me left and right through intimidating and extremely cruel psychological tactics.

It is a perversion, those who derive psychological pleasure from their abuse of other people; with the sense that such people have nothing inside, where for most people heart and soul, or decency or remorse would reside. It is still an open question for me, as to whether I should just leave the situation as best as possible; trusting in my own vision for my work, as well as the sense that ultimately the relationship among Sophie, Sam and me is bounded by love; and will outlast these folks no matter what anyone.

That again speaks to the notion of letting go and letting God. It may be that the sheer designation of David Nathan Myers as a psychopath is a victory for me; and God will do the rest. Not to mention however, David Nathan Myers intimidates my parents Morey and Sondra Myers, and wreaks so much havoc on so many. It truly is unfathomably important to keep my joy, not to mention my wits about me

This is where an element of "forgiveness" can come in, because the sheer understanding that someone is a psychopath or potentially personality-disordered provides some buffer for you, irrespective of how destructive they are, ultimately at least you are solid in the knowledge that you are dealing with an extremely corrupt and impaired individual; once one learns how to emotionally distance themselves from such a person, one is much less prospectively hurt by them.

This is one of the strokes of genius from my life and experience. when a person is so hell-bent on bothering you, and you become so psychologically strong so as to not allow them to bother you. This is one of the facets of my own development with The Science of Inner Strength; when you develop your own sense of self and vision; it becomes much harder, if not impossible for other people to bother you.

In some ways letting go, can be part of the ultimate revenge; in terms of a person who perverts their very sense of reality so much that at some point, you are just able to ignore them. I must say these type of thoughts puts my mind wonderfully at ease. Rather than seeing the perverted mindset as a direct threat on you, see it as the truly horrific mindset that it is, and how disconnected from their own heart and soul such a person really is. Our own spiritual development can be such a protection and buffer.

I am grateful I have Calm Interventions and the orange dove, to promote forward at this juncture. I mean major questions arose, for me, as to whether I should pursue another round of legal action against my family, or pursue reconciliation with them; even when they seem to convey no interest. This is the brilliance of life, in an "odd" way; in that I have what only can be described as "the third way." The third way is a way of letting go; and to my understanding goes back as far as Jesus. I am familiar too, with a sentiment of the Buddha with respect to the sense that in life, we must find the middle way. Yet the middle way is not about merely going to the middle; it entails going from one extreme to the other, in order for us to discover the middle way itself. It is such a wonderful concept, the middle way, to be discovered in this amazingly experiential manner.

The third way for me, may well mean eschewing the

notion of revenge or even justice; it may preclude the sense of inordinately reaching out to people to bring them together; and instead it means moving on with my agenda that I have spent such time and energy developing. This is where I am inordinately grateful for the years spent of seconds, minutes and hours of exquisite work actually developing something, while people were so perniciously working to abuse me.

There is much discussion of the Law of Attraction these days, and while I find it to be an interesting notion able to help us keep a positive attitude at times; I do not find it to be the be all and end all. Instead I find, in a less cosmic and more practical sense we can make ourselves more attractive by having a main commitment, a theory, an underlying authenticity and purpose in life. We create a sense of attraction for ourselves by having a skill, a talent, a notion that we can walk anywhere in any direction in the pursuit of our dreams, not being held back by people who are not making the investment in us..

In the spirit of forgiveness and letting go, it may as much be the ultimate position of strength in the relations with my family of origin to sincerely have the capacity to walk away and pursue my dreams. Thus, while I was in this psychological prison that they had kept me in, I was not idling; instead I was in phenomenally painstaking capacity creating a better world for myself; to the point where I can walk away from them as need be; or at least for the moment, I am walking in pursuit of my dreams, literally and figuratively.

Letting go, means that I have created a better life, true lemonade out of the lemons they were throwing at me. I love the expression from former newscaster David Brinkley somewhat along the lines: "The key is to build a foundation out of all of the bricks that have been thrown at you." In some ways, the spirit of the Brinkley quote is the essence of The Science of Inner Strength, as well my whole approach to life. We have gotten sucked into a whining, self-entitled culture, where people are smart, but do not show it, through the verbal assaults and hate on on-line commentaries and things like that.

Having a brother who is psychopathic, or at least acting in a psychopathic mode, while unfathomably painful at times; ultimately were some of the bricks to build the foundation of my life and my science. This is where pain became so useful to feel it, and absorb it, not in some masochistic sense, but buffered solely on the basis that I had a goal in life, children and business that would see me through this 500 year storm that he was able to send my way. Letting go, may entail my capacity to not inordinately seek out justice against him, but rather to focus on the true gifts I have gained in the process. Moving forward as I did today, with a mailing to residents of Scranton, PA with a positive vision of my life and my work.

I did, indeed, run into a massive iceberg in my life. It was a trap; something unbelievably unexpected. You take all of the expectations from your family; all the things that they have raised you with, and all of a sudden they are not only not there, but they have turned viciously against you. Suddenly the ship you have been sailing is no longer a ship, and the little boat you are riding has been cast out far to sea. There is a British expression: "Calm seas, never a skilled mariner did make." It was navigate successfully or sink.

The rudder is your purpose, your underlying defining element that guides you through the highest, roughest seas, the darkest night, the sea monsters themselves. People can wonder how rough it can be, when the primary vehicle for the discord is an emotional one, a psychological one, and not as we have been previously ingrained a physical one. It can be record-setting with respect to emotional and psychological pain, if the inflictor of the pain is so malicious and manipulative that the tables are continually and deceptively turned on you; and thereby it can go on and on for "decades."[23]

Being basically a relatively happy, upbeat person, even empathic, I had no idea such a trap was being laid for me. It began evidently with the unrest that David Nathan Myers had grown up with, and berated my parents, unbeknownst to me, post our undergrad days, in the 1980's. The point being, the emotional landscape was shifted within our family without my knowing. What occurred I believe is that David Nathan Myers through the combination of his volatility and irrationality was able to overwhelm Morey and Sondra Myers. It must be understood that at that moment in time David Nathan Myers nineteen years old, when I first saw his irrational volatility rear its ugly head, showing up at my Oberlin college graduation in 1980, stating he wanted to "fight Dad."

In all his efforts at creating an extremely false and flawed emotional sense I believe that

---

[23] A term David Nathan Myers flung at me, with respect to his boasting he had had "nothing to do with me for decades."

David Nathan Myers was supported by his then girlfriend ultimately wife Nomi Maya Stolzenberg, who was wonderful in creating a false sense in David Nathan Myers of victimhood. Evidently the argument of David through the 1980's was that Morey and Sondra were, in David's own words to me: "Bad parents." Characteristics of extreme narcissistic, even psychopathic behavior entails changing the landscape from a rational one, to an irrational one, where the only true interest in play is the extremely sharp-edged one; that of the narcissist/psychopath, in attempting to falsely establish their hegemony.

The relatively rational landscape of our familial home and family life was torn asunder in the 1980's and at this point, I believe that the constant banging at the door of David Nathan Myers to falsely establish his hegemony was the driving influence, at least initially, if not substantially. Sondra Myers has elements of being divisive for her own benefit, but it is harder to believe at the moment that she could truly generate the velocity needed for this 500 year Perfect Storm. Still I was reminded of a wonderful thought this morning; people who hurt others are fundamentally hurt themselves. While this does not absolve them, it allows us to establish at times, an understanding, if not compassionate sense of their afflictions, while enforcing appropriate boundaries; no easy feat!

There is a part of me at this juncture that wants to set up a huge umbrella for my family and welcome them in. I recognize that they are emotionally not in wonderful shape, and their actions towards me are their own way of lashing out to help them make sense of their own lives. While the things they say and do have been historically hurtful to me; there are moments, when I just want to hug them and tell them it is all right, or at least to not take personally their antics towards me, no matter how hurtful.

It is a daily reminder that processes like letting go and forgiveness are processes and virtually constantly on deep matters, huge pieces of work. For me, it is a matter of working to see if I can somehow develop a sense of this compassion, which recognizes the hurt and pain of my family, and stands in to heal or at least deflect; other times, I say it is better to just leave it behind, and call it for what it is.

I suppose the defining element above all else is to determine a sense of who you are; then you can decide how you want to deal with people who nearly destroyed your life. For me, defining the psychopathic elements of my family of origin helped to buffer me. I mean I was handed this unfathomable level of abuse, perhaps not just to develop my own inner strength, but also to help society understand them, as well as to embrace a more compassionate sense of things.

Letting go entails, just leaving these folks behind, and proceeding with my agenda. It is asking the virtually impossible of another human being to remove themselves emotionally and psychologically from their own family of origin. On some level, however the antics of my family of origin seemed to have virtually demanded that I do that. The work of The World's Best Mediator must continue.

CHAPTER 18

DEFINING THE WORLD'S BEST MEDIATOR

So what is this world's best Mediator. The World's Best Mediator is many things. First of all The World's Best Mediator is my own living example of The Science of Inner Strength. It is the equal and opposite response of finding my own inner strength, my sense of who I am; the true strengths within me through the wonders of adversity. Adversity teaches us like slow drops of moisture in a cold cellar, drip, drip, drip; we must be extremely attentive to it. So first of all The World's Best Mediator is that of finding my true self, my true inner voice, and expression to this world as a whole. It some ways, I feel like bringing the Calm Revolution; a revolution of decency, of understanding and compassion for one another. To me, what began as a specific response to my specific situation and problems in the court system can well turn into a movement of, and for decency, That was my inner core being; that was what was inside of me, when exposed to the most massive case of emotional/psychological abuse that one can fathom. Inside me was determination not stubbornness, as well as compassion and insight. That is what twenty seven years of emotional abuse; twenty years in unfathomably intense fashion scraped away, and developed in me.

So much of the nonsense and stuff I, like most carried around, was sculpted, scraped away like being in the emotional dentist chair for twenty years straight. God in some "odd" way was having his way with me; with respect to making me a much better person than I had been before. Ultimately the human features of insight and understanding and developing a human touch were honed and honed and developed with me.

I want to focus for a moment on my younger brother David Nathan Myers, Even through David may well have begun this narcissistic landslide that turned into everyone's worst fears; I am continuing to work on the notion of forgiveness, understanding and compassion. Once a person has healed enough they can begin to look at situations and

people in different lights. Clearly people who hurt are hurt themselves; let's begin there.

Maybe I have acted in a strong enough sense, so as to begin to look at David in even a compassionate sense. Clearly his lack of direction and enormous violation of boundaries stems from both his own pain AND his failing truly to know any better. Does it not ALL come down to that, as Jesus is quoted: "Forgive people for they know not what they do."

I just read a fantastic article on the subject: "How to forgive by allowing a person to be ignorant." The article is wonderful in that it recognizes the psychology of people essentially along the lines, the way some people think, they essentially need their craziness. People get so tied in to their image of themselves and who they think that they are that they really do not recognize their own internal thought processes, and how locked into certain patterns of thought, as well as elements of *groupthink* they can get.

In pursuing the third way, I have looked beyond notions of forgiveness and revenge, and looked towards the notion of just basic fairness for me, as an individual, and on behalf of my children as well. When I think inside the mindset of the truly deviant, and again truly injured from childhood, I think of my biological father Morey Myers. I think people can begin to conceptualize the notion of a person, who is so injured from childhood, and when I say injured I mean, a very stunted, if not repressed sense of self-esteem, that they bring this limited perspective and vast sense of entitlement to every conversation.

I mean, Morey Myers has lived eighty-eight years and is viewed as a pillar of his community, and yet unfortunately has emotional elements that are equal to a four year old. I suppose I can see how my brother inherited this sense too. Let me be abundantly clear, I was locked into much of the same mindset until the events of March, 1996, But for this really extreme and abusive separation that they were orchestrating and my reaching out for some support on an emotional level, I would probably have remained trapped in that psychological prison myself, of enormous lack of self-esteem, lack of trust and massive anxiety about the world.

It is not that I am better than those folks; it is just that God provided me with a divine moment to learn unfathomable things about the world, and carry my quest and path for a better world forward. In this way, I can see my father for instance in a more empathic light, at least at moments in time. Perhaps I am even bending backwards too much at times, to avoid conflict, although the thing I do not want to do is get into a fight with a person with a personality disorder at their level. I must make sure that my efforts and my interests are all about doing positive things, and not fighting with negative people over negative things.

What does all this have to do with The World's Best Mediator? Well, for one, it is part of the science of human behavior that I am developing. It seems to be my assignment from above, to learn above and delve into the world of the person with the personality disorder. There are many people talking about and writing about the psychopath and narcissist on-line. Two entities that come to my mind are an organization called PsychopathFree and Melanie Tonia Evans. In encountering these entities they particularly advocate No Contact as a major remedy; which virtually intuitively I began to question.

When someone is absolute about something as the only way to go; I tend to challenge that assumption. My work aims to go beyond some of that thinking. In my view, I work to see if the world of the psychopath or extreme narcissist can be better understood and ultimately broken down into more human terms, so that in essence the psychopath or narcissist can be emotionally disarmed. I am literally taking the hardship of my personal situation and using it as a laboratory to study this science. Although

I use the personality disordered as a pushing off point, towards compassion and fairness in society.

The extreme narcissist or psychopath, functions emotionally like a Great White Shark, and it is my sense to study this animal, with the sense that if and when we can penetrate and quell the hurtful energies of this figurative animal, we will have solved prospectively a lot of the hateful and even violent energies of the world. work That is partially my goal, to penetrate the mindset of vile and violent behavior with the aim of providing the help and insight to the world to understand it, if not overcome it.

That is where the title of The World's Best Mediator comes from in part, in developing this profoundly deep understanding of human behavior that essentially can turn off the violent switch, can stop unnecessary conflict; and can help people find their inner strength so that increasingly people are coming from their true strength, authenticity and kindness, rather than lesser and hateful energies. So it is not a mere title, it is an advancement, if not revolution in understanding of human behavior. I am working on getting to the root of what makes us tick; in terms of what is that choice that pushes people away from strength, and towards lesser negative, hateful and harmful behaviors.

The mode, in which I seek to move mediation if not the human condition is to develop an understanding of deviant behaviors, and thereby conflict, as well as human conversation that goes beyond where we are now. It is as if, we as human beings are somewhat stuck in this lower level, conflict ridden type of interaction, when most of us, actually seek more and intuitively know that we deserve something better. I am seeking to move the human conversation to our intelligence and true strength.

When I say intelligence, I am in the main talking about something that is accessible to most of us, irrespective of their status or position in society. The maintenance person has as much access to common sense as the President, the nurse as much as the CEO; and so on and so forth. Much of what is going on is that people are so consumed with profits and survival that we are teaching one another a very crass way of interacting, rather than coming from our true strength and intelligence.

I must interject however, today, February 17, 2016 there was a true breakthrough of sorts with a number of current topics. I am constantly learning, and this morning, an article by a person last name Wilson really spurred me on the topic of forgiveness and letting go. What inspired me, is the sense that I cannot fully be The World's Best Mediator, unless and until I am deeply healed myself.

However deep, the injury or the pain, I needed to cleanse it to fully be myself, as well as to function well in my work and my world. I am trying to think of the topic that truly was the tipping point, with respect to embracing forgiveness fully; perhaps it was just that, it was the internal pain I was carrying around, by not forgiving, even though I had "rights" not to forgive.

It seemed like relatively speaking, I did just let go and I suppose, let God; in essence forgive. What was forgiveness in that moment to me? Forgiveness seemed like a lightness, a letting go, a willingness to be in the moment, a healing. Perhaps it was my greatest victory to date; to say that I have endured this unfathomable abuse and pain, and was able to forgive, able to declare my health and happiness for that matter. I am inspired because as I allude today is the 17th and my daughter was born on March 17th and March of this year will make a twenty year anniversary of the journey of my spiritual growth. So, I feel like there is some cosmic alignment with things happening on this time schedule. My kids are still involved in mourning the passing of their mother and I love and respect that.

Yet, I can solely deal with the things within my control, for me the recovery from the abuse; the strengthening of myself and my agenda, and finally the capacity to forgive releases me deeply from the harsh ways that challenged me.

The way of The World's Best Mediator is to develop a profoundly humanistic view of the world that does include appropriate competition and also recognizes that we all participate in a greater game, which relatively requires our respect and gratitude. Having experienced what I have experienced, what moves me most in the world, is to see human beings be kind to one another; to listen to one another, to respect, even "get" one another.

Harmony and positive communication move and inspire me. Having felt the anguish of non-empathic behavior, I am deeply inspired when I see other people offer kindness to one another; it is almost orgasmic with regard to how deeply it moves me, I say with a tad of a chuckle about myself.

The fundamental issue in society today is to retrain society on both a micro and a macro level. One key element that we must begin to reward is the notion that kindness is a strength. It is attitudinal; it is our mindset we have worked ourselves and trained ourselves into a notion that being cutthroat is what is needed, and we could not be further off. Being antagonistic, being hateful runs contrary to our best human nature, and hurts ourselves greatly.

The crucial element and the revolutionary thing about what I am saying is that people believe we will sacrifice our productivity by being kind and considerate; and I am saying the opposite, we will actually become stronger and more appropriately competitive by playing by reasonable and appropriate guidelines of engagement. That is the essence of the Calm Revolution: To bring out our inner strength, and recognize that coming from a sense that we are good at root. Once we realize that we are good at root; we will need less punishment and restriction; and more encouragement and development of our abilities. As society grows in this area, the spectrum of behaviors will follow.

It is as if a gigantic billboard or website at least, lol; needs to go up in society that says we are good at root, and we have the respect and encouragement to be ourselves. Think back to many of our childhood days and the message was often the opposite; that we were flawed and needed to be corrected. So much of the hatred in the world comes from people not feeling respected and validated. It is slow and steady work, and doable, and a revolution nonetheless.

A crucial element in this, is that of trust; trust of the process of life itself. The notion of trusting life also goes very much against the grain of our previous upbringing. Even, when it gets painful; that is the precisely the moment to trust in life, and even trust that there is a higher purpose working its way through your life. I will give you a current example from my life. My ex-wife recently passed away; and I have not really heard from my children, since before the Memorial Service. I am reasonably confident that my parents and other extended family members are at work, working to seek to further denigrate my relationship with Sophie and Sam; even mixing in legal facets pertaining to my ex-wife's estate and all of that; in the main a home that I had purchased.

The emotional challenges are deep at this moment; when you have your own parents acting in such ruthless fashion against you, especially when your very own children are involved; and yet, I seek to move myself to higher concepts of possibly forgiveness, healing, and keeping the steady pace with my own life. At this moment, while I am not doing cartwheels because there is pain, I am not running from it either; I am allowing it to exist, taking it in, with the confident sense that it will teach me something and/or mold my character into even a higher level of functioning. I read a wonderful column on Chabad.org last night about how to respond to evil. This Jewish website, was aligned with some thoughts from the New Testament, with respect to responding to evil. On some level; the focus was on either ignoring evil or overcoming evil by doing good; the latter a prominent notion of the New Testament, as well.

It is inspiring to consider just ignoring the evil being conducted by my family of origin, and due again to the notion that I have created something plausibly greater in the way of Calm Interventions Inc., The World's Best

Iceberg

Mediator, and The Science of Inner Strength. The thought of ignoring people who are in such a concerted pattern of attempting to hurt me, is an amazing thought. Would that not be a prospectively stronger action than fighting directly with those scoundrel-like actions?

It takes a ton of inner strength to ignore that degree of evil; and perhaps I am ready for it. The concept I am working with in my work as The World's Best Mediator, well there are two, one is the Calm Revolution; and the other is that of using the term "compassionate genius" to describe my work. Does it take chutzpah to describe oneself as a genius in any way? I suppose on some level, but if Kanye West can do it, I suppose I can as well, lol; from my part, with genius being two percent inspiration, and ninety-eight percent perspiration, it is earned.

Speaking of Kanye and his recent request for $53,000,000 in help; I am reminded that the only requests that matter from this point forward are those that are geared to helping the world. From a Science of Inner Strength perspective, I would see that Kanye would have to do something that was about improving the world in order for him to truly raise that money. The distinction being that if those funds are just to bail out Kanye that may well not be, with all due respect all that wisely used; on the other hand if and when Kanye developed a way to mold his considerable platform into truly working for the world's benefit he might well find a way to raise those funds in question, if not much more, along with his wife Kim Kardashian of course.

Which brings me to my key point in all of this; the notion that all actions from this point forward must truly be about helping the world. That is my revolution in an "odd" way; nothing really matters from this point forward unless and until we develop a mindset to help the planet. Well actually there still are a ton of people stuck in just survival mode, and yet we must recognize that just mindless pursuit of profits or anything else is ultimately going to push our one planet perhaps beyond what it can endure. We need a little TLC for virtually everything that we do.

That is my commitment and work as The World's Best Mediator to introduce this sense of kindness and gentleness into the culture. It matters not as to whether one's agenda is the environment, or crime prevention or fiscal responsibility; any and everything must be done, with a sense of love and care for our planet; a sense of both purpose and gentleness. If we cannot talk with, and to one another; how can we resolve conflict?

Today, February 23, 2016 is an important day for me in my journey. There have been incredible forces aligned against me, and I dug deep to find a way to proceed and find that inner strength within me. The path to proceeding today, was not to take on rivals and enemies directly, but rather in the mode and spirit of the third way to press on with distributing brochures for Calm Interventions and The World's Best Mediator. Sometimes it takes more strength to walk away or not confront what we perceive to be an evil. It is finding that special gift within us. Beethoven would not have used his time well, fighting the neighborhood bully; his time was better spent playing the piano.

My gift is helping the world understand that humanistic and kind communication is a considerable strength; and it is a better and more sustainable way for our planet to proceed. Aa vast number of people confuse bitterness and derisiveness with strength or even intelligence., That is where and why you find so many on-line commentary boards filled with disparaging types of comments. Think of it, virtually all of those, are voices that want to be heard, and for some odd reason believe that putting another down expresses one's intelligence.

The point is, that a lot of these people are in fact intelligent; they just don't truly believe it. A person who truly believes that they are talented or intelligent does not need to spend a lot of their time putting down another. What I am talking about, is learned behavior on top of learned behavior on top of learned behavior. People are coming from fragile, with all due respect slightly injured senses of self, so that that they believe that their voice will only be heard if they put another down. Or similarly people believe that putting down another demonstrates their intelligence or strength.

Think about it; when a person is intelligent, then it exists on its own, without an overwhelming need to compare oneself to another. The revolution that we need, entails beginning from a place of our goodness; and embracing that about ourselves and others.

Problems in society are mainly solvable, and if they aren't for that matter, they aren't; all of our efforts at problem solving are greatly enhanced by honoring our goodness in ourselves and others. Surely, as well in this age, when terrorism is a true threat, there can be a tendency to overreact with respect to clamping down on our freedoms, and tending to label us with too broad a brush, when most of us are good.

CHAPTER 19

THE IMPACT OF MY STORY

I find myself needing, for accuracy's sakes to return to the impact of my entire story; as I am not certain yet, as to whether it is properly understood as to both the gravity of what I endured, as well as the license that I believe it gives me to speak in such deep and moral tones. Unless you have really been in a relationship with a person with psychopathic, extreme narcissistic or borderline personality characteristics you may not understand the concept of a person acting with a pointedly malicious intent or no rational basis for which to continually wish to cause you emotional distress. The intensity of abuse brought to bear by my family was unfathomable, and then again, by Science of Inner Strength standards, provided the opportunity for me to grow that much better and stronger.

In my case; that I had entire family and extended family, and ex-wife's family turn against me extremely viciously for more than twenty years, using my very own children as a focal point; I believe is ultimately unprecedented. The entire occurrence seems to me to be a once in a millennium type of event, if that; along with what I ascribe as the divine purpose of my developing these human understandings, as also an extension of the divine, as well as human necessity.

It is not my ego at all speaking with reference to what I believe; it is merely an honest and objective assessment on my part of what I believe has happened. The notion of "everything happening for a reason" is profoundly at work here. I recall again, the story from childhood of a mother being able to lift a car off of a child of hers that was trapped. In the same way, I was able to form a protective barrier to the most insane and vicious amount of emotional abuse that a person, could fathom. This endurance, is why I take issue with those voices on internet chat forums and the like who laugh and encourage others to toughen up. Unless and until one has truly experienced deep emotional and psychological abuse, then people really do not know what they are talking about.

I liken the situation to gamma rays or some intense Star Wars like force being directed against me, and due to the fact that I had a sacred purpose, protecting the emotional and psychological well-being of my two children for one; I was able to withstand those rays for "nearly" twenty-five years. Not only was I accomplishing a specific purpose, but I was essentially becoming greatly changed, if not transformed in the process. It was as if God was using some ex-ray like sculpting tool to "perfect" [24] and change me into a person, of extremely deep values, with a message to heal and help the world.

To sit in the midst of great abuse, fighting it yes,

---

[24] On any human basis I surely do not claim perfection; I am only referencing the mission that I believe God was giving to me.

but unable to completely overcome it at points, was unbelievable; and rather than compare myself to others, I empathize greatly with any and all who have experienced abuse, of any kind. Perhaps I differ a tad with some, with respect to my urging people to use that experience as a strengthening experience, which is a challenge to some, and yet it has become my mission in life.

The words are rather "indescribable" to use the word from my daughter to really describe what one feels. Emotional/psychological abuse is one of the perversely outrageous situations that a person can experience. Not only are you being defamed and demeaned and ostracized, but those who are on some level torturing you, are enjoying the process; and stake a special delight in ridiculing you further when you confront them on it, and/or even bring it to the attention of authorities. Because your position has been so demeaned, and you may have been pushed so far to the edge emotionally and/or financially or both; you are further ridiculed as having mental health issues or even being crazy.

Because you are functioning from a rational standpoint, and believe that most people will listen you try harder and harder to convince others. Some can grow weary of your perspective and tell you to buck it up, and even those closest to you, begin to doubt your rationality. The mantra of "patience and perseverance" served as my guiding light often enough during the saga, because if you really did not have a long-term perspective on eventually overcoming it; one could not make progress. Perhaps most important, albeit extremely challenging is working yourself into a sense that the individual challenge is not your enemy per se; but it is a gift, a challenge from above, for you to learn much greater things about yourself and the world.

There is a grave danger in personalizing the struggle or sensing that because a person with a personality disorder is assaulting you so much that they are your enemy. On the most disturbed level, the person attacking you is coming from an extremely impaired sense of themselves, and may well be grabbing out at you, in their own extremely impaired way for attention or their own sense of help. Of course, we cannot allow another human being to use and abuse our lives, but through The Science of Inner Strength and developing our own strength, we can simultaneously while protecting ourselves fight back the pain; as well as at least intellectually develop some sense of a buffer of understanding that we really are dealing with a very sick person!

Society as a whole must know that people who are acting in hurtful ways are indeed hurt themselves; it is not an absolute protection and yet it is a buffer for us to develop understanding, if not a tad of compassion for these folks. As I have moved more towards the elements of forgiveness in my own life; I have been able to inculcate these senses of understanding into my life. It becomes extremely important to understand that people who act in systemically hurtful manners, have what I like to call a lack of light in their lives. There is no true sense of God, light, universe, decency; that buffers them from their hurtful feelings, and what amounts to be a sense of severe self-entitlement on some level.

Today is March 1, 2016 and I feel like I came to a major breakthrough/affirmation of this entire saga. I confirmed something that I have played around with for a long time. In my mind, at least as of today; I identified on a much deeper level Morey Myers as the iceberg, the source of this unfathomable emotional abuse that was directed towards me. It went down like this. With the passing of Margaret; Morey had an opportunity to provide health care coverage for Samuel and me, which I appreciated. True to form it came at a price however.

Yesterday it came to Morey's attention that I was working on getting some of the paperwork together, some of which was taking time, as some info I needed was from a person, who was out of town. I got these emails from Morey, talking about my "failure;" when indeed it was under control, I had taken all steps within my power. Then however for the topper, he signed off saying "answer immediately." I mean his entire tone, I would not speak to a broken down dog that way; it was so abusive.

As painful as it was, it was as if he finally showed his hand after all these years; not that I did not know it anyway, but it just seemed to come crystal clear. After following through on the things I needed to do with the health care; overnight it hit me at the core of my being how abusive he was, and I could overlook it no more. I called him out on his bullying, and essentially implied that he is never to talk to me like that again. I sent a letter out to family members with that insight. It seems like prospectively a historic moment. I had also added in the email and the letter; that I saw Morey Myers as the one with the mental health problem. I feel like this was a rather historic turnabout; after having Morey Myers point the finger at me for more than twenty seven years, the truth is beginning to see the light of day. Morey Myers has occasionally this impish sense of cuteness and has hid often enough, behind his sense of civil rights and this kind of thing; so who would believe it?

While I still in pain for this last round of emotional abuse, I feel like this could be the beginning of the great victory in this situation. On some level, I am surely calling it as such. The deep element and the iceberg of ALL this, is that Morey Myers is a person of such limited self-esteem and understanding that he became threatened by my very being and sense of success that I could achieve in this world. This is truly the nature of emotional/psychological abuse; it is people with such an underdeveloped sense of self that their only way of being in the world is to be pernicious and/or hurtful to others. It really was a desperate situation that Morey Myers constructed.

The degree of psychological sophistication to keep another person locked, essentially imprisoned, if not tortured on a psychological basis was just extraordinary. This is what I am getting at, as to the unprecedented nature of what my daughter aptly called "indescribable." The number of factors that were brought into play: The irrational volatility of my brother and his wife; an ex-wife who would do virtually any bidding against me; having two amazing children, who virtually everybody craved after, and having the lawyers with the capacity to influence an already ruptured family court system, and my families' betrayal created this asteroid like impact on my life. It is the vicious confluence of these factors that makes my story so astonishing.

The equal and opposite response was for me to dig

in, and to develop my inner strength to turn this unbelievable harm intended for me, into generations and generations worth of lemonade; with the help of God, of course. Emotionally it reminds me of the heroism from the movie from Afghanistan "Lone Survivor" of the four Navy Seals that took on seemingly hundreds of Taliban type fighters, although I must bow to our soldiers for facing awful physical weapons. Because I had at my core protecting my two sacred children, a purpose; it gave me this unfathomable staying power. God willing, I am not celebrating too early; but I feel like on some level the mere identification of Morey Myers as perhaps the source of this conflict is a phenomenal victory unto itself.

I can just feel his sickness; the irrationality of his mind; and how it was used to abuse me, and control others. Along with merely coming through it, and developing the genius to identify the source of all of this, I find my spirit uplifted. One element of emotional/psychological abuse that is hard to discover is the parasitic nature of it. Morey Myers was able to couch much of what he was doing to me; behind the guise that he was just trying to "help." It is part of the iceberg effect; some people just cruise their lives, virtually undetected by others, albeit for Morey at eighty-eight years, he was discovered.

This is the genius of Calm Interventions Inc., my mediation and coaching company; developing the capacity to work through these most complicated of situations with a compassionate accuracy, even genius, as I love to call it. If a scenario like this. enters a typical court hearing; as this has done, the chance of people butchering it, with all due respect are extremely high. Can you fathom the pain of being in a deeply challenging situation and having people perhaps not get it right, and rub salt into the wound? That stuff is extraordinarily painful. The genius of Calm Interventions Inc. is to find the compassionate accuracy of these situations, surely beginning with this accuracy: It is so hurtful to be being abused by another person; and to have them get away with it.

So, the discovery of the illness and the source of Morey Myers is a huge facet of the making of The World's Best Mediator. The challenge with society today, is to find the honesty, the accuracy if you will. People yearn for truth, and there is deception on so many levels, from political to economic to legal; it is a true wonder that the ordinary citizen can stand it at all. Perhaps then, it is virtually with a sense of desperation that people are turning to Donald Trump in this day and age. The Trump phenomenon is two fold for me. On one level what he is representing is this need on the part of people for something really better, given those senses of corruption that I have described. Yet, unfortunately, with all due respect, Mr. Trump as a personal messenger seems to be mixing in some of those iceberg like qualities that I have described, to attempt to attain his goals. Sadly Mr. Trump may be being artificially bolstered by a media that is thinking about its own ratings before the accuracy of the American situation.

Still I must revert back to one item pertaining to my own personal discovery episode. This morning, I seemed to have a wonderful insight. What I came to today, is the sense that the crowning piece to the unfathomable story, was on some level the adamancy and exaggerated sense of superiority of my sister-in-law Nomi Maya Stolzenberg.

That is the genius of the situation, essentially recognizing that Nomi provided the figurative match, to the kerosene over the pile of wood if you will. In an extremely complicated situation, particularly familial, there can be an incredible mix of personalities and behavioral types that confound a situation.

The wisdom that is descending upon me is that how much this dynamic can be affected or altered by marriages that come into a family. Wowsie, as my late Grandfather Samuel Z. Myers used to say. In some cases, especially when boundaries are not well established, a whole other families' baggage can be added to the mix. One of the true points of vulnerability of my family of origin, was around the issue of divorce, as divorce had not been a common occurrence at least among my grandparents and parents. I was at each of my grandparents fiftieth wedding anniversaries.

It is emotionally like an elephant is afraid of a mouse. My family was so terrified of divorce that when Margaret and I separated for a period of time, one year into our marriage; my family had to concoct some far out reasoning as to why this happened. In addition, the fact that Nomi Maya Stolzenberg was a distinguished law professor with an interest in family law; she inappropriately saw an opportunity to assert her sense of legal muscles on this family, readily taking up and advising my ex-wife as the entire separation and divorce thing unfolded. To the degree as well, that David and Nomi's marriage may not have been so solid itself; my marital challenges gave this family "ample"[28] opportunity to create this outrageous narrative about the problems of this family. In essence, as I have said, I was targeted as the family scapegoat, and every problem that affected or even afflicted this family was deposited at my doorstep.

Yet, today on some "odd" level, I am still choosing to forgive. This is the inspiring and unfathomable notion that given that truly massive emotional impact that plowed into me; I am choosing to forgive. There is again, where The Science of Inner Strength comes in to play. While I was being attacked and put through an emotional and financial purgatory I was also growing and changing as a person; kind of like how a caterpillar changes into a butterfly, or how plants sprout from the ground. That kind of growth and change can be hard and even painful. Again, one must be versed in the notion that one has a goal, and also profoundly attuned to the notion that God, or a higher power, is working some kind of divine purpose upon you; meaning that while you may not enjoy each and every moment of pain, you can almost feel the growth as it occurs.

So I sit here today in a Whole Foods café wondering if indeed the identification of Nomi Stolzenberg as the crowning piece of all this, is indeed icing on the cake. As I say, I am confident enough to pivot from this scenario, knowing on some level that I have essentially done all that I can do. It feels like a rest my case moment; "odd" in that it has all unfolded over a period of at least twenty years. This is the moment when forgiveness can and must occur.

So what does forgiveness mean now? Forgiveness means the capacity to let go of some stuff, and to have outgrown the problem; to not be so affected or taken aback by other peoples' somewhat vitriolic actions. It is the capacity to have built in a buffer, of a sense of self so that one ultimately is not prone on some level to other peoples' perspectives. Forgiveness, ultimately becomes the capacity to see another's statements as a reflection of him or her; and not an accurate characterization of you. Maybe even on some level, it is developing a pity for a person, who has chosen to. so voraciously and blatantly violate your life; strong work indeed.

CHAPTER 20

THE CORE OF ONESELF

"It is not what lies ahead or behind, it is within..." Henry David Thoreau

The crucial element with all of this is developing a sense of oneself, from an inner perspective. If human beings do not have a sense of decency, a sense of respect beginning for oneself, and spreading out to others then they will be much more prone to violate another human being. Again, it is hurt people, who hurt others.

In my entire evolution today seemed to be a special day. This is Sunday, March 6, 2016, and it seemed like this morning, maybe I nailed the entire scenario I have been working on for twenty years and in some ways more. The entire notion of Iceberg, has to do with what I consider to be extreme narcissistic, borderline and yes even psychopathic behavior. It was clear to me that the entity that I was dealing with, comprised of my family of origin, ex-wife, extended family and the courts was a psychopathic situation.

For so long my efforts have been to get to the centerpiece of the entire thing, so as to prospectively identify it, and with truth as my sword put a stop to it. Today, with a reasonable degree of certainty after twenty years of the most extreme iteration, I seem to have identified my biological mother Sondra Gelb Myers as the focal point of that entire dynamic; lol, yes it does evolve on a day-to-day basis. The aggressive, even outrageous behaviors of my father Morey Myers, and my younger brother David Myers, seem to be reflections of their manipulated sense of loyalty to my mother Sondra Gelb Myers.

I am not certain. but the end seemed to come in an unusual way. When my brother and I were growing up in Scranton there was a woman, named Mrs. Bear(sp?) who we would often and seemingly randomly walking all around Scranton, a very elderly woman with gray hair. Mrs. Bear may well have been a wonderful woman; yet it seemed to us a rather odd sight as kids to see this woman kind of pop up wherever we drove. Today, I stumbled upon the brainstorm of calling my mother Sondra Gelb Myers, Mrs. Bear; conveying the sense that my mother was an elderly lady randomly wandering around doing things, with no offense to Mrs. Bear, whatsoever. Clearly I do not in the main approve of the tactics of Donald Jr. Trump on some larger scale; yet in tiny doses designating an opponent in a certain way can be extremely effective. To give the sense that Sondra Myers is not some other worldly icon helping to change the world for the better; but rather a person, who acts virtually viciously and totally for show; I designated her as Mrs. Bear, albeit with no disrespect whatsoever to Mrs. Bear, again.

Iceberg

We shall see the total effect of such a designation but I have a sense it could be the crowning piece in the struggle; lol, I have said that before. Not to mention, virtually immediately afterwards, I watched, as I often do on Sunday mornings Joel Osteen, and Joel's sermon seemed particularly apt this morning. Joel's sermon was about the resistance we get to our big dreams, and essentially to never give up on them. I have been having a wavering thought or two recently; and Joel's sermon was perhaps that last steady boost to move me forward on virtually every level; leading me to the point of something that I call the Calm Revolution in my work on behalf of Calm Interventions/

It was like another crowning piece or pieces of certain things. Actually Joel did say to be careful about sharing your vision, so perhaps on some level, I should just keep quiet about certain things today.

Today is a new day, March 7, 2016 and having appropriately taken down Sondra Myers a notch or two; I am left on some "odd" level with the perspective of David Nathan Myers as being the dominant energy remaining. There was a huge iceberg, at the point that he falsely intervened in my life in September, 1988 that runs like an axe through the situation until this day. I have no animosity towards David, as a human being; albeit the competitive part of me, does want to win this contest on some level, in the name of truth.

A person with a personality disorder, as David seems to embody, is so doctrinaire about their perspective, that they are virtually blinded, and continue their actions towards you with this outrageous sense of self-entitlement. Perhaps the root of people who act out this type of behavior behavior is their exaggerated sense of victimhood, and accompanying entitlement. Let's be clear there are legitimate victims in this world; although I believe somewhat optimistically that true victims tend to want to work through their pains and develop that inner strength.

David's victimhood is virtually all a concoction. It is not to say that David as a younger brother did not lose certain contests as a kid; but I mean that is par for the course. If there are two brothers, unless they are twins, essentially one will be younger and one will be older, there seems to me to be no logical way around that. To attempt to make one's basic position in life, as a basis for victimhood, is a reflection of true weakness. David received an excellent beginning as I believe that I did, and for him to somehow comport that he has at age fifty five, a basis for life-long rage, is just bizarre and disgraceful, not to mention harmful to others.

It would be truly "fascinating" if David was the true root cause of all of this; bounded and buffered by my response in terms of the unfathomable personal growth that I ensued. This would be the fascinating point with respect to the notion that one person could essentially tip over the entire weight of a family to such an unfathomable degree. What I am getting at, in a more general sense, is how one person's personality can impact a situation so enormously and for so long. This outrageous dynamic has been in place for more than twenty seven years now. Think of the capacity to apply these understandings to dynamics in businesses, families, organizations' to recognize that one person or at least one mindset can so definitively influence a group like has been done here.

I used to wonder about the Israeli strategy or the USA even, with ISIS of targeting leadership, but there may be more wisdom in those strategies than I was aware; it really can be that one or a small number of personalities can influence much larger, more destructive group dynamics. Wow, on some level I must pause, as I am truly stunned myself. Of course, with me, I am only referencing appropriate means, such as my pen, and not the sword.

When you are in an emotionally abusive situation, where essentially the group has lost their mindset, if not their collective minds there is an enormous amount of pain and trauma that you and the group are going through. It is hard to come to the logical essence of what is going on, and in that regard with all due respect I credit myself for having developed what I call a "compassionate genius" in my role as The World's Best Mediator, with respect to understanding the underpinnings of group dynamics and human behavior.

I say wow; because I was the target of the abuse, AND the scientist who figured it all out.

A sort of magical thing happened today; I found myself removed, even possibly above the abuse.

What I found was the true me, in greater proportions, my inner core, if you will. I find myself more and more oriented towards the goodness and decency of the world. That truly is my contribution to make; the influence towards a world of decency, revealing to people that true strength resides in things like kindness, respect and determination.

We live in a world, where some value the "toughness" of things; where a Donald Trump can do his "tough" talking and try to impress people. True strength resides in positive actions that are imbued with a respect, if not kindness towards others. Think about it, ultimately we need the buy in of other human beings to progress our agenda, and most human beings are intelligent and will respond better when they are treated respectfully and intelligently. That is what the deep abuse brought out of me, a true kindness and humanity, like a diamond from coal.

It is worth saying a few words about kindness. By kindness, I do not mean, people pleasing, or doing things just to win the favor of other people. By kindness, I mean being in healthy and good shape yourself; and then having something extra to offer to our fellow human being. Clearly it is strength, if we are not trapped inside our own perspective of life, and rather we can offer something extra to another human being, in the way of empathy, listening, and understanding.

To really touch my fellow human being in a warm way; that is my essence; that is my contribution here on this earth. Critics will point to the incredible journey I had to travel, and the fact that I could fight really hard to forward my agenda. One way of looking at it, is that greatness is truly forged by fire; those deepest of fights that not only bring out our inner strength, but our true inner core. Arguably we need a fight of the level, to define ourselves, in essence to scrape away all of the gunk that society has deposited upon us. In an "odd" way, my families' fight with me, was ultimately to control me, and to shape me into some form of them, of which I would not conform. Unfortunately for them, I had a destiny that exceeded who they wanted me to be, and probably with all due respect, who they were, themselves.

At its core, that is our divine imperative, to become who we are meant to be. Good parents, will support our full progression and growth as a human being. It will pain some as I say this, but we cannot be wedded to the past, or to other peoples' expectations for our lives. My story is an extreme example, and yet I do not know everything, but I know there is a divine reason to my story, and in that regard, my general message to the world, is that it is our divine imperative based on our goodness, to become the person we were are meant to be. Some may fear that I am talking about living almost lawlessly; instead I am saying that as we develop our goodness, we live by our own discipline of appropriateness, rather than a mere fear of the law.

Appropriate is a wonderful word; something I have learned to love over the years; and reflective of a high rate of growth and development as a human being. All of the political correctness and that kind of stuff can be reduced to a sense of respect and dignity for each and every individual in a generic basis. Once we understand that we are good, and that we and other human beings are worthy of dignity; then a lot of our fight with others, can dissipate.

What is the fight that most human beings have? It is a fight to express ourselves; a fight to overcome our feeling of a lack of worthiness and recognition. What if instead we started to base society on the basic worthiness of every individual; as not something to be feared, but something to nurtured. It does not matter, straight/gay; black/brown/white; woman/man/transgender; ethnicity, anything; let's begin from the standpoint that every human being is worthy of dignity.

Imagine the changes in society when we begin from a premise of dignity and respect. The need to fight decreases by at least half; what happens when society values one another as a human being. People will say impossible, due to economics, but we must rework our sense of economics, and it may not take such a major shift. Like tires on a car, will last longer if treated better; human beings will work better, more happily and productively by being treated fairly and with dignity and respect. Here is the revolution in a sense; for the most part people want to do well. We are not square pegs to put into round holes; we are healthy and happy human beings, by encouraging and supporting our health, happiness, and positive development.

Clearly there is much as far as families and parenting; that society can learn and make adjustments. The notion of healthy and happy children is gaining credence in the culture. One thing that my experience has taught me, one grain of truth perhaps within our court system is that we really cannot be solely pals with our kids in the long run. While there were many humanistic aspects I brought to my parenting in my early years; it is viable to suggest that I needed to add some starch to it, as well. My generation has taken a step forward with respect to empathic parenting in response to the strictness of our parents' generation, and yet maybe in some ways we have gone a step too far, and can calibrate.

As painful as it has been, the eight years or more that I have been alienated from my sacred children has made me a much better father and parent in general. I am not so inherently deriving my joy from my children, and rather recognizing the sacred role of being a parent; and treating it a tad more like a job. I have honed more of my energy towards my children, in terms of their true benefit, along with joy, which is are hard skills to master. Especially with the passing of their mother, I am heartened that I have taken on that role; not in an authoritarian way, but in a way, I would dare to say, filled with wisdom.

Today, March 8, 2016 seems like a monumental day, with respect to keeping a sense that David Nathan Myers may well be at the root of this historic conflict. I am writing at, of all places McDonald's; for some reason their expression: "You deserve a break today" stuck with me. It is a rather unfathomable journey, chopping through this emotional ice or even iceberg as I am. It is hard to see my younger brother David Nathan Myers ever coming to a rational place within our family. Maybe the best I can envision is to apprise others of what I see the truth to be, and let it go from there.

I can't really complain, if David had not gone so far off the ranch; I would never in thousands of years have gone through the emotional development that I did. The things I was just discussing with respect to parenting and all of that, The Science of Inner Strength, none of it, would have come about but for this extraordinary process. The thing is, my family is still involved in working to keep my children from me, and I see it as the best method to change that dynamic by emotionally breaking the back of that irrational hatred directed towards me. It stands to reason that not all the members of my family can equally feel this irrational hatred, and over time, those less inclined will lose their energy, particularly by isolating David's hatred, if that is indeed what is at root in this situation.

It has truly been a monumental journey, an emotional saga of virtually unknown proportions. If your family of origin turns against you, and is willing to use your very children against you; you are for starters having the emotional screws turned ino you, in the most unfathomable of ways. It is kind of like if you were on the old torture rack, just stretching and stretching your emotional growth and wisdom, until you virtually could not stretch any more. As I say, God is using me for this very purpose, so I cannot complain too much.

When it comes down to it, I can only take it one day at a time. Enjoy each day as the gift that is. There is a lot of emotional pain though, when people are putting the screws to you. I suppose that is the most fascinating part; working to find ways to use the pain to your benefit. Like lemons themselves, in the spiritual lemonade factory, the pain can rest withme. What do I suppose is the source of the pain? Beyond the emotional pain itself; some Buddhist and like minded philosophies suggest that pain is the result of things occurring different to our expectations. Perhaps if I could be totally in the moment, as someone like Eckhart Tolle suggests then I would feel much less pain. That is actually a wonderful notion, although the pain has its benefits.

You know there is "fascinating" concept in there somewhere, that is peoples' sole intention is to bring emotional pain down upon you; then one way to defeat it is to on some level not allow the stuff to hurt you. I must confront some of my feelings about my children on that level. Why does it outrage me, that these folks seemingly are working to keep my children from me? Maybe when I trust my children to discover the right answer on their own, I can let go of a ton of the load. If I was not worried about my children; it would just be a beautiful day. Just like McDonald's would have us believe, lol. Trusting in life, it is.

A breakthrough of sorts; I am leaning back towards Sondra Myers as the true source of this emotional tsunami. People may not understand the constant return to that scenario. I sincerely believe that it is a once in a millennium type of event. I mean, after twenty seven plus years; you have your eighty eight and eighty one year old parents, working to try to keep your very own sacred children from you. As just one bottom line result, has anyone heard of such an outrageous thing? I mean my ex-wife passed away five months ago, and it seems rather than lessening the desperate efforts to keep my children from me they have intensified. I mean, as cold-hearted as my ex-wife could be; I am not certain it was really her impetus at the middle of this unbelievable effort. To think that eighty eight and eighty one year old parents would work to disenfranchise their own son, from his own children; is an other worldly happening.

Some would have me, just not pay attention to it, anymore; like Esther Hicks of Abraham-Hicks, essentially would have a person virtually ignore a negative event. I suppose for me, it is really a matter of developing my genius, my science in this area. It is intriguing for me, to attempt to decipher, who is most at root. Is it Sondra? I cannot tell for certain; it is somewhat like an octopus that moves and wields around.

I suppose what I do know on some level, and it is extremely sad to say, is that such behavior does verge on evil; actually it is, as far as I can see. For the moment I am allowing God to fight my battle for me. There are notions from the New Testament as far one way to fight the darkness is by spreading light. I do not know everything, but I know that it would be a tragic mistake to blow my cool. At times the patience of the moment really does stretch me, at least in terms of entertaining thoughts as to whether I can heal them in any way, shape, or form. Yet, I persevere.

It does seem amazing that when I look at Sondra in an emotional sense; I just see this dark mushy mass, kind of like a huge grouper that lives under sea, in a cave. One of the true breakthroughs of all of this; is that a lot of people live their entire lives, full of resentment from childhood, and then given an opportune moment unleash all of that pent-up rage. Sondra, in some ways, has Morey wrapped around her finger, and thereby is able to act as viciously and disrespectfully as she wants; essentially knowing that he will back up her every move.

Competition is all new to Sondra; never having participated in it herself; and she seems to think she can be as vicious and invent as many rules as she wants; essentially working exceptionally hard to uphold this bind around my life. On some level, this is an amazing breakthrough to discover that Sondra is working recklessly to wring tight this bind on my life. This is news to people; that there are people who are emotionally, sadistic. This is the new reality of today; heretofore people looked for a rationale for a person's actions, and for most us of that rationale is a sensible, even "interdependent" agenda, as Sondra purports; yet does not fulfill.

For people with a personality disorder, reason and rational are not the parameters, by which they play. Personality characteristics such as being in control, or even being sadistic are what makes them tick. Think about the notion of being "sadistic;" it is the sick idea of deriving pleasure from another person's pain. There are people in this world, who patently derive pleasure, from another human being's pain; indeed, they seek to create it.

The on-line communities around psychopathy describe things such as the psychic bond, and for narcissists; narcissistic supply, with respect to the actual sadistic, parasitic type of energy that a psychopath or extreme narcissist will derive from the pain they are inflicting on another human being. In my situation then; my sacred children became tools for Sondra Myers and others to use, mainly with the idea of inflicting pain upon me. Each statement, each word becomes a vicious tool, for how to offset me, or brainwash my children, in a direction different from the humanistic one that Sondra would know that I would want to see.

I am describing an unfathomably sick behavior that forms the essence of evil. It is crucial for society to know of people who act and treat others with such desperation. While this may be an extreme example; I do not know everything, but I know such behavior is festering, if even in tiny ways, within society as a whole. People interested in rational and decent outcomes are frustrated by people, who have no interested whatsoever in inducing rational and decent outcomes in society. The sole interest of such deviant behavior is not only self-centered, but interested in inflicting pain itself, which is a new phenomenon in this form for society to know.

On some level, it could well be an aim of mine, to create a social understanding around Sondra and others in this situation, so that others can begin to see how deviant, and malicious such an agenda really is. Most people once they develop an understanding that another person is acting patently maliciously will not support that kind of behavior. Sondra is able to hold everyone's attention through her social orchestration and manipulation of family communication and events; so that all communication is channeled through her.

I must repeatedly and abundantly make clear that the purpose of my writing is the illumination for society as a whole; to bolster those who have gone through such things, and for whom this will ring a bell; and every bit as much to point society into a more decent direction. It has been an awesome piece of work, with respect to prospectively identifying Sondra as potentially the source of this; and yet, from where else would my brother have developed such rage, at such a young age?

A profoundly narcissistic, if not psychopathic mother, could not stand the closeness of her children; she would view it as a threat to her; and would work deceptively to drive a wedge between her children as she has done here. Indeed, the light in my life, must be such a threat to her, in terms of my joy, and sense of purpose that she has muckraked so much in the efforts to bring me down. Failure, lady!

Nonetheless, the title of this chapter has to do with our inner core. On some "odd" level the real life experiment, that that I am conducting has to do whether I can essentially stretch myself so much during this situation to have my love and/or my compassion, not to mention my genius if you will; to overcome their hatred, not by "defeating" them, but by illuminating them to the error of their ways. That is truly the intriguing thing about all of this, because no other approach would have advised this course; or precious few. I mean there is a woman, whose name may come back to me, on the internet who suggests that there may be a level of growth that a person can achieve essentially grows beyond the capacity for a person with psychopathic or extreme narcissistic tendencies to be able to hurt you anymore.

This morning, March 11, 2016, an inspiring notion was that of accepting these people as they are, which is a challenge unto itself, and a severe adjustment from having parents, for instance, who are 100% in your corner, and instead maybe ten percent, and accept that ten percent; and/or work to slowly and surely raise that ten percent through virtually pure positive or at least constructive behavior towards them. It is said that necessity is the mother of invention and that is really the situation that I found myself in; as my sacred children, if you will, were trapped behind enemy lines at least temporarily.

That is the psychological bind that I was getting at, throughout this entire scenario, which has made this situation so unfathomable and pernicious in "odd" ways. It was my own parents who were spearheading an effort to keep my children from me. The levels of psychological hurt that that can inflict are astronomical. Fortunately I was clear enough about my priorities in the vein of The Science of Inner Strength so that protecting the emotional health and well-being of my two sacred children, and not on adhering to or even worshiping my parents, as their psychological needs at times, seems to demand.

Can people really picture that? One's own children being brainwashed and worked to be kept from you, virtually totally unjustifiably, and it was one's own parents that were doing it. The problem with really going off the rails about it, and that kind of thing, is that if you protest too much, it makes you seem like what people are saying about you is true. In that regard one must go immeasurably slowly at times, to effect longterm change.

The strongest position is, to assure yourself that you will be alright no matter what those folks do, or do not do. I wonder if it would be better just to leave them behind, and yet because of the position of my children, I have not been able to accomplish that as of yet. Common sense must take hold at some point, and as long as I am reasonably bringing that forward, I am in a wonderful place. These are high level skills, in terms of prospectively dealing with people who would emotionally take hostages.

The challenge is to interject oneself into the realm of hurtful people in a way that calms them, and on some level assures them, that you will not do anything to make the situation worse. People who are hurting other people, are themselves hurt; often we must come back to that constant reminder, in terms of defusing rather than escalating situations. Of course first we must contain the negative effects of their behavior. Once that primary goal is achieved then we might begin the meeting the hurt person at the point of their hurt.

I am getting at a really key point in conflict resolution and as I say in general, dealing with people in hurtful patterns of behavior. Yes, we as people and as a society must stop those hurtful behaviors, and then whenever possible we can work to assuage, if not heal that hurt person, if possible. I feel this way, at times with my biological father Morey Myers. Morey's with all due respect, hurtful behavior towards me, is not only stemming from his own hurt, but to my mind, a large part of it, may well stem from a lack of recognition of his own sense of self.

A person, who has not fully developed or even moderately developed their sense of self-worth, goes out into the world feeling deprived, in many, if not most of their interactions. It matters little how talented they are; they can virtually always focus upon what is lacking in their lives. This is the unbelievable part about the role that I have had to play. On one level, I am the person experiencing this phenomenally intense emotional/psychological abuse; on another level I set up this emotional laboratory to use this situation to study the issue; and finally utilize the results of that profound scientific study to attempt to offset, if not heal the hurtful behaviors of those who are abusing me. It is, if I can say for myself, a rather miraculous process.

So in looking at the core of my being; I find first, I suppose a susceptibility to having been abused in the first place. Perhaps I put a naïve trust in Morey and Sondra Myers, and did function in the world, like I could do whatever I wanted without having earned that right. Then when the tsunami hit the fan, so to speak; I began to discover this core of inner strength, my core values, and where I stood. That part was probably the part that my critics and challengers grossly underestimated within me, as it had not evidenced itself until these times. Probably like my family of origin, I was exhibiting at least some elements of bullying type behavior, and as most of us know, a bully is acting in a cowardly fashion ultimately. That was the extraordinary wake-up call that began in my life on or about March 22, 1996; which is about eleven days short of twenty years today.

That self-definition stage was about building determination and if people can see the distinction here, to replace the stubbornness that existed previously. This stage also included learning about my spiritual, trusting nature, as well as coming into much greater touch with the gentle and/or compassionate elements within me. It is worth noting that on or about that date in 1996, I had a tiny bit of marijuana which I tossed off a look-out point on my way into Scranton, PA, and have never looked back as far as that substance, and did go three years without a drink; and now drink quite sparsely. Yes, I do believe a limitation of substances can have a somewhat liberating facet on our lives, as well.

In the third phase, I see myself taking those natural and appropriate steps to branch out and find positive ways to share the fruits of my transformation with others. It has been multi-dimensional with respect to sharing my stuff with the world at large, in the form of Calm Interventions Inc. and The World's Best Mediator; and working to reach a point of interaction and healing energy for my family. On some level, I am feeling that by reaching my family I could prospectively reach virtually anyone, and if nothing else they have provided this unfathomable sense of a laboratory in which to develop my skills, to truly make me The World's Best Mediator.

The net result being on some level, I see the healing energy coming forward as what is at my core; I have taken to calling it a compassionate genius. That is a lofty position to uphold myself in terms of pointing towards a genius; and yet with all due respect to me, lol; I believe that I have earned it, and believe genius resides within many of us. It is merely following the adage of genius being one percent inspiration, and ninety-nine percent perspiration!

March 12, 2016: This is turning into a journal, at least in this part, lol; in any event, today, I feel like I just reached a point of willingness at least to sever the relationship with those people, or at least "forgiveness" to the point where I am trusting God, the universe, truth, logic; call it what you will to resolve this situation. Again, it is with a sense that I truly want to dedicate myself to being The World's Best Mediator; and yet it pulls on me, somewhat to go back into court. I am following a precept of the New Testament, with respect to taking my position and then letting God fight the battle.

The position that I took today, clearly delineated three main points of the abuse to the abusers: 1) That they had defamed me to a core; without ever once allowing for a fair hearing; 2) That they had ostracized me to such a degree that they had actually replaced me in my family of origin, with my ex-wife; and 3) That they had and continue to conduct a merciless campaign towards my sacred children to outrageously attempt to sever our relationship. There were clearly other things including physical assaults and vandalism and the like; but those are the three main ones for sure; along with this just insatiable hatred that they direct towards me.

And on that basis I chose to forgive them, in the way of handing this entire problem over to God. I mean God is big enough, he has handled bigger, lol. I shall see how that goes; my position is clear. I must say the number of times that greater and lesser miracles have entered my life over the last "nearly" twenty years is innumerable, and God has not let me down yet; even though it has been quite a roller coaster. The only thing people in that state feel; to the degree they "feel" anything would prospectively be loss. Any kind of fight no matter how big or tiny; they relish.

I did have a breakthrough of sorts along the compassionate front that I was developing yesterday with a neighbor. This person has a personality disorder, and acts out in small ways, when he is upset. When this person yesterday did something to cause distress in a shared environment I went to him, and talked for a while, and actually later on in the day, he disclosed to me that he was in intense physical pain.

The theory of people in pain, being the ones to inflict pain and distress was borne out; It is just impossible to me, with my family for instance to maintain a constant, at times even a modicum of compassion towards them. It may be that the capacity to leave them is the only meaningful thing on my part, and even with a slight chance to theirs. After leaving or even being willing to leave a distressful situation, one does feel a void and I do feel some of that today. I am not sure I am at that point of a total departure yes or no; but it does feel like a part of me was left behind.

It is a matter of believing in the orange dove of Calm Interventions, and what my sacred mission is. Hey maybe God really did call me, perhaps that is what it is all about.. Maybe I really do have this humongous mission to influence the planet in some overarching way. Hey what do I know? I just work here. One of my favorite spiritual columns uses this principle which I love. It talks about writing down a list of things that you really wanted at the time; and did not work out. How in retrospect we are glad, it did not work out; instead better things have occurred.

For instance for me, at the time I wanted my marriage to work out and now being thankful that I was divorced. Everything that is happening along the lines of The World's Best Mediator is virtually a function of something else not working out; although I have kept to my basic principles. Even if this does not work out; I trust something better will take its place. It is also a matter of having faith and trust in God's timing or timing that is much greater than ours. We see precious little of the big picture sometimes; especially when we become narrowly focused on, one way of things working out for us.

Being happy is key. I do believe that being happy is a point of attraction for success. Perhaps not an overly smiling outward happiness; yet an inner sense of calm and solitude on some level. It seems that if we only spend time pushing ourselves, we cannot allow some of the changes to solidify and take hold. One of the favorite expressions of Pastor Joel Osteen is that God will take what was meant for our harm, and use it for our good. Joel has his good days, like the rest of us.

I mean the last twenty years of torpedo like emotional and psychological abuse directed at me, was turned into something terrific on my part with respect to my own inner growth; and the development of an agenda for The World's Best Mediator. So the question becomes or remains: What is the meaning of my story truly for the world at large? What in the cosmic sense was the reason for all of this? What can it mean with respect to future world change?

CHAPTER 21

MY STORY AND THE REST OF THE WORLD

"I'm just a skinny little boy from Cleveland, Ohio" Alex Bevan

Thanks to a gentleman by the name of Bill Ferguson; it seems like I took a quantum leap in the whole sphere of letting go this morning. Bill has some wonderful videos on the internet about letting go and facing our fears. Essentially Bill's premise is about allowing the worst of our situation come true in our hearts, not in our actions however, and stop resisting so much. By allowing it to come true in our hearts our actions can be, broader in scope and more effective. I must say that outside perspective inspired me greatly today.

Essentially I was able to write to my family and emphasize some positive points, a few points where I did not agree; indicate my desire for things to improve, and my confidence in self if they did not. I love aspects of Bill's philosophy; with respect to a sense that our fear to certain things, is essentially based on a childhood fear or two. I am trying to think what mine might be. Most of ours has to do with a sense that we are not worthy or good enough. In the main, I seemed to have passed that bridge, albeit, it is not a work of perfection, lol; by any means whatsoever.

My childhood fear, would probably be some fear of rejection, of not being good enough; in particular too, our family seemed to bring a huge sense of retribution when you made an error; whereby the tiniest of mistakes may bring out, not a huge punishment, but a very condescending attitude. If a parent is doing that, I suppose one develops a fear of making mistakes, and an avoidance of taking responsibility if an error is discovered. Another component of Bill Ferguson's philosophy has to do with saying to ourselves that even if the worst happens, we will be okay.

For some reason, I developed a financial dependency on my family and my father; it was like his promise was so great in that area, and then funds were inherited from my Grandfather, that when the rug was pulled out in many ways, my financial self went tumbling, due to circumstances beyond my control, I must add. To compensate for that fall; I developed what I believe to be a philosophy and a resilience in self, that has not yet manifested itself in the way that I desire financially as of yet, and still I believe that it will, perhaps much better than ever imagined.

I am not afraid; I am trusting immeasurably that it will work out. At the same time, I remain committed to my dream and mission of spreading mediation, and substantially influencing our culture towards decency and a truly kinder, gentler way. In that way that is the miracle of my story: Faced with unfathomable abuse; I essentially developed a commitment to inducing the opposite of everything that happened to me. That is the way of adversity; it can make us or break us. I could have become an unfathomably bitter person, and instead I used those lemons to become much the better, kinder and wiser.

When people spewed abuse; I responded with inner strength; when the world pushed me to be cruel, I am became kinder; when some demanded stubbornness, I developed determination. At the core that is my message; that ultimately strength is comprised of qualities such as, determination, kindness and decency. Contrary to much of our current cultural discourse and even recent Presidential campaign; for society in the long haul, first, we must treat each other as human beings, and not as machines to wear out; and two, true strength must incorporate decency and a sense of understanding of others. Otherwise we are looking at cruel, and even ruthless modes of interaction.

In the realm of iceberg kinds of things; I suppose I must take on the element of the Trump factor, to some degree. In that, one of the crucial elements of the iceberg phenomenon that I am describing, with respect to different behavioral and personality types is our behavior; it is shocking on some level to see the degree to which Donald Trump can turn things around, and make it about him. I saw an interview with Mr. Trump on CNN yesterday; and he attempted to turn the conversation around to how he was unfairly treated by the press; rather than beginning from a standpoint of acknowledging how much Mr. Trump has benefitted from the press in general, it seems. With all due respect, even CNN must reflect on how it contributed to the rise of the Trump phenomenon, something its own President admitted.

In general I am talking about extreme narcissistic or even psychopathic behavior when a person, essentially takes no responsibility for any hurt that they have caused, and instead turns the situation around from a fifty-fifty win-win proposition; to when they look to extract 100% from virtually every situation. So, it is not enough for Mr. Trump to be treated fairly; say one negative word about him and he may attack you at the level to rip your throat out. I am somewhat surprised as to the degree that Americans are supporting, him, and yet from a historical or even psychological perspective it is somewhat understandable as the worst thing that I have referenced is that people, especially our parts of our government in many ways are being dishonest, and the one thing that would drive people nuts is to be lied to, and then have others benefit from those very lies. So, in some way America is getting what it bargained for, with respect to a volatile type of prospectively political revolution, although on some level I do not necessarily perceive that Mr. Trump would be the terrific revolutionary that he portends to be, if he is elected.

Instead, I am initiating some type of Calm Revolution; a revolution of thought and spirit, aimed to uplift the positive within people. At the core is the sense that we are good at heart and that we not only must align with our goodness, but our government and our leadership must begin to reward our basic goodness, rather than the crass nature of human behavior that seems to be markedly on display today. We have an upside down view of society;

which has been built upon the notion that meanness is strength, rather than the opposite, meanness, is ultimately a sign of weakness, and true strength resides in respecting and uplifting others.

The premise that I am raising will take a real shift in our societal, as well as our emotional perspective. But when you think about it; why not reward goodness? We will not see society as a whole flourishing unless and until we stop division; we must set the tone that we value each and every one of us as human beings; and that our inner goodness is the most enduring and most economically viable quality in the long run. There needs to be a revolution of spirit; it might as well be a calm revolution.

I must move back towards my story for a while. This situation provides the backdrop for me being The World's Best Mediator. When I break the back of the hatred; I will have done an unbelievable feat. To take narcissistic/psychopathic rage directed at me, and break it down would be a terrific event. If I don't, well at least I suppose I will have tested the current theory to a "nearly infinite" degree. What I definitely am doing is revealing that families do matter, and whether this one can work out "outstanding[25]" issues, remains to be seen; nevertheless it is providing me with awesome experience in figuring out where the beginning and end points are, for certain kinds of human behavior. I am learning responses, if not remedies for those types of behaviors as well.

It is wonderful to be alive with a story, to live within a

---

[25] In a court document for Morey and Sondra Myers, Richard S, Bishop stated that Margaret Carney was doing an "outstanding" job in her role in the family. I am not sure about that one.

virtual human laboratory of understanding and discovery. The endpoint that I would like to get to, in terms of the net effect of my life and my story on the culture at large is indeed to influence our culture towards decency, and positive conversation. To boil this all down to its root; that is one outcome that is encapsulated in the Calm Revolution; demonstrating that kindness and goodness are strengths, and increasingly worthy of economic support and reward.

Decency has become such a part of my essence, my "political" agenda and everything beyond that. If I do nothing else in this world but to exhibit that decency is strength, my life will have fulfilled a lot of it mission. Of course, I love having fun too; and in recent years that has been put on the back burner, albeit this work is fun, the discovery is fun. It is the development of genius that is so inspiring.

Everyone, at least most of us, have genius somewhere within us; it is a matter of digging through minefields and mines to find it. Speaking of which, I implemented something yesterday that may bear significant fruit. I have been emailing on a regular basis to my family, to help them find a positive way through our situation. Yesterday, I took David off the mailings for what I said was three days. I am communicating to Sondra and Morey directly now for at least that time period. What I am starting to see, although I am not absolute at this point is that the dynamic of Nomi Maya Stolzenberg and prospectively her mother Judy Levine that has brought this hyper critical, what I have described as nuclear level of criticism onto this situation.

My family would have its jousting matches and that

kind of thing growing up, but virtually never would it take on this go for the throat mentality, which could essentially desecrate another human being. If Nomi convinced David that he was a victim, essentially of his growing experience, which I do not know everything, but I know that David was anything but a victim; then they created this hyper tornado-like emotional dynamic that has run through this family for more than thirty years. It seems possible that Morey and Sondra essentially got blindsided by the emotional dynamic, and in essence the basic fabric of the situation was overturned.

Rather than a sense of a supportive family; it became a hyper critical emotional whipping chamber, where I became the designated target. In a general sense I believe it is very relevant for the public to know how much a family dynamic can change because of the entrance of a new wife or husband, especially if and when there are children involved, as belief systems change. Nomi's mother Judy Levine, a therapist, began introducing psychological theories into my family that seem, with all due respect, hair brained at best.

It seems that Morey and Sondra were swept up in it, and blindsided to the level where they somehow found it expedient to essentially eviscerate their first son. Nomi is a very adamant person, who to me, could have a chemical imbalance or something, which makes her advocacy frenzied, and her capacity to see a viewpoint other than her own, very challenged. That is, where my analysis takes on a genius level, with respect to seeing this thirty year pattern of behavior, and tracing it back to find the roots of it.

Now it feels kind of stunning to sense and emotionally

feel the emotional umbrage of Nomi Maya Stolzenberg. It seems "ludicrous" that one person could both be so imbalanced, and seemingly catalyze such an emotional avalanche over a matter of decades, if Nomi did have that effect. Just sensing that one person is in that much pain; or has that much misguided righteous indignation to essentially feel that she had a right to bang the drum so long and loudly to the exclusion of everything else, is again to use Sophie's word "indescribable;" as today March 17, 2016 is Sophia Rose Myers's twenty sixth birthday. Happy Birthday daudsie.

The essential element introduced by Nomi Maya Stolzenberg was this hyper-critical sense that something was not right; that David was a victim; and essentially the rest of his family must pay an unbearable price. The first problem with that analysis and accompanying chain of actions is that David was not a victim in the first place. When you make a gargantuan error in the first place; and then push everything downhill from there, you can get a relatively tragic outcome; but for my capacity to hang in there, and essentially outlast all my enemies, rivals or whatever you want to call them.

In my work as The World's Best Mediator I have developed a sense of Compassionate Genius, so if the genius was coming to and discovering prospectively Nomi's enormous role, then the compassionate part is now something I must consider as well. I mean what would prospectively be the compassionate response? Stay tuned.

Well today is Saturday March 19, 2016, and on some level I may have adjusted my thought process a tad. I may have settled on David Nathan Myers as at the root of the great emotional tsunami. This would be historic, I say with a tad of irony, as David is an esteemed History professor at UCLA; evidently, he did not learn his own history lessons of decency and a sense of morality in what for most of us, occurs in the first grade or two, not necessarily in an advanced Ivy League education.

The hardest part of this story, given the age of skepticism that we live in, and the notion where everyone can portend genius, is to convey the level of emotional intensity that was posed against me for more than twenty years. Today, I am approaching a twenty-year anniversary from the start of my spiritual journey, which began on March 22, 1996, and in other ways on March 26 or so, 1996. I suppose I am seeing David as the engine of this giant airplane of emotional abuse that was directed at me.

I am reminded of virtually comical notions of The World's Strongest Man competitions on ESPN and other networks where these huge men, pull jet liners. It is such an amazing image. I feel like between the courts, David's bizarre hatred, my ex-wife, my entire family turning against me, and more, I had the equivalent of a huge jetliner of emotional abuse posed against me for twenty years; and there again is where The Science of Inner Strength comes in, because due to having a sense of purpose I would not yield, I would not be overcome. Emotional abuse is the plague of our time.

In my own quiet way, I trust it is one of the great feats of humankind, as I am aware that others as well do heroic things, in often obscure ways. Yet, I do not know everything, but I know that my story is truly one of unfathomable emotional focus and strength. I am not bragging; it is just a kind of strength that needs go forward in this world.

There is so much misunderstanding in this world, as far as what is strength and what is intelligence. The hate and animosity that we see showering over the internet and that kind of thing, much of it, is people looking to appear intelligent, by outdoing one another. Don't get me wrong, my message is that a lot of these people are indeed smart and strong; it is just that we are teaching people the wrong ideas of what intelligence and strength really are, and people are learning inaccurate things.

True strength and true intelligence ultimately need no comparison to anything else; they are not accomplished by taking down someone else. Intelligence exists unto itself; strength the same. There need be no comparison. Indeed, true strength on some level resides in the capacity to recognize the strength and intelligence of another.

We in society are teaching ourselves and each other the wrong messages, by not recognizing that humanity is a shared game, there is a collective intelligence, surely not embedded in just one person, man or woman. Cooperation then becomes a great skill and a form of intelligence and even strength unto itself. This is the revolution that I am talking about; understanding what our true strength and true intelligence are.

On some level it is very hard discussing or talking about such things as intelligence and kind communication in world where things such as a overwhelming array of nuclear weapons exist; and yet there is something deeply embedded in our human spirit that compels us towards peace and better human understanding. It is incumbent on us, as sometimes tiny human beings in the grand process, to move towards peace and better human understanding, to find our true strength and intelligence.

So, the unfathomable message that I am talking about, is again how "nearly infinite" adversity led to this equal and opposite learning on my part. It is when we create those "prisons" of adversity that the deepest learning takes place. Like Nelson Mandela, exited prison after twenty-seven years and said that "maturity" was the one thing that he learned; it is when we create that great crucible of pain and even emotional torture that the deepest and truest learning takes place. While I was in this emotional prison, unfathomable growth was taking place in a way that virtually had to mean that I had a sacred role to share in this world. Don't worry, my ego will not go amuck; as I sit in a Dunkin Donuts, waiting to pick up laundry, go to CVS and catch my bus home, lol; the rigors continue.

From the depth of that pain I was given a life and a message to share with the world. Virtually every ounce of that emotional pain, every emotional tear that I would have cried, if I had the time to cry, was transformed into something deeper and better in the way of human beauty, in the most general sense. The true beauty was uncovered and shaped, if not forged by the pain.

CHAPTER 22

OUR PRECIOUS PLANET

"If not for you, I couldn't hear the robin sing…" Bob Dylan

In a brochure I just created, well actually with profound gratitude to JTC Printing too, I highlighted the phrase "Our Precious Planet." It really is our precious planet, when all is said and done. Where are we going; what are we going to do with it? I mean there may be forces beyond our control for sure, but then again, . I am mainly speaking to the things we can control; if we cannot control them, then why worry in the first place?

It is like we need a timeout, to reorganize, realign; albeit such realignment is taking place as we speak. The world really does not stop, as much as we would want it too, perhaps at times. There are a multitude of ways to come at the world's challenges, and I must confess this is mine. My view is that unless and until we develop the capacity to work together as people virtually nothing else of true meaning will get done. I must pause for a moment, in my own loving tirade, lol; to come back to the notion of forgiveness itself. Why? Well for one, forgiveness does on some level, open the door to joy; and frankly when all is said and done. I do want to be happy. The expression it is better to be happy then right; or better to be kind than right, is sprinting through my mind, as well as the Carly Rae Jepsen song: "Call me maybe." I mean we can all try too hard sometimes, surely me included.

God is in control. That is the main thing. On some level, perhaps our biggest challenge is not hurting ourselves and the precious planet too much. So everything matters, perhaps…perhaps I will get protested by The Black Lives Matter movement preposterously, even with my ingrained history of equality and fairness, for saying that, but everything matters really, Black lives, brown lives, the environment, men, women, airplanes, schools, insects, everything matters.

So, a few things seem to have come to a head, in the last few days. For one, March 22, 2016 will mark twenty years, since this spiritual journey began; I suppose on some level I could also use March 26, 2016 as a date, but March 22, 1996 used to always be the date that I used. Yesterday I took a leap and identified Morey Myers as the source of the conflict on some level; I kind of just made it a relatively simple issue with respect to calling it bullying on Morey Myers's part, or even "terrorizing"[26] mine and other peoples' lives. It was wonderful yesterday that I got a much deeper sense of what emotional/psychological abuse

---

[26] I use this word in quotes, because that can be a word that is falsely used in police-state like divorce proceedings, to tip the balance wrongfully in another's favor.

is, in coming to terms with the pain Morey Myers and others has caused me. I feel the abuse from Morey, because I trusted him so much. What emotional/psychological abuse is, in its most precise sense is essentially an assault on an angle of one's mindset, and our sense of being.

For instance, if you raise someone; as a parent, invariably does, you clearly for the most part, get to know the child's emotional composition, how they think, the way that they respond to things. So what emotional/psychological abuse is, is an assault on a particular angle of the way a person thinks, feels and operates. For instance, if you know a person has a certain weakness, then a true abuser, will assault on that particular angle and press it to the hilt, putting the screws to the other person continually along the way.

Morey Myers knows my mindset; he knows the way I think, or at least used to; Morey Myers knows that I looked up to him, and yes to some degree depended on him. Thus, to inflict the maximum amount of pain, Sondra and Morey Myers could find the most injurious assault on my heart and brain, knowing me as well as they do.

Emotional/psychological abuse feels like someone has placed a tire iron on the side of your brain, and just continues exerting pressure on it; sometimes painfully, sometimes, in a dull ache way, but virtually always aimed to have a sense of control of you.

Because of the depth of my family values, and for sure my family of origin's capacity to viciously co-opt my ex-wife and financially manipulate my children, they were able to create this insufferable vice-grip life emotional/

psychological hold on my brain for twenty years, more or less. Yesterday when I wrote this letter to other family members, on some level it truly was my breaking the yoke of Morey Myers' hold on me, or at least a significant step in that direction. Also, I was finding more of the divine within me.

I designated Morey Myers at the root of this, and equated his behavior with an illness, albeit on some level, I am still dealing with the behavior itself. Morey is either being substantially manipulated by others, or has a deep illness, or some combination thereof. This situation reveals how one person, can set up a social and/or financial system aimed to abuse, if not emotionally imprison another person. Again, I must underscore, this situation is so unique and like a perfect storm in terms of having courts, parents, an ex-wife and others ALL willing to go along with this extremely deviant behavior.

I suppose the miracle, or at least the miracle in the situation would be if Morey would ever take me up on my offer to assist him with his emotional well-being issues, and/or other family members start to understand what is really going on here. Here, one family member has been massively scapegoated, and then again I have taken it on as the extraordinary challenge of my life, to develop the skills and inner strength to overcome this situation.

To pose things again in The Science of Inner Strength sense; it is developing this science and this human understanding in the midst of adversity that is an exact expression of Sir Isaac Newton's third law: "That every action has an equal and opposite reaction." The more brutal and grotesque the treatment of me, the more it pushed and moved me towards a determined humanitarian outlook for our precious planet.

Perhaps in the ideal I would be able to leave Morey Myers's actions behind, and really unify and pose a way for a better family out of all of this. I have kept this naïve sense or deep trust and faith that it would all work out. I have been living on this extremely narrow rail in greater or lesser extents, for more than ten years easily now.

This is where I get into divine faith and divine purpose; the fact that I uphold a sense that I am going through this all for the benefit and development of my children, makes it possible for me to hold onto this extremely fine line of support and life, for well over a decade now; along with the abuse, which proceeded that by another decade or so. On some level I want to give myself great credit on the verge of the twenty year anniversary; on another it is really just one day at a time; where I work to make progress that day.

Another major element that I actuated today was the order of a major order of the Calm Revolution brochures. That is yet another major step forward over the last several days.

Things came together with JTC Printing for a major step towards this revolution. I mean, I know in my heart, what I am after is a more humane, emotionally whole society, with built-in recognitions that goodness is strength, and contempt for the bullying behavior of these days. This transition is what the Calm Revolution is about; it is about a societal shift that helps people understand kindness and goodness are strengths; and must be built into our business practices, and basic ways of life.

The message of goodness and empathy as strengths, is something that society clearly can grasp, and is within our reach in both an intelligence and human strength level; it is just that we must start working to inculcate those positive elements into our basic business practices, as well as our societal norms. I love to remain abundantly clear that this entire message of humanism arose out of the unfathomable emotional abuse that I received; once again the notion of a diamond being formed from coal under intense pressure.

CHAPTER 23

THE WAY FORWARD, HOW TO BECOME A CHAMPION THESE DAYS.

*"Well, I've been out walking; I don't
do that much talking these days."*
These Days-Jackson Browne

Well before jumping ahead, I am steering back to the notion of the cause of my familial volcano that erupted; and on some "odd" level I am circling back to the notion of a critical moment that arose between Nomi Stolzenberg and David Nathan Myers. It seems to me that on some level a sense of David's victimhood was created at that point of their coming together, which then provided the backdrop for David's ongoing rage and rampage through our familial setting.

The only reason this is truly noteworthy is that this particular dynamic is stilling manifesting itself twenty seven years later; well going on twenty eight years. On some level, what I am getting at is the effect that one person can have on a situation be it a familial, employment or even societal. It really does seem true that one person can influence or distort an entire "political"[27] situation to permeate so much hatred and vigor and other unpleasant type of stuff. The equal AND opposite reaction, if you will is that it pushed me to become a giant with respect to goodness and basic humanity, which I look both to share in the world, as well as to "impose"[32] my basic goodness on this family.

A crucial point in my new brochure, is an ending quote that I do not know everything but I know that calm focused action is stronger than loud bullying behavior. This notion of strength is precisely what I look to be invoking in my family; that no matter how volcanic and bombastic David's actions were, my equal and opposite actions of humanism and strength are stronger. People will be tempted to criticize me in that I had to fight extremely hard to develop a philosophy a way of humanism, The Science of Inner Strength. It is somewhat like the old adage a former colleague Ed Cyr imparted on me, while on the Cambridge City Council: "There are two things you never want to see being made, laws and sausage." In the same way, you do not necessarily want to see the making of a philosophy. In this case, given the opposition

---

[27] I recall the words of the then City Manager for the City of Cambridge Robert W. Healy, at the point I first became elected to the Cambridge City Council when he said to me: "Everything is political." Lol [32] I was told in recent years that Morey Myers wanted to "impose" fiscal discipline on me; even though his actions helped to drive me to near homelessness, due to my commitments to Sophie and Sam. Go figure.

that I faced; it was a truly brutal fight, in some ways, and while I developed calm methods, I could not back down.

People cannot confuse my basic kindness with weakness. Well the whole thing kind of reared its ugly head the last few days. David seemed to come out of the woodwork with an assault on my mental health and all. It is funny that I had a dream about a snake biting me, and the next morning David appeared with his psychological assault. Fortunately I have done enough work over the years to fend it off, although it was an unbelievable challenge. My belief is now relatively firmly that David is the psychopath, or at least one with psychopathic behaviors in the situation. It is "fascinating" how the psychopath can strike totally at what he perceives as your weakest point, and stridently go for blood. A psychopath, in an iceberg type of sense portends that he owns you and your life; that is the disdain that he or she will pay you. The psychopath feels like their assault on you is their entitlement or right.

An entire family is infected by this creature, and I wonder if I would have done better to just walk away, albeit I am glad I took the stand. These people have been in a threatening posture to me for thirty years; either they have something going for them or they don't, at some point. AND they don't!

After a day or two's reflection I am on some level delighted that I seemed to identify

David Nathan Myers as the overarching source of this conflict. It is rather unfathomable to come face to fact with a person with psychopathic capacities. Again as I am reminded by on-line discussions and the like; psychopaths for the most part are not the bloody serial killers that we first think of. Instead they are these exceptionally devious, and torturous people, often in positions of power with our governance and other places.

What I am getting at, is that an entire horrific familial dynamic for more than twenty seven years, was potentially inspired by one person, who was able to cajole and intimidate others, into this ferocious point of irrational antagonism towards me. I must confess, recebtky, March 17, 2016 I read a wonderful article from 2012 by Melanie Tonia Evans, which talked about not being afraid of the narcissist in her case; perhaps psychopath in this case. This article emphasized not spending one's energy attempting to defeat the narcissist, but more so in trusting and caring for ourselves.

With all due respect I do believe my path did walk an extremely fine line, with respect to not wanting to do any of this defeat David, but rather on many levels to survive, then thrive and further my own goals for my children myself and society as a whole. As I did put David off of communication with me for thirty days; I am "fascinated" to see if and how this effects the group as a whole. I wonder if even the small removal of this anaconda like energy will diminish the tension in the group as a while, and in essence begin to restore some rationality.

At least for me personally I surely feel less of a feeling of dramatic struggle in the thing. There was another facet of Ms. Evans' article that talked about once we have for all intents and purposes created the proper separation from the deep narcissist, we expose how vapid and essentially weak they are. The article intimates that the narcissist and personally I would include the psychopath, needs our energy to derive any strength whatsoever: In particular our fear, our stressing out, our trying to figure out the right strategy are the very thing that the person with the deviant personality type depends upon.

This is the analysis I have alluded to earlier. The psychopath is essentially a morally and spiritually empty human being; there is nothing there, virtually everything in their lives is a take off, a mimicking of something else. There is no spirit there; no breathing soul functioning. The psychopath strictly functions in desperate efforts to win. That is what is alarming on some level, in the current Trump campaign is the emphasis on being a winner or a, to use his word "loser."

Most people do not have the luxury to think in terms of winning and losing so profoundly as a way of life. I mean most people want to go to work, raise their children well, that kind of thing. How about every time we got to a traffic light, we thought in terms of winning and losing? Rather than having, some order of a civilized community, we would be running into one another left and right; defying the very essence of society, which on some level is to have a peaceful society with a purpose. At least those lofty goals are how the founders of our Constitution envisioned the United Stated of America, overcoming too, our horrific slavery. Thanks to Abe Lincoln and all those who fought for equality.

The reason my story is relevant, is because I am identifying one of, if not the great impediment to peace and civility within the United States of America. Yes, we have threats from outside, but I am continuing to advocate the true greatest threat to America is our less than uniformly honest function of our governmental entities themselves from our Judicial to our political to our economic system as well, along with perhaps worse the emergence of the narcissist/psychopathic personality. Let me be clear again, I believe in America; I do believe most people are honest and want the best.

The outrage that has been capitalized upon by the Trump campaign and other sources is pulling on that sense of dismay with the American system. Yet for me it is the Calm Revolution; it is the realm of doing things well and honestly. If the American system is weaker on the inside, because it is not being overly honest with the American people, then we will meet huge challenges.

This is why with respect to the political agenda, I believe it is necessary to create the capacity to talk to one another; more than staking out one particular position. We must create consensus at times, if not total agreement around the seventy or eighty percent who truly want what's best and right for us as a country as a whole.

My personal adventure continues today, March 29, 2016. It is funny as much as I seem to have drawn on line with David; well who is to say. I am wondering if Sondra is really behind it all, but who is to say at the moment. What is clear is that I was hit with emotional abuse of epic proportions. On some level, after you have been hit by a 100 foot Anaconda, and you survived it, I almost want to tame the snake.

That is really the unfathomable part about me. The entire situation has brought out on some level my love of humanity; my desire to love and be of support, especially on some moments to those who have been hurt, or who are acting in a hurt manner. My point is this; that people who do the most egregious acts in our world, are essentially hurt children, and what if for one, we developed that awareness, and for two, developed societal mechanisms as to how to deal with, if not heal such pains and traumas.

It is on some level my calling to create, or influence us, towards a more compassionate and humane society. I suppose at the core is the sense that kindness and determination are strengths; or better barometers of true strength. Strength is not what is often posed in our current state of world, with respect to bluster, dog eat dog, and loud voices. Consistent, unrelenting and purposeful action is what comprise strength. David's rage is a function of his lack of emotional development, which comes from Sondra and Morey as well. This is why, my emphasis on purpose is so important. Finding our identity, our purpose calms peoples' hearts and minds. This is where we must educate society.

That is at the heart of the Calm Revolution, teaching people that our inner strength is really about purpose, working together, determination, rather than stubbornness. One of the key words in all of this is the notion of "necessary." So many actions and types of conduct are mainly unnecessary these days, or even harmful. These are times, when we need focus and commitment to certain ideals and goals; I mean a lot of people don't really recognize or acknowledge that we have some massive challenges facing us.

Greed has blinded people, and I am all for capitalism and doing well; it just must be integrated with true purpose these days. There can and will be a shift in our collective consciousness sooner or later; it is just that I would love to see it be sooner. I mean the integration of a holistic type of attitude. For one, such an attitude will not limit business, rather it will accentuate those businesses that are able to define a public purpose as well as an economic bottom line.

These theories and philosophy are what came out of me when I was abused to the core by my family of origin, late ex-wife, and the courts. This true compassion and sense of love came out of me, along with purpose and determination for sure. That is one of the most miraculous ways to find your true core, one's true essence; although I am a huge believer that adversity in general, can and will be that kind of defining element for you.

CHAPTER 24

HOW EMOTIONAL ABUSE RELATES TO EVERYTHING ELSE.

First of all, I am inspired as usual to update this particularly interesting, if not precarious round of my story; in the emergence of the serpent's head of David Nathan Myers, in a figurative sense. I must confess it is an enormously startling experience to have a human being with iceberg like or even psychopathic like tendencies confront you in such a guttural sense. The psychopath is essentially going for your jugular, in any given situation, given the opportunity, based on their spiritual and emotional emptiness.

It leaves a few tremors after having been confronted by, and even appropriately addressing the psychopath. I mean I sent a letter outlining my views to familial members. A key is once again, the capacity to detach from the energy of the psychopath, and profoundly related to my goodness. This is an ongoing journey for human nature, and I would be remiss if I have implied that I have perfected it, as I have not. What I am simply implying is that I have reached a level where I am worthy to teach this stuff; not that I know every iota there is to know on the subject, or for that matter that I do not continue to learn and grow as I do, which is a blessing and a beauty.

Indeed the recent encounter prompts me to lurch towards another level of my goodness, and that is what it is really all about, goodness. If and when we as human beings use our goodness as our center point in our lives; our go to place, rather than our neurosis and our worries, we then gain a sense of trust and confidence that we have not really anticipated. That is really what it is all about; finding, affirming and establishing our goodness, and using that as the building block for society to make its moves forward.

Currently most rubrics of society have our pillars built on fear and intimidation. I need not necessarily go as far as love, but let us rebuild our pillars of society on trust and encouragement, if not love. In the same way American bridges, schools and infrastructure must be rebuilt; so must our psychological and emotional framework to begin from a more trusting, loving and caring framework. If the old model was that people were idiots and needed information pounded in to them, my old school desks nailed to the floor in Scranton, PA as a reminder; now let's begin with the premise that most people are smart and need to be encouraged and developed, rather than beaten down.

This shift in consciousness that I am proposing, is something that, for one, is coming anyway, so we might as well get out ahead of it, and two, is enjoyable, productive and well within our grasp. These premises infer that we cannot be our own worst enemies in all of this. We cannot allow human stubbornness to stand in the way of what is going to happen anyway. We are moving towards a more fluid open society and the essence is to capture this energy and ride with it, in a positive manner.

Of course, the fear based notions will try to grab us and pull us back to constructs of irrationally based fears. We must develop the sense that we will overcome all obstacles, and that bad things are going to teach and strengthen us, not bring us down. This attitude is the attitude of winners and champions as stated in the most recent Calm Interventions literature piece advertising the Calm Revolution.

Today March 31, 2016 marks that date that the Calm Revolution began; as the first mailers went out this morning. It was a rather momentous occasion for me getting the first batch of these mailing pieces out in 6 x 9" inch envelopes with the Calm Revolution posted on the outside. It is a wonderful moment for me, to let go and watch this take place. I wrote a kind of interesting personal note to go inside the envelopes.

The spirit of the note was along the lines, that this has all just happened to me, or rather in essence that I was called by a much greater force to work and act in this way. I had a funny line, in the note, along the lines of "Who am I to argue?". That is the way it all unfolds. I am reminded of this while making a stop at Dunkin Donuts, and talking to gentleman by the name of Chuck originally from Philly this morning. When I told Chuck just the beginning of my story, the very tip of the iceberg, in terms of how I came to the Boston area nearly thirty six years ago; Chuck already said that's "quite a story." I said to Chuck I am writing a book, perhaps you will see it; and that is the essence of my life.

I spent time pondering the details of the mailing; whether, the last minute note and that kind of thing was necessary, and all of a sudden in a spontaneous splash I just set off for the Post Office with the first mailers, and wouldn't you know it, I chose the butterfly stamp to put on the piece. On some level, the symbolism is right on time; both the sense of a butterfly being free, and also this article that I have relied upon; believing in the process of change, as the caterpillar goes through the course of its change into a butterfly. I am blessed, and I also put that into the note, as it is extremely rare that a person gets to live one's life in the enormously spiritual nature that I do, and then again, there is no better way to fly, but to be in your heart and soul.

Perhaps too, in that I made a last minute change in one of my quote's on the brochure, that my core was about helping others to learn how adversity and challenge, can be the great teachers and opportunities in our lives; it is similar to that process of helping a caterpillar become a butterfly. That is my role in life to help people turn challenge and adversity into better times and opportunity. There is a secret to it, and it resides in, or at least, is closely aligned to The Science of Inner Strength.

The hardest thing on my journey was that fact that virtually the entire thing was uncharted territory; so there were innumerable occasions when the question would arise about turning back and even questioning myself, and yet something kept me going forward is the best and worst of times. On some "odd" level, I trust it was ultimately a belief in fairness or goodness itself, but not giving up on the notion that my life for myself and my two sacred children, would be about fairness, and that ultimately my work in the world would be geared to inspire us along the same lines.

I was going to talk more about in this chapter about emotional abuse and how it affects us all so much; and yet today, I seek to discuss more the results of being liberated. On some level, the timing of David's pathological assault on me, and my pushing through for the initiation of the Calm Revolution seemed to be a relatively massive one-two punch at the end; with respect to my dismissing and bypassing David, and then figuring out the way to unfold the Calm Revolution.

My spirit seems much more liberated than in previous times or even days; at least in this moment. The final note that I wrote with the Calm Revolution brochure was key. First, from a design perspective it was wonderful, in that I was able to write nearly 100 copies of a handwritten note in blue ink on half-sheet letterhead, no small feat unto itself. Yet, it was the note, itself that moved me by putting myself in the place of a relatively unknown person in many cases; and beginning from that point of uncertainty.

I began with something along the lines, that you might be wondering about my journey; as if to clarify why I was indeed writing to them; and then it just naturally flowed that I was essentially writing as an expression of the divine. I am not certain how this will impact everyone, if at all, but it was similarly super in that I ended with a sense that it was not so important to me whether people accepted what I was saying or not. Liberating again;

perhaps previously I had conveyed a sense that I needed people to accept me, and this time, I kind of just let it go, and it felt great.

The crucial element again is the ability to overcome obstacles, and turn them into advantages. There was too much inspiration, let alone perspiration, and momentum inside of me to be turned back, and even for instance, I did see David's assault on me, as a frontal and desperate last chance type of assault for him to contain me, and keep me at a certain level. I feel in some wonderful way that David's efforts failed. Anyway, what can you do; being in the moment helps.

It might be time to express some appreciation to people whose writings and work have helped me along the way. I am thinking of Bill Ferguson for one, Esther Hicks, Louise Hay, Wayne Dyer, even Melanie Tonia Evans at moments. The key for people to understand is that it would be my considered view, that you must develop your own philosophy, your own mindset in the first place, which others can help you do, you keep moving with your mindset and then others can help.

Stuck is an interesting notion as once I made the commitment essentially that I would not ever quit; it was not ever really that I was "stuck;:" it was just that it was not happening at those moments, and in those moments I would fall back upon prayers and poems pertaining to trusting God's timing. One of the most wonderful things in the world, and such a high art form for the most part, is learning, if possible to let go, and sincerely living in the moment; just allowing the natural joy of life enter.

I find myself in such a letting go moment; having

released a fair number of Calm Revolution mailing pieces yesterday and today. It is kind of the notion that no matter what your circumstances, do you work, then let go, and be in the moment, essentially not worrying at all. For some "odd" reason I find myself with such a sense of feeling and lightness right now. Contemplate that, not worrying at all; truly being in the moment. I suppose that feeling comes about when we feel that we have worked hard in a certain area and have that sense of pride, however temporal.

I was going to talk about emotional abuse in this chapter, with respect how its fundamental dishonesty is affecting society on such a profound level; and yet there is more than one way to skin a cat, as they used to say. In this chapter, I have much more used my spirit itself as a positive vessel of illumination to demonstrate that emotional abuse and that kind of thing can be overcome, by shining the light on positive human behavior and modality; we overcome negativity that way.

A recurring underlying theme in a more general sense, is that I got hit with an asteroid like impact of emotional abuse over a more than twenty-year period; and as challenging as the abuse itself is, the notion of how it transformed me, as a human being. I feel like a guy in an old movie, from around the 1st century or something, who was hung in chains in some dungeon somewhere; That is the net effect of emotional/psychological abuse, aiming to keep a person psychologically imprisoned or chained to a circumstance.

The one thing the abusers cannot count upon, is what happens inside a woman or man. You can chain a person to a wall for twenty years, and yet within the man or the woman, an unfathomable change can be taking place, in an emotional, psychological and spiritual sense. Maturity and true learning can take place solely within the heart and the soul; in fact; are furthered and chiseled by the sense that the adversity itself is dripping beads of blood, sweat and tears of emotional growth and change, while the person is hanging there; certainly furthered as well by the sense that if and when one develops a purpose or a determination; it almost becomes a contest or an amazing education unto itself, to not be broken by those very circumstances.

I read an article today that was illuminating from a person who had experienced a physical disability, essentially saying that the disability was not a disability at all, but rather an opportunity for a different kind of learning to take place. There was sense in the article that the God provides each person an opportunity wherever they are to have that kind of learning. That learning is the ultimate in turning hard times into better times or adversity into opportunity.

So my particular prison was this unfathomable twenty plus year period of emotional and psychological abuse, ridiculed, ostracized, isolated, you name it. This was, and these are the circumstances God allowed for me to develop this unfathomable sense of learning, because I had a purpose. While I emotionally hung from the wall, in my figurative chains, I was learning; growing stronger virtually every minute that I was there. That growth and that learning is the function that the abuser never counts upon; they think that you are lassoed to the wall in a "permanent" sense.

That is the M.O. of the abuser; the abuser virtually never grows and indeed, stays stagnated. The path to ultimately overcome the abuser is through spiritual growth and development if physical circumstances do not afford the opportunity for immediate escape or the life that one has imagined. It is vital to understand the psychological need that the abuser has to keep a person trapped or imprisoned in some way. Think of Ariel Castro, the deviant personality from Cleveland; he literally set up a repulsive prison type environment for those girls.

An abuser, depending on the degree of their abusive mentality has an extremely malformed psychological profile; so they need to keep someone attached to them physically, emotionally, psychologically, because spiritually level they are not able to stand on their own two feet. Not only, do they need that dependent relationship, but they mix-in their amalgams of hatred, even parasitic, sadistic, and overly cruel behavior.

I am considering the grotesque compensation that my younger brother David has concocted in his life. On some "odd" level David probably leans on, and depends on me, dating back to his childhood. Yet David has never developed any positive realms of communication, even understanding, let alone expressing his emotions. Instead David, creates this insanely concocted world, rather than express his appropriate emotions, like:

"I love you;" or even "I am upset;" or whatever David creates this insanely concocted world, where he has perverse attachment to me, predicated on his delusional sense of superiority and concocting bizarre theories of my life and the world.

All along what is truly on display is David's bizarre leaning on me, and creating some false narrative to rest his shoulders on; rather than acknowledging his true human emotions. This false narrative I first noticed in David dating back to his being in fourth grade, when he came to me and said that he no longer was going to fool around in school, and that he was going to focus more on academics. I mean this was a wonderful choice in a narrow sense; and yet it was almost like a part of David died that day. David was fun and humorous until that time, and he adopted an overly strict attitude, perhaps it came from Sondra on some level; influencing him to give up our relationship at a young age.

Still, it seems as if David channeled so much of his personality into this intellectualized version of who he needed to be; essentially leaving things like emotional development far behind. It is not a particularly benevolent way to look at things, but no one, really wants to be oblivious and harmful and that kind of thing; it just happens, I suppose with an overemphasis on intellectual development and "achievement" at the expense of emotional and social development, people can lose their sense of empathy and humanity.

The last few days have seen perhaps a quantum leap in my perspective; early this morning seemed to have prompted such a leap. I am reminded of an expression: "the wounded deer leaps the highest." Sometimes, one really never knows how thin the line between success and non-success really is. This morning, I had a dream that seemed to spur to me to take another leap.

Specifically, I somehow put behind my parents'

treatment of me, even the brainwashing of my kids; and saw them as very fragile eighty something year old people, who clearly needed support in some way, be it around their home, emotionally, but support in some kind of way leapt off the page to me. This insight coincided with some sense of my getting the final eight brochures out via mailing for the Calm Revolution to the Massachusetts Supreme Judicial Court.

So perhaps the final leap out of this emotional prison is starting to occur. I must continue unfailingly to trust the process. It is really a fascinating integration of my new experience with my former one in Pennsylvania. I mean even the Calm Revolution on some level is a leap on some level; to put myself out there with respect to a revolution in the world is quite a thing, when it really comes down to it.

I continue to explore the parameters as far as my family. I am discovering as to whether my diminishing contact with David, will take the steam out of the hatred of my family as a whole. As far as my own involvement I have found this compassionate angle with my parents; I mean they are eighty eight and eighty one years old. I can see myself being supportive albeit on some level, I wonder if I would just do better to keep to the Calm Revolution; and leave them responsible for their own actions.

The Calm Revolution is my fight for the world to become a more decent and humane place. I suppose that is really it, in a nutshell. It is an unfathomable message in a way; and a fascinating way to seek to make a living, if not thrive financially. That is the point I suppose, to truly make it in this world, and demonstrate to the world that the path to success in this day and age *is* by being kind and focused, and relatively sober for that matter. Perhaps that is the long and short of my story; having suffered unfathomable abuse to have developed focused compassion, purpose and sense of direction for the world and me.

It is still an open book as to whether I will find the key to un tap the peace and natural empathy of my family; or whether I am wasting my time. Well either way, I am not wasting time, as it will be unfathomable research on a human scale. I have sought to intuitively challenge the No Contact movement that says the only way to deal with those with personality disorders. Instead, I have committed considerable personal resources to discovering whether I could penetrate, and in essence, break through the veneer that separates those personality types from a caring and empathic world, melting the iceberg.

I mean it was divine light that entered my life around March 26, 1996 that took me off of the path of narcissistic darkness, and my sense is, that if it happened for me, it can be done for virtually anyone. The work involved in this situation is immeasurable; as for one, I believe that my parents Morey and Sondra do have some natural empathy buried deep inside of them somewhere, although deeply buried.

Then again, there is only so much that I can do in one day. God grants me only so much room to play. and fun on a particular day, even if it disguises itself as work.

CHAPTER 25

THE KEYS TO FINDING YOUR INNER STRENGTH IN THIS WORLD

"In the midst of winter, I found there is, within me, an invincible summer." Albert Camus

Enough about me; it is time for me to share with you, how you can find your inner strength, and what are the keys for doing so. Well I must detour again. It feels like I am getting very close to a home coming. I cannot describe it. After dreams that seemed to push me to my edge of understanding; I relatively speaking emailed Morey and Sondra and said that I could not go on any longer; I needed to separate myself from their abuse. Then a flash of insight hit me; with the sense that perhaps they could achieve the breakthrough needed to come closer to their own sense of their divine purpose.

That is the key issue on some level. It is about; can I breakthrough the veil of narcissism and other severe hurts that they carry through? It happened in my instance; and I know that there is goodness within them somewhere. It would be an awesome accomplishment to be able to reach them at that level. Yet, nothing is guaranteed, and I feel like, it is mainly uncharted territory.

Basically, I feel like over the last month or so, perhaps week in particular I have pushed myself about as far as I can go, in terms of the Calm Revolution brochure, the accompanying mailing, and my outreach towards family. It would be nice to look towards the weekend as some time off; although this situation has consumed my very heart and soul. I do feel like a tad of a breakthrough has occurred, and it is rather "indescribable." Something may finally be turning the corner towards success. No worries, one way or another.

I must believe in my basic goodness; and continually develop my trusting nature, towards God and life itself. It is an amazing circumstance to develop one's faith in the midst of pain and adversity; as our common reaction would be to say, I will develop my faith after the adversity passes. God however, desires for us to develop our faith, during the adversity, and that is the key. All of these things speak to the higher level of life that we are supposed to discover, and the divine nature of adversity.

It really is a blessing; to be exposed to life on this deep a level. I cannot help but believe that this is on some level the way that life was meant to be lived; with this level of experience, if not pain at times. The key is clearly, having a purpose; and thereby inspiration to turn the pain, into learning and other fruitful interests. The pain that I have experienced, must have that meaning, and that sense of virtue.

When I read, or at least thought about my most recent Calm Revolution brochure; yesterday I was alleviated to feel that yes, it really did all make sense no matter how far I chose to put myself out on the limb to accomplish it. That is where I must pinch myself sometimes; as I sent out 102 mailers to people, who in the main, have not given me one word of encouragement. While I am not attempting to win over my critics; I am looking to implant ideas about our present and future that ultimately will appeal to people.

When you are so far out ahead of the curve; it can be unnerving to one like me, who while born into a reasonably talented family; it was also mainly a relatively cautious one. So being on the leading edge of thought and actuality does not always come easy to me. To convince oneself that one has indeed been given a divine purpose; is one thing; at the point it readies to go unto the world, it becomes tougher, although I am ready.

It makes the most sense to accept the principle of divine light, applies not just to me; it is a part of all of us. It is just my calling to have discovered it in my way; and to be called forth to share it with others. It does, indeed come back to that notion of divine light; that sense that there is a higher purpose, which has not yet been translated onto society as a whole. That is the test of leadership itself, in these times, to define purpose.

Unfortunately, our political process does not seem to be speaking to our sense of purpose.

That is what calls out the innate sense of frustration;

some would call anger at these times or even fear. People want to do well; people want to find their purpose, and from there people want to express their purpose, particularly in ways that will be economically and societally rewarded. This is why my ideas are on some level a revolution. We have not raised people so much to think in terms of their purpose. Our economic system is not set up to honor and accentuate peoples' sense of purpose and inner strength yet.

Merely to continue in the same way, and at the same rate, is for one, going to leave a lot of scorched earth, and perhaps even more so, is just plain being dishonest to the people of our world. People deserve honesty, and they can feel it when they are not receiving it. Indeed, almost as much as anything else; honesty is the issue for our world to deal with. If and when governments and systems are dishonest to people; people will rebel in spirit or at least turn off, in some profound ways. This year's election cycle in the US is a representation on some level of manipulation it seems. For one, Donald Trump does as I alluded, seem to have some of those iceberg-like qualities; essentially turning any attack or even questioning of him, into an assault on the other person. Yet, equally if not more disconcerting is the media's promotion of this phenomenon essentially as a link to ratings, and thereby its own profits.

I am not against peoples' pursuits of revenues and profits; I am saying that such pursuit must be tied into a basic morality, a sense of benefice for the world and the country. If the media has influence as it surely does, it must work harder to clarify that its intention is actually the promotion, survival and even thriving of the planet.

I am all for profits; they just must be linked into positive outcomes, which we basically know what they are, when we see them.

In other words, the Presidential election for instance, cannot just be an extension of a game show; or a display for entertainment purposes only, if so, it need have that warning attached to it. Coverage of the Presidential election among other things must clearly be tied to the benefit of the country. There must be parameters, that we are going to actually and truly discuss issues, such as the national debt, American education, the number of murder deaths in Chicago, and things like that.

I see little clear evidence, that virtually any of the theatrics so for, are really predominantly geared towards the improvement of the country. The Democrats might be slightly better; surely Hilary Clinton presents herself that way as a candidate, and yet there are lingering and substantial questions as to the motives, with all of the garbage pertaining to the Clinton Foundation, her emails, and other issues of credibility. Bernie Sanders at least has a philosophy that has linkages within and a view as to how to improve our world. Whether it is sustainable economically is entirely another question.

That is where, I at least dovetail with the world, in that I have a philosophy that I am fighting for, and at least for the moment I do not and have not had to compromise with political entities. It is a philosophy that I have worked on, for over twenty years at this point; if nothing else it is mine. I have to smile, if not laugh as there is a song, playing in the Dunkin Donuts I am in, that seems to be saying that: "it is mine." The universe coming through with some big time synchronicity; thanks a few billion, lol.

So if politics is the art of the possible, how to we get from the overriding corruption that we are facing these days, to a more humanistic, altruistically geared society itself? A big question for sure. I mean I know what I am doing with respect to The World's Best Mediator and The Calm Revolution is my personal expression. The first step on a broader societal basis, is something along the lines that kindness and decency are strengths. The fundamental message that we must begin to deliver is that recognition that kindness, decency, respect, appropriateness and all of those things, are indeed higher values and strengths, not weaknesses in society.

It is a matter of education in society. It is, a oh so subtle change from the top down, smash square pegs into round holes, "bottom line" mentality to an acceptance of the wonder of economic achievement, but only, when it is melded with kindness, as well as societal good.

So I must confess that I have been feeling the weight of emotional abuse at times recently. I reached a breakthrough I thought last night; when all hope seemed lost. I was able to identify two major feelings that I had towards my parents: One being love for my sense of upbringing as a child; and second is the virtual disgust that I have with their actions towards me as an adult. At times today, I have been feeling what it is like to be utterly hated and dismissed from you own family of origin, for no substantial reason.

As much as I know these folks are just nuts; there are

psychological burns and scars for sure. I must continually remind myself that God has brought me here for a reason.

That is the real question is it not? Is there really a reason to all this? In the most optimistic, faith-oriented sense, I have maintained a sense that yes, this is all happening for a reason. Today I came across a Biblical reflection ironically about David, who went through a period of questioning and lamenting towards God. Can it truly be so arithmetic that every lemon of pain surely; does become lemonade? I live ast if it is.

I am in a quandary today as to whether I need a new pair of walking shoes, to initiate the Calm Revolution. Funds are tight, and yet I am pulled by a sense that a new pair of shoes after many pairs that did not fill the fill, will be the right move. The larger question is whether I can help my parents Sondra and Morey find the light; or whether those efforts have been in vain? As I say, at a minimum it is research but what an amount of research. It is this mission towards goodness; can I reach and ignite their goodness, or help them find and believe in it? It does not seem utterly impossible at this particular moment; whereas a few years ago, even month ago, even hours ago, lol, it did.

The questions being do I commit fully to the Calm Revolution now or do I continue to try and entice Morey and Sondra or essentially de-program them from ALL of the hate of David and Margaret? Perhaps it really was that psychic connection between David and Margaret that ignited this situation in the way that it occurred. I mean it would be hard to find two more, with all due respect, psychologically manipulative and ultimately hurtful people

Iceberg

underneath the surface. It is easy to see how people with some goodness could get intimidated and confused by them.

So I do return to this recurring point of the unfathomable hatred that stirred up and spawned towards me. I mean it is just the most bizarre feeling to be ostracized, defamed and scapegoated so maliciously. Well, I will surely take solace in the notion that today is just one day; and on some level it was extremely productive, especially with this writing towards the end. These are amazing questions; along the lines of: Can narcissists be reached and detoxed; I am essentially sensing that David cannot be reached, and as to whether the whole group is beyond reaching is an open question at the moment?

I am feeling more optimistic today on the subject of reaching those who are "confused;"[28] at least in part. The challenging thing is, what I am describing is mainly uncharted water with respect to reaching people with extreme narcissistic tendencies. Many who advocate in the narcissism field encourage strictly No Contact; such as Melanie Tonia Evans and those affiliated with Psychopathic Free; I have been inspired by this situation to take it a step or two beyond those conventional wisdoms.

In part, that inspiration comes from the sense that when I have encountered people advocating those

---

[28] While I have used this word to describe Morey and Sondra; let also give significant credit to Esther Hicks of Abraham-Hicks note. Esther used that word in a video I watched this morning to describe people
who were not acting with their best interest, or in what I would call "divine light."

perspectives they are not uniformly empathic and kind. I do not know everything but I know that to truly be effective in the line of assisting and helping other peoples' lives one must be relatively kind in one's outreach. The element of kindness, or at least empathy is a noble truth of my work. This is another of the deep principles of breakthrough, that I have achieved with respect to the entire topic of self-improvement.

If a person does not really understand how the process of change occurs in a human; then no matter how prophetic their ideas are; to me, they can be fruitless. That is the great advantage I have relative to a lot of other approaches, I have walked the walk in a most amazing of fashion with a very empathic sense to myself. I understand how challenging and awe-inspiring the process of change is, and the pains that one encounters in the process of change.

The last thing in the world a person needs to make meaningful and lasting change, is to have the additional burden of an insensitive, not well attuned person seeking to help implement these changes. The true champion of helping others and encouraging others to make changes will have personal empathy and understanding towards other people and the process of change itself. Having this great deal of personal empathy and recognition of the process of change itself gives me the opportunity to consider going beyond what traditional approaches to narcissism and psychopathic behavior would suggest.

For instance, isolating David's energy does at least afford a tiny opportunity into the world of Morey and Sondra Myers, who ironically even though they are a generation older, seem more possible, if even remotely to make positive changes in their own lives, than David. Narcissism is virtually by definition a shutting down, and a person accepting a nihilistic mean view of the world, rather than an upbeat, understanding and optimistic direction. The task that I have applied myself, at least in a small way, is to attempt to reach points of previous kindness and understanding of Morey and Sondra Myers, particularly pertaining to their good work with me as parents in my growing years.

Part of Morey and Sondra Myers's "confusion" there is that word again lol; is to my mind caused by the essentially mobbing or bizarreness of circumstances that was brought upon them in the summer of 1988. The collective energy, of, for one David's, with all due respect harmful behavior, my then temporary separation from my ex-wife, Margaret, conspiracy around the estate of my Grandfather Morris B. Gelb, all collectively induced a much changed psychological backdrop, and an element of great confusion for Morey and Sondra Myers, who while probably good people, were unprepared for the psychological avalanche that started to be rained on them. Once Morey and Sondra Myers had their psychological view, shifted by Judy Levine, and Nomi Stolzenberg and Gelb money as well; then the entire mob shifted its attention to me in vicious, albeit irrational fashion.

The key facet I am pointing towards is that in the confusion that bombarded Morey and Sondra Myers; one of the critical legs of the chair that was knocked out was the sense that they were indeed excellent parents. This is the work of a person with psychopathic capacity; to essentially stun its intended victim like a cobra would stun its prey with spit, and then move in for the kill. Once Morey and Sondra Myers lost the sense, or with all due respect did not assertively stand for that position on their own right; then a psychological vacuum, if not chaos could occur within a previously stable situation.

At all points I would still say that it is great that this happened. I would never have been able to achieve such amazing personal growth but for this most extraordinary of circumstances. Part of my genius too, in my work as The World's Best Mediator is to pinpoint that point when Morey and Sondra Myers's perspective changed from benevolent to malevolent. This is a matter of prospectively teaching people who were acting in an extreme narcissistic fashion that their behavior was not merely not right, but was not even ultimately in their own interest, because the position they adopted was predicated on the notion that they were not good parents, which was fundamentally untrue. As their first son, who grew up in a six block area bounded by four long-living grandparents, a school and a temple I do not know everything, but I know that I am an excellent authority on their parenting.

So the question becomes can I eradicate through God's work of course, lol; the hatred that David and/or others has implanted in this family, and can I overrule it with love? I must be able to do it right? Love does conquer hatred; I am of two minds, on some level. So much of the world has also implanted in me the notion that being able to walk away is a strength as well. I did this evening, April 13, 2016 see an image of how Morey Myers was in essence, intimidated to the core by David Nathan Myers.

What I do know is on the occasion of my graduation from Oberlin College in late May, 1980 David Nathan

Myers showed up wanting to "fight Dad." What I can vividly recall is the look in David Nathan Myers's eyes that was eerie and chilling.

David's level of irrationality with all due respect had not been seen in our family before; and I can see how it would have penetrated and totally shaken Morey Myers. This is still a theory of course; I am not certain I would call it absolute science at this point, but if some part of my mission is to restore a sense of decency and understanding to Morey Myers and Sondra Myers; then they deserve better for their work as parents.

This is where trust also enters into the equation. There is a Biblical note from the New Testament that emphasizes not to lean too much onto our own understanding, but on God's. So, on some level it is not for me to figure it all out; this is where patience comes in. That is truly my godly notion; that of patience and perseverance, both pieces are needed on a profound level.

Emotional and psychological abuse are such cruel tools of usage; as in addition to the abuse that is inflicted; there is this extremely cruel element of denial and indifference to another person's plight. In any event, I seem to be coming to a sense at least as of today that perhaps David is not fully at root. I sense a deeper level of psychological disruption from Morey Myers; which could then be the source of David's actions and ultimately what is happening from the family as a whole. I mean some things point towards Sondra and yet Morey's sense of psychological disruption seems so blaring and so clear. Then yet again, these folks present themselves and position themselves as societal "icons" [29] so it becomes very hard to penetrate that veneer.

All of a sudden, I do feel the rise of some compassion for Morey Myers; as he clearly does not know what he is doing, or he would not be doing it. As much as people can be sadistic, if they were able to act in kind and benevolent ways they probably would do so, if they knew how. Earlier today, I am grateful to have watched a video by Melanie Tonia Evans, to whom I must give thanks; as the title was along the lines of: "When your friends and family cannot understand what you are going through with narcissistic abuse."

I must confess this stage of my journey has seemed to entail my circling back through my familial situation, to see if there are elements of it that are worth preserving and/or whether Morey and Sondra Myers have been victimized by David Nathan Myers? You see, what I am getting at is that perhaps my parents in some "odd" way have been innocent victims, and are worth preserving then by all means let's do it. That is the line of distinction I am seeking to make. Who really is a root in all of this; and can the family survive above and beyond, all of what has happened.

On some level, I must first be concerned with my own success; and it seems as if Monday or Tuesday, the next day or two at the latest, I will launch another round of my Calm Revolution brochures. Tomorrow is Marathon Monday in Boston, so I am not certain if I will do it then,

---

[29] Icons was a word used by Angie a wonderful worker in the PA courts, when I went to file something around 2009 or something.

or take one more day of rest with the holiday, which is rather wonderful, as well as working on the familial piece. Ahh, one day at a time; it will work out one way or another, lol. Actually getting back to the video by Melanie Tonia Evans; it did bring a note of validation to what I am saying.

The opening segment of this video, was essentially saying that unless and until you have experienced narcissistic abuse, you have no idea of the utter irrationality, the depth of pain and trauma; and in essence how foreign such type of abuse is to our everyday experience of commonality. As much as we know these kind of ideas, it is crucial validation; also it hones me to a deeper spiritual sense that this is all happening for a reason, and on some "odd" level accept the experience unto itself, in addition to creating a greater or opposite reaction.

This plausibly in an "odd" way brings me back to the theory that I have been recently advancing: Of David Nathan Myers essentially being of psychopathic energy; and his capacity to tilt, if not establish a reign of terror among the entire group. Even if, what I am postulating about David Nathan Myers is true; on some level I do see him as a human being, who is simply impaired somewhere along the line. Even in those worst of circumstances, I would still after resolving issues of safety and security to the rest of the group; see if there was a way to be beneficial to him perhaps; that is a big ask though.

First things first. The first things have virtually always been about getting Sophie, Sam and me to the right and best place. "However,"[30] I wonder if there is a spiritual reason that Morey and Sondra have attached themselves so much to Sophie and Sam; perhaps it is their way of ensuring that I do not run off from them. Ah…the universe surely moves in mysterious ways. Sometimes I just feel like the old expression: "What do I know; I just work here;" yes even The World's Best Mediator, perhaps especially, lol must bow to higher powers.

What this last two or three weeks on some level has been, is pure grit; at times I felt like I was emotionally almost lying flat-faced forward barely walking or crawling forward. This stuff to work through with my family; even the production of the Calm Revolution brochure all pulled me virtually to the end of my rope. I must regroup a little; and inhale the feeling a little deeper of just being The World's Best Mediator; being a little more assured in my journey.

Yes, this article by Melanie seemed to take some pressure off the situation; as I was able to send it to Morey and Sondra; and perhaps they might be able to gain some insight from it; just in terms of the phenomenon itself, and how it impacts others. How also isolated I have been. Nonetheless that cannot be my ultimate final notion; for me it is much more about putting one foot in front of another with respect to the Calm Revolution, well AND the benefit of the family too. At root as well, is that this rather unfathomable pain is working its way through me, like that process of a caterpillar turning into a butterfly.

---

[30] Last night I received a text message from Sam, describing his pain and sadness at the loss of his mother; and then adding "However…." how much he loved me; quite inspiring.

It is that notion of understanding and accepting what I perceive to be a divine purpose. The notion that the deeper the pain, as long as one is able to withstand it, the greater the transformation into forged positive qualities. That characteristic of sticking with one's goals, is an unfathomable one; trusting in, yearning for that sense of logic and fairness that one believes must be there at some point in this journey; or even perhaps accepting that transformation itself is so worthy. God has filled me both with the pain AND the capacity not just to survive it, but to learn from it, to grow stronger in the process. It is also that belief that the pain is not the endpoint; that I will get through it better and stronger with a bright light for society.

Recently I have slipped a little, maybe worked too hard, in that I have allowed everyday people to get on my nerves; and yet even that serves its purpose, perhaps best by bringing me back to my purpose. It is this path of internal growth, of accepting the hand one has been dealt, no matter how tough, and then learning how to play it. The best poker players don't just win with the good hands; I suppose anybody can do that; it is learning how to play and even win with the bad hands that makes for the greats.

Some people would undoubtedly believe that my familial situation has become so toxic that it cannot be preserved. I am testing if not challenging those notions. Morey and Sondra Myers are eighty-eight and eighty-one years old respectively. It would be rather late in life on some level for them to learn new tricks so to speak. Yet they have hung in there for one reason or another, and the life and well-being of my two sacred children seems quite intertwined with them; so this is the hand of cards that I must play.

I am not saying for David's sake one way or another that I want David to be that type of personality type; and yet it would be an unbelievable feat to rescue others from that personality type if it turns out that David is at its core. I mean, I am such a believer in justice and fairness that on some level I'd love to see that synchronicity, but then again, I also an acceptor of what the universe actually delivers. Although in the third way sense; I also have these virtually irrevocable commitments to certain underlying beliefs so that I believe I will find a way through, no matter what.

I am laughing out loud now, because my spirituality is that wonderful mix of determination, acceptance, a little humor; perhaps bit of a mutt as they would say, but a beautiful mutt at that. Speaking of acceptance I read a wonderful piece on acceptance by a spiritual leader and coach Connie Chapman yesterday.

Today marked a prospectively "fascinating" type of breakthrough. A MBTA bus driver jumped on my case erroneously over the weekend, for standing at a bus stop where there was no sign, but other drivers assured me, it was indeed a bus stop. The guy kind of went off on me, and worse he had a friend there standing near the front of the bus go off on me as well, telling me the bus stop was not a bus stop. I researched it a tad, and found out is in fact of bus stop.

So I filed an online complaint with the MBTA about the sign, this guy's attitude, not to mention the other passenger. I realized through the night; it was kind of one of those where: "Do I want to be right or happy?" These days I am erring often enough on the side of happy. Clearly sensing that I did not want to get into a big argument or fuss about the thing; that event seemed to help push me miraculously on the familial situation.

This nudge if you will from the universe, helped me articulate a position this morning to Morey and Sondra that was much more prospectively supportive; as well as even left some glimmer of possibility of being able to reach David. This all seemed to come about with the sense that I really do not want to be fighting with people, much if at all any more; at least not on more than one front.

I cannot even remember so much what my words were to Morey and Sondra; just encouraging them on some level to see the truth of the situation as I outlined it. I recognize that it is unfathomably hard work on some level that is going on: Confronting extreme narcissistic or even psychopathic behavior, and a nearly thirty year frenzy, Parental Alienation all at once, even the loss of Margaret for Sophie and Sam, has made facets of this stage to be a brutal emotionally, and on some level I give Morey and Sondra among others much credit; and especially on some level Sophie and Sam, who for goodness sakes were born into all of this.

CHAPTER 26

WHAT IS REALLY GOING HERE?

"I am not necessarily smarter than others, I merely stay with problems longer." Albert Einstein

On some level, I must be somewhat clear about what is going here; and on another level I work to continue to put this into context, as when one is assaulted in a psychopathic sense, I tis hard to understand.. In short, I am virtually in the midst myself of an iceberg. The iceberg is what I, with all due respect consider to be psychopathic abuse. It is still very hard to find words to describe what it feels like to be confronted with extreme narcissistic and/or psychopathic abuse. Essentially your entire emotional world has been turned upside down, and in addition to the unfathomable pain, you are virtually forced to defend yourself, for not being perfect, or at least trying to figure our your next move.

The psychopath will find virtually any imperfection about you to attack mercilessly. So when you get tired of defending yourself, the sole refuge that I can find is the development of a spiritual place; a deep and abiding true sense of self, one's personal life, work, and everything about him or her. That is the antidote to this unfathomable form of abuse; is like the notion of a caterpillar turning into a butterfly again; the development inward of all kinds of beautiful qualities that you did not know you have or had, in addition to fending off the hateful and hurtful behavior directed against you.

It is that sense of the divine again, or as I call it divine light. To the degree that I am in Newton, a la Sir Isaac Newton, I maintain that every action has an equal and opposite reaction; the equal and opposite reactions to extreme narcissism occur on a couple of levels. One is that virtually by definition, narcissism is the absence of divine light. Again, it is not that every person must or need adjoin themselves to organized religion, often the opposite. For me it is the notion of accepting something on a level higher than we are. By definition extreme narcissism and psychopathic behavior are the elimination of a divine source, and the sense that that individual, in their minds is the highest power.

Then, by virtual force the extreme narcissism and psychopathic behavior of some, pushes people, in equal and opposite form, into a spirituality, almost automatically; as most sane and rational humans are repelled by this hatred; they almost intuitively search for something deeper. When a person experiences pain on such a deep level, either they will accept the pain on some level, or virtually naturally develop a deeper sense of life and spirituality. Thus, through the unfathomable pain the narcissist or psychopath is doing us a great, albeit, abnormally painful favor.

Clearly offsetting the rampage of the extreme narcissist or psychopath is human nature itself; that spirit, the inner strength and resilience that does exist within us. That is again the beauty of what is going on, as horrific and scary as the age of narcissism is" when ideas about our basic goodness, take hold; then all this hatred is through our inner strength, pushing us towards our humanity.

My individual story is merely a revelation that are well underway in our culture. The degree to which mine is so pronounced is only an acceleration of what is already underway. The person or persons, who invented cell phones or computers or whatever were not necessarily the repository of all the information on that subject matter. Einstein is quoted along the lines: "I am not smarter than others, I just stay with problems longer." The fact that I have developed this insight and even a genius into narcissistic and psychopathic behavior is not because genius is about intelligence. Indeed it is much more to do with "staying with a problem longer;" and thereby collecting information and understanding that is out there. My situation provided a personal laboratory, and for the most part, I am extremely thankful to God and others for allowing me to sustain myself during this work, and keep dreams alive.

This morning April 21, 2016 I reached another deep insight with respect to the notion that the unfathomable rigidity in the situation is coming from David's wife Nomi. The logic would be that David at some point capitulated to Nomi, in a psychological sense developing a false sense of David's victimhood; I am talking when they were in their late teens and early twenties. David, in a psychological sense became subservient to Nomi; and they created this landslide predicated on David's relatively non-existent victimhood.

The level of velocity AND certainty that David and Nomi can collectively bring together is unfathomable and may well have provided for the asteroid-like impact that was rained on this family. This is astonishing if this is near to an understanding. The question then becomes should I deign to communicate this to David; and if so what is the effective route? I mean David's entire psychological state has been developed around this lie, going back to 1979 or so.

The good news is, that it is a combination of their energy may mean that in the strictest sense David is not fully psychopathic or something, but rather acting out of a desperation of his marriage. When I say desperation, I for one, could mean a fear of losing a marriage, which many men have, and thereby it makes them very susceptible in divorce situations. David also seemed like he kowtowed to the psychological faux expertise of Judy Levine, his mother in law, with respect to his psychological understandings (sic).

So essentially David did not stand for the fact that he came from a good family in its roots; and instead accepted lesser notions that his family was so flawed, which, while having much room for growth, it was not; and that his married family had some psychological hegemony, which it did not. Like a cobra these two, meaning David and Nomi struck with false psychological certainty; first at Morey and Sondra Myers claiming that they were "bad parents;" when in fact they were not. I do assess the intentions of Morey and Sondra Myers as basically excellent in our growing years.

Well a sense of revelation seemed to open today. I have been working a great deal, as you can see with the concept of forgiveness; what it is, does it really clear away room for other things to occur? The issue at hand; being I sent a Passover forgiveness email to Morey and Sondra Myers presumably to be shared with other family members, if such a gathering is taking place. I had just read a Christian sermon about forgiveness and loving our enemies, and even wishing them well; so I did that, in relatively eloquent form. I wonder if I am wasting my breath; I do believe virtually every human being is reachable on some level; at least in a non-iceberg world.

Which does bring me back to the notion of what is forgiveness anyway? Forgiveness on some level is letting justice unto God. It is a relatively risky proposition in this day and age, when people seem fixated on the notion of standing for themselves and not getting pushed around and all of that. I go back and forth on these things. It is in part why I write this book; to explore some of these questions. I mean, I love the idea of forgiving people and yet not needing to be a part of them.

Giving myself license to walk away, to repudiate certain kinds of behavior are part of my DNA at this point. A major theme of this book, is the entire idea of Iceberg and deviant or challenged personality types. Yet, another notion however, is that at the point one grows so much as a person; developing emotional maturity, one can become much more "immune"[31] to the behaviors of others, such as my family. On some level the capacity to rise to another level exhibits emotional growth on my part, to not only wish them well, but also to make the statement that their capacity to hurt me is diminished, as well as specifically if one of their modes of getting together, is to exclude me AND hurt me; I have defeated them yet again.

So maybe that is a wonderful word equated with forgiveness; that of "immunity;" it provides a certain cover and buffer to keep one above the fray, and in a magic bubble of protection from bad forces . I am thinking in terms of a great article by a woman by the name Donna Labermeier I read, who talked about four impediments to our dreams manifesting. The second one had to do with pulling out our weeds, as in forgiving old grudges and the like. So I have been focused upon forgiveness; as it helps me not to think about the element of emotional abuse, when I think about specific people and their roles.

Other facets of Ms. Labermeier's article entail other things I love, such as trusting the universe; as well as getting out of our own way. That last point has to do with not trying so hard, to force and cajole things, but allowing wonderful things to come to us. This notion is something that is contrary to much of our training and perhaps actual history; coming for instance from old coal mining Northeastern Pennsylvania, where backbreaking work was

---

[31] I laugh at the word immune; as on one occasion an email that I sent to Richard S. Bishop and family members alarmed David; and Rick's response in an email not meant for my eyes was that he had gotten "immune" to the things I said; I had to laugh as that was six or more years ago, perhaps.

seemingly a necessity for many, around the turn of the twentieth century, and from the late nineteenth century. I do like hard work as well; and for that matter the ideal of reaping what you sow.

Still there is a natural ebb and flow to the universe, and no matter how "successful" we appear; we really cannot overrun the world order. Take Donald Trump again. I mean this person seems to believe and he has said so that "dog eat dog" is the way to roll. I do ultimately, pose my Science of Inner Strength and the Calm Revolution for that matter as alternatives to the dog eat dog approach. My approach is predicated on human ideals and human improvement to sustain the species; putting aside the notion that "winning" is the only thing that matters. Winning matters, as does how we treat each other.

I wonder about the net effect of this year's election cycle, and whether Hilary Clinton for instance will be able to truly move forward, if for that matter, she is the Democratic nominee on an agenda that emphasizes love and not hate. Secretary Clinton has mouthed those words a few times, and yet it remains to be seen if she will truly make this a centerpiece of her campaign, which would take real chutzpah. I believe, unlike a lot of politicians probably that it is essential, as an act of courage to have an issue that is so meaningful that you are willing to lose the election it is so innovative and progressive. I am not certain Mrs. Clinton is there, but it would be enormously gratifying if she was able to move the American discussion to that level.

So forgiveness seems to be working so far, lol; as it seems to have inspired me to talk about other things for the moment. The Calm Revolution for instance, what is it really all about? Well on some level, it does pertain to The Science of Inner Strength in the regard that we must understand what true human strength is. On some level, that is one of the main, if not the main message of my story, and the divine purpose if you will, is identifying what is true human strength and helping people get there.

There it is in a nutshell. Defining true human strength and helping people get there. You see how and where we are operating now, is not our best human strength. When I say best; there may be levels way beyond what I am referencing, but I will settle for mine in 2016. Society, currently functions from a reactive and defensive type of interaction in somewhat kneejerk fashion where we are not using our highest modes of intelligence.

Saturday April 23, 2016; there seems like an interesting twist; waking up with a sense that Sondra is at root. An inside secret is that my nighttime dreams inform my direction for the day, at least on this project greatly. Without going into detail; my dreams are rich and seem to throw challenges, if not monkey wrenches into my thought process causing me to think in ways that I could not logically come up with on my own. This inner work provides an enormous boost to my capacity to work on this case.

So when I say this case; what am I talking about? I mean seeing if somehow I can get to the root, to the shut off valve if you will of this obscene hateful dynamic directed against me. This dynamic is clearly an amalgam of different peoples' energy; of taking a collection of their own worst feelings and energies AND directing them at me, in some familial scapegoating capacity.

The hard line perspective of Nomi Maya Stolzenberg seems quite strong in this situation. I mean bi-polar and that kind of energy could take the form of this extreme rigidity and narrow-mindedness, insisting upon one realm of answer to the exclusion of much broader, more expansive perspectives. For instance, it seems quite plausible that Nomi Stolzenberg, her Harvard Law Review editor role aside, has a locked in hateful, ostracized perspective from her younger years that informs her familial, political and -social perspectives; this is my hard-earned assessment after "decades."

Nomi may well have formed a perspective in this situation, geared towards ostracizing me, in her late teens even and has not the temerity nor intelligence of thought to adapt, reevaluate and God forbid admit she was not right about something. What I am dealing with here; is an interjection of an extremity of perspective into my familial situation that was not there when we were growing up. Sondra and Morey Myers had a normal amount of craziness as most parents do; present company mildly included, lol; but Morey and Sondra Myers did not oversee a home of unfathomable violence or hatred; it was strict very, but still relatively normal and quite supportive on some levels.

My own rebellion against the strictness was football, and all the partying that that entailed at Scranton Central High, and then rugby and all the "fun" at Oberlin College, but however festive these were relatively normal outlets for the seventies. David may not ever have found out those structured outlets from the strictness of Morey and Sondra, and essentially panicked in the early eighties that something was really not right. I am not saying that he has no point at all; I am saying that perhaps the lack of outlets, along with his overstatement of the problem, and connecting with Ms. Stolzenberg may have enormously exaggerated David' sense of the problem.

What is alive in me, is that I do not want this inordinately false perspective to overrun me or my sense of family. I mean my children are involved, I am involved; my entire sense of family; if Nomi Stolzenberg was at root and/or that kind of thing, I would be relatively idiotic to let this all go down without doing everything to reverse it, in my power. Ah, anyway, it is life; that is one of my growing expressions; it is life, just go with it, ride it. That perspective is such a change unto itself from what I was given in Scranton; when everything seemed so orderly and just the way things were supposed to happen.

Now the expression, "it is life" is more like surfing, riding the wave. Life itself has its own energy, along with our goals and visions; just ride the wave as well. Do not get flustered, good or bad. David is a parrot or a puppet under this scenario; it is Nomi that has gotten inside his skin or brain; and in essence terrorizes him to these bizarre thoughts, with respect to what is going on. Wow, I wonder if this is approaching my bottom line analysis of what is going on in this situation; perhaps a miracle unto itself.

Well, well, well today, Monday April 25, 2016, the figurative head reared its ugly head for real; and it was promptly and appropriately handled. It was David himself who popped up, after I included him on an email group with Morey and Sondra; to opine his vulgarity one more time; in his typically hyena like fashion. After I had talked about forgiving him, and attempting to vainly point out his kindness perhaps as a child; he reared his head. My response was swift and immediate with the essence that he was now officially on my No Contact list Ever Again. It was a rather severe action, and yet it seemed so spontaneous and fitting. I must say I feel on some level elevated today; not worrying, or feeling so under the gun.

It really may be that that psychopathic behavior was at the root of this all along; and forms the iceberg for me, and many other members of our family. It is strange when in an emotional sense there really is a large python like figure in a family; who is not only deceptive, but who has no real interest in the well-being of others. I am proud of myself for having the wherewithal to be able to respond in that moment. I am reminded of a story in a book written by I believe it is Neal Clark Warren, the founder of Eharmony. Dr. Warren described an airplane pilot who had maneuvered a plane out of the path of another oncoming plane, and essentially said that he had trained his whole life for such a event, and was able to respond within a second or two.

That feeling of intuitively responding with a matter of minutes, making the determination that I would not have contact with David again under this dynamic, was something that I have trained in this situation for over twenty years, on my spiritual path. A person with psychopathic behavior perverts and causes chaos in an entire situation. I did not know everything, but I know that there was no middle ground in this situation with such a person. I mean, for God's sakes, he is fifty-five years old. What was I going to give him another fifty years?

In addition, there are others to think about, first and foremost my two sacred children Sophia Rose Myers and Samuel Morris Myers to risk having their lives contaminated by such filth of a perspective; as well as Morey and Sondra Myers, who lives prospectively are being intimidated and overrun by this person. If they are really with him, so be it, but it is hard to imagine that they can support such vile behavior so completely. We shall see.

So on some "odd" level that seems like a monumental accomplishment of the moment. It is something that had to happen, or in God's world was destined to happen. I just follow God's plan for the most part. This had been brewing; this particular juncture for a while it seems. I can only speak to how I feel; just a much more focused, decent kind of feeling.

Because it seems quite possible that I was dealing with a full-blown psychopath, it becomes crucial to continually set the context of what is going on, as most people are still not at all accustomed to the damage and the deviance that a person with a severe personality disorder can create Such personality types defy our sense of reason, commonality and common sense. People will look at things and say: "Oh that is nothing;" or "You must have done something to provoke it." Unless and until you deal with a person with extreme narcissism or psychopathic behavior; situations like this will challenge one's understanding to the core.

People are not yet accustomed to a sense of a fellow human being, who is in essence a "vile" emotional predator; a person whose interest is to tear good people apart for no reason other than the blood sport of it. Today was, April 26, 2016, was relatively revelatory as well, in an almost shocking kind of way. Let's just say that I had some really intense dreams as the day was breaking this morning that through some dream work I was able to turn into a relatively astonishing breakthrough on this situation. Without going into detail, I had a kind of scary ending of a dream, and then I studied stuff about dreams for a while and came across again the notion of re-scripting dreams, giving them different endings with us being heroes and essentially conquering the enemy. Well this was amazing because one tidbit of the dream had a man, hiding in a crouched position under some rocks, as if to attack someone.

As I worked on the concept of re-scripting; I recalled a family picture from more than fifty years ago, when David as a little boy was kind of cowering off to the side, in a crouch reminiscent of the man in the dream. I re-scripted the dream to the point where the man, was really a little boy, and David was that boy cowering off to the side. In essence I came to the sense that David really was at root a coward, or at least acting on coward-like energies these days, and there came a moment where I could appropriately confront David on being that coward-like person, with his cheap shot like tactics.

This interpretation magically, may get at the root of this entire saga, as David has been using these abundantly clear cheap shot tactics; not to just to outrageously get at me and my children, but essentially to tilt the entire balance of the family against me and fors him. I also felt like a fair portion of David's energy was fueled by the Stolzenberg-Levine wing, and yet he arose with such a snide comment again today, that it is hard not to attribute a great deal of this situation to David himself.

If people wonder, how can a single comment be so revealing, I would say; if a person has been enormously abused for twenty some years; a single comment or two can tell a great deal about a person's attitude of indifference to you and/or your plight. The things David says are so vile, so base, so course; it is truly as if he is on another planet. One of the messages of today, it seems is that no matter how long the night is, daybreak is coming. It depends on context; if a person was hanging off a cliff and another said: "Oh it's a nice day, let's look at the view;" it could be horrific.

Well it seems like a certain daybreak came this morning April 28, 2016. Something just hit me, during the night; God I suppose, lol; and I somehow came to the sense that I must love my enemy. If and when I had a chance at one final word with David, it came in the sense that I would love him. There seemed nothing else left. The argument with him had devolved to an entirely nonsensical point AND even though, it was, in the main about my life, and my children; I could not argue any more.

For one, I have also been working on a fair amount the last few days of letting God handle it. Ironically yes, for me this stuff came from Christian ideology in some "odd" way, given my deep Jewish roots, but I could think of virtually nothing else this morning, given on some level the absurdity of the situation. I came across a reasonable sermon as to what it meant to love your enemy, with the bottom line being, to be there for them if they ever needed you to be there; and that is something that I thought I could do for David, his wife and his mother-in-law.

Coming to such a point was truly a way of letting go for me; as also yesterday in a bottom line sense I decided that I believe enough in myself as a person, and in my work that I was willing and able to walk away from these folks. David's email and my processing of it, kind of jarred me back in a way. It ended up that the piece about loving these folks was an add-on, in addition to the barebones version of it, essentially saying that if I could ever be of service to them, I would.

Having reached such a point, it seems there is little else for me to say, and indicate but to be willing and able to walk on with the Calm Revolution. The question is, am I really done with the family stuff at this point? I trust I have left it in God's hands. It is the most "odd" thing in the world to have people obsessed with my life, in the way that they have been. In that way, I do ascribe a lot of it, to not just David, but to his wife Nomi Maya Stolzenberg. Some people irrespective of their accomplishments or standing, have personality characteristics that are not about any joy unto themselves, but about scrutinizing and critiquing others.

In this case, these folks have had a fanatical obsession with my life. I have had every word, every action painfully scrutinized, while they are the ones working effectively to deny me basic human integrities, such as life, liberty and the pursuit of happiness; denial of access to my very own children; and so on and so forth. Still for the moment, I am allowing God to handle it. I can write about it however.

This Nomi Stolzenberg seems to me, like she brings energy from another planet. The thing about extending love to these folks, is that if nothing else will, it will probably be the thing that chases them away, lol. Unlike other people, deep narcissists and those with psychopathic behavior are repelled by love. Perhaps that is one of the secrets of overcoming narcissists and psychopaths is developing the inner strength, to ultimately be able to love them; even if they act in pathetic and underdeveloped ways.

The thing that love does, is lessen virtually all resistance to them, and almost intuitively dissipating the significance of their all important (sic) opinion. That is another thing about narcissists; they live in a world where virtually the only thing that matters to them is their own opinion. That is the ultimate goal when dealing with a person with deep narcissistic and psychopathic tendencies; to somehow develop the emotional resilience and strength, to profoundly reduce their emotional impact on your life.

What if, I do not ever need that families' financial support again; in some way that would be the ultimate victory; even with all the "loss" they inflicted. In any event, what I wanted to focus on today, was a couple of things, one of which is just the person that I have become. It has become a most extraordinary journey; and as something I read reminds me, no one can take way the person that I have become. Supplementing that point is an accompanying feeling of worthiness. Feeling that you are worthy as a person is one of the profound keys of life.

In some ways that is what my journey is about; finally feeling that true sense of worthiness. Many families perhaps; my family, inherently feel a sense of lack of worthiness. In some "odd" way that is what this journey is really all about. Even if they had a billion dollars or more, and a castle on the hill, my sense is that members of my family would still feel unworthy. Nothing we attain outside really addresses the feelings inside, unless on some level we have achieved those things in fair and honorable ways; which is why I should celebrate today, having received a payment on the minimalist, albeit wonderful legal settlement that I received. To me; it is worth billions.

I have done a ton of internal work to feel worthy, and today I find myself feeling that way more and more. It is the training of our families and culture historically that have ingrained this sense of fear and unworthiness into us. Still, it is my journey towards worthiness, and earning good and pure dollars that matters. Once we come from our sense of worthiness; then we have the upper hand in virtually every situation; as no amount of fear mongering or manipulating is acceptable to us, or can sway us.

A couple of key readings helped me on the road to worthiness today. One was one by a Coach Doug, found on the internet under the search topic: "Let go and trust." Letting go and trusting is one of my favorite notions; as Coach Doug, written in 2009 talks about relaxing into our spiritual nature, and following more of our divine path, rather than cajoling and moaning to make things happen. The other article I was reading again, also was about one of my favorite expressions these days, of "Letting God handle it." Whenever I find myself sweating or moaning about any of this; I trust, and then immediately say God will handle it. I apply this concept to virtually anything that I fear.

See, this is the true war that is broaching on our collective horizons. It is not

Democrat/Republican; not solely America versus terrorists; the even greater battle is for humanity, with light replacing narcissism and psychopathic behavior. That is where my concept of divine light comes in; and working to reverse, or at least influence centuries and centuries, of human turmoil.

What I am getting at is that there is a continuum in life say of 1 to 100; of psychopathic to light or enlightened I suppose. Everybody falls somewhere on the continuum, with one being most psychopathic and 100 being most enlightened. So I see the world as a realm to not always confront things so much head on, but to shift the human consciousness more and more to the higher end of the spectrum. It is hard for people in economic systems to consider shifting, and yet change is coming for sure, technology is ensuring that. We are coming to a day, when creativity and positive ideas will more and more appeal to the masses, by competing successfully with the top down, fear based ways.

The thing is, that people who are in a narcissistic way, cannot really create or move themselves to a higher level. What they are very good at, is controlling systems or environments that they are a part of; perhaps having bludgeoned or played dog eat dog their way to the top.

Light and truth does win out in the end; the only question is how soon, and in what way and all of that.

So my way, will win out; or it is really more God's way or light itself, there is a progression, it just takes much struggle, overcoming hatred and retrenchment from those inappropriately in control; who eventually realize they were not really in control anyway. There is a sign on a church nearby that says something like: "Love can overcome hate, it is just not easy."

More onto the positive; I am feeling that is about this notion of trusting; trusting, trusting and more trusting. Yes, there are things not to trust in this world; yet what happens when our nature became more and more trusting. That is a major component of my recent journey, and perhaps the crowning piece of The World's Best Mediator. What if our life and our work about trusting that things would work out? This is where the rubber meets the road, in the collision between my family and me; they have such a fear based perspective, even though in a material sense, they have more than me at the moment.

That is why in a divine sense, I went through this experience, to essentially strip down so much of my previous frame of reference; and to replace it with this determined, visionary and even trusting perspective for myself, my children and the world. Today, May 1, 2016, yay, actually it is the merry month of May, Sam's and my birth month. This morning I heard and watched a wonderful sermon by Joel Osteen; as I often do on Sunday mornings. The sermon seemed to affirm many of things that I have been working on recently.

Well first actually this morning I woke up with a

whirlwind idea, the development of an idea that I have been considering for a little while; the notion of having an artist sketch of a person's inner strength, as the seventh hour of the Magic Assessment. I have a pal who it seems can do these sketches, which I need to affirm; and I took a little leap in sending an email to Sophie and Sam; and Morey and Sondra cc:d this morning, the first time I have ever mailed that collective of people. On some level it was an extremely intuitive thing, and seemed to have the net effect that no matter what opposition was thrown at me, I would overcome it.

I must say I feel more relaxed, confident and at peace after such an email; that in some "odd" way seemed to culminate a massive period of work. It was the best repudiation to David and his history of hatred that I could muster. Joel's sermon was very much affirming. Joel's sermon was about preserving our secret space; that place inside of us, where nothing can really affect or deter us; from major opposition to insults hurled at us AND ALL the rest. Joel's words mattered to me this morning, especially as I had sent that email prior to the sermon itself.

Yet, I believe we are getting to a very key point here; which once again really has to do with the entire notion of inner strength itself. The key element is that once, one adopts a sense of inner strength, a goal, a vision even; it is not necessarily that important that we reach it perhaps, as it is that this particular vision, goal or inner strength provides the wherewithal for us to essentially go through any amount of abuse or nonsense that we must go through.

There are crucial elements of inner strength. One is, that it is authentic to us; it is close to or at the core of our very being. That inner strength must be true to us; a piano player is not going to play professional football for instance; and preferably having had emerged from one defining moment, such as adversity; or the Magic 6 hour x $600/hour Assessment or something that truly defines who we are as a person. Second, that element of inner strength must also contain a goal that we can commit to; so that once we understand who we are, we are ready to put our inner strength, our effort, our vision into action. I am a believer that life has a purpose; and through adversity and/or our inner strength we begin to understand that purpose and apply ourselves towards the appropriate meeting of our goals.

Our inner strength, then, is not just something that we develop for ourselves on an inner level, but it becomes a shield if you will on an outer level to impel us forward and protect us from ALL of the grief and nonsense of the world. Having an accurate sense of self, and a positive sense of where we want to go, comprises, in part a winners' and/or champions' attitude on this earth, because if we cannot muster ourselves to the degree of saying that we deserve to be here, and we deserve not to be pushed around, then there is little point in working with that person for me.

My inner strength in this situation was, and is, an amalgam of a few different things. One surely, is the health and emotional well-being of my two sacred children Sophia Rose Myers and Samuel Morris Myers. The commitment to those two people has provided a spiritual anchor to me, to endure massive abuse and twenty years of crazy psychological, social, financial and legal assault against me. That is the crucial element and what is "missing"[32] to a lot of people who have not stepped up to find their inner strength and true courage, is the notion that they are more than the criticism and hatred and opposition that comes their way. There is something called purpose and determination.

A person with no inner strength, essentially is bowled over, cowered, almost permanently skeptical about another person reaching their dreams and goals, while a person with their inner strength developed has something to impel them forward. It must again be emphasized that one's definition of inner strength must be an appropriate goal, and basically lawful, surely as well in a moral sense. If one adopts a goal and it is not appropriate then that is, a losing proposition. You have to, on some level, be rationally based; fully believe that you are right in what you are pursuing.

Without being right; a person is just hot air, or an antagonist or a bother to society; and it is truly walking this fine line that is all the difference between success and failure. I learned that particular sentiment from a little book of Jewish wisdom, which specifically wrote that the line between success and failure is very thin. So the goal, the inner strength must be an appropriate one, a just one, and one to which we fully commit.

---

[32] Upon a trip on Scranton around February, 2016, when my own biological father Morey Myers "granted" me fifteen minutes of time, wrapped around a twelve hour journey; Morey Myers said I was "missing" something; to which I replied he was ultimately missing love,

In my case, it is abundantly clear to me that I was a person, if not the person, who truly cared about Sophie and Sam. If their mother was essentially using them against me, and she was attempting to alienate them, that excluded her, and if the courts were not functioning in an appropriate and just manner; and my family of origin was abusive and was totally misusing a seat at the table; then I had wonderful moral latitude to press on this issue and against the entire abusive dynamic as, along as, I could appropriately do so.

While I suffered "loss" after "loss" if you will; the fact that I was morally right AND willing to stand for that gave me wonderful leverage to do my work, as I pleased. In addition to my children themselves, the development of my company, and the entire notion of honesty and authenticity in our world became major commitments for me. When I say honest, I must be clear in saying none of us are perfect for perpetual faultfinders, there is always something about someone that can be attacked or ridiculed; I am talking about a basic comprehensible human honesty, and good societal intentions.

I am talking about establishing fair and comprehensible standards for us going forward, not in an overly politically correct way, but in a way that acknowledges, even embraces our humanity. Given my profound respect for adversity, no person, worth his or her salt has not confronted some kind of challenge, and benefitted enormously from it. I am putting on the world's table the notion of a basic decency or a true commitment to positive qualities, as essentially a barometer of our assessment of human beings; along with the sense for sure that there

Iceberg

were no truly disqualifying events, like major crimes or sexual abuse, or violence, in one's past. While I believe that all people deserve chances; truly harmful events must be understood and disqualify people from certain types of interactions and societal participations.

For the rest of us, which to me, is the vast majority of Americans and humanity; we must be given the freedom and latitude to be who we are, in an appropriate sense. This is another point where the shift towards inner strength must come. We must be allowed to become who we are meant to me; and indeed encouraged to be so. Clearly society is going through a time of substantial dissent and dissatisfaction regarding our political, judicial and economic institutions, with more and more people stating that things are "rigged."[33] There are fundamental challenges, which again for me, relate back to the basic honesty or not, of society as a whole, and what I would put as the basic desire on the part of most Americans for things to be honest and fair.

This is where the iceberg notion comes in again, because it may not be that the greatest impediment to societal greed, is just human greed, ; instead the greatest impediment, may well be the emergence of the psychopathic personality type, and its vastly undue influence on American society as a whole. When I say psychopathic, I am indeed talking about points on the narcissistic spectrum; so without unilaterally declaring a person to be

---

[33] Political people as disparate as Donald Trump are pointing out "rigged" elements of society; others such as Black Lives Matter point towards our criminal justice system, and those in the know, know the horror within our divorce and family court system.

psychopathic or not; again the tactics of Donald Trump at least early on in the 2016 election cycle had elements of narcissistic tendencies, such as turning every criticism into a verbal assault on others; and using at times abusive language to appeal to a certain base. Mr. Trump seems to have toned down at least part of his rhetoric so we shall see how that plays out, and as I say, he is tapping into a legitimate sense of frustration, if not dishonesty in the system.

May 3, 2016, back to notions of David Nathan Myers, on some odd level. The problem is not as much in the individual, as it is in the sense of what society values. If society puts achievement over humanity on every level, then we are going to reward dog eat dog; an almost rat-like existence. Yesterday I saw a wonderful quote from Einstein about how "compassion was the true genius of humankind" or words to that effect.

David took one angle of our existence and pushed it to the hilt. In other words, my two grandfathers came from Poland and Hungary one before and one after the early 1900's and essentially for all I knew had virtually nothing; one for sure. In Scranton, PA, one grandfather rose to be a doctor and the other a successful lawyer/businessman. They lived in a world, where the pressure to rise and be a success, was great, and could have felt like life and death. Morey Myers pushed hard to be successful as an attorney; initially being associated with Martin Luther King and the civil rights movement, so my notion of the law was a positive one.

David took that notion of doing well, and seemed to have made a beeline through his academic career, through Ivy League schools, to a tenured professorial position at

UCLA. Generically speaking all of that "success" is wonderful; and yet if and when it replaces our humanity; it can not only become neutral, but hurtful or even abusive if one's behavior is unchecked. All I could convey to him this morning, is that he would not bring me down, no matter what, no matter how much he tried; so he might as well give it up. This message was wonderful in a way; in that I seek no fight with him, I have too much work to do; and yet I am also drawing a parameter to say that spend your time harassing someone else, or even better growing up, the latter, which I am not certain about at all.

It falls back again to my belief in myself and my mission; which is after all what the Science of Inner Strength and my work and my philosophy is all about. No matter how small my work may appear with regard to prospective outer world success; I believe in it more than whatever negativity or loss of family that David can threaten me with. That is the key point having something that you truly believe in to get you through virtually any and all turmoil; and for that matter, not be fazed by the bullies of the world.

This is an essential notion that we must have a sense for ourselves of what is right and what is not right. For me, in a relatively naïve, albeit enduring sense, such a sense of right and wrong, was given to me at a very early age. I virtually always carried this sense with me. The great learning lesson of my life in some "odd" ways, was learning to "adjust"[34] to people. Clearly what is right and not

---

[34] I had a wonderful little exchange with D. who does laundry for me this morning, a woman of Asian descent, where we bantered about how people must adjust, her word, towards each other.

right cannot be applied unilaterally to people; everyone has their own perspective. Interceding in another person's life or even stating our opinion, in less than tactful ways can be inappropriate.

It is finding that ebb and flow of life; that trusting of the divine or some higher power. Narcissism, carried to an extreme, even psychopathic behavior is the absence on some level of that sense of a higher entity, or at least a sense that our opinion unto itself, is not "King."[35] The Calm Revolution is about accepting a sense of our higher self, of our shared interests. Climate change, terrorism, financial issues, schools; we cannot solve any of this stuff, it seems to me, unless and until we create a reasonable dialogue and a capacity to work together. That is the truest me: Working for and helping to create this common agenda where the sensible part of our world, will ultimately rally around, in all likelihood, beyond the spectrum of my physical years. Maybe the best I can do for the moment is begin the discussion, and move things forward as much as I can.

The interweaving themes in all of this, have to do with a basically being good person, who was confronted with an avalanche and a landslide of narcissistic and even psychopathic abuse, and from the rubble of this landslide was able to create a science out of it. To be so inside, so seemingly trapped in this abuse, although I was fighting a lot of the time for American values it was like a pressure

---

[35] Even my daughter Sophia is not exempt, as she wondered about who is King of our family? To me, the King is God or at least truth. Truth in a compassionate sense is King; not really any one of us.

cooker, for me to dwell inside, and develop a science. Adversity that deep, not only makes or breaks you, when it is so deep, it add layers of character and thought, and even beauty to your very being.

Then, once that character and being are formulated, it becomes the task to take that process of learning and work out to the world at large, in terms of viable concepts that people will do extremely well to consider, if not adopt.. The notion is, is this country/world on the right track and if not, what can we do to get it on the right track? There are many elements of The Science of Inner Strength that can get our country on the right track. Specifically, for one, coming from a place of our true strength, and then learning how to communicate with and work with others, in the vein of our true strength.

The work that I am most interested in doing, is pointing society towards our true strength, and our better nature. Like a butterfly hatches from a caterpillar; it is from the deepest recesses of pain and abuse that true human goodness can emerge. Consider some of the inspiring words of Anne Frank, the young Jewish girl in Holland who hid in her attic for years; often speaking to, pointing towards the beauty of humanity. It is from the worst that we produce the best; it must be so.

Well a little twist with respect to my living space; in that the landlord is working to sell the building, using shall we say tricks of the real estate and building industries. A bit of a challenge, but nothing I cannot handle; indeed, I will let God handle it, lol. It is once again an opportunity to trust my process on a deeper level. My work must rule, must provide the light for me, and where

I am heading; I cannot be fazed too much by any lesser energy at this point.

I did have some time to reflect today on the wonder, of what I am really doing. Most of the time, I am either doing or thinking about it. Let us say there is this rich caliber to my work; that is what comes out to me, in the course of this real estate stuff, and how the politics of the city of Newton works. There is a part of me, which just wants to do my work right up until the move out date; and not think about it at all. God did seem to direct me, to some minor types of action on the situation to protect tenants and me.

Back to the notion of letting the air out of David. You see on some "odd" level that is what it really about; as need be to expose how empty he seems to be; that is the stunning thing, there is virtually zero there underneath all of his bullying and intimidation of others. I am pointing out the true iceberg nature of the psychopath, there is nothing there underneath. They can accumulate great things, influence many people and yet there is nothing there, evidently in a spiritual or substantive sense.

I am getting at the nature of the psychopath; the vast image, the capacity to intimidate others, and truly nothing, there; AND look at how much wreckage has been done in their wake. I must say that it gets lonely at times doing this work; working to induce change in a world that is so resistant, enduring the abuse. I guess I have "adjusted" my mindset to it so that like Nietzsche suggests both "what doesn't kill you makes you stronger;" and "he who has a why, can endure almost any how." So, at times, I grow, if not comfortable, at least peaceful with the pain, trusting that it is working its way through me for my betterment as a person.

Challenges also reveal our resolve; while the stuff about housing and the city of Newton can be annoying, it starts to bring out my deep resolve, as in these folks do not know my story, so to speak, and thereby my strength. I do believe on many levels most of my fighting days are behind me; so as I said today, I must be careful not to be baited by people, and drawn into conflicts that are unnecessary, and not worthy.

Bottom line I am very grateful to be me, with the extraordinary richness of experiences of my life. Even or perhaps especially, being pushed into very hard economic circumstances has its plusses. There is this grit; and this relationship to people living at an everyday down to earth level, I write as I sit in a Dunkin Donuts again.

Another piece is that at least today, I feel warmer towards my parents; I am beginning to believe that on some level they really have been intimidated and influenced by David Nathan Myers; and my work on some level is really to extricate them from this nonsense. Still that is a relatively precarious route, with no assurance that it will happen, as I wonder as to whether I would do well to cut the cord with them more fully.

Yet on some level, that is a component of what makes The World's Best Mediator; that capacity to truly untangle this thing on an emotional level. If so many people were in the hateful dynamic and one or two really drove it. Well who know really, one day at a time, as it goes; I can on some "odd" level feel the innocence of my father Morey Myers. I am not fully certain as to whether, that is all thoroughly real, or whether that is my desire underneath that my parents are innocent. I mean, they have done too much good in my life, to be utterly guilty.

Who knows? It is not a perfect world, albeit the Earth is remarkably round, and spins on its axis and all of that. Well enough for now. A nice little piece of research with a Starbuck's employee, who was just a tad rude, last time; and today was all peaches and cream. Well that is how it goes, people can make errors; I gently asked if I had gotten in her way last time, and she said: "No you are fine;" which was wonderful for a young lady. All's well that ends well.

I love people so much, and I have so much to offer. It is either a matter of me, improving my methodology a tad, or people letting down their guard a little or both. Patience and perseverance. Reminding me that I came with a barnburner of a concept pertaining to the Magic 6 hour x $600/hour Assessment; called the seventh hour; whereby we will produce an artist sketch, along with the person's magic words identified. I raise that concept because I have gone back and forth a little as to whether I will use the term "Compassionate Genius;" or "Patience and Perseverance" for my own descriptive words;

I also thought of another, but pretty much on this little jaunt I leaned towards Compassionate Genius, as on some level I just love it better. It does take some getting used to, and that kind of thing. Compassionate Genius is a product; and patience and perseverance has been my process; so I will also await the artist and see what happens there. I am enjoying this Starbuck's decaf, although wondering if the caffeine will hit.

I have a lot, I mean a ton of empathy for my father. You see, I still see him as a man who is virtually universally intended well; albeit trapped inside some of his emotions. This is one of those moments again, when I must trust God to handle it. I foresee wanting to spend time with him; perhaps I am making him more heroic than he will ever be, but I truly see his humanity on some "odd" level. Still like all folks he must also be responsible for his own actions.

Today, May 6, 2016, I found a substantial facet of moving on, as the expression and a piece of reality goes. I had a couple of small dilemmas pertaining to the town of Needham, and a mailing address and shoes of all things. I went to the local UPS store, where I have a mailing address, and a wonderful little piece of courtesy unfolded, as Eric, the store manager extended me an extra month of rental as a courtesy, based on a minor misunderstanding. Let me be clear, it is wonderful to be welcomed, and kindness itself is such an inspiring, almost orgasmic thing for me in general. Then I went to the local shoe store, and I was looking at my quintessential walking shoe to lead the Calm Revolution. I have been looking for a few weeks even. Allen Edmonds was supposed to call me back on their walking shoe; and yet today, in the local Needham store, there is style of the SAS shoe, actually called Moving On, that they can get for me for tomorrow morning.

It seems like a sign, and if nothing else, a mighty warm welcome in an "odd" way from the town of Needham, which is terrifically appreciated at a time like this. I did start the day with a couple of emails that contained a certain amount of push back with respect to the real estate situation that confronts me, as well as my familial situation. You know what? In the UPS store, I leaned in with trust; and on these larger things I will lean in with trust as well, to truly trust that things will work out.

Of all things it is great to see myself as a good person. For one, it took an enormous amount of work, and two, it is its own safe haven. The icing on the cake surely has to do with trust and letting go, and all that stuff. I mean you do the work and you let it go; you put the ingredients together, and then you put the cake in the oven. You say the prayer and then you say Amen. You plant the fields and then you let them grow. That is it.

Perhaps Moving On is the shoe for me, lol at this point. I wrestled with this quite a deal. I liked it three weeks ago and they did not have it in my size. Looking for and purchasing this next shoe has been a journey unto itself. One issue being, is getting to know the terrain in Newton and Needham. The terrain is more rugged and casual then downtown sharp. I want a shoe to lead this revolution with, and perhaps this shoe is it. The shoe is due to arrive tomorrow, Saturday morning.

Saturday it is and sure enough the shoe did arrive and fit well. So the Move On shoe was purchased. It is truly a miracle unto itself, as I was patient over a course of three weeks or so; also working through my relationship to some degree with Needham, and all's well that ends well. In addition, this morning; I seemed to reach a degree of spiritual breakthrough. I really focused on one central idea after more than twenty years of spiritual growth and development. This may be a certain icing on the cake; with respect to the notion that I consciously decided and continue to work to drop anxiety from my life. You know that feeling of being anxious; what if I was just able to drop it?

What an opening and a freeing of energy, if we really stopped being anxious, and stopped worrying about things. Think of how much happier and able to do more productive things we would be.

CHAPTER 27

COMPASSIONATE GENIUS: MY GIFT TO THE WORLD

This morning I also reflected on the concept of Compassionate Genius, and what an awesome concept, if not reality that it is. On one level, it is so much work to reach a level of Genius; and if and when people do, that means that they can help others. The compassionate component has to do with, with then being able to be a part of people, close to them, figuratively touching, healing if you will. That is the most extraordinary of concepts, and I admit conceptually there is some sense of awe on my part, in terms of theoretically melding those two concepts. Yet practically I may have already done so, without my knowing; actually like breaking in new shoes, lol. Follow the synchronicity; in and of itself, it contains magic.

So what is the genius part? Well a saying of Esther Hicks is true; "you can't get it wrong, and you'll never get it done." Genius is essentially a never ending process, as there is virtually always more to learn. No matter what level of life one reaches, there is virtually always more to learn and develop; especially when one is talking about human behavior, where there is a virtually endless amount of knowledge, change and new information to learn and absorb.

The genius does indeed have to do as a start or at least as a pushing off point from the notion of Iceberg and the recognition of the personality disordered in today's society. The genius begins by starting to understand the unfathomably complicated web, that human emotions and behavior can weave, and to stand for calm, solid and rational behavior. It is not enough and surely not fully understood, how a person with a personality disorder can so deleteriously affect a group dynamic; and in the process move it away from the core human values of fairness and decency that we desire and deserve.

Once beginning to understand, and disconnecting from the emotional energy of the personality disordered; it then becomes a process of finding one's inner strength and ultimately goodness. We must develop the strength, confidence and courage to act on our inner strength, and use that as our guiding light going forward, rather than our fear of the bullies and tyrants of the world. A very challenging part is that it is not known and understood the subtle ways that those with personality disorders wreak havoc, influence and control on our American institutions. In this way, one person can influence ten others or more, in non-positive and deleterious ways.

This all pertains to inner strength, by adopting the premise that most people are not just good, but intelligent in their own way, and yes somewhere in there, contain their own genius. It is almost solely a matter of education, with respect to understanding these challenged personality types and their effect on society as a whole. In essence, anything that takes us substantially away from fair and decent treatment is prospectively getting into the range of a person with a personality disorder; although in some, if not many cases, it can merely be a matter of people who truly do not know better.

For the most part society has raised us and inculcated in us, with the notion that toughness, if not meanness is virtually a vital part of success and progress. I cannot argue with the past, and unfathomably challenging circumstances that people may have had to deal with; I can solely work in the present with an ideal towards the future. We are at a much different point in 2016, with respect to our "potential"[36] for spiritual understanding and a prospectively intelligent redirecting of society. Resilience is strength, not cruelty.

Part of the genius, perhaps a large part is the recognition of those twin points: 1) The understanding of the impact of the personality disordered, such as extreme narcissistic, psychopathic and borderline AND; 2) The equal and opposite point that true strength resides in determination, purpose and cooperation. This is why on some level, the Trump phenomenon is possibly destined to fail, because of his unwillingness to truly incorporate concepts of kindness and decency into his presentation.

---

[36] "Potential" was once a wonderfully important word in my life, as in when I first met Margaret Carney she was promoting a game called Pente, developed by some folks in Stillwater, Oklahoma, and an incredibly important concept in that game was the one of a moved associated with "potential,"

The substance is important, and perhaps half, of the equation; and yet the style is also important, because if we cannot relate as human beings, how are we truly to make progress?

Personally when I look at Donald Trump, it is still an open book, as to whether he is truly a person with a personality disorder type, or as to whether he is merely following learned, bullying behavior in terms of "winning." Some glimpses into his personality recently as of today May 7, 2016, indicate that he does indeed possess some capacity for introspection, even if it is undeveloped, and there may be some true intelligence there in a emotional intelligence sense that could be developed. Perhaps a landslide loss at the polls might be the best thing for him and for that matter his family, if I could be just a tad honest about it; although the corruption occurring in our country must also be confronted.

That to me, is the miracle of life and The Science of Inner Strength for that matter, it is "nearly infinite" in its capacity to be open to human growth, and human change: It relies on the concept of life itself that when we can grow and change, miracles do happen. So the Move On shoes may well have inspired me to these heights today, lol; as I sit in a cool place called "Bagel's Best" in Needham. In the name of full confession and possibly TMI, I feel my Prostate has been stretched a tad, as a man with a numerical age getting into his later fifties, albeit I am virtually irrevocably young at heart. Perhaps it is a function of the enormous amount of work and even anxiety that I have encountered. Still using one of the concepts of the day, with respect to dropping anxiety and instead trusting. I will trust that it is a relatively minor flare-up and something God can handle.

It is also probably wonderful that my internet could not connect here at the bagel shop, as I believe I was able to come to a clear sense of the dual relationship between understanding and moving on from challenged personality types; and how the science of inner strength is an antidote for those personality types and behaviors, as I reference I in the Calm Revolution: Speaking of which this morning, May 8, 2016, I felt I was getting near the end of my rope with the familial nonsense and then ran across a really deep article on forgiveness.

I read the article and really tried it with my family. I am looking at ways to alleviate the emotional pain they have caused, and once again I circled back or stumbled upon the notion of forgiveness. This article by a Reverend Chip or something took it a step or two beyond forgiveness to love our enemies, as well as pray for their healing. Why not on some "odd" level? I am giving this a try, albeit the tricky part of this one, is that many of their abusive elements are still in play. That may be where it is a matter of trusting my vision and proceeding onward anyway.

I watched a wonderful sermon with Joel Osteen this morning, and it was entitled: "It's all good;' meaning that whatever is happening is good or for the better. This notion is in the ballpark of my own philosophy of things happening for a reason, or at least providing us with an opportunity to develop our inner strength. Inner strength, by the way, is not always about doing; sometimes it is having patience and allowing room for God to function, which is kind of what I am doing now.

A little room passed, lol; and today May 10, 2016 is an awesome day. I had a challenging piece of resistance with regard to my work and the Calm Revolution over the last day or two that caused me to use virtually all my skills, as well as some newly learned ones. It was funny, I was encountering some resistance on one particular item of business; and it went on some unusually long that I associated it with the craziness from my family. It almost seemed like a make or break moment that really tested me, and through effort and sheer momentum at one point I pushed myself through. I chose to even allude to walking away from a somewhat cherished relationship, but we seemed to have gotten through that test; presumably to push us to higher ground.

Speaking of walking; I received a phone call from a Victoria from Allen Edmonds today, to advise me that another pair of shoes had arrived for me. Yes, I had purchased the first ones, and they seemed wonderful; and yet here I am downtown preparing to look at another pair of shoes. I am pushing it and yet I must say that with all of the shoes that I have; leaving those SAS shoes in my closet for one day, seems like a loss. This may fully allow me to walk on the Calm Revolution at least five days a week, which is a miracle unto itself. Let's see what happens.

So I went for the Allen Edmunds blue shoes. It is a daunting task working to change the world for the better. To take some of the pressure off; I suppose a lot of it is done, through the work, as the person we become. Our words and our actions are highly relevant, but perhaps it is just the person we become that is equally important, if not more so. At times I work to convince myself that the work of the last twenty plus years is already done; that there will be significant harvests to reap no matter what; so just relax.

There are a lot of pieces in play of the Calm Revolution right now. For one, I was able to get brochures out already this morning. I am going to look at artist's work of my concept of the sketches of those who achieve their inner strength. Third today, rather unfathomably I began to develop a compassionate sense of David. I saw that Nomi and her Mom could well have influenced him; if falsely. Once we start to see the underlying rationales for peoples' behavior, we can begin to understand them, if not feel compassion, or some sort of support.

This has been an unfathomably long road, in an effort to essentially prove my point, or points that I have learned. The person, who ultimately cares the most wins; the person with a genuine stake in the situation ultimately prevails. Indeed, today, I did come to a wonderful breakthrough with respect to Morey Myers, and then I turned the situation over to God again. The breakthrough was another layer of understanding with respect to emotional abuse.

Still perhaps I am better talking about leaving it up to God, and letting go, once again.

Yet, I suppose that understanding was a point of genius for me; so worth noting here. What I really came to, was how much Morey Myers had his emotional clamps so definitively posted in me, as a virtual constant stream of his own negativity; if not through his words, then through his actions.

Even so, for now, I am better off leaving things to

God to resolve on some level, as I did a couple of things to follow up with that. Then there was a breakthrough with my printer JTC, coming through with a small piece I am doing leading up to the Science of Inner Strength honor, a pre-advertising piece that I am looking to insert into the Calm Revolution brochure. I was so inspired with the entire Honor that I moved to do this interim piece; a placeholder we are calling it. Not only did a wonderful design come through today, but I got a sense that it could be completed by tomorrow afternoon; so we are cooking with gas.

Well, it did come through, and here I am on Saturday May 14, 2016 late afternoon, just having mailed ten copies out to my family. It was kind of a bold move at the end of the day. I went strong with the notion from the New Testament of: "Do not overcome evil with evil, but overcome evil with good." On some level that is truly my work. Being a happy fun-loving person raises concern in this day and age, especially in the era of intense scrutiny and political correctness.

Nonetheless my heart of a champion, serves me well in any day or time. I am blessed that I have developed the personal style to work well with people, or I would have been trampled on long ago. Taking on David's mother-in-law appropriately seems like, in some ways the hardest and most precarious fashion of all this. It could be possible that she is at root, the psychological mastermind to much of this; putting her nose into my business. Judy Levine seems like her role is to stand behind her daughter, and urge as much narcissism and false superiority for her daughter Nomi as possible, while condemning my family and me, without knowing us barely at all.

It is my belief that truth ultimately wins out, but what a long and winding road. Maybe that is a breakthrough. I mean the entire area of psychological ostracizing seems like in some way it comes from Nomi, if not even more so Judy Levine. The entire area of narcissism is an unfathomable area; which on some level is what the realm of iceberg is about; that which goes on beneath the surface, the unfathomable torturous world of the narcissist or psychopath.

David and even Nomi could well psychologically be intimidated by Judy Levine, and that could be how this entire avalanche started from that naked desire to ostracize, to demonstrate that one is better, by seeking to impugn and do harm to someone else. Perhaps, that is an extremely crucial point of identifying Judy Levine, as a head honcho here; perhaps then the healing can start to occur. We shall see.

It probably is not her true intention to do harm. This is an example of about how when a group of people get into a group dynamic how out of control those people can get. I go back again to the notion of an elephant being afraid of a mouse. Maybe that is truly how and where the story begins and ends. I mean not totally but perhaps the avalanche can be stopped, if not reversed; in terms of repairing damage.

I am grateful that I can break at a little restaurant called BrickFire pizza a new entry into the Newton Upper Falls area; playing by the way, seventies rock and roll in the background or even sixties: Stones, "Jumpin Jack flash," right now. Today, Sunday, May 15, 2016, forty five years from my Bar Mitzvah, I am at a Dunkin Donuts. There seemed to be yet another breakthrough today, in an unexpected manner, albeit dovetailing with some previous communications.

In the main, I stumbled upon the notion of Morey Myers as a bully today; nothing more, nothing less. So, I rather calmly and kindly requested him to stop, in essence appealing to his better nature as well. This has been a most remarkable journey; the likes of which most people who subscribe to a strict No Contact kind of thing with narcissists, would never advise. Still it is virtual necessity that seems to encourage and dictate my course; so I am allowing my sense of genius to swim into the process.

Who, in their right mind, could ever fathom such a journey; being psychopathically mobbed by your family of origin, ex-wife, and the courts; and then working my way back through to essentially wear out and overcome ALL of those obstacles. If I stop and think about it, I honor my journey so deeply. The part I reference in terms of who could fathom; your own family, in essence working to psychologically destroy you; and then you going back, as if to heal them.

I go back in the main, which perhaps they know, because they keep my children psychologically, not to mention financially imprisoned in their little world. Hey, why complain; just continue to work through it. So the piece having to do with Morey Myers as a bully, is potentially a wonderful breakthrough, because for one, my family of origin, and even my cousins, are familiar with the notion of bullying, as their fathers, my uncles seemed to have elements of it to greater or lesser extent. People understand what a bully is, and perhaps collectively we can "contain"[37] Morey Myers on some level, if not really encourage a cessation to the element of bullying within our family and collective families. What a familial breakthrough that would be.

So we shall see, where this goes. In a way the stuff pertaining to the Stolzenberg/Levine family is a layer of the onion to peel back, before this one. Maybe at its core we are dealing with Morey Myers's bullying run amuck. The "odd" thing is that I can really see through him, how in his case, bullying really is an indicator of fear and insecurity. It is fascinating how some people really are fearful in life; continually in a state of worrying.

The notion of trusting, is another element of the Calm Revolution; as to how we as people develop a trusting notion in life, rather than a nearly endless cycle of fear and worrying. People cover up their fear with bullying and cover-up their insecurity as well for that matter; anything they do not want others to see, they cover up by pushing others around. I persevere as I do, to restore my financial position and the place for my children; those two items being my twin goals, not necessarily in that order.

Life is good; today I feel a sense of buoyancy at times; really hearkening to being in the moment. I was worrying a bit because I wrote a letter to the Mayor and the twenty=four Newton City Councilors about our building being sold and the process; my first and preferably nearly

---

[37] "Contain" was a word of Morey Myers himself, in my growing years, when would watch football games, he would urge: "Contain them, contain them."

last or surely infrequent foray into local politics. Even referencing it makes me nervous, lol. Some bit of work this afternoon brought me back to a sense of being in the moment, and thereby basically happy, and not worried about a thing. I do better to focus on what I consider my work of taking on the bully. I developed an ancillary concern that my mother Sondra Myers was also perhaps in a historical sense prospectively being bullied by Morey Myers, although I have no first hand evidence of this. I recall a story of an elder cousin, demarcating to me that Morey Myers intervened with his father to prevent any abuse of his mother; it would be "odd" if history were to be repeating itself, with respect to my interceding in a way to protect my mother, in addition to my children and myself. I have no direct evidence of this; but it a concern of mine, although Sondra, in her own way can bully..

I am extremely grateful for this cup of Dunkin Donuts decaf and yes, the banana chocolate chip muffin that I had as well. My refrigerator died at my little unit, and the landlord in the process of selling the building, may not fall all over himself to replace it. We shall see what tomorrow brings on that front. What a country; I get to sit here at a Dunkin Donuts and write my memoir; let's call it for now.

The entire notion of trusting rather than worrying is an ongoing topic. Could we really trust, rather than worry as a way of life? There is so much abundance in the universe. Just think for a moment of the number of stars; I mean that is a lot of something; yes, our planet has challenges. On some level we are raised to come from a caveman mentality of fear; but what if it is true we live in basically a universe of abundance?

Even more, that is where the basic notion of goodness comes back in. How about, if and when we live and breathe in the essence of our goodness for humanity; rather than the fear of our demise. I am totally excited about my insert for the Calm Interventions piece. I am following up on my notion of trusting, because along with a generalized notion of trust; I also rely upon the notion of a farmer having planted many seeds; one of my favorite quotes is along the lines of my "harvest coming to fruition."

In my life, I must remain cognizant that I have planted many, many fields in personal and professional life, and it may well be that they come to harvest any day as far as I know. I cannot determine the timing; those things are in God's hands. I do not know everything, but I know that in human terms, I have planted an awful lot of seeds and fields of goodness over the past more than twenty years. I am truly blessed for this journey. Joel Osteen's sermon this morning was that along with blessing, comes burden; ending up talking about how to reap great harvests, we must go through a lot. Oh brother, you can tell me about that one, lol!

My life is living testament to those kinds of things about blessing, burden and harvest. The sermon buoyed my spirits and relatively speaking centered me again to alleviate some worry and suffering; and extend more patience to my effort and cause. When something has taken twenty years more or less; there can be points of frustration and that kind of thing, which in the main, as they did this morning provide yet another opportunity for learning, patience.

The patience became a wonderful thing today, in coinciding with this afternoon's notion of being in the moment. Being in the moment; if and when we can get there, aligns us much further with things such as love, gratitude, faith, and joy; which to me, are some of the deep characteristics of God; and essentially where I desire to be, at any given moment. So in its own challenging, if quiet way, along with hitting the nail upon the head of Morey's bullying, the notion of being in the moment, and actually being there is a wonderful saving grace today; in the midst of familial abuse and a landlord's movement to sell the building and a resonating eviction. Just be in the moment, I say, with a smile on my face. Did I mention I am writing at Dunkin Donuts, that it is forty five years from my Bar Mitzvah. Wowsie, it is wonderful to be alive.

Today, May 16, 2016, I wrote a letter to my family essentially outlining what I perceive as David's integral role in this situation; it was somewhat cathartic, and a calm and thoughtful letter. Still I have also taken a step further, with respect to openness to the element of forgiveness. I just read an fascinating article by a Phillip Moffitt entitled "Forgiving the Unforgivable;" on his website Dharma Wisdom. It was a revelatory piece that I have read before. In particular, elements in Mr. Moffitt's article address the notion of still seeking fairness, while offering forgiveness.

This is pretty much where I stand on one hand, I want this conflict over, and yet it seems right to request funds, and non-interference with my children. Although it is tempting on some level to just move on, with the full confidence of my business and my work. Today, I decided to fully commit to the notion of Compassionate Genius, at the center of my Science of Inner Strength Honor. I was going back and forth with some other versions, but Compassionate Genius is it. That is my talent, and what I can offer to the world for the next twenty years or whatever it be, and here I go.

Forgiveness is what? That great question again. Based on Phil Moffitt's article I did garner some additional buffer with and for David, with respect to separating him from his actions, along the Jesus lines. It would be clear enough that David really does not know what he is doing. Perhaps that is the winning point of all; the capacity to see it in that manner. David is truly reckless in his actions and develop the capacity to see him that way; not as much as a threat. David really does not know what he is doing. The emotional implosion he for one, set off in this family was almost an act of desperate innocence, surely feeling dispossessed not just from his own heart and soul, but from the gravity and impact of his very own actions.

These are rather splendid insights I am coming into today. Having developed that emotional strength and distance to be able to strain to see innocence in David, if not David's actions is progress under the most challenging of circumstances. Yesterday, I moved things along further with the sense that Judy Levine, David's mother in-law was actually at root for some of the craziness; as she perhaps in subtle ways demanded emotional subservience from David and Nomi. We shall see.

Today, May 18, 2016 was an odyssey unto itself. It is astonishing what every day can bring. I had a very intense dream that seemed to be a catalyst in some ways, first in letting Morey know how unacceptable some of his behavior was; and then through this rather magnificent emotional journey reaching a point where I touched upon a great point of love for him. In other words, if he has been emotionally hijacked by David, Judy and Nomi on some level; I am very protective of him, ultimately, as I honestly do love him. One of the blessings that has been bestowed on me, AND that I have grown into, is that I am a human being who is able to love. It has added another layer or two of depth to me today; as it is one of those days, when I feel like I am on the verge of tears; even having shed a few, and for that I am thankful.

Will love penetrate even the seemingly toughest veneer is a question that I am dealing with. These are fundamental societal issues. Can hatred be turned back? Surely, on some level, but this unfathomably insane familial situation, can I drive through and reach some point of rationality for the group as a whole; or must I fully consider leaving the group? Or letting God just take its course, or some combination of all three?

It seemed there was great resistance on some level to get the Science of Inner Strength project moving forward at the printer. I needed a gut check moment; when I backed away from it. First, I realized that the Science of Inner Strength was something that I really wanted to see through. Next, I realized even that the specific project with the printer was something that I had a deep commitment to, as I saw it as a culminating piece to more than twenty years of work, and I pushed it through irrespective of any real and/or imagined opposition.

Boston is one of the toughest, if not the toughest place to start something along these lines, as it is by nature with all due respect, somewhat provincial and even defensive; yet it is where I live for sure. I have learned to work with and respect, and as need be, get by with the local loving Boston attitude, but it can be yet another challenge, on more than one occasion. All making the eventual success that much more, sweet.

Louise Hay on Facebook this morning had an affirmation of gratitude; and so I did adopt that today, and it was the piece that allowed me to go back to Sondra and Morey one more time, with the depth of my love and encouragement. Such affirmation also reminds me of how blessed I really am, to have a positive mission as I do in the world. Indeed, aligned with the sense of the toughness of Boston, is all the more reason that I want to have an office, maybe even street level that is the emblem of positive attitudes, actions, and vibrations. I am now schooled enough in the Boston culture to embrace it.

That is one thing Boston and New England have taught me on some deep level, is respect; to listen to the perspectives of others first, and to have respect for people; not fear, but respect for sure. New England is an amazing place unto itself; the work in getting to know the people and culture of New England could be a virtual lifetime learning unto itself; while I admire that, I have other work to do as well. We shall see how it all plays out. Tomorrow, could be something when the first of the Judy Levine letters arrives; with respect to identifying her as a spiritual leader in the hateful dynamic in this family. One of the other facets of my dream this morning was to trust my process even further; not to worry. I have come all this way, and something great will happen.

Well it is a tad fascinating with respect to the sale of our building. The landlord has in the main posed things in a way that does not seem overly fair to the residents, especially the long-term residents, people who have vulnerabilities. So it seems like a multi-pronged opportunity for me. For one, I am working with most of my fellow tenants to articulate a position of fairness for those who may need some support in moving out of our economically challenged scenarios. On the other hand, it is also an opportunity for me, to develop more understanding with city officials. Things seem to be unfolding in a wondrous way. It is but another opportunity to use adversity to my benefit. It is kind of fascinating how this dual track has emerged on another level as well; the tougher the challenge, the greater the reward as is said.

I have been wondering if I would choose to go back to court yet again, with my family. It may reside on the fact as to whether the negotiation with the landlord is successful, because one endpoint of that process would be going to court on an appeal. I wonder if I would then being having the opportunity to figuratively kill two birds with one stone. I have been working on the notion of letting God fight my battles, although it does seem that a necessary component of that must be, to be prepared to fight as need be.

Ah well, one day at a time. A fellow tenant named Jim provided a certain impetus and did a heroic job by delivering the letters to City Hall today. It is a matter of developing faith that no matter what happens we will be alright, or if not, I will deal with it. Living in a state of fear is the worst. It was kind of funny how this coalition among the tenants came together. I would have thought it was impossible to get six signatures from 10 p.m. last night until this morning; and yet they came together in virtually that timeframe; connoting again the sense of just trusting. I led the effort and then let go.

So it is really important to just stay within confidence and trust. The position we are articulating as far as the city, is an eminently reasonable one given our circumstances. I must say I was really moved by a Louise Hay affirmation yesterday as well. It was something along the lines of: "Put aside being normal; and focus more on being yourself." That was a wonderful word of encouragement for me; to put myself out there, even a little more and do so in a way that acknowledges that I may be different, but I am me. I am accurate and appropriate, as well, and I am being me, once and for all.

Not to mention the underpinnings of both my familial and landlord situation, in the simplest senses putting aside notions of bizarre personality types, is the notion of standing up to bullies. I mean, if and when you cannot stand up to a bully, and feel reasonably great about it; then what are we doing being alive? It is again, as Thomas Jefferson is quoted: "Be like the rock with our substance; and like the river with our style." Take the challenging stand, the courageous stands even; but do it with calmness and consideration at virtually all times. Indeed, the capacity to remain calm, is a humongous strength unto itself, as the enemy will flip and threaten and cajole.

It is a matter of having a joy of life itself; knowing that

being involved in challenging situations is an adventuress part of life. I must say this is one, working for the tenants, I do not feel that I could have done alone, nor did I want to. The inspiring concept was really the plight of my fellow tenants; the betterment of the whole. In the same, perhaps it has not totally emerged as of yet, but the work with my family, and for my family is for the benefit of the whole, if and when that ever comes about; surely with my children as an anchor, but it has grown to a commitment and an interest in goodness itself.

I am delighted I have grown, beyond the point of who is right as far as my familial matters, but more so to what would be right and best for as many members as possible. A little wrinkle with respect to advocating with the tenants. I got some negative feedback from one of the signers of the letter, and you know what? It is a cause that I really do not believe in so much; when the signers of the letter do not want to stand for it themselves. I am back to trusting God on that one. You cannot get out in front of people too far to lead. I must take care of myself first, and see what happens.

I wrote a letter with respect to Morey Myers today; identifying him as the source of the conflict on some "odd" level. I am conflicted. How much can one person give to the noble cause, with not a whole lot of return as of yet. In any event, I do believe that I was honest and accurate with respect to Morey Myers, and that is what matters.

What do I know about Morey Myers in this situation? Morey Myers has essentially adopted a sadistic role with respect to my life, organizing and managing this perverse familial dynamic that seeks to denigrate me and keep from my children. What an intelligent program, NOT; I must say with a tad of a laugh.

On some level the thing that I am feeling today, oddly even in a positive sense is the pain that goes with this situation. I suppose the goodness of this pain; is that I am clear that it is in pursuit of a purpose, a relatively divine purpose, and in that regard I am inspired, uplifted even. I take it as still an ongoing test of my tenor and fiber. Today May 22, 2016, a lead headline in the wonderful Boston Globe is literally "In custody case, Clinton took side of a father." That is a direct quote, as if in 1978 and reviewed today, it was a crime to represent fathers in our society. What is our society coming to; as if in some general sense it is not right to represent a father, even thirty eight years later?

Society in terms of our leadership is threatening to lose its soul. That is the Boston Globe with a lead headline; as if there was never a father, out of the two main genders, who ever deserved representation in a custody case. Rip Van Winkle, please pinch me. The science that I bring forward entails an honesty in life, for a culture that has lost a ton of muster, with respect to just speaking for our basic values of decency and respect in clear and cogent manners. Well I have made it past 90,000 words with this book/memoir; that is an accomplishment onto itself.

If I had to stop right now, and summarize the three major themes of the book so far, I would say: 1) My ongoing perseverance through whatever, to get to my goals, as I truly chuckle. Chuckle in the sense that it surely has been an uneven line, with so many zigs and zags; running into this tenant today, after I put myself out to the City Council was a piece of work unto itself. It is important, lol, to see virtually every experience as a learning experience; and that is again where the science of inner strength comes in to have that underlying; 2) Surely the notion of the iceberg personality, that Cluster B personality type that dramatically affects culture right now; the wolves in sheep's clothing, as I recently called them, and our need to realign and reeducate society due to them; 3) In more macro senses of 1 and 2; it has to do with the major corruption within our societal systems and our need to delve forward with to our honesty, decency and purpose; once we have divined our purpose, in a societal sense. We cannot be afraid to press forward with our honesty and things we know to be true, in terms of basic decency and honesty as a society.

In even a more general sense I would say that my life is a work of art. It is not easy to convey as to what it is like to in a state of emotional and psychological abuse for decades. That is where a sense of humor is relatively mandatory. You must be able to shoulder things in life, to laugh on occasion, even if it outwardly so funny. For some "odd: reason, today, is a day I can share a few of those laughs. It is as Kafka might suggest an absurdity of life, albeit I maintain a much more positive outlook; it seems rather stapled into my inner being. For the last twenty years that positive outlook even stems from no artificial substances, and precious little alcohol.

It probably is what bothers people so much about me, is that I am a happy person. Some people hate upon you, just because you are happy. I am blessed on some level, to have learned that painful lesson over the past many years and inculcate it into the fabric of my being; there are people who just hate my joy. Joy is, in terms of our divine blessing, my internal love is something that I have worked hard to establish in my life; and not something that I will give up for anyone. In addition, that sense of joy, when properly cultivated helps us endure the most harsh and challenging situations.

That is one of my great lessons, is keeping alive God's light within me; through the most arduous of circumstances. It is developing that inherent resilience, that sense that virtually anything can be done or overcome with the right attitude. I would say on some level that attitude is well cultivated within me. What happened today, with respect to some vituperative feedback from another tenant that could well come from the landlord, previously might have stagnated me for days or weeks. Now, it is a little pain, yes, but also a sense of humor, in that that is life itself running its course, it is bigger and stronger than me, and I have learned not to fight what happens in life, better to respond.

My fight is virtually totally on behalf of my sacred children and Calm Interventions and that kind of stuff, and society. As long as other stuff does not inordinately throw me off of my game; I will reach my goals: Which resonates to the Science of Inner Strength in terms of knowing that resilience, and capacity to know which fights to accept and which to let go. It is clear to me that some tenants are intimidated by the landlord, but I will not waste time and energy trying to convince them, unless they ask. People can make their own choices and stay in the type of situations they desire or create for themselves.

It comes back to that joy stuff; or at least that notion of an ideal and a goal, and determination to follow it through, and overcome challenges that pushes us towards greatness. My landlord would like nothing better than to engage me in a fight over this issue; and that is bait that I cannot accept; although in fairness he wants to sell the property and move on. It is not my work to engage in local politics. Although on significant matters I do stand for fairness.

May 23, 2016, it is, an amazing day unto itself. A little event entailing a returned piece of mail from my cousin, brought home to me, how much I love everyone. Wow, conflict, it really is something; it is a learned thing. Underneath people really do love one another. Life is precious; there is so much we take for granted. Society has taught us, evolved to the place that conflict is natural and perhaps necessary. Listen: sometimes it is, but probably not in the way, and at the level that we have been raised.

Underneath, most of really do love, and we have just not been taught appropriate and healthy ways to love each other. We are not taught to value love, and that love can and will be a significant strength. I see this now, in this little returned envelope from my cousin as she moved; in wondering what it could be, I realize on some level how much I love her, even though we have not been very much in touch since childhood, and even not a great deal even then.

It is nothing less than societal retraining that I am advocating. Yes, accept what is good from the past which is significant; and yet there is a fundamental retraining, realignment, rethinking of the human condition that we must undertake. "The work"[38] is truly about helping ourselves acknowledge and align with that kind and loving part of ourselves; a

At a time yes, when economic systems virtually tear apart human lives.

It is a "fascinating" stretch. It seems like as hard as heck in a way; so I stopped into O'Hara's Pub in Newton for a relatively rare beer. On some level I have worked so hard it is unfathomable. It is an amazing act of faith, belief and trust for that matter to have gone on so long with little if any positive feedback, other than my own trust. It is very important to stay in touch with my humanity, as an occasional beer will do.

Actually this morning there was a relatively significant act that seems worthy of celebrating as well. I just spontaneously offered some forgiveness, to Morey and Sondra, with a sense that everybody was forgiven for everything; although I did leave a caveat that reconciliation was not the same. I stated forgiveness took a ton of work on my part, and reconciliation would take work probably considerable on their part, and I suppose on some "odd" level that is the best way to leave it, at least for the moment.

I drafted a profile of the tenants and their interests to present to the Mayor and the City Council in Newton, which seems like a very heavy project as well. There is only

---

[38] "The work" is a methodology strongly used by a spiritual leader Byron Katie to describe her approach. I do not totally subscribe to her method, but I love her expression of "The work;" to describe her method; and it does have some wonderful stuff.

so much that I can do. I am working as well, on allowing God to fight my battles, a deeply Christian, rather than Jewish notion on some level; and it also is a nice way to go, surely as compared to worrying about things.

A beer or two, literally no more, lol; for me does provide a sense of perspective on life. A little backing off is wonderful; this is also a terrific time to trust life, with things up in the air as they are. There is just the trust as well, of the farmer who has planted so much that he or she knows that something is bound to come to fruition. I had a wonderful conversation with a couple who used mediation to save their marriage, and that is what the world is about; to use a word that the woman Leah used, moving towards a more "thoughtful" world.

So much of what I desire to see is a more thoughtful, more emotionally intelligent world,, that is what it is ALL about. The key is influencing the culture in such a way that people do not sacrifice, but actually, bolster their economic success. It is hard when people are so locked into their mentalities of success, to convince them that there can be more effective, more emotionally intelligent, more economically productive models beyond what we are doing now.

The personal transformation that I have lived so far; for some "odd" reason I am believing that it is my sacred mission to share it, if not substantially actuate it on some level in the world. To me, the Science of Inner Strength and for that matter the Calm Revolution are facets of the tough decisions we must make to survive and thrive in the years and decades ahead.

Today, there was a rather "odd" turn in my

understanding of my familial situation. I actually had an inkling, a teeny bit I would say of a pleasant dream involving my brother David, ending on the sense of his almost listening to me on some stuff. As I did some true dream reflection I came to the sense of how Sondra Myers has worked to cut off so many of my relationships in life; from my brother to my father, to my ex-wife, to children and on and on. Those qualities of controlling relationships of working to isolate a person, are Iceberg characteristics of extreme narcissism and psychopathic behavior. Still, as I work to understand peoples' energy itself, perhaps I can break down these people, to bring them and "restore"[39] them to their sense of humanity.

I was then able to take a next step, which is similarly significant in raising for Morey Myers a question. The question that I put to him in a firm and yet compassionate sense, was what was causing this aura of antagonism that seemed to surround his life. In thinking aloud at the moment, I would not be shocked if Sondra, through those narcissistic qualities of jealousy and the like was essentially tying Morey into that aura of antagonism, as a function of her way of keeping him, and even more so, her status where she wanted it to be.

Families are these very complicated entities, where there can be ALL kinds of energies, emotions and agendas at play. It is a blessing and a curse, lol; I suppose for me in believing in fairness. A blessing in that it is such a wonderful quality and value to embrace; on the other hand,

---

[39] "Restore" a word used by Sondra back around 2005, perhaps the last time we got together, when she referenced wanting to restore relations with me.

it can lead us into taking stands for things, on occasion more often, than we would otherwise choose. Alas, not everything is perfect, lol; AND for that matter I do not aspire to be.

Well a fascinating day in some ways, I seemed to have walked away from the relationship with my printer.. I am proud I had the strength to walk away, a more newly defined skill in me, not inherent to my family of origin. I also got out a wonderful letter to the family; I included David on it, I almost feel toxic for including him. Part of my emerging theory, is that it was the collision and amalgam of energies that brought this unfathomable dynamic to a head, surely with David playing a leading role.

It takes a village, as they say. It takes a village to engender such hatred; people play off each other, and feed into each other, and create this dynamic of the sense of their own invulnerability, which is solely in the own heads. These folks are playing by such a sense of violating all rules of humanity, and functioning that way solely because they can get away with it. That type of behavior is behavior of the worst kind, being so violate only because they can get away with it. On the other hand, I did offer them some forgiveness today, and we shall see how that goes.

It really is a matter of a carrot and a stick I suppose, and with God, for sure. The carrot being to wear them down, with love as well. Why do people act so hatefully? Because they are without love. The stick being to identify and call out their behavior. I have taken to calling David and Nomi's perspective "birdbrained;" with the notion of hitting them exactly where they think they are strongest, their amazingly exaggerated sense of intelligence. I am not sure if that is a hard enough, but in a group dynamic it can be quite effective. Judy Levine, as well, is another one, who sought to put her false genius on the group; and clearly that comes from a sense of disconnection herself. Again, it is that amazing point, healthy and happy people do not intercede in other peoples' lives, especially falsely.

I am glad to have been willing to leave some past work behind, and we shall see now, as I can focus more on Calm Interventions stuff. I do have this eviction thing, based on the landlord's sale coming up in five weeks or so, and yet I am trusting that God will handle this, at least or more my work with family will pay some substantial dividends. I suppose the main thing is not to worry about it. I am inspired to do my work with Calm Interventions. I received a wonderful phone call from a prospective client today; that seemed like the right kind of client, perhaps the work is finally sinking in. It seemed like the most wonderful affirmation that I have received in a long, long time.

I love my life; and on some "odd" level, I do love my parents, and I would love for them to see their way through this situation. It is surely moments like this, when I am happy that I am alive. Life itself, a wonderful gift; moments exist unto themselves. There was a great quote from Louise Hay the other day, that was along the lines of taking life like a learning experience and doing our best. No matter what phase of life that we foresee ourselves at, it is a wonderful notion to take each experience as a learning experience; and just do our best with it at that moment. I was inspired by that notion of Louise Hay; thank you Ms. Hay!

Not so fast with the printing stuff. The work has a life

of its own; I was able to drop off a revised version of my stuff to them, over this Memorial Day weekend. I mean the Science of Inner Strength is moving forward sometimes, in spite of the challenges involved, and that is the nature of divine inspiration itself. While it is challenging to learn; it is deeply reassuring to know that even if I get in my own way on occasion that the work will continue. It has been twenty plus years in the making, and sometimes things that would hamper more regular human relations seem to dissipate like dust, before the Calm Revolution.

In this particular case, I took the bus and chose to walk the last piece to the printer they have said that they would leave some envelopes in the mailbox for me. I wondered if I should bring one, "just in case;" and decided not to, with the sense that if it was meant to be it would be. Sure enough the envelopes were in the mailbox.

Now, it is Memorial Day weekend, May 28, 2016; and my birthday is on Monday, May 30, 2016, which was the original Memorial Day. I have much to be grateful for; I could have a little party, if I so chose on my birthday, which was not always the case. I have just all this forward energy for the work, and I am not where I thought I would be.

Yet, the thing is, I do a lot of work about being happy where you are; and for that matter, a spiritual sense that I am exactly where I need to be. One spiritual principle is to feel the feeling of how you feel after reaching your goals. For me, it is more than attaining my goals, perhaps the feeling that I am seeking, is in overcoming this obstacle, of being defamed, ostracized from my family and their working to heinously cut me off from Sophie and Sam.

Yet, the thing is, even in overcoming this once in a millennium thing, there could well be other obstacles after that. It is still an open book for me, as to whether there will be a moment of great victory in this situation, or reaching a place that will give me relief in an "odd" way.

One thing is that whatever it will be; it will be new, and there will be adjustments to it. I am getting that feeling now that everybody will know me for my work; I will do wonderful good for humanity, and be happy, healthy, prosperous with a wife, my children and community or some compilation of what God has in store for me.

May 29, 2016; I had a really nice conversation with a compatriot Jim, who has been talking with me about the prospective sale of our building. I totally enjoyed talking calmly with people and even ending up with a common understanding. Nice conversations are a blessing unto themselves. I was able to push through in a way with my family, to gain a better sense that perhaps Morey and Sondra were victimized by David, and that is how they adopted such a awful perspective. It is such a function of groupthink, being confused and/or not fully standing for one's beliefs.

That is one thing I virtually always had, even if it was not so developed, at younger ages, is the capacity to think for myself. That is another main reason that I was cut out to be The World's Best Mediator; is that capacity to think and stand up for myself, in ways that are accurate, and in keeping with moral standards on the part of society. That sturdiness is a function of my upbringing on some level, albeit I do not know how much I would have had those characteristics on my own right. I do attribute that capacity to stand for what is right to Morey and Sondra; even if, in my mind they have not followed through, in a way that I might have thought.

Originally, I had a very rigid sense of right and wrong; with respect to relating with other people. New England will fix that rigidity in a hurry. Massachusetts is very self-protective, do it your own way, and rough, very rough, even mean often enough. In short, Massachusetts proved a wonderful training ground, to take my rigidity, and meld it into flexibility and ability to work. with people. Rigid will get you run over in Massachusetts.

So, to be clear, I have an eviction notice for June 30, 2016; limited financial resources, a very intense emotionally abusive dynamic in place from my family; and the development of the science of inner strength and Calm Interventions Inc. In other words, as the old expression goes: "I've got them right where I want them." Oh, I am also working on praying to God and letting God handle it as well; so that is wonderful. I believe that things are happening at this moment, and in this manner for a reason. I have basically seen the sale of this building as my ticket out of 1110 Chestnut Street, after seven years.

Of course, too, with respect to God working; I am also developing deep notions if not of forgiveness, then of compassion, and truly insight as well. The notion of David being a catalyst, is a "fascinating" concept, which is not iron-clad, but perhaps redeeming. I am deeply moved on some level by all of what is going on. It is an opportunity to know life on a very deep basis; that is what adversity does for us, it puts us closest to some of the most real things on earth.

When adversity occurs, we are seeing things on the most base, even pure level. There is no sugarcoating or putting on spin, it becomes what it is, buffered for sure with faith in God, and a sense of the divine, but still very real elements of life in play. One thing in my favor is that when I see people acting in very baseline, even greedy ways, I make up my mind that there is no way that such low-level actions are going to beat me. I was also inspired this morning by a talk from Joel Osteen, who emphasized the role of being a peacemaker, and letting other peoples' craziness go.

Which invariably brings me back to forgiveness again. Forgiveness has become necessary for me often enough, because of the pain involved in holding onto the conflict. Forgiveness does also convey a higher moral ground than those who would oppress us. I have become not only more trusting of the unknown, but at moments like this, standing back and enjoying it, like a scientist.

Forgiveness for me, on some "odd" level has become working for what is right, by having an encouraging and non-punitive outlook on things. With the sense that most people desire what is right; and most people will ultimately go along with truth and wisdom, and the wrongdoers, may not be unduly punished but will be evidenced to people as being the nutcases they truly are. It is so; truth must prevail in the long run; there can be nothing else. That is the astounding confidence of my belief system and plans. Adhere to the truth, and then be prepared to go through anything and everything to get there; like a diamond itself, under the most unfathomable pressure as a piece of coal, molding and melding into its brilliance. A rock dropped out of a window, will fall downwards due to gravity. Certain things are bound to happen, based just on natural order. How and when remains to be seen, for sure. God lets us know.

So for the moment I sit in the café at Whole Foods market on Walnut Street in Newton, on this late Sunday afternoon, May 29, 2016. I enjoy life, and allow its dynamics and all that occurs to fall like snowflakes upon my shoulders, for the most part. I got a wicked burst of hay fever or allergies all of a sudden yesterday, our first really hot day. What I also enjoy about adversity is that there are people trying to do no good in this world; and I am still standing, not allowing them to accomplish their missions. So the conversation cannot only be seen through the lens of my "winning;" but also the fact that my stand, in and of itself is, a victory for consciousness, and a better way.

Well, I leapfrogged over my birthday for writing, as it was yesterday. Fifty-eight, fun filled years as we say. It does seem like there was a key piece that fell to the ground, in my assessment. That piece had to do with perhaps deeply discovering that Sondra Myers is more at root of this viciousness, than perhaps any other. On some level it has been rather monumental work. Indeed it does feel like Morey and Sondra Myers "together"[40] have created the possibility of the unfathomable viciousness to unfold, with Sondra being the more manipulative one.

Why you might ask would parents not just allow, but support and strongly urge others to mob and vilify

---

[40] Again there is amazing irony to the word "together;" in that there was a day and a time, when Sondra assured me that she was "together on this" with Morey.

their own son? . It does go back to the Iceberg notion of extreme narcissism leading to psychopathic behavior. Narcissism, as described is this spiritual darkness; I at times, call it insect-like perspective; of these little creatures scurrying around on the ground, without much of a thought process.

The deep narcissist has no real developed sense of self, and is continually in a dog eat dog, survival mode. There is no real positive vision, no sense of togetherness or comradery on the part of the narcissist; it diminishes down to this very narrow outlook on life that seems to entail solely room for the narcissist and their needs, like a shark or barracuda. I recall once, a guided exercise from a woman Cara or something, I will look it up at some point, with respect to narcissism free. The guided lovely meditation ended with us cutting the cord, with the person we perceived as the narcissist. I was shocked at the last minute in doing it, as I went into thinking that it was Morey Myers and at the moment of truth the person I clearly saw overseeing the narcissistic effort was Sondra Myers, my biological mother.

So, what is shocking to folks, in this day and age is that there are mothers that can act so hatefully to their children. The image of apple pie and motherhood, is not universally applicable. Ironically I did see some positives from Sondra, when I was growing up in childhood. Sondra, took on these more monstrous proportions, when strife came into our family, and also around the time of her father's estate in 1988. It is as if all of the hidden rages from Sondra's early years came forth and exploded onto the scene. Suddenly Sondra saw her moment to act as mean and controlling as she wanted.

While I am generally aware that Morey and Sondra Myers had some marital problems in the day; it does seem like the psychological decision they made, as part of their cover up was, to denigrate and scapegoat me. That decision really pulled the rug right out from me. I remember Sondra calling me in July or so, 1988 with a very supportive tone around, a then temporary marital separation, and a week later calling me with a very different tone. Something profoundly changed around that time; and it seemed her decision to turn against me, was beginning to take place.

I suppose the key phrase when it comes to narcissists of a very deep level is "without conscience". It is an unfathomable process in life to be hated by your own mother, essentially for no real reason whatsoever. When she begins as a wolf in sheep's' clothing; it is a staggering emotional adjustment to wrap your arms around. Wow, there I said it; perhaps on some level the entire psychopathic Iceberg that was set up for me, in my own family was established by Sondra, or at least with her considerable role.

I attempt to work my way to things like forgiveness, and even compassion; at the same time considering further court action at this rather vulnerable moment. Sondra has gone her more than eighty one years, without anyone really saying no to her. She told me on a limited basis once that her father, did not get involved with disciplining her, and that Morey really seems to be unable to hold her back from essentially doing whatever she wants. Thus, Sondra's M.O. is to travel without any sense of restraint, respect or boundary; particularly in a familial situation when she can attempt to hide it, and further scapegoat me. There is plenty of literature on narcissism and scapegoating around.

It takes this equally unfathomable walk of faith on my part to work my way through this. I mean, there is a great deal of commentary on-line and stuff that states that a narcissist or psychopath should not be exposed, because their image is everything and that they will respond in the most vicious ways. I am relatively expecting that, but when your own life and destiny and sense of children is on the line; it does seem pertinent to attempt to work through it, if not expose the truth, no matter how painful at times.

The alternative I have played around with is, the sense of leaving it to God. Often though when I leave it to God; I get this inspiration, what I reference as my genius, and that lends me forward towards doing the work. It is the unknown for sure. I mean I do not do FaceBook. I have a profile that I have not used in five or six years at all; so I get two messages for my birthday, of what I could somewhat justifiably call "brothers" from Oberlin College. It is a nice feeling. On some level I have been battered into the ocean by these folks, and I guess what I have to show for it, is being The World's Best Mediator, for one; not to mention a wonderful guy, and perhaps even better father. Whoa, that's a load to share, and it is cool to have people who remember me.

Wow, it has been six days since I wrote; what a time-frame. Much of my energy has been dedicated to the effort to work with and support myself and other tenants to make a positive transition to better housing from our current challenging situation, with an eviction notice hanging over our heads for twenty four days or so from now. It is a rather miraculous feats that I was able to inspire, if not lead and encourage an effort to engender a voluntary Resolution for consideration by the Newton City Council for the tenants.

God has planted on my path an attorney for the "other side" who I knew from twenty four years or so ago in Cambridge. From everything I have seen so far, Terry's work has been a gift from God, as he has worked to use his words in "kindred spirit" with me to draft an amazing resolution that will support a positive transition for the tenants. We came up with a finished draft yesterday, and Terry shared it with me, City Councilor Deb Crossley who has agreed to take the lead on it, and the prospective new owner, his client and the current landlord: A wonderful step of progress.

The landlord hit the fan, with the whole thing; even though, and really began verbally assaulting me. Terry was wonderful this morning in indicating that he will talk to Dave (not real name) strenuously. I cannot help but wonder on some level if Dave is tied into my family of origin in some ways; some of the terminology seems to tied to them. I offered some forgiveness to Dave and even to my family this morning.

It is such a bizarre feeling, albeit I am partially accepting it as a fact of life that your own family is working in insect-like fashion feverishly to bring you down; Wowsie. While I still try to snap them out of it, in an appropriate sense, perhaps "oddly" I am getting used to it, in a way that it least it does not bog me down so much. It really was a boost for Terry to respond so vigorously this morning as an affirmation of God's will at work. Joel Osteen is wonderful with respect to not allowing or paying attention to people who talk behind your back to bother you.

It is funny Joel is coming to the Boston area on July 8, 2016 and I could almost consider going to a Christian rock show of sorts; although I am not committed to doing so. Not bad for a little Jewish kid from Scranton, PA, lol. In the meantime and almost incidentally the Science of Inner Strength Honor came together almost miraculously as well. Too much good is happening to worry.

Things were getting a tad challenging in creating the Science of Inner Strength Honor with my printer. Then one morning I walked over early with some changes made in hand, old style, as the computer did not seem to making that connection. I was fortuitous in getting there a few minutes early, and running into their owner John, before opening time, being able to convey my changes and the like. Within hours things started to happen that the previous weeks were not able to materialize and we had a program. It was kind of like I needed the one burst of final energy to push the thing through. I am wondering what it will take to get my family eventually in line with me, but then again; that is a matter of trusting the process and God to make it happen.

So the unfathomable journey is continuing. I am not sure at times if the epic nature of the journey is coming across, in mere words. I mean fighting against this emotional/psychological abuse of the past twenty plus years is unbelievable and perhaps even more unbelievably my efforts are often enough to tame the abusers into nonabusers, as they have my children behind enemy lines.

Compassion: Another Chapter of this journey: "Rejoice in your troubles."

I have found myself "oddly"[41] veering into areas of love and compassion, forgiveness; ALL of these wonderful things over the past week or two. It is moving beyond peoples' remarkably hurtful behavior and finding the strength to see that their hurtful behavior is for sure, a function of their own hurt. Perhaps like the Dalai Lama would commend, finding the strength to have compassion for one's enemy or tormentor; is perhaps the ultimate test of my journey, to truly reach and turnaround people who have been so hateful and not acting in their own best interest.

It is a work in progress.. Time will tell what the results will be. It is a trade-off or intersection of our own interest versus the sense of helping the group will help all. Those are the circumstances, the hand that I have been given. It does seem the possibility is there that I am getting close to the end of a twenty year cycle; albeit perhaps more so; I have more have moved to trusting God's timing.

On some level that is similarly as large, perhaps even larger than the compassion piece; is the entire notion of trusting God or the unknown, the universe, the process whatever you r want to call it. Trusting is so much against many peoples' natures, I would suppose; and perhaps particularly so in my family of origin. Every family has its rather ordinary neurosis. My family even in its starts, perhaps due to Eastern European Jewish roots, and people

---

[41] Actually Sophie's word was "oddly;" not odd in her seminal college entrance essay.

living so long, has high levels of anxiety and lack of trust. I believe, they have gone way beyond in this situation what normal anxiety might be, in terms of controlling behavior.

I am laughing out loud in a way, with the sense of still believing that there will be a day and a time that they will snap out of their absurd behavior. The abuse from my father, the pushing of his fear and anxiety onto me, is an amazing challenge of my life.. Morey's love and care for me, has gotten so twisted around that the only way he can express his feelings unfortunately is through abuse, and browbeating; and all this kind of thing.

Wow, that is an amazing breakthrough of sorts, to more deeply discover that Morey's, bullying is in all likelihood predicated upon his fear, and guilt, and all of that Jewish, ;actually human type of craziness. That is the truly absurd part of it, what if all his bullying and browbeating is actually a function of how much he loves, albeit in his disturbed and undeveloped way.. That could be the breakthrough of breakthrough: That their crazy behavior is based on fear. By understanding that breakthrough, one can then address their two percent of real fears in sensible and reassuring ways.

That understanding is possibly a big piece of the iceberg if you will that I have broken off. Honing in on the notion on some deeper levels that peoples' harmful behaviors are truly functions of fear. How to convey to the world as Bob Marley sang: "Everything little thing is going to be all right"?

Well my work, today, June 11, 2016, seems to have veered back into the realm of forgiveness. I sent out one more, perhaps last familial letter honing in on the notion that perhaps David was at root. Maybe my work was done there. I was able to include the last insert piece relating to the Honor of Inner Strength into the brochure, and that could be a realm of completion of the past twenty years.

It is funny, and I am nearly laughing to myself with respect to the number of people who have sought to challenge me and bring me down. Forgiveness is near by, when I can even fathom laughing about this stuff. Breaking this stuff down is very useful; I mean if David is at root then David is my younger brother, he is not going to bring me down.

Forgiveness is an amazing piece of work in some ways. What is forgiveness today for me? Forgiveness is the willingness and ability to extend prospective kindness to those who have sought to bring you down, to cease on some level to feel the pain of their present or past actions. As I write those words it is a victory unto itself; I have an image of me standing at the top of a mountain, with my arms outstretched in victory; forgiveness is a reward.

Even more perhaps is the notion of healing that is going on in my life. I find myself in more peaceful and calm states of mind, virtually all the time. Today, June 13, 2016 was a wonderful example. I went to look at a short-term place to live in Newton, and the people and I really seemed to hit it off. I really seemed to bring a calm presence unto the situation, and I was really inspired; looking beyond credit scores and all that jazz, the people seemed to like me very much, and that was cool. I live in a very rough place right now; there are no two ways about it. It is a place to live, but a little calmer, softer place may well be a step in the right direction.

I continue to do the main work of my life; for one being, a father, and running my business; but also working on trusting on deeper levels. What if the world trusted, rather than feared, in the manner we grew up? It is a very hard transition to make, in some ways, perhaps more or less challenging than the one Caitlin Jenner is making before our very eyes. Looking to transition to trust, from fear, and then spreading it out into the world. I am inspired by that. The one thing I forgot to say to my family was that they really mean something to me; oh well, nothing can be perfect I suppose. Can I really change and inspire the world, and make a ton of money from it, and be healthy and happy, the way my vision is relatively speaking unfolding? I mean can the joy I have worked so hard to create, now come into vogue? I am excited; I suppose I am reminded of some of my early work twenty years ago, when I read Thich Nhat Han, one of whose books is "Being Peace." More and more of me, is being peace; and/or at least promoting that development in the world.

Today, June 14, 2016, Flag Day, yay; brought some interesting stuff. For one, I continue to wrestle with the notion as to whether Morey and Sondra inspired David's hatred or David's hatred ran over Morey and Sondra; for the moment I am seeing it as more the latter, as I grew up in the same environment as David. I had youthful rambunctiousness and that kind of thing to work through and grow out of; and yet, I was not ever a hater. David is my brother, and if it turns out that Nomi, his wife and Judy Levine set him up in some way; I will eventually side with David on that one, albeit that is not where we are at today.

Today, I continued to encourage Morey and Sondra to see the light on things.

In addition, after drafting a draft press release, I heard back from the Attorney on the real estate transaction of our building, and he is planning for the resolution that we worked on together to go through this coming Monday night. I had gotten a tad confused with some of the dynamics; still it does seem like the resolution is there, perhaps fitting with Flag Day, as in our "flag is still there." I am back to supporting the needs of the tenants, and communicating to them, in the best manner that I can.

I tend to see virtually all people who attack me at times; if and when I catch them in a vulnerable moment, as suffering from pain in some ways, and then my empathy kicks in, once their very hurtful behavior stops of course. In my parents, case, I am using the empathy and compassion as a tool to attempt to shut off the hurtful behavior, through the power of love. I am blessed. This seems to have been one of the most challenging moments; and yet I have not yielded; even at some moments when my strength seems almost gone; then I pray or trust; just trust things will work out.

PRESCRIPTIONS FOR GREATNESS

On some level, I am laying out the criteria and handbook for greatness, with respect to what it takes to conquer a great goal. It is both the patience and the perseverance. Again, in the moment it seems like I am occasionally back at square one; I continually remind myself that I have been at this for more than twenty years now. While I often use the date of March 22, 1996 as the point of demarcation and in some ways it was; it was also on or about July 5, 1996, when things took on a life of its own.

Margaret and I had reconciled briefly around May 11, 1996, and we were together for a few weeks, and then she announced that she was going to Europe for two weeks or so; probably at the orchestration of Sondra Myers "oddly." That was quite "weird"[42] and off she went, going back and forth between calling me repeatedly and being independent. Then to top matters off, Morey and Sondra Myers flew to London to meet with her, right before her return; ostensibly to plan more separation activities. Sure enough, the morning after Margaret landed, on our anniversary BTW; I had the audacity to suggest that I could discipline

---

[42] I remember a court worker describing Margaret's behavior as weird as one point.

Iceberg

her cousins while we were in Oklahoma to keep things calm, if needed.

Margaret and I had rented a house in Oklahoma on a lake where our kids and her teenage cousins and the like would spend parts of a month. Margaret in wonderfully (sic) clever fashion had gone to great lengths to rent out our marital home for the month, little did I know her intentions. In any event when I suggested playing a role in disciplining the kids in Oklahoma, Margaret lost it. Margaret began screaming that I had to control everything and she grabbed our kids and began marching off, as we were at a local café. That might have been the relatively irrevocable moment, as this was around June 19, 1996.

From there, the plans became: Margaret was to drive to Oklahoma with our one car, and I was going to fly there around July 3, 1996 with Sophie and Sam. Sure enough when we arrived in Oklahoma the battle lines were relatively drawn. Margaret basically refused to interact with me; her older sister Kathy was also going through a separation with her husband Ray Reins at the moment, and there was all of this crazy energy in the air.

The coup de grace was a shocker. After watching the fireworks in Tulsa on July 4, 1996, Margaret changed her mind and said that I could go out to the Lake House and stay there. Finally at one point we drove hours and arrived there, twenty miles outside of Tahlequah. Once there I admit it, I lovingly got on her about her smoking at one point, and attempted to hug it out with her; that was it. Soon thereafter Margaret asked me to drive back to the store to get three items, napkins, maybe peanut butter and one other; I happy obliged.

When I returned the legal war had begun. Margaret handed me a note at one point telling me that if I did not leave by noon the next day the sheriff would come and get me. I was like for what? I did nothing wrong. I eventually told Sophie and Sam, who spontaneously burst our chanting: "Daddy's right, Mommy's wrong; Daddy's right, Mommy's wrong..." I decided what the heck I had paid for half of the house; our house in Cambridge was rented out, our car was with Margaret, wonderful divorce attorney planning; so I was almost checkmated.

Instead I gave Margaret a note in return, saying I had done nothing wrong, and that I was going to make a sign and sit peacefully by the front door, waiting for the sheriff to come. In a minor miracle; six year old Sophie handed me a notebook/journal to utilize as she and Sam were dragged out the door by her mother and aunt on the way out. Pardon me, the exact date of that occasion was probably July 6, 1996; so in some odd way that in all likelihood was the date that things really began to hit the fan, and this July 6th or so will mark twenty years of that true craziness.

Who really knows? I am trusting God's timing for the most part, but then again twenty years would make for a wonderful end of the craziness. As I have often mentioned that was like the first scene in the Indiana Jones movie, when the big ball comes rolling down the track at Indiana and sets off one amazing escape after another. That was like those what three days waiting by the door for the sheriff, who never showed up were like.

I am shaking my head, because it is truly an amazing moment to trust God; I have done enough, have I not? Speaking of which, I received an email today that the new insert with the Calm Interventions Science of Inner Strength Honor was just about ready to be printed. That piece also seems to reflect a twenty-year cycle of the development and a philosophy of Calm Interventions Inc.

Indeed, as of today, June 17, 2016, the insert piece was printed, in what seems to be record time, and it seems wonderful, as I discovered the printer seems like he is taking a mini-vacation or something. Mini-vacation sounds wonderful. There is so much going on. It seems like the city of Newton called me out a tad, with respect to this resolution regarding the positive transition of tenants of the building we have been living in; not to mention the landlord too. I suppose people seem to think that my basic kindness is a weakness; and I found a way to respond, with a tad of my old school stuff, If nothing else, I have been so tested during this process.

Nonetheless, I like fighting not at all; I hardly recommend it, for the most part my fighting days seemed to have faded; now for loving and working. Speaking of which I wrote a significant Father's Day card, to my father Morey Myers. I had a wonderful interaction with a cashier at Trader Joe's yesterday evening, where I purchased the card. He mentioned a heartwarming kind of story to me; and I shared with him, a story..

Wait, I am not sure I even shared the miraculous baby story from the other day. So I took a little break and went to downtown Boston. I saw Neighbors 2, the movie, had a very nice slice of pizza from Sal's Pizza, and then got on the subway, to ride home. The subway was mobbed, it was an old car, and it was hot, and I was fortunate to get a seat. Right next to me, wasa parent, with a little baby on their lap, and seemingly their grandmother next to them.

Well sure enough, at some point into the ride, the baby began screeching its eyes out, screaming and everything. It was quite annoying on some level in the packed subway car. I waited and waited; as I could not really intercede and disrespect the parent. Finally, after a while, a magic moment arose; I had my little journal in my hand, and tore out a half a sheet of paper, and slowly handed it to the baby. The baby took it, and instantly stopped crying; at which point, ten people laughed and breathed a sigh of relief.

These are the skills of The World's Best Mediator and Calm Interventions, in one having the insight to see a solution; and two to have the human touch to implement a solution. I did not really realize how much that commotion was causing on the subway. It was affirmed as I shared that story, with the checkout person at Trader Joe's; who found the story to be kind of miraculous. Yet, another small and meaningful miracle, in the course of a life of miracles.

It seems that today, I hit upon a "fascinating" notion in my assessment of this families' virtual nightmare, and corresponding opportunity for that matter. The central question that arose today, had to do with whether it was ultimately David or Sondra at root? That is it; that one tiny question. My gut, wants to believe that it is David on this, with the essentially psychopathic behavior, at the most extreme sense. Sondra clearly has manipulated and taken stark advantage of the situation with my children; yet for the moment I am more concerned with whether Sondra initiated it all or David. David meaning also his wife Nomi Stolzenberg; if not mother-in-law Judy Levine.

That is truly the fascinating question. If that is, really the question to be raised. Is there one inspiring negative influence on their side of the ledger that inspires and keeps the embers burning for the hatred and negativity towards me. The word "hatred" may well be a clue, because on David's part it does really seem like hatred. The question being then, is David being pushed forward by Nomi Stolzenberg and her mother?

There is little question that Sondra is extremely deceptive, and has often sought to control my relationships with people, from David, to my ex-wife to my children. If it is Sondra most at root, then it becomes clearer how things could have gotten so messed up; as the emotion in play relating to a mother and child is very deep and can be, with all due respect, somewhat of a mess; if it is not properly understood. It is almost too painful to assess that Sondra is at root. I mean Sondra was a great mother in some ways, somewhat narcissistic, I suppose, but very supportive in our daily life, and at my sporting events.

Maybe it is not my destiny to figure it all out. This is where I am supposed to trust God. Yet God gave me this heart and brain. I do know that David attacked Morey and Sondra first, as being "bad parents;" and that has me in a rational sense, thinking that it was more David. This is where forgiveness comes in too. I mean, no matter how challenging the situation; if and when I merely proceed as being The World's Best Mediator, and do not rock the boat too much otherwise; perhaps I am in wonderful shape. On some level, I did reach an achievement, in the creation of the Science of Inner Strength Honor, so that world is very enticing.

Even further, it does not matter so unfathomably who is at root, as in the bigger sense, I have God on my side. I mean, another minor miracle occurred today, as I set off to my laundry, and I did not want to totally pay the woman $23 to do it; and when I arrived she told me she was going to New York and that she could not do it today. Instead she set me up to do it in the machines on my own, and it cost me $6.75 so far. These are kind of miracle solutions that without God, would not be occurring so regularly. Speaking of miracles, tomorrow night LeBron James goes for his third championship; I had to throw that in there, it would be wonderful to see him do it.

So on this little walk between Dunkin Donuts and the laundromat, I started to say to myself: "Self…,lol; no really what difference on some level does it matter, if it is David or Sondra, it is just hatred, and I will succeed anyway. These are more thoughts aligned with God; not worrying, not fretting, perhaps God is giving me a big test on this one, with respect to no worrying, having faith and trusting in God.

Yesterday I was thinking that David was acting psychopathic; but that does not necessarily absolve Sondra. It might mean that the entire situation is so toxic, that precious little can be saved from it. The work in Newton is positive; perhaps that is just the direction in which to proceed.

My fear on some level, is that I have done so much

work and that it will not come to fruition in the way that I want. That is truly my fear, in its most open sense. Goodness itself cannot be stopped; is my counterpoint. The adjustment has just been finding out how fierce the opposition can be, and not worrying about the future. Worrying makes no sense; just live life one day at a time!

The work that I have done is so much; and I have become so much a better person than I was before; and I sincerely want my work to translate financially as well. I believe it will; I have faith that it will; it is one step after another, one step in faith, confidence and trust after another. Perhaps walking off from Morey and Sondra is what I must do at this point; just letting it all be.

Where is the fear coming from? The fear of looking like a fool, in front of the Newton City Council. I mean why am I giving them so much influence. How much power do they really have over me? I have come too far. All I did was push back a tad, with the resolution that they sought to make tighter. It does seem like the whole land sale move was at least in part designed as another obstacle for me. The question there becomes what does Morey Myers really want from me, beneath his repressive, controlling and even abusive behavior?

Most human beings want love and affection. That is what unhealthy people do to get attention, and their own sick sense of affection. They create one unhealthy dynamic after another to get people to respond to things, because in the main, they do not know their own emotions and needs; and surely then cannot express them in appropriate and healthy ways. So Morey is acting very bitter and sad, who acts in the way he does, due to his failing to understand his love and express it appropriately.

So maybe beneath Sondra and David, lies Morey; perhaps by accident I am coming to an answer. So much of life has to do with people hurt in childhood, growing up with these repressed rages. Every family has their own thing, with all due respect sense of rage and temper on my father's side, comes from a sense of hurt, "what about me-ism," as I would call it, deprivation. That is how people were raised; virtually every ethnic group and the like has been scorned or discriminated against somehow, someway.

People grow up with this sense of deprivation or sense that they have been mistreated and then it manifests in all different ways. My father Morey Myers is a wonderful person, in there somewhere, and yet he represses so much of himself that the way he had learned to communicate is through repressing feelings, tempers, and controlling; rather than expressing the love he has, to share.

To greater or lesser extent; so many of the world's harmful behaviors in addition to legitimate discontents have to do with this notion of people being hurt, and feeling deprived from childhood. That is truly where my sense of healing comes from, I suppose. Maybe I am going overboard on my father, as perhaps it is even more my destiny to utilize those talents and skills locally, beginning here in Newton. Perhaps that is the answer to just go forward with my mission and not worry about the rest; it is a phenomenally intriguing idea.

Well, one day at a time. If money were not involved, would I want to go back and see or even heal Morey and Sondra? Not really is the answer. Perhaps that is another

Iceberg

fear on my part; with respect to not having cracked through, to where I want to be financially as of yet. I am fearful that I need my family to succeed. As Byron Katie would ask through her "Work" theory: Is it true? Is it true absolutely to God? What does keeping this thought do to me? What would I think or be without it?

I do however have a sense of honor for Morey Myers. It pains me, the empathic soul that I am that Morey Myers put so much into our familial situation, and seems to be so confused, by all that has occurred and is opposing his first son for no rational reason.. First, I must protect myself and yet; I see and feel his vulnerability at the root of his anger and tension. So, what can I do, but take it one day at a time.

That was my bottom line, with Jim, a fellow tenant with respect to our Resolution that is pending for tomorrow night. Perhaps I have quelled the opposition. It is fun and kind and soothing to be happy; as today, I am at McDonald's of all places. A woman looked at me, in kind of condescending fashion yesterday, with respect to my writing at Dunkin Donuts; and I just shrugged it off and laughed, and said yes, you can write a masterpiece at Dunkin Donuts and McDonalds. I suppose that would be a major shock for the literary world. It will not be the first or the last shock that I pull off.

If I can somehow tame Morey Myers and my familial situation that would be a miracle of epic proportions. One potentially major breakthrough of today, was stumbling across the notion that the entire element of exclusion, which is what drives my opponents, may well be a psychological tactic embedded in the six year old mindset of Nomi Stolzenberg. For starters the entire mentality of excluding Jon is a six year old, or relatively speaking first grader type of action; everything geared around let's keep Jon out, let's keep Jon away from his rightful stuff.

Indeed one of Nomi's major articles of years ago, was entitled something like: "They drew a circle to keep me out." I would not be shocked if, in addition to the childhood divorce of her parents, a compelling element of Nomi's young girl life was to be patently excluded from some circle or set of events. That entire notion opens up an entire another door unto itself, in that similar to her husband David; Nomi may well have channeled all of her emotional development into academic excellence; rather than focusing on developing other human qualities. I say this kind of thing with an aura of compassion; as people make the choices that they make a six year olds; not out of malice.

It would be rather illuminating however, if the issue of exclusion is important in Nomi's life, and she is taking adult level ferocity to six year old level of development; which is the stunning thing about this situation. People with high positions can have childhood like emotional development; that is indeed what helps to create the iceberg effect: People who are in positions of influence or power, and have not developed the basic skills of fairness and working with other people, and instead rely on harshness, judgments and excluding others as their way of making themselves feel better.

All of this helps to get to the essence of what I would love for my contribution to humanity to be about. Helping us find our inner strength, which is our goodness, our sense of the divine or life itself, along with our positive purpose. Then we learn to cooperate and work together in positive win-win type of discussions. I mean I really believe it is my sacred mission here on this earth, to bring forth this really unique perspective that I truly am uniquely qualified, if not divinely blessed to do.

That message and that work is really my divine blessing and irrespective of what outside circumstances are reflecting; I am committed to bringing that forth no matter what happens I suppose. It takes me a lot to put myself in that situation and follow through and all of that; and yet, it surely is a function of the twenty years of twenty-four seven work. This is a fascinating moment in my life.

It is so clear that I have encountered so much opposition that it is unfathomable, beginning with my own family of origin, to local communities, to our court system. I must sense that so much opposition "oddly" means that I am on the right path, or otherwise why would people use such underhanded tactics to oppose me. I mean if I was in error; they could just use regular tactics, but instead all kinds of rules and procedures away from basic fairness are bent and broken to attempt to dissuade me from my path.

So as challenging as that is; as painful as it can be at moments, I must take it as an affirmation that I am on the right path. The greater error than any that I could make, is that of the level of dishonesty, we are tolerating in society. People accept that corruption as a given; and yet I say corruption and dishonesty will ultimately bring us down, or putting it positively by playing by fair rules, our society will rise.

I am imbued with these kinds of sentiments as I saw

the way that the Newton City Council handled the resolution pertaining to our building; clearly after repeated promises from some, the thing was relatively buried. C'est la vie; it did afford me with an opportunity to get out my Calm Interventions piece, which probably what was best all along. In this way, I was able to communicate with the Council in a gentle and encouraging way, rather than getting upset. I am sure in the main, the world is waiting for me to blow a fuse; AND I really do not believe that it will happen. I am keeping to my message and my ways, in these most challenging of times. In and of itself, keeping to my agenda and keeping calm is a deep victory unto itself, as there are clearly people who are attempting to do things, to purposefully thwart or at least demean me.

I suppose I should take a bow for myself, as another "Jon;" named Meterperel, a Boston media type would say: "Take a bow." Just staying calm, is probably the last thing in the world that these folks meaning at City Hall, my landlord, or my family, expect or want to see. Then again, it is a matter of having a purpose.

When a person has a purpose; they are able to proceed in life; and in the main, disregard the 998 things out of 1000 that could prospectively challenge, distract or even tempt a person, into an artificial, or at least unnecessary conflict. This is where I am proud of myself again, because these are decisions that I am making, not just not to escalate, but to deescalate and/or pose better ways out of challenging situations. While these things are more part of my nature; I have also chosen to push myself into these areas, touching upon compassion and this kind of thing.

My perception of forgiveness has grown and expanded

over recent months and years. This has been a controversial topic for me, and many I suppose. When dealing with people with Iceberg type personality types, surely there were phases as most community forums and online communities promulgate to essentially adopt No Contact. No Contact did not seem so relevant to me, at many points, as the people who I would pose to go No Contact with, were essentially controlling my children; thereby I had to develop other strategies. These strategies, while accomplishing some of the same emotional buffers that No Contact does, to not allow people to hurt me,, furthered my strength, by allowing me to develop insight into their pain, and even compassion for their "illnesses and conditions."[43] It is a remarkable struggle to see if the people that sought to falsely stigmatize me, can ultimately be reached, even turned into empathic human beings.

That exploration is really a major part of my life, on some level; seeing if the haters and other types of despots can ultimately be reached through the approaches that I am developing. It is one of the great questions, if not the great question of my life; well along with just developing programs and approaches for society. It does seem however, that the masses on some level, due to the corruption and dishonesty that I have referenced, are being substantially influenced, by those less than straightforward influences; still I believe in our goodness, That is the positive side of what I am looking to accomplish, to reach people

---

[43] Illnesses and conditions, is a phrase of family, probably derived from Judy Levine; kind of reminds me of
"Silver and Gold;" sung by Burl Ives in the Rudolph, the Red-nosed Reindeer TV program, lol.

with the aim of helping them understand that our good part, our honest side, is the source of true strength within us. Our goodness is our path forward.

I suppose on some level it is my responsibility to share, if not teach. It would be a pretty lonely world, to have developed all of these insights, and then not share them. I am not committed to being a hermit type of person, lol. This is it; I have been given a mission, which I chose to accept, lol[44] to help the world understand smarter, kinder, stronger, more respectful types of interactions. Indeed, at least from what I heard, there is a letter with prospectively twenty one City Councilors signatures on it, pertaining to the work we did; on the sale of the property.

I was just a little deterred wondering about that letter and this morning, I received an email from Councilor Crossley indicating that she now had received twenty two signatures on the letter; meaning twenty two of the twenty four Councilors, with one being absent and one a neighbor recusing himself: What a miracle. Today, June 24, 2016, Councilor Crossley showed up with a copy of the letter, with no signatures, what a hoot, patience and perseverance.

Anyway for today, I really want to focus a tad on the notion of the hurtful mindset of Morey Myers. I mean it is a work of art. Let me preface anything by knowing on some level that Morey is somewhere in there, a great man, who is just psychologically lost. The work I am doing has to do, with whether I can reach him. It is kind of like my landlord too. Can I somehow rise to the degree

---

[44] That was a line from the old Mission Impossible TV show.

of recognizing their rational position even if they are not articulating one, and look past their negative behavior?

It is, as one of my fellow tenants said to me, the work of Job. Maybe on some level that is what I need to do. To rise to that level; that is one path. The other has to do with this notion as to whether I can reach unreachable people like Morey and others for instance. Will positive reinforcement and love eventually reach these folks? Common wisdom of today, would say to write them off. Who knows!?

So, I have come back to an amazing concept at this moment, which is once again, to allow God to fight my battles. I seek to be calm, and place this entire battle into God's hands. Perhaps that is the route to go. It is something that I have been doing a lot of work on, and it is not easy. God has brought me so many tiny victories, medium sized ones; perhaps I am ready through his work for some bigger ones.

It is so wonderful and soothing to think in this manner; that perhaps this is the moment of truth in the twenty plus year work and battle of my life. Perhaps on certain fronts there is no more work for me to do. Rejoice in God, victory is mine. It is kind of funny, signed or not; Stanton, one of the tenants said to me, this afternoon: "You won." It was the first time someone so directly uttered such words to me, in a long time.

I have heard reference or read reference on more than one occasion, with regard to "the peace that passes all understanding;:" with regard to our work with God, and this seems like some of that. Being at peace with God at this moment; trusting deeply in the work that I have done, as well as the essence of God himself. God is present.

June 25, 2016, what a day already. For one, I seemed to come to a sense that Morey Myers was at root, with a mental illness, and I sent an email and a letter out on that basis. Further the internet and presumably cable TV are leaving our home today, at least for the moment, and that will surely be a change in life as I know it. Then I had a conversation with one of the tenants from our building about the entire program that I had put together, and it was kind of inspiring. It seems that this program with tenants both has the capacity to profoundly influence these lives for the better; as well as firmly establish Calm Interventions and The World's Best Mediator in Newton. This may be a moment or the moment to make it all come true; or at least substantially move forward. On some level, I am clearly engaging the city in a high level philosophical discussion about my work and the opportunity to begin to leave my footprint on the city, through this discussion.

It surely is a moment of very high impact to a significant number of people; and I go back and forth between being fully engaged, and sliding out a tad, as these tenants, as well as others, surely challenge my leadership skills, and as I say, I am mainly in God's hands. I mean I was going to let it go for today, and a few days even, but I ran into Anthony today, and life kind of just happened. It is so important not to worry about anything at this juncture. Trusting in God and the universe is virtually the highest priority, before any individual move that I might, or might not make.

The notion of trusting is just amazing. God does send me messages and commands I suppose, with respect to when to act, but I must just push and adjust myself further and further towards a trusting attitude. I kind of threw a fast ball down the plate to Morey and Sondra; not to mention a challenging, well actually passionate note to Sophie and Sam; yet I guess that is just what the situation requires, who am I to question? This has been a productive little run to Needham for now. I cannot be afraid, it is more a matter of trusting that God and the universe has my back.

A "fascinating" little run today. It hit me that the program aimed against me by my family really was evil; and as that word sank in, I thought about David's role. Then amazingly however, in a saving grace type of thing, I began to see a way, where it was not entirely David's fault. The scenario that I began to see, was one where David was both goaded, and mesmerized into taking this vitriolic position against me, to the point of evil, but it essentially a group position. Almost like the Oliver Stone "JFK" movie, where there was this vast mob-like mentality, and no one person was truly responsible. Wow, that is a point of genius; even compassionate genius, as I tend to forgive people, who were goaded.

Everyone kind of likes a fight, and perhaps Sondra pushed David into this position, in taking me, on; where ultimately he stood a risk of getting smashed on some level, in taking me on with respect to my children. Like Margaret Carney was pushed into fighting me, by women and others, who would not have done it on their own or in their own lives, such as Sondra Myers, Pat Rebsamen and others. This is why it was so unwieldly and hard to take on the giant because, it was not a true representation; there was really a group behind, pushing and misusing David to the point of his bizarre conduct.

In that regard I can become my brother's keeper, because people who misuse my brother are dealing with me prospectively. Still David is somewhat accountable for allowing himself to be used in the capacity that he was, if that was the case. Margaret Carney was pushed into fighting me, and it was not a good use of her energy. David was pushed into this position, and he has felt the pushback so to speak. In this way, evil can be created and not one person is truly responsible, like a perfect storm. Other than the unbelievable growth and learning that I did; it was such a misguided use of peoples' time and energy. Ah, everything happens for a reason, if not the best. Nomi may have pushed him out there; although the Scranton energy is stunning.

So today, June 29, 2016, I received a copy of a letter with twenty two of the Newton City Councilors signatures on it, to provide for a positive transition for the residents of our building. On some level this is an accomplishment worthy of The World's Best Mediator. It felt like I was taking on the whole city of Newton with this one. It feels like a genuine accomplishment. I was able to put out a lot of my philosophy and on some level it was accepted by a diverse twenty four member body; no easy feat in this day and age. Props to Terry Morris. Councilor Crossley, President Lennon and everyone.

This result seems like a wonderful affirmation of Calm Interventions and The World's Best Mediator methodology. As I say, it seems like it could be culmination of a twenty year cycle. July 5th or so, will make twenty years since this thing really hit the fan in Tahlequah, Oklahoma, or twenty miles outside of Tahlequah, as I am prone to say. I have pushed up the pressure against Morey Myers, who still seems to have a leading hand in all of this, perhaps accelerated by Nomi Stolzenberg; that is my analysis of the moment, and I am sticking to it; although it is fluid. I am sticking to the process as we say, lol.

What brought this family down to this level? How did my biological mother capitulate to this thoroughly lesser energy? I mean a sheer feeding frenzy broke out around my life. This last stretch has been the most challenging that I can remember; virtually physically bringing me to a standstill; with virtually every shred of my energy expended, and left on the floor. It was a wonderful feeling in a way. You see, it does seem like the entire eviction process around my home, was at least on some level directed at me. Other tenants did not have the wherewithal to fight it per se.

It was virtually like the combined energy of my landlord was correlated with my biological father Morey Myers, and they saw this, as the moment when they were going to take me down. Turning a proposed eviction; into a letter signed by twenty-two of twenty-four City Councilors in my favor is a miracle, so to speak. Some of the tenants said to me: "You won;" and perhaps being just a touch naïve, I did not necessarily correlate that it was a personal victory, as for the most part, I was invested in the cause.

Today, July 1, 2016 I received some blowback from the letter for sure, in the form of, my landlord who is working to get all the tenants out now or "yesterday" as he put it. The truly ironic thing is that Doug feels a lot like my father Morey Myers, in his presentation of things. Not the first time, I am wondering if there is any connection between Morey and Doug; it does seem that way to me, which has led me to the point of sensing that it really is Morey that is behind this unfathomable hatred.

The energy is just so focused, so sadistic; I mean it is really strange to have your father hate you in an irrational way. That is part of the theme of Iceberg itself; the notion of these personality disordered, who have this hatred unto itself; that they just attach to another human being. It is the weirdest phenomenon to have people, particularly blood relatives who hate you for the mere fact of your existence. There is a part of me that is enthused to experience this stuff. Hey, I would surely rather experience being on a beach in Hawaii, but as long as this is what is coming down the pike, it is rather "fascinating." Fascinating directs me back to David, and yes it would be better if David and his people were at root, as I would not have to write another letter, for goodness sakes.

Could it really be that the Stolzenberg/Levine family triggered Morey? That would be a classic unto itself. I would love to let it all go this weekend, and do something fun or rest; and begin to get out brochures on Tuesday, after the fourth; that would be the greatest upset of all. Well the brochures are still a possibility, however the relaxed weekend, is being challenged a tad, as of the last day or two; today being July 3, 2016.

The landlord is trying to put up a fuss about our moving out, or "oddly" it seems like his wife is. I wonder to the degree that my family prospectively has influenced these people. I was thinking of calling Doug, the landlord today, but I let it go; I had talked with him a few times already on my initiation, essentially offering some support to him.

It has been quite a weekend already; as I did two or three mailings yesterday, including one to law enforcement, where I bared my soul a bit. I have either been demonstrating unbelievable courage, or pushing a tad too far; time will tell. I cannot fault myself too much, if I did not call Doug today. I believe I am good enough and that is the main criteria to follow; as I drank some diet coke today, and that also seems to spur a tad of energy unto itself. It is nice to come back to my center in writing this book.

Hemingway himself, is quoted as saying that he always would leave a good idea to write for tomorrow. This situation requires me to be really focused, and that is enough I suppose. I am vigilant, I am plugging in there. Getting Allen out of the home, who is the most vulnerable loosens things up for the rest of us; so one day at a time. I surely could not ever have predicted my life like this.

It is a test for sure. I wrote to Morey today, to ask him to refrain from alcohol. I mean this is all something. I am a great person, and I just need to be calm; I mean it is really the other people that are freaking out; I must remember that. They are threatening things that are not even remotely legal; which kind of implies that they are not talking to a lawyer, in great detail on this.

This is a moment for me not to yield in my method and my approach. There is enormous opposition aligned against me, and yet I am taking it on, in reason, and purpose. The saying I have fallen back on recently is something like: "The opposition is the greatest, right before your greatest miracle." So the thing is to be patient, resilient and calm. I am not wavering, and I am conveying a sense of benefit for all; what can the problem really be? So if I was not perfect today; it looks like I will have a shot at another day of excellence tomorrow. God bless.

This seems like my final exam for something or other; life being this ongoing test that it is.. I have developed a greater appreciation for people who pursue Doctoral degrees, I suppose; the rigors of exams and final exams and all that kind of thing. I mean, I see my project as a larger scope, but then again, I am fifty eight years old, not a twenty something pursuing a doctorate, so immense love and respect to those who pull it off at that age.

What do I mean by final exam? Well, maybe it is forgiveness. What would forgiveness be, in this situation? Letting it go, for one, letting God handle it, and just doing the things that God directs me to do. For the most part. that is what I believe that I have been doing. I must continue to remind myself of forgiveness though; it puts a smile in my heart, some joy on my steps, even as I walk towards a sense of greatness. I have not yet resumed brochure distribution, and tomorrow could be that day; albeit one thing I said I would put on the back burner is the brochure distribution, better to take things one step at a time, and to enjoy myself.

I got a haircut today, and "oddly" that was really fun. Not thinking, not worry, is a wonderful thing, which is also part of my final exam, I believe, although that could be a never ending one. As the process of trusting will seem to repeat itself over and over in one's life. This does however, potentially seem to be a moment, where the work of the last twenty years; the clash even of two ideologies, comes to a head.

Well, it is really more than the clash of two ideologies, I think. What has challenged me, is some of the most mean and hateful of things; still they probably do represent an ideology of "do what your told," and the person with the money gets to abuse others, I surmise. My ideology is about love and light and fairness; which probably scares the heck out of people, who have spent vast parts of their lives beating down other people. You must wonder, or at least I do, for instance that with regard to Morey Myers, my biological father, there is a ton of guilt that stands in his way of acknowledging errors, and making requisite changes.

That is again, where forgiveness comes in, and letting people know that they will not be irrevocably punished or perhaps punished at all, with respect to their past errors. For me as a healer, illuminator type, life is much more about helping people come to new understandings, rather than criticizing or pummeling them for past mistakes, as most people grow up thinking that that is what will occur, and emotionally, if not physically cringing when errors are pointed out to them.

That my dear friends, is a huge portion of my work and message; healing, teaching, inspiring, and not in any way attempting to bring people down. Drawing appropriate boundaries, yes, to reveal to people, places that they cannot go, but not unnecessarily chastising or browbeating people, who for the most part are so sensitive anyway. That is, in the most optimistic sense the work that I have posed for my biological father Morey Myers; we shall see how it plays out.

What is truly extraordinary on some level is that this intense set of letter writing that I did, actually ended up with one coherent theme, at the end of the day. In and of itself that is a miracle, lol. I mean I bounced all around, with respect to who was the person or persons most at root in this situation. The theorem that I ended up engendering was that essentially Nomi Maya Stolzenberg, Judy Levine and David Nathan Myers, were the axis that invoked this horrific psychological axe and psychological fault line within this family. Essentially that fault line spooked Morey and Sondra, and on some level really psychologically devastated them, to the point where, up became down, and down became up, as in Alice in Wonderland fashion.

There were four or five communications over the past several days from me, and somehow or other, they pretty much all ended up in that similar place. So that was a work of genius unto itself. The compassionate portion being that somehow or other, it was bounded by a fair amount of forgiveness as well.

So, a crucial element is, that the letter from the city seems to be doing the task; after the landlord has really taken out his antipathy on me. Anyway, that is how it goes. With all due respect, there seems to be layers of challenged behaviors in play; the type of behavior that is forever entitled no matter what the situation; you have always wronged them, and virtually not ever can you please them, two twin elements of narcissism.

Speaking of which, I issued a challenge of sorts

through the attorneys to David Nathan and Nomi to essentially have a contest as to whose perspective is more accurate in this familial situation. On some level, that is the act of genius itself to put them both on the spot together. Something tells me that they are unfortunately not strong, as a couple and truly depend on their ability to intimidate and back people down; with virtually little or no validity to their adamant presentations.

I would love to appropriately crush, as need be their arguments, and yet on some level I feel so little need to do it, personally; it is just in the familial sense that it would be worth it. I already skipped ahead to two main points in my challenge; one being that there is virtually zero validity to their presentation, and two, there is a world of difference in our intents. My intention is to heal or restore, while theirs' would be to stigmatize and demean other people; which in a familial setting, I would love to turn back.

Quite a start to the day today; as a long time tenant and often nemesis moved out of the building. I actually helped him take a bag out to the car, and shook his hand before he left. I received a virtual death stare from our landlord, who is clearly attaching his total angst about the world on me. My response on some level was to go back at Morey Myers; as I still at least somewhat, attribute the negativity directed at my life to him. Still, again, I am wondering if I can just forgive my way through it. Forgive these people, over and over again. Does that work? Jesus said seven times seventy.

People with that much negativity; it takes an amazing amount of work to address and deal with them. Would I just be better leaving my father behind at this point? What is the access that he has to my head? I mean it is diminishing on some level. There is still the notion I am developing that Morey was infected on some level by Nomi and that is where and how he lost his mind essentially, on all this stuff; which is the miracle angle of ALL miracle angles after all, of this nonsense directed at me.

That is such a fine line to walk that it takes a great deal of Wallenda-like balance on an emotional tightrope. If I am able to pull that off; then on some level the landlord might not turn out to be such an opponent of sorts. The view on that level would be that Nomi is like a giant hornet that has stung this family, and will not let go. "Oddly" it has fallen to me to be the one to correct this, as a brother-in-law from 3000 miles away.

Well that is just God driving me; I suppose I am just along for the ride. God has given me this ability and I have developed it to this degree and. I would just like to get along with people; I have worked so hard to be able to relate to people, and to date virtually all of it has been in challenging situations, very little in relaxing social situations. Oh well, I cannot rally complain; this is the task that God has given me.

It is really important as well, in that Nomi is the mother of three children; which is a most high of honors, and she in the best sense of the word ought to be recognized for this as well. Everybody needs to be recognized on some level; it is virtually everyone's sense of disenfranchisement and fear that hinders them so much. A tough day for America, July 8,

2016, with the shooting of police officers in Dallas.

We surely need a national conversation, and the Science of Inner Strength can help.

On my home front, it has been quite a battle; working to see if the family can turn around and respond, dealing with a building, which has become somewhat opened due to the owner's process of selling it, and today working with Jim a fellow tenant. Jim came to me, and encouraged me, which was good; and yet I ultimately had to strongly encourage him, as the premise of our Resolution is obtain "a safe, serene, and better home." Jim's issues was that he was not convinced that he deserved a better home. In that regard, I said, how in the world could I advocate for him, or others help him get there, if he did not believe himself that he was due better housing.

It seemed like a tough and yet necessary conversation, which Jim and I needed to have. Jim may not have liked it so much in the moment, but we shall see how he responds, as it just does seem that we have to believe we are worthy of something, in order not just to receive it, but to appreciate it. For me, it was a great opportunity to get involved in the baseline level of another human being's life, and really work with them to make a choice and move ahead. We shall see what happens there, no guarantee on that one.

Today, July 9, 2016, a massive chunk of forgiveness seemed to break off my own personal iceberg, lol; well actually perhaps it was resentment or bitterness over what they had done to me, or whatever it was, forgiveness kicked in on a new level. Forgiveness on some level diminishes other peoples' capacity to hurt you, and lets go of some of the pain. I mean things with my children and business are not straightened out yet; but leaving things in God's hands, has a lot of merit as well.

I am so sick of human bitterness; it seems almost everywhere, and I have had to or chosen to fight so long and hard; there are times I would just like to transplant myself to another planet; and I suppose that is what it is about for me, it is a fight for peace. My agenda, my philosophy is a fight for peace in a world struggling to find its true voice.

Maybe my time is truly coming; with respect to advancing my agenda. I mean these shootings and all of that, is really reflecting this kind of chaos in American culture.

Still for me, it comes back to an issue of honesty. A culture that is not honest, in a fair amount of ways, is going to create substantial disenfranchisement and sadly antipathy. I am not happy about that at all; treat people disrespectfully and they will scream, if not rebel, in lesser and perhaps even greater ways. For me it begins with our judicial system, and the moral crisis that I faced with respect to my children and our court system. Unlike the racial tensions; the divorce stuff, is able to be swept under the rug, and it is horrific for sure. Our court system is at the core of American democracy.

Not only do we need honesty, but we need a common understanding of human purpose, and compassion in our outlook and actions towards one another. The pace of society is also confusing a great many people, with respect to leaving behind basic values, and that includes the economic pace and demands, even created by technology. Large corporations and their employees are becoming quite confused by the values in play these days. We cannot really survive and surely thrive without values that have something approximating the Golden Rule in them.

Today, July 12, 2016 I declared David Nathan Myers, once and for all the source of our familial discord. In keeping with the theme of this book, David is truly the iceberg, the one with the psychopathic behavior. Albeit today, July 16, 2016, it seems a tad different. Perhaps it was a matter on some level of clearing David out of the picture that I came head to head with a sense of Morey Myers's illness. So there we stand, at the moment it seems like Morey and I are head to head; I have run into his irrationality.

Flash forward a bit July 20, 2016. It is an unbelievable journey. The reason I suppose that I have shifted to this virtually journal like quality recently, is that on some level, maybe I am in the final stages of this unfathomable fight with the devil or someone like that for my soul. God must want a lot out of me, because the battle for my soul, and indeed perhaps the cleansing of it, have taken on, an other worldly dimension. It is has been twenty years or more, of this unfathomable struggle, with Sophie and Sam at the core.

I mean I put it into spiritual terms, and yet it is also about Massachusetts in a way, and a lot of things. I continually fall back into forgiveness, as a needed buffer on the journey, as it seems that taking on all this alone, is too much for any one person for sure; forgiveness is perhaps where God comes in; albeit seeking as well to maintain a fine line of justice. Yesterday was a time and a moment where I surely did feel like God came to bat for me. I made a decision the day before, to take the leap and get produced my own Science of Inner Strength Honor, as it too seems fitting, and capitalizing on a twenty year process.

I am almost on my knees these day, with how rough and tough this phase of the journey with my very home due to be sold somewhat soon, and the threat of eviction swirling out there somewhere, along with all this other stuff. Intuitively it hit me that the creation of my Science of Inner Strength Honor was the right move in the midst of everything else. Yesterday I went to pick it up, and funds are low at the moment, and I did not know how it would go with the printer, and then the framer, with respect to the economics. Plus I almost rented a Zip Car, for a short spell, as the walk seemed daunting.

Nonetheless, the timing was such that it seemed that I should walk it, as that is a metaphor for the journey. So I got to the printer, and that went unexpectedly smoothly, leaving me relatively beaming for the walk next to a major road in the heat, to the framer. Indeed when I got to the framer, he was out, and his assistance was jovial, and had me leave my piece. I did and returned in a half an hour, and told the framer, Jordan that I came to him, because he once did a small act of kindness for me.

Beyond expectations, Jordan was able to identify color schemes and even terrific pricing for the frame. In short, the Science of Inner Strength Honor was created; Jordan even asked me if this was something that I created, and I said, yes that it had taken me twenty years; and so I guess there is an unfathomable sense of accomplishment there; even though I have not seen all the fruits of success as of yet; while trusting God's timing.

There were several moments with the Science of Inner Strength, when I seemed stuck, and something just came over me, and helped me to push through. I am working to adjust my thinking these days, that I have actually accomplished something great, even though it has not materialized yet. That is the unfathomable thing about this journey is that for virtually the entire twenty years, the light came from within, as it needs to. Yet I was given precious little opportunity to rest or gain applause from the outer world. I cannot complain; something pushed me for sure; and perhaps my own spirit pulled me.

That is why I talk in terms of the journey being one of finding myself. The journey entailed this constant thirsting and questing for the next thing and the next thing, without the rest spots of comfort that some have gotten accustomed to in life. But I suppose even more so; it is fun to return to the notion of letting God guide my path. Clearly in finalizing the Science of Inner Strength Honor, there were just acts of God from John the printer, and Jordan the framer that opened the door to its completion that under normal circumstances, would not have occurred.

I must just believe that the past twenty years will release a wonderful reward, and leave it at that for the moment. I mean some of the work on forgiveness that I have read, does reinforce the notion that we should insist upon justice, and not revenge in our situations. I go back and forth with that, and allowing God to handle things. One passage from the New Testament, says to hold your position and be still; as God will fight my battle. One day at a time for sure; as this has been a rather unfathomable final period or testing period, whatever the case may be.

I am working on proving the theory that if you care enough about a result you can essentially do whatever it is that you set your mind to doing. We shall see, as there is much uncertainty to deal with. That is the astonishing thing about all this, to proceed for twenty years, on some level, just on faith, and the way things are supposed to be; with virtually zero positive feedback for twenty years. That is faith; and now when things seem close or tight; I must just take a deep breath and redouble my faith.

So, I got a news flash today that perhaps the root of the conflict is really David and Nomi's marriage. Today is July 22, 2016, btw, lol. The root of this conflict on some level is David and Nomi's marriage, could that really be it? I mean, it is not David's fault; we only know what we know, but on some level he seems to skim through life on such a superficial level. That is narcissism too, assuming things, buzzing along without really being connected to people. Especially when you have money as well; it makes it just that much easier to buzz along, without really knowing people or situations.

That is the astonishing thing about my experience; when you are put into adversity, emotionally and economically and especially for an extended period of time; you are virtually forced to get to know life and people in a much different manner. It is also a part of being in New England as well, which is a very challenging place. In order to really get by, you are virtually forced to be respectful, and if you have high goals, as I do, you must be calm and being clear that you are not there, to cause any harm, in making progress.

Such an experience can teach you the deepest and

most adept of human skills, so you know people on a much better level, and you are connected to a life. It may not be the life you most desire at that particular moment; yet it is a deeply rooted life. So David and Nomi transplant to the West Coast in the 1980's and get involved in academic settings, and a Temple and kids school stuff, and all; but it is my experience that those experiences are not necessarily deep community experiences, where you really get to know the culture. David and Nomi are both a long way from home and family; and if their interpersonal communication skills are not that developed, they can then be in a somewhat challenging place.

It would explain why they travel around and look to blame me and others, as a virtual raison d'etre for their life. Maybe it is simpler than that; David is just horrific in his presentation to life, and I as his older brother would know that. Perhaps I should just let him sink or swim, or I suppose I was wondering does, Nomi and her mother, really push David into it. David is so repulsive and failing in some ways as a human being in his actions; irrespective of his outward "success."

Today, July 23, 2016 being another day, in a grander ship of forgiveness, I am seeing David in a more compassionate light at least for the moment. Every person who hurts others, is hurt themselves, right? It seems possible to break down the group dynamic of hatred, and perhaps "impose"[45] some respect and decency on the group. Whatever is happening is surely taking every ounce of energy and then some.

Although, this morning, I had a great insight, following

---

[45] Morey Myers's word

a reminder of letting go of my favorite excuse; which is something along the lines that this must be worked out in order for me to be happy. When I let go of that notion, and am just happy unto myself, it brings me closer to God for sure. So the entire notion of trusting God and riding in God's stream of greatness is a wonderful thing, which is accessible to us, at virtually every moment. Being happy in the moment is such an inspiring thing, and it tends to bode well for future events, because, when we are in joy and in God's stream, things pretty much, must go well. In being in the moment is such a hard thing, in some ways, as it goes against our conditioning. There are any number of ways to approach it; one of my favorite is a passage that I keep on my Kindle Fire, entitled: "Let go and let God handle it."

The notion of such a thing is that at any given moment of stress or heaviness, to let go and tell yourself to let God handle it, with any challenging situation. I really am virtually laughing out loud, as it goes so much against our grain; and I must say that it may well take considerable spiritual work to get to a place, where you can even contemplate such a thing, to have that trust in what is occurring, and not struggle or fuss all over the place. It is a fine line, although the thought process is that God will reveal to you the appropriate course of action at the right time; so all of our fussing and worrying is unnecessary, and in fact contradictory to allowing God's good will to occur.

For instance my family has ostracized me for twenty plus years, my landlord is going nuts on the sale of the building, we face eviction; the funds are not there, and I am just riding in God's stream, being happy and upbeat, actually using this situation to insist that the right solution will occur in time. So, it is only stressful, as I allow it to be, or let it go, and sit within the joy of God, trusting that the right answer will occur, bit by bit, or for that matter, in what ever manner God allows it to occur.

It is almost scary as I recite it, prompting me to wonder what must I do? Is waiting patiently enough? Or for that matter, I have taken my laundry to be done, and here I sit at Dunkin Donuts, and the next bus is not due for ninety minutes after this. Will I be okay for ninety minutes at Dunkin Donuts, just writing and stuff?

MELTING THE ICEBERG

The question becomes on the notion of an iceberg, such as David; is it possible to melt that? I mean, I have no idea as to whether the goals that I have are even possible. Can you turn the entire dynamic of hatred that was erroneously directed at me for all these years, into love and a normal family again? How far will it go? It is an exhausting journey. I am going to settle for anything rational, I suppose. Yet suddenly today, I see some possibility of breaking down David, or seeing through his hatred, and/or pain.

I am a little nervous, I just spontaneously applied for a credit card on line, without having had one in a while. Shockingly my credit score survived the financial storm; and it was recommended on a credit website. Still, I feel a little up in the air, after submitting the thing. Oh well, it is not like I did anything illegal or anything.

Stick to what I know for the most part at the moment. I am kind of shocked that I am seeing David in a slightly different light; with some softening of that image. The unbelievable thing about this journey is how much is dealing with the unknown. Very little of this kind of thing has ever been done before; to work or attempt such a long range reconciliation or mediation, which was based on such a level of hatred and animosity. If on some level they did not have my kids trapped behind enemy lines, perhaps I would not be doing it; yet that is the hand that I am dealt.

The other question I play with, at times, is whether I would do better just to drop that entire thing; and move ahead with my business. The problem is, that people are patently brainwashing my children, and as their father, it is appropriate for me to intercede. Better again, to lean into God's understanding, and not to try to figure too much out on my own. Keep in my joy zone. For today it is a matter of getting laundry done, and then RCN is due to check on my internet service.

It would be wonderful to get this familial situation to a better place. Perhaps on some level I would do well do understand that maybe it will not occur; or better said due to the strength of my business idea, I do not need it to be resolved. One day at a time. God will direct me to the proper course. This was underscored through a communication with the Attorney on the real estate transaction for our building, Terry, who indicated that God would direct my path, and then pointed out that it was the Book of Proverbs 3: 5-6; which urges us to rely on God's understanding, not ours.

It is a wonderful notion for not worrying, and trusting that God will be there in the long run, and at every challenging moment to catch and to guide us. So, the question becomes how much of our thought process is real and how much is worry? Is so much of our energy kind of useless thought and worry? That is what Eckhart Tolle would tell us that the mind is responsible for so much wasted energy and fear; and that it is our heart and deeper presence that is what we are all about, in a much calmer and more peaceful way.

On some level it should not bother me if my family comes around or not. The disconcerting thing has do with the financial piece, and yet somehow I must trust in God, that I am a person of profound worth on this planet and that it will get understood somehow. Then there are my kids and worrying about whether they will return or even dealing with the injustice of their being redirected away from me. One notion again, would have God handle it all; which is really something.

Could I just look for a small living place now, and move; and trust that everything will get sorted out over time? God will decide. So I submitted an ad on Craigslist entitled: "A great addition to the right home;" so I am willing to look at new options. My point of leverage does seem to be to get this right on this go round. My business may really be my greatest strength at the moment; other than my all around good nature. This is a liberating feeling; this notion of letting go and just being in the moment, even releasing my need to know and all of that; considering other less heavy options. Indeed, my shoulders are a percolating with energy, as if a burden was lifted off of them.

I will be alright financially no matter what. I must believe that. Not only have I gotten to know New England in a much deeper way, but my ideas are unbelievable in terms of what the world needs now. The media is so obsessed with the Presidential election, due probably to the revenue that they create, and yet this is a deeper philosophy that will probably not get captured in this election;

and that is okay. I am open to a new life at this point. Well it seems like I am making it for those extra ninety minutes at Dunkin Donuts, on this Saturday morning. It turned out to be fun, and rather enlightening.

Today, July 24, 2016, I find myself in the same scenario, with an extra hour and a half at Whole Foods; so today, I am not nearly as worried, with yesterday's experience, lol. I just shared with my kids a funny little anecdote, which told me that everything would be alright. I am here at Whole Foods, and I step up to the deli counter, and order something that I rarely do, a third of a pound of roast beef. So the next dude after me steps up and orders a third of a pound of roast beef, and then another gentleman steps up and orders a third of a pound of roast beef. We kibitz about it, and he says, he "never" orders a third of a pound. This little roast beef episode was a wonderful piece of synchronicity of the universe, and somehow I am taking the leap of faith to say that everything will work out, especially pertaining to this real estate situation, business/finances and family.

I suppose God is still testing me so that I do not panic at this critical moment. If nothing else, I am exhibiting my abilities to stay calm under pressurized situations. Maybe it is the final stages of the coal being turned into a diamond that intense heat, of the shining process. I survived another round of verbal abuse from the landlord. I am not certain why it does not bother me more than it does. Again, it relates to staying calm under pressure.

I am more prominently feeling like it was David and/or his related parties that put this overarching animus and rancor on this family. It is hard to say what to do about it. I continue to speak the truth, within the family. To the degree that Morey and Sondra were victimized by it, more than initiators; that dramatically diminishes the requirement for more court action, if they were victims. Still, I am not going to get overrun by people, no matter what. As I say, it is a matter of faith, to lean in to God's aura and trust; and wait for my instructions from that.

Perhaps trusting that all will be well, is enough. Maybe identifying David is enough, for my part. We shall see. Today, July 25, 2016, I am wondering if I must force open the doors of the situation, driving to Scranton, for instance. Also this morning, it is worth interjecting that I resumed my brochure distribution for brochures of the Calm Revolution today, and I really felt great. It was that feeling that that was the real me, which is the feeling I must keep alive and kicking.

I suppose there is a theory that I am really the center of gravity in this family and it is their efforts to ostracize me that are so bizarre. I am grateful for all I have; that is such a wonderful place to begin. So what do I have? I have confidence, I have a dream, I have two wonderful kids, I have clothes, I have a few bucks in my pocket, I have a heart, I have kindness, I have a vision for the world; so what else could a man ask for? Let's talk about the dream for a moment. What is my dream? My dream is that the things that I have learned will translate into economic success and an ability to make the world a better place, as well as to revolutionize the world possibly. Why those goals? It just seems like I have the ability to do those things, and I would like a great life for myself.

Is there something wrong with that? No, actually it

seems like I am rising to my God given ability in that regard. Today, July 26, 2016 seems like a watershed day. I came to the conclusion that Morey Myers in particular was so irrational and thereby he was entitled to forgiveness, with respect to the notion that I could have just nothing to do with him. His current state. I could not spend energy trying to change him or control him; and thereby forgiveness seemed like the plausible option. It was pretty revelatory for me. He is, who he is; it was a rather brutal process in terms of letting go; and yet, I did, and even let other members of the family know my opinion as well.

It is a seminal moment. It is like I just stumbled into this understanding in miracle fashion, particularly in coming up with the last line of this letter that I wrote. A person who emotionally abuses you; it can almost be like a hive of hornets in your head, or a drill going into you. I am grateful that I have persevered as long as I have. On some level, maybe Morey Myers will finally get the sense that I am more important in my own life than he is; that is another horror of the emotional abuser, they are so misguided emotionally, they think on some level that your life is their life.

Forgiveness seemed to be virtually the only way to break that bond, given the degree of family ties involved. I keep wanting to feel like it is over, and I am not there yet. It is these letters I write; they are such a fine line, between being accurate and really pressing the envelope, with respect to what is appropriate. At least I ended on a note of forgiveness. It is such an incongruity to have your own family in an emotionally abusive situation for over twenty years; our mindsets just do not think in those terms. We have these views of normality, and it is taking these iceberg like phenomenon to really change our perspectives. Well, I must keep speaking my truth or not; as forgiveness may overrule. Could I really forgive it for good, and go on with my life? What a miracle.

Forgiveness to me, is giving things back to God. God can handle this thing. I must sever that emotional connection to my father, as keeping it open on some level, allows him to penetrate my mind in a hurtful fashion. I surely will pray that he gets some help; as no one really deserves to be in that much pain. Still, it seems very much beyond my control.

Well, I put myself out on the limb somewhat this morning; writing to Doug Turcotte, essentially that he did not have a great legal position in things with our building, and to back off, and let the letter signed by the twenty-two City Councilors take effect. I am ambivalent about doing these type of things these days. I went through so much conflict; I am sick of fighting with people. Is it possible just to be a kind and caring person in this day and age?

I suppose as is the theme of this book; it is a challenge in a world where there are people with personality disorders. That is where our tough outer covering must come in. It reminds me of some wisdom, my late grandmother Mae Gelb shared with me, an old

Israeli expression: "Be like the cactus; tough on the outside and sweet on the inside." At the time she told me in 1996, I realized, probably like most people that I was tough on the inside and sweet on the outside. If nothing else, I have done that successful work of becoming oriented in the right way as a human being; I am now tough on the outside as need be, and sweet on the inside.

I am tired though, and boy could I use a rest. I feel like taking a day of vacation in the midst of all this. Where would I go? Is there a one day Cape or Berkshire thing that I could pull off? That is kind of interesting. I keep telling myself to trust the process; it is possible that this conflict could come to an end today. I read a nice article last night the theme of which was to trust God's timing, it could be today, tomorrow, twenty years from now; the date is already set, so let go and trust.

I also a came up with a, or the stellar angle with respect to our familial situation. I realize that Morey on some level is really not rational, and that he truly does need some help. I was able to put it in helpful and constructive, if firm tones today, and that is liberating. At that localized level, I am beginning to believe that it is more than possible to eventually get him to have the right conversation about taking care of his own needs. This is a breakthrough,; albeit I am so groggy with this situation that I can barely feel the feelings associated with it at the moment.

Maybe I really need to leave these folks, or at least be willing to do so. Even if it means my children at this moment, what can I say. I mean, I believe in Calm Interventions. I must trust that whatever is happening is happening for my benefit, no matter how hard it is. I did have an awakening through a dream today, and on this element Esther Hicks has some good stuff; that bad dreams can be a lack of belief in ourselves on some level. One cannot rush the process.

I must trust what I have become, If my family repudiates me totally; then that is the way it will be. I can only say this must be the most irrational, the most unfathomable familial repudiation of another person in history. I mean, I really feel that way. That is my solace; that is my redemption, in a way, to have survived this, to have become a better and stronger person through the process. Maybe my familial thing will never work out.

Yes, "oddly" that is the upside: To have survived something that one should never have survived. Maybe that is the story of my life. I want to put this story in its proper context. In this age, when people will criticize you for anything, the comprehension of something like emotional abuse is so far removed from our modern understanding and yet, I am convinced that understanding emotional abuse is the key to a better society. It is only by understanding emotional abuse that we can open the door back up to decency.

Understanding emotional abuse is the iceberg, by which we must begin to understand that the meanness and coldness in our culture cannot continue. It is only by understanding how much we do not like cruelty; that we can then affirm how much we embrace caring and respectful behavior. In that regard it is recognizing that a man who was put into a psychological torture chamber like me, could well then develop this intense commitment to humanity, respect and decency.

It seems like the first moment that I am seeing that; maybe it does not depend on resolving things with my family, or at least what I have become stands on its own, no matter what. That according to Esther Hicks would be one of the problems with interpreting dreams and the like; it means that I am claiming myself as a champion; not lacking in anything at the moment. To believe the things that I have achieved, and the process has generated genius. I feel much more at peace in a way; intuitively on a deeper level, like this was ALL meant to happen.

This is a feeling of confidence in who I am, and feeling like the journey was really worth it. It seems like the first time a feeling of ease has come over me; I am a little skeptical after a dream during the night, but it is a matter of believing in myself intuitively. Maybe the dream was pushing myself towards this breakthrough. Emotional abuse can do that to you; make you question yourself on a deep and dark level. Even while in the outer world, I feel confident enough to be The World's Best Mediator, my inner world was not totally there for some reason. Now I feel more aligned with myself.

It feels like a major piece of an iceberg just melted off me. That is funny; I was perceiving a lot of the iceberg to be from others, and perhaps it was, but now, I see I also had my own wall of an iceberg up as well. Wow, what an experience to go through. To live your life at this level of introspection and self-discovery; it is a blessing unto itself.

Perhaps that is the story of completion, to be able to walk away from my family; or even more on some level to sense that I am a full and healthy man. I mean I have been saying it, but feeling it on the inner layer of our being is a great feeling for sure.. That is the thing, we all have a kind of inner membrane of us that relates to our feelings, and until things have settled on that level, we have not fully inculcated the changes into the fabric of our being. So we shall see how I sleep tonight, as to whether I really have made these strides that seem possible.

This whole manner of relating with harsh people is hard, as a lot of me, just wants to be this kind and gentle person. Perhaps I just need a tad of a break from the old game of life; even taking an hour or two of quieter time today is wonderful.

July 30, 2016, the heat is on; the landlord is pushing his eviction stuff. I suppose on some level, I am leaning towards the conclusion that Morey Myers is most at source in this situation. Morey certainly has the capacity to deflect attention from him, and towards people against me. It is such a weird feeling to have your father hating upon you, after raising you in a certain manner. In that regard, maybe my life was always about him from his point of view and not about me.

July 31, 2016, this morning, I heard a rather inspirational sermon by Joel Osteen, who was talking about my favorite topic of the moment, with respect to forgiveness, and letting go of negative energy. It kind of inspired me, with respect to letting go of all of this stuff; maybe my re-work is sufficient as is, and perhaps it is the best way to reach Morey Myers, is to meet him at the notion of his goodness; surely he cannot need a great deal more strife; even if his behavior is so out of whack. Could he just need love? While I began to draft interesting court documents; could love reach the same result much better. Maybe too, with forgiveness, there is no urgency

Last evening, I had an epiphany with respect to Morey Myers; that he truly does have a mental illness. I have said it before, and yet it really hit home with me, how offbeat he is, on some level. I do believe this was kind of a breakthrough of the likes of a piece of the iceberg falling off. What is truly amazing, is that this conflict has gone on so long.

Today, being August 2, 2016, I must comment on the long-running nature, both in terms of my unwillingness to yield over the course of more than twenty years; and their actually holding onto such hatred for so long. Stumbling onto the deep notion of Morey Myers having a mental health challenge, as I put it today, could be the beginning of the end on some level: Mainly because, I am committed to defeating it through patience, firmness and love, if possible.

My body is feeling some pain in the magnificence of the journey, and today I blogged about rejoicing in adversity; that old Biblical sense that adversity is how we get "perfected" and God's purpose reveals itself to us. So after twenty years of adversity; I say bring it on; I am figuratively, not masochistically rejoicing in my pain; like a boxer in the fifteen round, who now smells the championship.

We shall see, as again, one cannot predict God's timing. Speaking of the notion of acceptance; I did read a very interesting article that made a distinction between forgiveness and acceptance this morning. It is a wonderful distinction and illuminating in some ways; albeit, on some level, I am still dealing with the unacceptable, and while I can accept people for who they are; I am still working for a better resolution.

This Friday, Morey Myers is expected to turn eighty nine; and that is starting to get old, and perhaps then he can accept the handwriting on the wall that he will not bring me down. Who knows, in addition to stumbling into the notion of Morey Myers's mental illness, I also came up with a "fascinating" concept in which to present myself, prospectively in court or anywhere I suppose. Actually I will give some credit to a preacher by the name of Joyce Meyer, who talked about "Letting God handle it;" after praying and meditating after watching a talk of hers, I came to the notion that essentially someone was not supposed to survive what I went through, I am winning already.

The amount of emotional distress that I have endured over the past "decades" is precedent setting and off the charts. It is the kind of thing, where you could expect the doctor to come out and say; he was not supposed to survive that, but I did. That could almost be the secondary theme of this book, if not the main one: "He was not supposed to survive it but he did." It is a line that would allow me to go back into court, essentially stating that what I have done is unprecedented, and blah, blah, blah.

This is why I can go at my own pace these days, I suppose; and believe that my honor is worth it, and in essence I deserve to act like a champion, even though all the fruits of those efforts have not yet arrived. Still my body is really sore, and each little errand seems like reaching for the stars at this point. Like I have some medicine to grab and even food for tonight, and yet I seem quite happy just writing this book, and taking it a moment as it comes. It feels like heaven sitting in this pizza shop.

Well, I am ordering an Italian sub to go; that ought to hold me until tomorrow; the medicine antacid stuff is not due until tomorrow so one day at a time. There is truly a joy in that approach. I am reveling in just the simple stuff; writing in the sub shop, and the Italian sub to go, as the bus is due in six minutes, so we shall see.

So a rather seminal point came yesterday, or today even. Today being August 4, 2016; yesterday I submitted some court papers pertaining to Morey Myers, and yet today, I seemed to come to the solidifying element. I realized that above all else, my bottom line was that Morey Myers was involved in excessive bullying of me, along with Sondra Myers, and that was the moral element upon which I would be able to stand all the way through. Nobody can truly bully another person, and that is a piece that gives me both confidence, as well as a sense that they will come to their senses sooner rather than later.

It has been quite a journey and that really could be the culminating piece, or at least close to it, with respect to moral and emotional solidarity with myself. I feel like it gives me the upper hand, finally after twenty some years. One day at a time.

The key is also being happy in the moment; you cannot be too obsessed about court fights and this kind of thing. I mean yesterday I listened to some Esther Hicks stuff, and she was advocating against court fights, as it takes us out of our joy spot, our "vortex" as she calls it. I was influenced by her arguments, albeit not completely; it is what led me to break off my writing at the point that it got too painful, and just write what I feel comfortable in writing and go with that; so that was a breakthrough onto itself. It reminded me of one summer when I was a kid, and some counselors put me into a boxing match. I was working on technique and trying to be a boxer, and the other guy clubbed me down a few times; to the point where I just started to wail back, and all sudden I knocked him down a couple of times, before his backer moved in and stopped the fight.

There are some nerves about the whole thing, but I am not really afraid of the whole court thing that much. I have done all that I can at the moment, and that is the important thing; leaving room for God to do his work as well. It has been a most amazing journey. Yesterday Magdalena, Doug, the landlord's wife showed up and we had an interesting conversation. I am fearful that I shared too much with her, but what the heck can I do; I will reach my goals, God is with me.

Magdalena reminds me my fight is a Biblical level fight. So it has been awhile. I have been immersed in the legal mindset; doing some studying of the Esther Hicks stuff, around forgiveness, and this kind of thing. Esther Hicks ascribes that essentially we should not do anything that does not feel good, that in essence takes us out of our alignment. So at times, this court stuff feels awful. I feel called to do my philosophy and the Science of Inner Strength with the world; that energy seems to be calling me, if I let the family stuff go.

The thing was, I submitted the documents, because I did not want to be bullied anymore, and on some level there is nothing wrong with that. It just takes so much energy on some level, even prospectively thinking about it. Can I move on with my philosophy, and stop trying to convince my parents, not to be abusive? It is evil however, to be brainwashing another person's children.

Well, a tiny thing happened this morning, August 11, 2016. I received a text from Magdalena Turcotte; the landlord's wife, asking about my move, in a positive and encouraging manner. It was kind of a miracle to have, at least entered into congenial conversations with them, and that stands as a small, yet very important piece in terms of this situation. Doug, for unexplained reasons was a real negative at me, and it seems that I have neutralized, if not turned around that situation, at least towards win-win, which kind of leaves my family, as prospectively the last remaining obstacle.

Virtually right after the communication with Magdalena, space was cleared for me to communicate with Mike Perry, attorney for Morey and Sondra, with the aim of engendering some win-win thought process on their part. It seems clear to me that David really is the impetus for this twenty eight year cycle of negative energy, and there must be a moment when common sense will emerge!

One day at a time. Emotionally, it is quite a lot to take on the whole court thing; the thought of these big law firms, the court, ah yes, lions and tigers and bears, oh my. I have worked through my position enough to affirm that I just want to be treated fairly and that is the reason for my taking this action as well as to protect my sacred children; I have even developed some understanding for those who have challenged me so much, so what else can I do. My landlord started a tad of harassment, but I was unclear as to whether I should let it go or confront it; I kind of let it go.

What else can I do; I am a wonderful person, I cannot

get into every fight. There was a city letter that carries more sway. Ignoring people is not something that I am great at; what it will do, is inspire me to get my notes out to the remainder of the City Council. Just be happy sometimes, is what I tell myself; do not into the sink pit of all things going on. I am just being loving now, feeling very loving.

That is an ideal, to become love itself. One must maintain boundaries too, in this day and age. So the saga continues, I laugh. God must have wonderful faith in me, for giving me these challenges to handle. It is one of these deep questions, as to when to attempt to heal a situation, and when to let it go. I kind of let a medium sized one go recently. I did not really like the tone and tenor of things with my printing company, and I essentially walked away from them. It was a rather fascinating one, it happened like Ali taking Foreman in the eighth round; it just happened suddenly. On some level, even through all the pain, I am laughing at the situation with my parents to some degree; it is so bizarre for people to turn so unfathomably against you. I am also working on the notion of handing it over to God. What else can I do on some level? God does rectify things.

Maybe the sooner I hand things over the better.

Wow, I kind of did that, now what? I seem to have a lot of extra energy in my life, not to mention a void, where worry used to exist, lol. It is slightly funny, because I do not know how long these feelings will hold, how long can I release things to God. My father is my father; he is a different person than me; even saying that I develop an enormous amount of empathy for him. That is the problem on some level, I feel for him; I want better for him. I may be better off, letting him be who he is, but what a painful lesson, what a loss for me temporarily.

That is a crucial question: What is the loss for me? The loss is that innocence; that sense that things will be well; albeit, by substituting God into the equation, rather than Morey it is supposed to be the same result. Better to depend on God, than Morey is the lesson perhaps. What did Morey mean to me? Morey meant a sense of dependability, a care for me, a sense that things would be okay. I still have this love for all things; it kind of makes me love him more, not solely for my sake, but his.

So today, August 14, 2016, I received a warning type of thing from Mike Perry Esquire, not to email him. I am saddened by how screwed up this familial situation is. This is where forgiveness comes in again. Do I dare just drop the entire matter, and let it go to God? Drop the entire court stuff. On one level, I can declare victory in declaring that David and Nomi were at root of all this. America is so corrupt right now, it is bizarre.

This is one of those moments, when it appears that people are coming in from all sides. Maybe that is my saving grace to go into an American court and just share how screwed up it all is; and then they might just deny me a hearing and make me look like the biggest moron in the world, prospectively. What would forgiveness look like?

It would mean victory to me. How? It would mean that I did not become an evil person, by the evil done to me; I grew stronger and better. What about money? I will be in excellent shape. How? God will provide. I must just trust at this moment; it is not the moment to give up. I am dealing with pure hatred, so it is a victory to stand against it, no matter what. I sense my mother Sondra as part of this too; it is so sad.

On that basis, it is a wonder just to consider standing against it. It is an honor, on some level to oppose evil. That is the dilemma; do I just do this patient and forgiving mode, forgive all together, or let it rip from the hip? Let's see the aggressive approach, would be to let it rip; the passive one, would be just walk away, and the assertive approach would be to respectfully bring it before the court, at this point. The other option too, is whether delineating David and Nomi is enough to stop it? Are they really the two destabilizing influences, and can something positive arise by identifying their energy?

Through it all, my capacity to take things one day at a time, is a real strength, is even my capacity to laugh. I may do the forgiveness thing, lock, stock and barrel. Still feeling the sting somewhat of Mike Perry's shot at me today; I sent out a note along the lines of forgiveness about Nomi today. I am walking a real thin line. Something pushed me into the I Ching today, wow, I got some nice readings. I am not certain, if I want to deal with that every day. The hardest part is the indecision, like I perseverated about calling Mike Perry today. Was that a chicken out decision on my part, or was I was not giving in to an obsessive type of thought?

On one level, I am not really worried about this stuff so much, and then I read stuff, like make peace with people before you go to court. There is so much craziness out there. Actually today, by being patient, I did come up with a wonderful angle as far as a response to their stuff, along the lines that there are really two different agendas: Mine is to bring peace and Mike Perry's is to bring division. Also I am somewhat losing sight of the notion that my original thing was, about, not being bullied.

The other thing is that if I was trusted God fully and was not worried about money, where would I stand as far as all this stuff. I mean honestly speaking if money was not a factor, I would just move on, and not even worry about these folks. What about Sophie and Sam? I suppose I would just have to let it go too. It would be kind of fascinating. On one level they are really being brainwashed and that might truly be a job for God to handle.

Well today, August 16, 2016, I seemed to take the big leap of faith. I moved to forgive the entire situation. Just like that, I also told my landlord that I would move out

September 1, 2016, and it was a major move. I could be right; I mean I made a move to let go. It is not what is in vogue in culture today, with the sense to "stick to your guns;" but what if, I would rather stick to my common sense and love, rather than my guns? I found an element inside of me, that decided to honor Morey and Sondra as good parents from my growing years, and stick with that element as the mode to end hostilities from my point of view.

It is a little up in the air, as today also I an anticipating the possibility of receiving a document from Mike Perry that is aimed to singe my rear end, but perhaps on that level, I escaped just in time. I am not certain that I must take on the legal system. Plus, I am trusting in God on a much deeper level to handle things. I continue to wonder as to whether this entire saga also was about me purging some habit of mine. One thing, I am also working on is the notion of not worrying about money.

Just by subtracting that element from my life, and perhaps even a dependency on my family, the world looks like a different place. Think about it, if you are not worried about money; then the world is wonderful. I wonder, on some level if money is just created to intimidate and partially divide people. The world is an open possibility at this point; we shall see. It was a courageous step to let go, in this manner.

It does challenge that basic notion of feeling like we must clamp on and control every detail. Some people are more detail oriented, The best me, is a spiritual, natural, handsome type of dude. I am a thinker, a mover; somebody who cares about humanity.

So, on the familial front, it seems that the Red Seas may be parting a tad; it could be too early to say. I am beginning to see a way to approach the court, if need be that is keeping in my spirit of peaceful and calm interventions, along with a forgiving and fair approach. It is like, my father has done a ton of good; it is just that he has an impaired perspective, that keeps him limited, and unfortunately is hurting mostly me, and the family as a whole, as well.

The key for me these days, is turning things over to God, and allowing things to unfold in the best and most peaceful manner. One could virtually never have predicted that it would unfold this way; yet it is, the way it is. I must continue trusting; that is the way and means. This is one of the most wondrous lessons to learn about life, which is to ride with the tide and the natural flow of events; doing your things as well, but mainly in accord with some of the bigger things that are happening. When a person sets out to do it, all their own way that the universe can push back, even with umbrage.

So this is wonderful what this juncture in life is teaching me, especially when there is inordinate pressure. Under such pressure and time constraints, it is vital to make accurate moves, and not the wrong move. Understanding the rhythm of life allows one to act gently and in accord with what the larger universe is doing, and not against its nature, which can be horrific. Well this is a relatively wondrous outcome for now.

I had a breakthrough seemingly today, essentially saying that Morey's illness or impediment was at root of things. I was deeply moved to say this, and then I forgot to send the court withdrawal thing; yet maybe that is best. I am convinced that Morey's illness is at root, and I just need to rely on God for the best way for this reality to rise to the surface. It truly is a "fascinating" situation, as I am twelve or so days from my move out date from my apartment, and I have neither a place nor money; yet just a trust in God and a belief I suppose in the logic of this situation, if not the merits of my advocacy; so we shall see how it all unfolds.

Not worrying is a basic parameter of many of the modes that I am following these days; so that is the quality I must follow. One day at a time; I must put my trust in God, one day at a time. Actually a breakthrough later today, August 20, 2016; it seems to me the true malice on some level is coming from David; I am moving back to the theory that he overran Morey and Sondra, and that is the root of conflict here.

So today, August 22, 2016, I went back to court, and filed some papers. Initially I felt very good; and then there is the sense that you are in somebody else's hands. I have just taken so much abuse from people, I decided to stand up again; so I am proud of myself no matter what happens. I feel like I should have done the same, with my landlord; it is different though by a substantial margin; one is more feelings and the other is more actions. Anyway, I did my best; there seemed to be little other way to go, after receiving an email from Richard S. Bishop, Esquire that my emailing Morey and Sondra seemed not to have positive effect. I mean, I have not ever heard of a group of people laying on another with emotional abuse for so long, in such a malicious and distorted way. I attempted to reach them through compassion, and that just struck out. Once you file a court action your feelings change; I mean I see their actions as the low of the low at this point, Morey and Sondra, goodness knows what they have been involved with over time

Only people who have done really awful things would act this way to another human being. The ostracizing, the defaming, the need to exclude me from my own life, the psychotic desire to cut me off from my children. It is unbelievable; today is almost twenty years to the day from my ex-wife submitting her complaint for separate support in Probate and Family Court on or around August 21, 1996; it took a while to go full circle.

What is interesting is that up until today, I was somewhat nervous about my father Morey Myers being eighty nine years old, and the prospects of his passing away. Now, having filed that court action, I must say that it matters less to me what happens. A man cannot abuse another human being for twenty plus years and expect any warmth or reciprocity at this point. Well, today, August 23, 2016, who knows?

It does feel odd, to enter a court action; yet it seemed worse to be the recipient of peoples' abuse. It is really the work of trusting in God at all times. If it was clear that I was not worried about money; then there would be a lot less to worry about, right? Life is fascinating right now. On one level, I feel relatively calm and peaceful inside. My landlord kind of freaks me out; well put that aside for now.

Perhaps it is significant that I took on the true bully of my life in Morey Myers, not to mention Sondra; those two can be wicked together. Still today, August 24, 2016 is a new day, and I must say, I am somewhat exhilarated by returning to the notion of one of my original themes that of how, challenge, can be the great wake-up call of our lives, and we begin to develop strengths, that we could not ever known we had.

I am beginning to see the possibility of this long, long conflict being over. For one, I somewhat extracted the energy of Richard Bishop, the asshole attorney from the situation; which opened up realms of understanding. I was back to some sense of compassion for people, and even moving back to the sense that Nomi and David had a lot to do with this. Even further I started to see some of the roots of Nomi's adamancy back unto her family, and I put out some vibes that what Nomi actually really needs is love and acceptance. I mean why on some level are people so extreme or adamant? I suppose because in the realm in which they grew up, they were not universally love or accepted.

Nomi was actually the editor of the Harvard Law Review; she was probably pushed so much into such a high level, and perhaps not really ever even accepted for herself. Nomi also has a very sweet and nice personality in some ways, and it is too bad that people are not encouraged and/or taught that being a good person is as high an honor as anything else in the world.

Mainly I am trusting as much as possible, during this extraordinarily hard time myself. It has pushed me more towards familial reconciliation and care, for sure, which is perhaps the beginning, middle and the end of the intention of the journey; we shall see.

The Science of Inner Strength Honor is what it is all about too. "Oddly" I feel somewhat at ease; actually I just took a wonderful detour to the Needham Public Library, what a gift of a place that is. I got to sit in relative comfort for an hour or so, for what seemed like the first time in ages. I listened too, to a couple of videos from Bill Fergueson pertaining to letting go and trusting; and they were just wonderful; one I even sent to my children. Bill focused on telling yourself; you will be alright no matter what; and that is an attitude I have had for so long.

Okay, so perhaps I got some footing. For so many years, I did not necessarily feel like I had footing in dealing with my family; it was like dealing with an octopus or something. Finally just yesterday, I served a court document that seemed like it was the turtle having passed the hare after a twenty year journey. In the document I used the word "evil;" that is a word, with which no rightful person can truly associate nor endorse such kind of conduct. I was able in a non-overly emotional way to insert the evil word into the discussion. Now we shall see what is what. I needed to come up with an overarching word that essentially could ascribe anything negative that they did past, present or future; I feel like it is a societal breakthrough, in beginning to define evil, with respect to the behaviors of narcissistic and psychopathic types.

In addition this morning August 28, 2016, I identified in a subliminal sense the overarching role of Sondra Myers in this, and that felt like an achievement as well. Perhaps the reason, it has been so hard to decipher between Morey's role and David's role is because maybe Sondra is the true linking, if not instigating element among the two. On some level, it is virtually comic but for its negative repercussions, Sondra has interceded and sought to negatively effect, virtually every significant relationship in my life, from brother to father, to ex-spouse, to children, to familial status.

That type of denigrating behavior is pertinent to a person with a personality disorder or extreme narcissism. I do believe that there is an element on the Gelb side of the family that has a somewhat extreme retributive sense dating back at least to my Grandfather Morris B. Gelb, coming to this country as a young boy, in the early 1900's and being mocked for not being able to speak English. Clearly the story itself, has lived on for more than 100 years, and the emotional impact must have been significant.

That sense of injury and repressed rage, if I am not mistaken could well be a characteristic of the Gelb DNA, whereas the Myers family, and its historic, with all due respect, tempers and the like were more visible; it cannot be underestimated the element of repressed and less obvious anger on the part of the Gelb family. The Myers family would tend to express its rages and then work to make up quickly revealing a latent compassion. The Gelb family is more like a permanent slow burn it. The anger with the Gelb's could actually be a more brutal and mal-intended one, than the regrettable but still somewhat comprehensible Myers outbursts of temper. One being simply a behavior that was not learned and overcome; and the other being a characteristic of vengeance.

Wow, this insight is a true breakthrough for me; notable, as well because it is Sondra's birthday. In other words, if I am coming to a prospective sense that somehow Sondra has taken on this notion of being offended; she could put into place this vengeful attitude, with seemingly no end. Maybe that is the element and the route upon which to approach her, to reveal to her, she is carrying this slow burning rage of her father, and who knows the ancestors before her. Sondra's mother Mae S. Gelb was generally good to us; yet she did not seem to be overly affectionate emotionally.

Sondra, may well have grown up in an emotional canyon of sorts, where a lot of simmering rage and this kind of thing lie dormant. Sondra had brighter days as our mother; and that is why this rage is stunning. Still today, August 29, 2016, I examined more of a sense of forgiveness, after reading an affirmation on Louise Hay's Facebook page about forgiveness. Forgiveness just feels great sometimes, like nothing can go wrong with a forgiving attitude.

I have been functioning at an extremely high and intense level on this stuff, and I would love just to give it a rest, as while I have the ability; it is not necessarily my true nature to have this conflict. My true nature is a bit of an artist, a quiet, calm, loving type of person, although I am competitive as the times demand. Yes, I am glad I have my rugged side, honed by lots of sports and stuff; yet my truest nature is this ruggedly calm and loving person. I am laughing out loud, as it might not have emerged, but for this situation, being basically sober, and allowing the good stuff to really rise.

I am chuckling again, because in three days or so, I have a landlord about ready to totally evict me, and I am relishing my goodness, and how it has risen to the fore. I believe in goodness that as we become better and better on the goodness scale, nothing bad can happen to us. I saw a quote along these lines, by Buddha, something like: "when a person is pure, we are indestructible." This kind of confidence is the opposite of an arrogant sense of invulnerability; this type of confidence entails getting our soul, in better and better shape, to the point where we almost float through the world with our basic sense of goodness. I am not making predictions mind you, but forgiveness helps to open that door.

Maybe even more than forgiveness, it is that sense of emotionally untangling from hurtful people and situations. So much of this is predicated on my sense of fear put into me around financial issues. Again that is where God comes in, when, I have no fear around financial issues, then I am grateful for today, for sure. That is the winning notion, functioning with no unnecessary fear, whatsoever.

It would be great to help resolve my familial thing; the stuff with Sondra is unbelievable, and I am delighted that I could develop that understanding. I just feel like getting along with people; what can I say? So much of my fighting side has dissipated. I am not certain what to do. given that I just filed a court action labelling their patterns of behavior "evil;" I suppose that is my ace in the whole, in the entire situation. No one wants to be on the side of evil, right? Quite a journey.

I had an interesting little experience; as there was a gent I know from a local business who bopped into Dunkin Donuts, as I was doing a little writing this morning, and he was kind of cold, and I said to "forget" him. Then I go back there at the end of the day, to pick up my laundry and he is there again. This time, we chat again, and I buy him a cup of coffee, and I make a point to give him some of my time, to talk some more, and a relationship was saved. I read an article that said "don't be nice, when people are mean to you..." don't reward that behavior, and who knows there is an opinion and article for everything these days. That article went out the window, as I talked with my friend.

It is little things like that ;that inspire me to somehow take over this thing with my family. I must be patient, albeit from God an answer can take place at any moment. I should have put in, a thing to have David Myers appear in court; I would love to see that skinny little, with all due respect punk-like behavior in a court room, and for him to see how things are really handled. Perhaps just let it go, and trust God. Do not at this point go back and forth. It is quite a struggle for me, to learn the court processes, as the one being abused, developing the science, and representing himself in court; Wow, that is a mouthful just saying ALL that.

Maybe that is my role in society: An evil buster, and setting the tone for decency, in the form of the Calm Revolution, and all that. There must be some very deep spiritual purpose, some overwhelming societal good at stake here; a person does not go through this for no reason. Today, August 31, 2016, I got back out to distribute brochures, and it was as if I found my calling, spreading the word of the Calm Revolution is my calling.

I wrote a nice letter about David today, and encouraging the family towards a better route. Not to mention, I feel like I finally found the right angle with Morey Myers, so I feel like things will work themselves through somehow someway. I am not sure that I want to fight anybody in a court room, perhaps my letters are enough. It is all about vibe and keeping it positive. Last night, I re-read a piece about letting God handle things, and it sank in to a deeper level, where I really felt relieved.

I sent a tiny note to the real estate attorney and City Councilor today, on an optimistic note, so much is out of my hands right now, trusting God, is the right move, along with the greater or lesser things that I can do. Trusting the universe is an amazing process. There was a package that I sent priority mail, as I mentioned that was due to arrive in Boston on Monday; today is Wednesday and it left Illinois earlier this morning. Those are the kinds of things that used to, stress me out, on so many levels; and instead now I am creative enough and trusting of God enough that I just let it go, and find reasons why there is more wisdom in what is.

Something this morning, took me over a hump with regard to forgiveness. I saw no other way out, and then it came into my life that I could not continue focusing on the faults of others in this situation; it was too painful for me. I read this wonderful article on forgiveness that I had read before, and it moved me, pushed me; I must recall the name of the author, I may have mentioned him before and I believe his last name was Moffett, anyway, it was an impetus. I started to see the event as one entire event; one asteroid like event that went off near my life; and essentially seeing ALL parties as a part of it.

In this way, I could categorize the event as a whole, as I write at "Whole" Foods, and see it as one composite event and attempt to categorize, and forgive it that way. To be inside the maelstrom of it, was just too painful. Being able to see it as one event, even though it was thousands upon thousands of events, allowed me to forgive on a deeper level. It was one attack, yes over twenty eight years, but rather than worry about the dynamics of each of the people, it became healthier, I believe, to look at it as one event that went astray. It did not kill me, so it made me stronger; and there was some financial harm to me; so I would just like to gently pursue that under a notion of fairness and equanimity and leave it at that; as well as what is best for Sophie and Sam.

If ALL of these people wanted to attach themselves to one group; I will just take the whole thing on as one group initiative, and at the end of the day forgive it, as it truly had nothing to do with me, for the most part, or whatever remnants did have something to do with me, have long since passed. It does have an enormous healing effect for me, to be outside the maelstrom, to see it as its own standalone event, and for me to observe it, as I would Old Faithful, or the Grand Canyon or something like that, as a phenomenon..

I do seem a lot lighter, on some level, and even people at the grocery store, seemed more in tune with me; so this forgiveness thing seems worth continuing no matter what. Maybe this is truly all I can do, and God must do the rest. Time to catch my bus…

Okay, in the role of The World's Best Mediator, I work to designate the source of the

"evil" in our situation, AND I swear I am getting close to its being David's emotional coldness. David's coldness seems to be the deepest, most stark, one dimensional element in this situation. Is it possible that David was able to so profoundly negatively influence a familial dynamic? Wow, that would be surely astounding, with David being the youngest member of our family of four. It is the notion of a person with a mean streak being able through very subtle emotional tactics to take down, or at least psychologically assault another human being, with basically nice qualities.

Wow, it would be a wonder of wonders if that was it. I mean I had gone too far perhaps, in associating the "it" with Nomi. David just brings more energy into this familial situation. At least, at this moment that is the assessment and a wondrous one at that, lol. I mean I must have fun with ALL this. The deep part would be figuring out the psychological roots of this situation, after for one surviving a psychological force that would have, could have, and perhaps should have destroyed me. Not only did I survive but I developed a science for the benefit of human kind, and prospectively figured out the roots of this unfathomable familial conflict. That is the thing with David; that not once since his initial psychological assault on me, twenty-eight years ago, has there been an iota of let up on his part, virtually not a whiff of humanity. It is all rather astonishing.

As I came to yesterday, like an emotional bomb that went off in this family that is what happened, like an asteroid hitting a planet, a monstrous impact. Did David do it on his own? How much did Nomi contribute to this berserk formulation of David as a victim in his life play into it? Those are the right questions. I guess that is where the notion of a person being a "ticking time bomb" comes from, albeit the behavior can manifest in any number of ways from emotional to physical, from violent to non-violent.

I am grateful that I could have developed such insight into the situation, for whatever happens from here, I have won. I am declaring victory at this moment at 2:29 p.m. on September 5, 2016, Labor Day at that.

Well, I took a little road trip to Scranton; what a journey that was. It felt like an awesome phase of the entire journey. In the main, I seemed to have identified Richard S. Bishop the attorney as perhaps a prime mover, if not the prime mover in the hateful dynamic. It ALL started in 1988, well even before on some level, but 1988, with the death of my

Grandfather, Morris B. Gelb, and the manner in

which his estate was handled; with Rick Bishop submitted an estate tax form of $2.1 million, when actually $10 million or so, was distributed. Morey and Sondra Myers were drawn into it, along with Sondra's older sister Bev and her husband Jerome Klein, the stockbroker, who managed the funds.

At the time, these folks were just so overridden with their guilt and fear probably, that they needed to pick an enemy, and "oddly" they picked me, who did not live near them, and really had no concern whatsoever with what they were doing. It was, their own guilt and delusions of grandeur that kept drawing me closer to them, as they were abusing me for no reason whatsoever, and it gradually compelled me to take them on, over and over again. Given that I am only one person, it was "ludicrous" that they did not try to make true peace with me. So deep were their narcissistic and bullying tendencies that they did not, in the least, know how to make peace.

Finally, as I was heading home to Boston from Scranton, after riding two buses through New York each way, I felt after some more derisive email from Rick Bishop that I just kind of in calm fashion of course, perked up, and realized that I had to take these people on again. This Rick Bishop has insinuated himself into my familial dynamic controlling my parents, and overseeing a process committed to cutting me off from my sacred children. All of this from a guy, who does not have a legitimate interest in this; other than to be an attorney hired to represent interests and who lied on my Grandfather's estate to the tune of $8 million. I wrote to him today, how he was maniacal and insane with his actions; we shall see where it all goes now.

I found the only time that attorneys retreat, is when you find an appropriate way to attack them. Otherwise they function with virtual total impunity with other peoples' money on their side, and other peoples' pain on the other. So, I took a step up today, and we shall see how it plays out. I mean if you can't stand for what is right, in the midst of the muck and the bullying then what can you do in this world. This guy is just a bully at the moment; I did give him some positive inspiration to grow up and change, but we shall see; stuff like what in the world are you people thinking, and you are acting like the dinosaurs of the earth. Perhaps I did over respond, because I had heard from my landlord, in his usual challenging way. Still that was just part of the challenges that I face. The question is could I make it to the end of the month, and the answer is yes. There are certain things about the way this goof is treating me; not to mention the landlord is very clammy, when I returned from Scranton, it seemed like he had another tenant sneaking around the house, to see if I returned.

Some people just assume the worst assumption and then attack you on that basis. I am in the main, choosing not to escalate things with my landlord, as it would almost seem too dimwitted to delve into. I reached a moment of virtually pure joy and serenity today, when I thought of one of the sayings posted on my wall, something like: "Rejoice in your trials. If you are being challenged you are being perfected and thus have a divine purpose." That really sums it up in a way, both regarding my personal development AND the purpose to help others. I am laughing with the sense that I do not like creepy people.

There are certain people you must realize are impaired on some level, and really cannot carry on a positive adult relationship. Today I read an article by a woman who was talking about an ideal of a really exciting loving relationship, where two people was so inspired by each other; that is my idea. Why be in anything mundane, where you are not fully enraptured and inspired by each other?

Well things are at a "fascinating" point, as for today, September 13, 2016. The landlord has moved close to eviction proceedings. I sent the landlord a world of information as to what I have been doing. Who knows? Doug keeps encouraging me to just get a regular job. I tell him that doing something amazing can only be accomplished through situations and times like this; so as far as me, I suppose I can only enjoy the ride. Like the sign in my bedroom says: "Trials are your way of being tested and perfected; and finding your divine purpose. So, "rejoice;" or words to that effect.

It is time to rejoice; virtually anyone who looks at me, knows that I am an excellent person, who is doing my best. We live in a world that emphasizes conformity and lack of creative thinking, and I am a true creative type of thinker; and will remain one, irrespective of what other people say or do. A lot of work these days, also has to do with trusting in God, and letting this other stuff pass by in some ways.

Just focusing on being in the moment and/or trusting are such wonderful ways to live. It takes so much work to work on trusting and not fearing what is going to happen.

Forgiveness is a wonderful tool, as well. Forgiveness brings me closer to myself and closer to God. I am inside myself with forgiveness. I am in a happy and joyous space when I embrace forgiveness.

Well, I must say the move situation is one of the amazing challenges of my life.

First winning another modest settlement from the folks in Pennsylvania, then fending off Doug the landlord who was ready to come after me with a vengeance, until I was able to share some stuff of my story with him. When I shared it with him, it was a almost a total change in tenor on his part, from wanting to put me down, to stating that it was: "interesting." That was quite a turnaround from wanting to take my head off. Also, it was quite a release to me, being able to share part of this story with someone, even a tiny bit, took a lot of pressure off me. I know the landlord wants to sell the building.

The issues being the story is just so unbelievable that a family would so viciously and mercilessly turn against one of their own for virtually zero underlying reason. It was also wonderful in going to Pennsylvania and being rebuffed in seeing them. What this does for me, is stop the entire process of my trying to figure out their problems. I feel much more complete and letting go about the situation for now. It met me at the point of my manhood, and the capacity to walk away.

If I am going to travel that far, and as "parents" you cannot see me then, that is with all due respect your problem, and I am done on that basis. Indeed, I am focusing a great deal of my attention to attempting to wrangle a one-bedroom type of apartment in Newton; evidently these things are very hard to come by. Again, like many things I must put myself into God's hands.

It is a time of true and enforced patience as well, with things seeming very tense and not necessarily moving at breakneck speed. As I write about rejoicing in our hard times; I do kind of relish it, with respect to accepting and wondering as to how much I am learning in the process, and how God is shaping me through this ALL. I cannot, but for the life of me attempt to accept virtually every situation as a learning and improving situation. If it is a hard time, I get right into the hard time and feel it, in all its wonder and glory. That is where the capacity of grit comes along; I can almost feel it grinding and accruing on a daily basis. Speaking of, accruing, my corporate tax forms are due tomorrow.

I have made substantial progress on them. We shall see, how much I must push to get them out by tomorrow. The Massachusetts' ones are very extensive. One day at a time.

As far as the apartment, I am looking at taking a risk to get the apartment; due to my belief in where I am at as a person, and the belief in my story..[46] Today, September 16, 2016, a lot of little breaks went my way. One that was not so little is that my landlord Doug Turcotte found my letter requesting a move out date of October 1,

2016 "acceptable" so that takes some pressure off there, and that is yet another example of The World's Best Mediator functioning under pressure.

---

[46] Ironic, word # 120,001, written at "Whole" Foods, thank you Chuck Gorman and Whole Foods of Newton Highlands, more or less on the Highlands.

Be not confused, albeit the huge results have not materialized as of yet, the pressure that I am under and the successes that are occurring, if even on moderate levels are astonishing. You know the expression of a diamond being formed from coal under pressure; these last several months have been unbelievable, even by the standards that I have lived by previously. On some level I really do enjoy it, because I do not know everything, but I know that a person would not be subjected to such pressure unless something major was really happening. It is like my moniker of "rejoice in your challenges…;" I am feeling it and I do believe some larger purpose must be unfolding related to ALL of this. So perhaps I do feel blessed after all. Some little breaks went my way, in terms of payments that do not have to be made at the moment, which gives me a little breathing room, perhaps with the capacity to have some fun i.e. nachos this weekend, lol.

Sunday, September 18, 2016, what a day. I went out to look at an apartment. It had possibilities. I am confused, God will decide. I had a rough time sleeping for a while, and then I moved into a sense of forgiveness for Morey Myers, and I felt much better. Then I had a dream about Sondra, rather leaving me behind, and so I am somewhat confused by that. Forgiveness is quite a thing, as I balance it with the sense of working out another lawsuit against these people. As I said, yesterday I felt like I reached a higher sense by calling their underlying actions "irrational" and not saying "evil."

It is such a confounding situation; I must realize on some level that Morey Myers's hatred and hurting of me, comes from his own pain, and yet that takes unbelievable strength to take, all that he is giving and be fair-minded about it. On a strictly fair sense these people would pay me some substantial amount of money; stop attempting to alienate my children, and we would move on. It is such a fine line to walk on some level, to proceed forward or consider proceeding forward without vengeance or retribution. Perhaps that is the genius position to uphold a position of virtually sheer virtue, without it devolving into a high-level fight.

That type of thing is something to consider, and may be my path out of this mess, and yet a hard way to walk. We shall see what God has in mind for me. I cannot be fearful or worried or doubting; it is a matter of talking things in stride and trusting that all things are working out for good. What a journey, what a walk it has been and continues to be.

That is the difference between me and a lot of approaches to self-help, and realization. I have actually walked the walk with these things. I have not left things up in the air, or just "tried" to do these things. Through a combination of necessity and a sense of adventure, I have actually taken these spiritual principles, such as" everything happens for a reason;"

"you are exactly where you are supposed to be;" trusting our divine nature and following it;" and essentially bet my life and my future success upon these things. Not to mention finding my inner strength as well.

That is truly at the root of it, in a lot of ways. Well, it is first accepting the nature of the divine, the heart, the sense of spirit within us. As I say, it was March 26th or so, of 1996, when I could feel a presence in the night that I called God enter my life. Even so, I was somewhat naïve with respect to the sense that the finding of the divine itself, would be enough to solve my problems, lol. I laugh because, that was just the beginning of the spiritual warfare that God had in mind for me.

Evidently God wanted me to accept his, her or its way, and then apply that way to unfathomable challenges facing the modern world. Some would say that the voice of evil or even the devil is alive, in virtually any age. Whatever you want to call it, I did encounter evil. it was God's way of testing me, to discover my inner strength and voice.

Ah, there is that phrase again "inner strength." So it was accepting God's way, and then learning and developing my inner strength to take on the great values. I don't know why I am talking like it is in the past tense at this point, those challenges. Perhaps it was a little nudge from the universe today, in the form of an affirmation from Louise Hay that referenced giving up a poverty mentality and replacing it with a prosperity mentality. I sincerely believe that such a sense of prosperity will come into my life as of now.

I have planted the fields, done the work. I am developing a sense of vigor and excitement about my future at this point. A sense that that the philosophy that I have developed is going to come to pass. I mean that piece with Doug Turcotte was incredible; he was so intense about it. We shook hands today, and acclaimed that we had an agreement, which I very much want to see come to pass.

I had a dream this morning, which concluded again with my biological mother Sondra Myers, and it concluded with her impugning me again. I used the dream as a release to affirm all that I am, rather than what others seek to make me; I had a sense of freedom. I used the dream to affirm that I am a peaceful, calm and kind man; and that that was the me that I really wanted to build upon.

Thank you; I say to the world in general, and for the wonderful blond brownie type of thing that I am eating at Whole Foods. Wow, that is great. I am thankful for my capacity to stand in there, and take on the devil, if that is what it was, and take on the very most challenging human types of issues. I am delighted for the skills that I have developed in all of this, and surely the world will call upon me, to put them to wonderful use.

Well a slight breakthrough on the new apartment front. I must say, that on some level this has been the hardest time of my life. On the other hand, if and when I remember to let it all go, and just trust that things will work out, at least in theory it gets a lot easier. I am working on these notions of letting God handle it all, after doing my part. It is kind of amazing to develop this degree of trust; It moves me towards faith. At times like this, when it can get dark and uncertain that is all that one can do. I received a call back on an apartment today, and on some level, I am starting to love the idea of moving very much.

One thing that I will say is that I have the utmost respect and love for an apartment, as a home this time. After having lost a lot and experienced so much; there is a great deal of love and joy, in the sense of a home. Nothing can and will be taken for granted this time; if God is to bless me with such a thing. I worked a tiny thing that seemed big, or a big thing that became tiny out with the printer today, with the right amount of patience and care. The other thing that seems hard these days, is the wall that Morey and Sondra put up with me. Even knowing rationally that it is their illness at play and virtually not anything to do with me, does not decrease the pain and sense of loss sometimes. Further, it is like Morey just insinuates himself in my life, in my emotional space, and somehow seems to believe that he can dwell there. I sense that I have the approach for that, or again, am I just better off leaving that totally to God.

Today, the divine hit me on an even deeper level, September 21, 2016, the first day of fall or thereabouts. The word that I took to heart after a meeting with old pal Terry Morris is that of "patience." Even now, as I have endured so long, it seems that I might have to be patient even longer; the divine directs my path, as Terry himself has commended to me. I guess I am wondering if I should be even more patient with my living situation.

Rather than accept the first apartment that comes along, after I receive a payment this week from Pennsylvania, should I consider not moving on October 1, 2016, and instead hold my ground in terms of what I truly deserve out of the situation. It would take unfathomable verve to stand up against Doug's wrath and this entire real estate situation. Oh well that is a question for another day, and I do myself no favor by focusing on it now. What is pleasant and positive today?

Should I go out to distribute brochures or check in with the UPS Store for mail or just let everything ride for the moment? It is fascinating I just called the UPS store and it was a wonderful little revelation. I realize the thing I love most is talking with people, and working with people in positive ways. In that regard keeping alive my business and just fully committing to it, on some level, is just my highest calling.

This approach offers an alternative notion to the notion of fighting, fighting, fighting one more round, and just leaving to do my work with The World's Best Mediator, and leaving God to do God's work as far as my family. That would be a miracle unto itself. I love my work that cannot be a problem, can it really?

Well last night was a revelation or a revolution of some kind. The long story, short is that I took an antacid pill without water, and it seems possible that the pill did not dissolve and worked its way through my system, causing massive upset. After consultation with my health plan on more than one occasion, the pill exited my body, in a most shocking and surprising way. Enough said on that front, just take your medicine with water folks, lesson seemingly learned., although it could be something else.

So today, it seems like there was progress in the housing front, as this place that offers real possibilities may actually be coming through. So, I am thoroughly grateful, at the moment, if my stomach is still a little wheezy. Actually as of today, September 23, 2016, it seems that was not an antacid pill, but some stone or something that passed through my system, rather unbelievable. Just another day, in the life of The World's Best Mediator.

Back to the mission; I gave an idea or three to this apartment we are working to put together in a part of Newton, presenting a live/work option. Living and working together, I believe is a winning option in this day and age. This will be amazing if we can put together this apartment deal. It is bringing out my creative energy so it is cool.

It did seem that God whispered to me today, as well as to a route for dealing with the familial stuff. Morey is kind of psychotic, and ultimately on some level, I believe rather hurtfully influenced by David and his wife, as well as others. The other thing on some level, I am thinking is that this is historical destiny; me representing the roots of familial values, with a contemporary twist and my sister-in-law representing extremist views, with my philosophy actually the much more evolved, egalitarian and thereby advanced. To me, as I have said before it is historical destiny that was supposed to take place, but who'd have thought within my own family of origin? As one of the last movies David and I saw together, "The Secret Policeman's other Ball;" F'ing Amazing Shi…!

What a day, what a life. Terry Morris, my attorney friend, if those two words are compatible sent me Biblical passages the last two days, and they have captured a fair amount of me, and I have loved one; particularly as he signed one today: "Have a peaceful day;" what a wonderful way to sign something and it was a thought that guided me, at crucial moments during the day.

Well today, September 24, 2016 evidently a check arrived from Pennsylvania, a little bounty check, well actually I do consider it a reward for my efforts, even if, not what I would see as fair. Yesterday God's inspiration hit me to draft a letter to these folks, so evidently I will not quit, abrogating in some way the coercive "Agreement" that we have. Coercion and agreement cannot coincide.

I do wonder about the notion of just moving on without them. We shall see, one day at a time.

It will feel great on some level to receive that check; alleviate at least some immediate pressure that I feel. God speaks to me through a gentle and guiding voice, with respect, as to how to proceed. I would be remiss to stray too far from God's command for me. So this letter as challenging as it will be, may be God's command for me. What a road to hoe, it has been an unfathomable challenge the last several months for sure; and that must mean that I am in at the deepest end, or where I need to be, or taking the battle on, in the manner that it was intended to be fought.

So, I picked up the check today from my mailing spot. I got the sense that someone else was possibly signing things for my father. His signature did not look exactly as I remember it. It is really sad, if on some level he has been controlled by my mother and this attorney Rick Bishop. Ittakes the heart right out of the family, in a way.

I am nearly in tears, with the sadness in some way, and also the recognition that these folks are on some level really are acting in a virtually evil manner: That raises the ante. I am essentially the only one who knows about it as well, or at least, as first hand as I do, and even remotely willing to speak about it. It is important at moments like these to trust God and put things in his hands. I must be patient when I do not understand.

So today, September 28, 2016 I made seemingly a choice. I decided to forgive fully. It was rather cosmic in some ways. I was just under so much pressure, and almost feeling hopeless, when the only mode that came to me was that of forgiveness. There is a rather remarkable twist to this saga of forgiveness. Today, I am scheduled to go see a woman about a place to live, who knows me. Indeed, more nearly ten years ago, she shared with me a story, where forgiveness was virtually the only way out of a sincerely life and death situation, she described. Unbelievable in that I am going to see her today, and this very morning it seemed for me that forgiveness was the only way out of this virtually life and death situation for me.

The mere survival is so deep and so intense, as it seems that so many people had it out to truly tear me down. It was virtually all God,, along with my God given ability and purpose that pulled me through. It is said by some that forgiveness is a final test of love, so perhaps this is the final too, of these unfathomably precarious predicaments that I have found myself in, that virtually defy human existence.

I would love to think that my death defying story will have a much higher and greater human good, but then again, a lot of that seems to be in God's hands, and I am just along for the ride. It is hard for people to relate to the notion that a person could actually live their life in a Biblical, if not profoundly spiritual way, but I am a person who relied a lot on deep Biblical, if not spiritual principles to inspire and guide me over the past more than twenty years.

Thank you to all, who have stayed with me in one way or another. It is an unfathomable story, because most people do not know what emotional/psychological abuse is, and for that matter have not adapted to the understanding that goodness and kindness are strengths. Most people can get caught up in the realms of coercive behavior and this kind of thing; and being mean as an expression of strength. Of course, in the true sense of the word, meanness is virtually the opposite of being strong, and much more so, an act of cowardice. One crucial element of forgiveness that I picked up from a video from Thich Nhat Han this morning, which I shared with my children was that of forgiveness, and a sense of compassion for those who are mean, and commit mean deeds. It is truly their own hurt and pain which causes their mean behavior.

So, I am blessed with these knowledges and understandings, and the wisdom or pure luck to resort to forgiveness, when in a deep pinch. Thank you to God, thank you for today, and let's move onward and upwards, as the expression goes. So, I saw the living space at a woman Linda's house, and facets of it seemed wonderful; for one is some decent space and two is the possibility of having some meeting room space for my office. Rather unbelievable when you look at it.

It seems like forgiveness was the way out for me, in the final analysis. I wrote a strong rebuke to Rick Bishop and ended it with forgiveness. Maybe I can just let the entire thing in God's hands, and leave it there at this point. I would love for instance for my younger brother, to get the memo on peace and maturity; ah, well that and life take time.

So I consider myself fully blessed today. What a day, what a few months. I mean the[52]

[47]pressure of this real estate situation was rather un-

---

[47] Antics, is a word that Mike Perry, Esq. flung at me during this escapade

fathomable compared to other things that I have done, with the result forgiveness. I do feel like forgiveness was my final exam or final piece of work associated with 1110 Chestnut Street. The building Itself was an old church rectory.

So, somehow I made it to Central Avenue, my new address, from 1110 Chestnut Street; it seems miraculous. A guy named Brian, who I spoke with about an hour earlier showed up to move me, otherwise, I am not sure what would have happened. Miracles happen. At the same time, I had a health scare with Ben Stiller's announcement about having prostate cancer; and scheduled the PSA test with my doctor. Considering my mortality, nudged me closer to seeing David as the initial massive source of hatred and animus, within our family.

This understanding can be a true breakthrough. This kind of understanding might alleviate some tension and pressure on Morey and Sondra. Time will tell. Here it is a few days later, October 7, 2016 AND I am still holding David, and/or David and Nomi accountable for a lot of this. I am starting to believe their "antics" supersede even the entire thing pertaining to Morris B. Gelb's estate, which is staggering.

Essentially the anger and bitterness of David, has driven like a hot branding iron throughout this entire family for "nearly" three decades now. Now that is some kind of destructive influence on the family. That influence is offset and then some, by my capacity to hang in there for the truth and real essence of this family and myself. Wow.

I am feeling really good on some levels these days.

Perhaps it is my new home, not drinking coffee for a few days, even no television. For some reason I feel lighter, even though the scale is not saying so, as of yet, lol. I also heard from Sam this morning on the topic of chess, which was wonderful. Just, be able to eat and conjure the notion of cooking, in a kitchen is an intensely inspiring image to me. That I have lived without these basic amenities of life for the past, more than seven years is astonishing; even though there are some who have less than that for sure.

I really appreciate these amenities more than ever. I have been without coffee and television for the past four days, and I have started not to miss television much, although I will probably enjoy it when I get it back; still, I do feel happier. Maybe it is hard too, to describe the circumstances at 1110 Chestnut Street; although I am not certain that everything will turn out better, but still 1110 Chestnut Street was on some level being in a prison, between the landlord, the tenants and the conditions themselves.

Again, I am not complaining; I am respectfully embracing the unfathomable lessons that I learned there; and how the challenge of that experience molded and shaped, if not forged me, which is of one of the major themes of this work, how adversity itself changes us as people. In some ways that is the theme of my life, along with helping others.

Diamonds from coal; how adversity made me, and shaped me both as a person, and in developing an agenda to serve the world. Today, October 9, 2016, seems like a wonderful day in some ways, as it seems like I pinpointed the sense that Morey Myers's illness is below all of this, perhaps going beyond David. I feel better having reached this point; I mean a fair number of people in the super market are talking to me and stuff, like a whole new lightness has settled in for now.

I would like to focus a little more on the notion of melting the iceberg. While I began this book with a sense of the iceberg, being particularly related to certain kinds of personality types, which I do believe very much exist; and yet for me the focus has shifted. The focus shifted towards me, being who I am, and how I could personally overcome those senses of iceberg in my own life, with which I was hit with an extremely severe version.

Beyond those personality types of narcissism, borderline and psychopathic, on some level, I am appropriately confronting a more general meanness or sharpness in our culture that we have gotten used to, or at least confused, with respect to what is true strength and what our true values are. Being crass or mean, can rarely if ever, be a necessary component of life.

Today though I seemed to have come across a major breakthrough on the forgiveness path. In researching narcissism, I came across the notion again that narcissists do not really know that they are narcissists, or are clueless about emotional stuff; meaning if they had the capacity to, in an ordinary sense become more empathic they would do so. It diminishes the sense of anger and even pain to anchor ourselves in the sense that no matter how hurtful their behavior is, on some level they do not mean it. It is not so far from what Jesus said:: "Forgive them for they know not what they do."

I was probably guided along in developing that

Iceberg

understanding, by re-watching a video by Thich Nhat Han yesterday, which I sent to Sophie and Sam, where Thich recommended that we are able to forgive, if and when we can understand the behavior. With respect to my family, in putting them in the narcissistic vein; it dawns on me that they do not know they are narcissists, if they truly had the capacity as it stands to be more empathic or more compassionate they would do so; not that they are not to be held accountable for their own actions however.

People do not want to be this mean, they just learn it, and somehow think it becomes the path to success. There is, the proverbial needle in the haystack for me, because it is precisely in showing people that compassion and empathy can be winning moves becomes the purpose of my work.

For me that is the melting of the iceberg. The issues presented by my family, are prevalent in society today. The kind of crassness and even cruelty is unfortunately what we are learning and teaching one another in many ways. There is no reason, in the world why being kind and considerate would detract from business; indeed to the degree to which, we are dealing with human beings, being kind and considerate is beneficial to business and economic success, not dog eat dog. President Trump extolled.

We as a society are learning and teaching inaccurate lessons, or more so, lessons predicated on fear. Yes, our world has changed since 9/11 and other events; yet if we lose our sense of trust, of enjoyment, of humanity itself we will have substantially diminished the human condition. Speaking of this; this is a really challenging notion to advance, with the great focus and advancement for women in society; much of which is due. It is about equality, not retribution. This morning I woke up and ascribed a ton of responsibility in our situation to Nomi, and in likely some psychological characteristics that she herself brings forward.

I say this, because one area, where the realm of women's influence is unfair and even somewhat cruel, is that of Probate and Family Court. While the end of men's abuse towards women is mandatory and advancement of women to all levels of leadership, particularly on merit is a welcome thing, there are areas where women's influence is unfair and even far too harsh. The very area that I have traversed pertaining to Probate and Family Court, is case number one of those harsh areas.

In that regard, I am pretty much like a salmon swimming upstream, and yet that is how a salmon does reach its final goal. I feel that with all the appropriate emphasis on social justice for African Americans, and persons of color, women, the LGBTQ community and others, we can begin with a sense of dignity for all human beings. My experience is such that as my elementary school integrated at an early age,[48] my father's association with civil rights and Martin Luther King and my own work in developing career based programs for low and moderate income youth in Cambridge, combined with the vast injustice of Family Court system, makes me a fervent advocate for dignity for all.

---

[48] I am want to say that my elementary school and the sense of diversity that it proffered was the best education I ever received, meaning diversity itself, alongside my Harvard Masters and Oberlin degree.

Iceberg

With respect to taking on Nomi for instance, within my own family, it is a matter of her having imposed some kind of legalist feminist structure on my family. As I often say, it is as if, it was historical destiny for me, given the intense familial upbringing that I encountered in my own family, to run into the female dominated realm of divorce and family court, with the advocacy on my part towards fairness for everyone.

So, it is all good, I suppose. This is all part of the process that God has delved out for me. Nomi is the kind of person, who I believe genetically has a hard time admitting that she is not right; so it remains to be seen, as to how a combination of love, forgiveness, and determination can overcome her sense of dominating me in my very own family; a scenario starkly too logically "ludicrous" to contemplate.

One of the redeeming themes in this situation, is how one person can shift, if not overturn the balance of power and the dynamic in a familial situation. Not to push too hard on this analogy it is almost like an elephant is afraid of a mouse, in general. I am not knocking Nomi's or David's talents personally; I am merely saying that in an extremely long running family like ours, in elephant like fashion, it was the specter of divorce or attacking someone's mental health; contrary to our actual experience and the truth of the situation that set the elephant into panic mode.

Well, recently I have tried putting my familial situation firmly in God's hands. I still do not know whether that means not doing anything at all, or if I get an inspired idea, do I go with that? Time will tell. For instance, I prayed to God for help after a challenging night of some dreams, and then the inspiration of Morey having an illness arose, and having compassion for that. I do not know the answer; so I will let God tell me. On some level I have said these kinds of thoughts to Morey, without his response; I am thinking that I will drop a note to family members on this, time will tell.

It is developing this compassion out of the deepest experiences, the most unfathomable pain. It is that level of pain, which can produce greatness, and true empathy. Perhaps it is the rare bird, who can take that pain and become developed by it; forged, by the pain, to the point, where it molds your core, your true being. In being compassionate, it is also important to act in a mpassionate manner, as well. It is not a theoretical issue, as I wrote to Sophie and Sam today, October 19, 2016; it is a true priority. An article by the Dalai Lama suggested that true compassion could only come out of a great degree of pain; Wowsie you said it Dalai!

So I am thankful that I have learned through my pain and pass it onto humanity. The pain through the dreams at night is a challenge. I sense that it is the pain and trauma of the actual abuse that I have suffered. There is no practical way to truly address it, such as therapy or work of that nature; no one would essentially believe or understand it, in a worthwhile manner at this moment. It is more the work and the challenge to integrate the pain and turn it into some form of growth; the realm of compassion for Morey, with an understanding of his challenges, seems to be the best proscribed route at this point, to lead the family if not by their formal acknowledgement, then by intuitive action.

Yesterday I did some work on gratitude, with respect to gratitude for everything, including our enemies. So once again, I do find myself thankful for all of my experiences, and these extreme challenges, which solely develop these really deep human qualities on profound levels. Rejoice in your trials, it is said!

God had provided me insight yesterday morning with respect to believing that Morey's perspective was a profound part of all of this. The essence of what I am doing is Compassionate Genius; the nomenclature of my Science of Inner Strength Honor. Wondering if I can penetrate this situation with both genius and compassion.

Today, October 21, 2016 is an important day. I resubmitted court papers to Mike Perry,

Esq. predicated, on the "leverage"[49] being Morey Myers's impaired judgment. It really ALL came together in rather miraculous fashion today. Yesterday, I was straining, feeling pain, and all of a sudden I got a burst of inspiration about which way to go.

Remember that this week, Joel Osteen talked about following God's daily direction, and I have really strained and listened for God, in ways that I had not previously, to find the right path in all of this. It was rather wonderful how God guided me to that point of inspiration. Still this morning, I was looking at having to compose

---

[49] At negotiation in recent years, Mike Perry said to me, I had no "leverage." I trust that Morey Myers's mental illness, could be the winning move, the point of leverage in all of this.

accompanying documents, and feeling like it would take days, if not weeks.

Once again, God stepped in, and reminded me that I had prepared supportive documents, previously, and I was able to reproduce those this morning, and able to get a thirty-five page document out this morning, in really miraculous fashion. I feel like this time, I needed to stay ahead of these folks, as who knows what will happen, as I have written some letters to family, contrary to what Rick Bishop sought to impose on me. I cannot predict the future; I can say that God's guidance seemed to impel me in the right direction today, and for that I am ever grateful. At the last minute I remembered to stick in there, a Calm Interventions' brochure, and I was delighted for that as well, as it keeps it about ultimately the progression of my work on all levels.

It has been a rather unfathomable three weeks on top of months before that. Moving, has pushed me to a higher level in some ways, as the person(s) who lives at the new place seem to be operating at a high level in some ways, and it inspires me to a higher level myself. We shall see if the issue of Morey Myers's mental wellness is enough to stop their crazy train.

If I had not listened to Joel this week, and been willing to do things differently no matter how much it challenged me, I probably could not have produced the stuff that I did. Anyway, it has been quite a week; the kind of week that each day seemed like a long time. I wonder too, if part of it, is that I do not even have a functioning TV at the moment; so there is not that buffer/excuse to lay back upon. So, I pushed myself, plugging to the next level, and these documents were one result. As I say, it was not something that I planned; it just seemed to happen in rather spontaneous fashion. Generally too, I would hem and haw about it, and yet this morning, I wrote a cover note, and just went to the Post Office and sent them out, Priority Mail that is. I totally let it go.

I must say in writing the documents, I did feel an element of the whip that has been on my back, loosen; so perhaps this was a vital part of the whole[50] process. I am in comfortable clothes, and I am rather shocked that it all went down in this manner. I just spent nearly ninety dollars at Whole Foods, and I am wondering about that a tad. Yes, the money is a focus; and yet it was all rather necessary and healthy at that.

I have had the notion that I must be willing to die in the fight, I suppose, again and again, and I have survived, if not won. This is a tricky one; yet I will come through easily, with God's leadership. This morning, October 23, 2016, I feel like a breakthrough, it started to happen last evening or so. I started to develop a notion of how everyone in the family could be part of a win. I started to see my entire advocacy, as part of my historical destiny to bring an advocacy to the courts.

At that point, it started to make sense on a much deeper and better level, and I felt a sense of comfort come over me in a way that I had not in a long time. I cannot say for sure that this is the reason for all this, but it seemed to provide a certain light at the end of the tunnel. This morning, even, I went a step further in recognizing Nomi's role in this, and at the same time sensing that David and she

---

[50] I say, as I write at Whole Foods.

have issues, or she having some of her own that have been directed at me. So, I am feeling some more of a sense of optimism about things, on some level, and for that I am grateful, and feeling well this morning.

Today, was a bit of a challenge, and ultimately, now at the end of the day, it feels very worthwhile. Worthwhile is, I got out to pass out brochures, which felt great; I also seemed to dovetail the court piece in with it. The connecting element is the science; it is all about the science on some level, I am feeling more and more like that is my deep selling point. I am not absolute about it, and yet it feeling more and more like a possibility. Specifically, I would be open to going into court and presenting the science, particularly on some level, as it pertains to David and potential personality disorders.

I have trained myself not to relish in other peoples' defeat AND yet, it I am feeling some prospective sense of satisfaction to actually on some level, pummel David's position in court. It may take further work to separate myself from knowing the pain he inflicted was more a matter of his illness and all of that. Still the irrational rancor David brought forward, might be worth that due satisfaction; albeit it would probably be better, if he were just to concede, and I could work to heal him. Well, I don't really know.

Also this morning, October 24, 2016, I heard from Rick Bishop in an email. Those folks must be getting just a tad nervous and all of that. I do not relish so much the prospects of pummeling Morey Myers, my biological father, at age eighty nine; David may have contained the backbone of the hatred and the opposition. Perhaps I am thinking too far ahead, and yet I do see the Science as the linking and binding element in all of this.

I even took up an issue within my home, as F. my flat mate seemed to perhaps have a sensitive sense of smell, which I related to a type of anxiety disorder, which was revealed on line in a general sense, and seemed quite accurate as I considered it.

Today, October 25, 2016 I met with my doctor. I am taking the PSA test regarding prostate cancer; I believe I am okay, we shall see. Still the larger issue is that I do not seem to have a great connection with my doctor. He makes snide comments and seems condescending. I was reading an article that talked about firing the doctor, and perhaps it is time for that.

I am working on trusting. I did take those folks back to court, as I said, and the thing is I am gearing myself to discussing emotional abuse. The court is not ready for that, in all likelihood. Who knows though? I did it. Gandhi says to speak, even if you are the only one. There seems to be no going back this time. The one thing is that Morey is so old; he just seems more bitter. I am not good at being rigid, we shall see.

Albeit, I have an insight, and I am reverting to the notion that I have encountered evil. Wow, I said it; I have said it before, and I will say it again. I consider that a breakthrough. It is wild, right after I came to that realization, the Fleck coffee shop where I am writing; kept their doors open a little while longer for me, and extended me some baked goods that remained from the day. It is as if the universe decided on a reward right away for me, having come to that realization that the familial dynamic is evil.

Evil is a word that most people have heard; even if they do not know the precise meaning. My work is to define evil, and raise peoples' sense of sensibility, along with collective outrage to defeat evil. The essence of people is too good to stand and allow evil to exist among us. We must take ALL appropriate steps to defeat evil. I am inspired suddenly; it did hit me that everything needs the right label. Few things are truly evil, and when they are discovered, we must take steps to address it.

Now that I think about it, evil is the great danger in the world and threat to our true lives. Evil must be understood better, and we must take all appropriate steps to defeat it. It is about the basic goodness of human beings that we are fighting for, and our very planet. This is a breakthrough today, and on this note, we are moving in the right direction.

All of the work has perhaps come to this point. The call went out and God answered. Amen. And then there is God, part two or part 5038. Today, October 26, 2016; I awoke essentially to see that I had a somewhat elevated PSA test result, as far as in the area of Prostate Cancer. The reading, while initially somewhat concerning, has "oddly" also too, had a mellowing effect on me. I do not mind my mortality; I embrace it. Certainly, I would love to live many years and contribute much to the world and my children; and yet also I do believe that I have met life at some of its deepest levels, and I am not afraid of death, for instance. While I would love to believe that I am due some great reward for my efforts; I am also at peace with where I am today.

In and of itself, this type of peace is a reward and a function of a journey to and through heaven and earth. It may sound morbid; it is just this temporary at least peace with life and the world, is a rather "indescribable"[51] feeling; so perhaps in that way things have gone full circle. Mortality has a way of bringing that feeling. I am glad that it seems to have infused virtually all aspects of my life at the moment. Having said that, well let's put it this way; I heard Rick Pitino of all people issue a second amazing quote today: "I live life on a one-day contract." That is all we can really ask, on some level, is to live life one day at a time.

It is just a feeling of peace. I did in that realm, get out a letter to familial members today, pinning things more on Sondra, which seems accurate, and then my personal note, was rather warm, loving and encouraging to everyone. I worked through some things with my printer today, as well; so that is a wonderful thing. It is a matter of taking things slow and smelling the roses; that is what this pre-cancer scare or whatever it is does do me, and gratefully, I am ready to receive that message, which is a high message indeed.

My life ultimately, may be a test case in human development. Taking a smart guy and high school football player from Northeastern PA, and making him a guru of sorts, lol. The magical mystery tour for sure. I am just grateful that I am alive today, is the message of the

---

[51] Remember Sophie's usage of that word in her epic college entrance essay.

moment. I am blessed; I am truly blessed for this adventure, and the notion of having this company Calm Interventions Inc., and a concept to share with the world.

It has been quite a journey up until today October 31, 2016, over the last week or so.. I have been studying cancer this week, of all things. I am coming to a sense that diet has a lot to do with it. Dairy is supposed to be somewhat linked to Prostate Cancer, as are I would think fatty foods, in general. So, I have been loading up on vegetables and nuts and things.

I believe that eating healthy is becoming a priority of my life. Wow, fifty eight years of a lot of junk and stuff. Anyway, I am due to go back for another PSA test, as my doctor gave me a rectal exam, which he is not supposed to do, beforehand, and my reading is not that elevated; still it is an eye opener. I came to the realization that the entire craziness of my familial situation, could well have been a factor with respect to emotional stress.

So, I am going slower. I studied forgiveness for a good part of yesterday, in a book, doing some exercises and all. It is good; it did bring out some compassion, albeit, I am not so worried about the possibility of going to court about it. Will I really get money from my family that way? Or is forgiveness better? Or is it just better to trust God and let it unfold? I am kind of wondering these days, with this Prostate scare; trust God it is!

This morning and throughout today, November 1, 2016 I withdrew my latest court action; I don't know the forgiveness work, the cancer possibility has me stepping back a bit; even just the possibility of being The World's Best Mediator in a healing sense. I mean it is fun, life that is. My energy level with this move and health stuff seems a little down, and yet it is, onto trusting God.

I read a quite interesting Christian perspective on handling evil this morning that swayed me. It is hard to remember now, lol; the essence seemed to be to be God-like, not to respond to evil with anger and that kind of thing, and to continually work towards forgiveness. Or also to leave a sense of retribution to God.

My aim, if possible would be to educate my family; it is this forlorn like desire. It may just be me, and something tells me that this group has to be reachable on some level, educatable, even. The situation does not seem to totally allow for a complete break; and they are acting so irrationally that education may be a possible goal. The other linking point is psychological/emotional abuse, and my breaking ground in the science.. Some of the things on forgiveness suggest that one cannot pursue justice on some level, and pursue your destiny. Other views suggest that one can walk an extremely fine line in terms of being able to pursue justice, in a forgiving tone, which is a rather unfathomable walk. So for me, it is a matter of a day at a time, to see which approach makes sense.

Perhaps that is such a key point, trusting myself under God's guidance to make decisions, not relying on other perspectives, such as solely those that I read. I am intrigued with the notion of developing a societal understanding of emotional/psychological abuse. My ultimate goal would be to help society become more humane and gentle; and thereby emotional/psychological abuse is a vital issue to understand in society.

The key thing is that I would love to have peoples'

support and in that regard beating it into them, does not seem to be the appropriate way to go. Forgiveness is a powerful tool; as it develops compassion for people. Can forgiveness win this situation? I mean there is no question that a certain part of their system is set up just to deny me. I do feel disappointed that I let go of the fight, I must confess. Somethings say that I cannot educate them. Let God handle it.

One key question is what was David, after when he imploded into my life in 1988? I mean it is somewhat psychopathic and yet what emotional need was he seeking to have met at that time? David was already married, for two years at that point, living in Los Angeles; his mother-in-law was in Cambridge, I was in Cambridge, having done well in an election. That is truly the odd thing here; on what level did David pose some kind of connection, or control of my life? What was he seeking? Perhaps, it was vengeance.

He must have wanted to look like a big man; like a tough guy in his new marital family; like a faux genius. On that level that is where I have won right away; to the degree that his efforts were to bring me down, he failed. And yet were David's efforts his own, or where the functions of others, even my own family. On some level, as I indicate yes, David was seeking to appease Judy Levine and Nomi. Yet how about Morey and Sondra?

Morey had been extremely vocal and supportive at my 1987 election effort. Things were changing too, with the advent of Gelb money, which was significant. Morey and Sondra, did make a massive error, in choosing money over my life; and that still could be, where forgiveness comes in.

Yesterday, I hit the nail on the head that it was David who forged so much of the rancor and animus into this family. Ironically yesterday was David's fifty-sixth birthday. Today, November 3, 2016, I also seemed to develop a winning vision for virtually all members of my family. I finally came to the point, where I could develop the notion of us, as a good family, with potential for great, as the umbrella, under which we must fit. It seems logical that everyone would want to be part of a good, if not great family.

That is one of the upsides of all of this, if I can actuate a notion of a good family, where all members are respected and feel valued. It is astonishing that this vision could begin to emerge. It is a matter then again, of trusting God's timing, because for ten years or more, I have been working to bring this conflict to an end, well I have been involved in it for a while; still it is only now that I can develop this vision of prospectively bringing this situation, even possibly to a better end. It is through God, or patience and perseverance, or whatever sense of a higher power, one would choose that this is happening for me.

I am taking this prospective cancer challenge, as true to my philosophy an opportunity for me to learn and grow, and blah, blah, blah. I already I can see where diet plays into this; even more perhaps is the element of stress and how the unfathomable pressure that I was under for the past twenty plus years could have factored into it. So, I am relatively renouncing that kind of stress at the moment, eschewing more fighting and that kind of thing, and leading in a calm and gentle, if not compassionate way.

That is a part of the true level of opportunity that this entire situation represents. I pushed back against my doctor a tad, and he still seemed to hang in there with me, so I am A-OK at the moment. Also even more so, I am trusting of God in general; as love and light and being happy are of the highest order, even in; if not especially in, times of challenge.

So, unbelievably the Calm Interventions philosophy of "Turning hard times into better times" and The Science of Inner Strength seem more alive than ever. It is just that I have worked to really slow down and smell the roses a bit, in the last few days, as I have been relatively exhausted on some level, after the move, the ongoing familial stuff, the change in lifestyle/medical stuff and on and on. It has been somewhat reassuring to slow down and just enjoy myself more, as in today organizing my home and work space; getting out some work, and contemplating the next version of Calm Interventions letterhead.

I am truly excited about color stuff, as it pertains to my company. It is funny that today November 5, 2016 I seem to have lost a day's work or so on this project for the moment, and it really reveals to me how valuable I view each day and each time I write on this book, even if it seems like I am just writing my views of that day. Losing even a tiny bit, perhaps indicates to me how valuable I view all of this, and what it really means to me. Every day I write is extremely valuable in terms of the evolution of the work itself, so if today, I take this time to reflect, it is due to the loss of a tad of writing; which in and of itself elevates the value of what I have done. Imperfection raises the value of an art piece,

Anyway, today was notable in the sense that last night I received a phone call from Dan Martin an old bestie of mine, and today, I felt somewhat taken advantage of by him, and I called him back to appropriately assert myself a bit. Dan was probably shocked a tad, as I am generally very mellow and yet, I felt he tread on my turf, in some ways, and I pushed back; so it was kind of out of character with Dan. It is melded in, with this PSA test, which is a possible reflector of Prostate issues, as in blah, blah, blah. The thing is I am realizing that men have prostate issues in general, and it might just be so benign type of thing; so I am changing my diet as much as I can. It is said onions and other raw vegetables can increase our health, and I am on that case at the moment. Who'd have thought that onions and garlic and stuff, could be a life-saver?

I am grateful for today, I got out a letter to the Attorneys. I am pushing on the element of new letterhead, with an elevated sense of the dove for Calm Interventions, and considering taking a financial leap on that one. Ah choices and decision; its seems like my life story. Then again, leave it all to God. So, it, is a Saturday evening, and I am here in the Newtonville Starbuck's writing with two bags of groceries nearby, desiring to catch the last bus home, twelve minutes and counting. I mean I bought some spices tonight, which can be expensive. Hey, I am cooking, and one or two are supposed to reduce the risk of the C-word.

I love you all, have a good night, wherever you are. Thanks! So here I am Monday morning November 7,

2016. It has been a whirlwind start to this morning. I took a leap of faith, yet again, lol; and ordered a great deal of more letterhead for my company, of a higher quality. I really do not have the funds as of this moment. I am banking on the sense that this familial situation must come to a resolution soon. I have honed in on the sense that Morey's irrationality is at root and that that must be rooted out in some way. Somehow or other, I seem to be on the right track.

Morey's irrationality is the issue from which all else emanates, it seems, although was he pushed by David? It is funny, I felt dead to rights at times over the weekend, albeit the breakthrough with respect to Morey was uplifting; it is just that a brisk walk in the sun this morning is really exhilarating. I feel up on my game. It is kind of like the cancer scare or whatever it is, is inspiring me, along with getting me to eat a tad healthier. I am in to my business. It is the orange dove. God is pulling me, and it seems our familial situation could be resolved very soon. I am not certain why I am so optimistic; it is just a feeling of the moment.

Thank goodness, I voted already. Also I have an ultrasound early tomorrow morning, which got me to get up so early this morning in preparation. Maybe I can resume my brochure distribution as early as today, tomorrow, Wednesday. I am so grateful to God that the sun was out today and that I could walk as much as I could. To enjoy just the simple things in life. I am not in a rush out the door kind of person, and yet I just caught the bus by thirty seconds or so; I caught the printer, a few seconds before

Iceberg

a phone call for him, came in; there is something divine about the timing of things today.

That is where the brochures need to come in; it is that sense of walking everyday. Perhaps it makes a tad of sense to wait until after the election; so material does not get mixed in with election stuff. Who knows, I am mainly waiting for the bus to take me back to Newton to decide, as I am in wonderful Needham at the moment: It is about the joy of being alive and living. That is another thing this entire journey has given me is the capacity to enjoy life and appreciate the moment. Yesterday I looked at a little quiz about happiness, asking if happiness was something we were born with, or not. The answer to the quiz was that no, happiness is not necessarily something that we are both with. My experience affirms that sense; as happiness seems to be something that is earned or worked towards to achieve; AND that is no minor point to me.

Happiness is something that I really worked on over the years; not consciously towards happiness per se, happiness is virtually a by-product of doing the right thing day after day for years at a time. Happiness entails cleansing out the hurt feelings, the misperceptions, the things that would cloud our minds and emotions. Happiness entails coming home to who we truly are. Today feels like a wonderful reward of that journey itself.

Well, today, November 10, 2016, I made a correlation between Trump's victory and my familial situation. I seemed to reach a point, where I was back to identifying Nomi and her radical ideology, as the strain that runs through our family like a political correctness virus, if not more that threatens our country's baseline. That is what

I am working with; it really has do to with basic human values surviving the earthquake like eruptions of political correctness and other things, which have elements of truth in them, and yet it is their absolutism that harms others, and thus diminishes their truth.

It was refreshing today, I kind of settled in some ways on the element of "finding your inner strength;" as perhaps the binding element of all binding elements in my life, relatively speaking of course. I took a break to speak with a couple originally from Ireland in Needham this morning. They inspired me to actually work to publish this book, so we shall see how it goes. Inner strength for me combines the sense of divine, with our mission, as well as our self-development into who we really are.

So it is quite an exciting day for me. I made a stop at Whole Foods, where I am now, and a couple of women friends, Toya and Denise gave me wonderful advise towards the frozen foods section for vegetables, rather than the fresh ones. I am working to change my diet rather substantially with this entire Prostate situation, along with the sense that my work is too important to have any major delays at this point, as least as far as I am concerned; God will decide. I am working to give myself perhaps an entire month of eating healthier to see how it effects my PSA and all of that.

Still settling on "Inner Strength" as perhaps the crucial concept to Calm Interventions seems like a wonderful breakthrough, and where I truly need to be. So…a wonderful day, today November 10. 2016. I had a little anecdote in Whole Foods, where I went back for a salad for my own lunch, and stood next to a woman, who was also getting a salad. Each of us did not have the lid on, I was holding mine, and she did not have one. I complimented her on her bravery, for taking the plunge, as we were both going to the little café area. We ended up at the same table, and as I ate my lunch, I had a little salad left, and ended using my lid. I shared this with her and added the comment that most things fall into place, if you are patient enough. She responded that it was a great life lesson. So that is kind of how I am feeling at the moment, light and airy and feeling healthy for my lunch, although I did have part of a brownie for dessert.

I am ready to write some notes this afternoon or something of the like; just spread the good cheer. I did receive some wonderful advice this morning at the printer,, who encouraged me to continue to use my older business cards, as well as to hone in on the sense of the Science of Inner Strength, more than "transforming challenges into opportunities." Whew, what a day already. Perhaps too, I am getting ready to start finding a way to publish this book.

Today, Veterans Day, November 11, 2016 was momentous, I filed yet another motion of court actions towards those parties. I keep knocking on the door, and look to find a way to get in. I received a phone call from Sophie recently, which was great unto itself, and yet there were too many things about her attitude and lack of respect in some ways, for me to just sit idly by, and allow this process to continue in the manner that it is. So, I responded, yet again, with these court actions towards my parents, as I see Sophie and Sam being manipulated. It was on some level an amazing response.

So we shall see, if these folks back down, get the

message, or we shall see. Whatever the destiny of the moment, it is what it is. Those documents mean so much to me; that I put my trust in the UPS store in Needham for the mailing as the Post Office is closed today. It is all rather amazing. My work is beginning to reach better color with the Calm Interventions stuff, and my book perhaps I am ready to start marketing. Who knows how it will all unfold?

What is "fascinating"[52] is that perhaps it is going around full circle; in that at this juncture I identified David at root here, AND also identifying that the entire family system is lying about and covering up, his illness and "condition"[53] and instead seeking to blame me with it. This unfolds as a point of genius on my part, with respect to figuring this out, and even then allowing for some compassionate response in that once the illness is on some level identified with David; perhaps some kind of caring response is then possible.

I did capture that spirit in the ending part of my motion and perhaps that is the spirit that can come forward. Well today, November 13, 2016, I literally and figuratively did some housecleaning. My housemate insists on our cleaning our bathroom and somewhat common areas, and I did that this morning. It was actually not that bad a feeling. Last evening I took a shot of this turmeric super juice and I virtually slept through the night last night,

---

[52] Again the word used by David and Nomi to describe a community they are looking at; let me say a prayer for the community, lol.

[53] "Condition" is a word that those folks have flung at me.

and so I walked again to Whole Foods today for another shot of the stuff.

The other housecleaning came as far as outreaching to the attorneys a tad, with respect to softening the groundwork for some kind of resolution here. Sondra is due to receive an award in the Scranton area, and I am ambivalent about congratulating her. There is a part of me, that is just allowing her to learn her own lessons, and while it is on my mind, I am not reaching out as of yet.

The big news also is that I came up with a new quote for the Calm Interventions mailing piece, which is: "My job is to help restore our humanity." It is lofty, if not ballsy quote and yet there I go again. I really aimed to have the word "humanity" in there, AND "job" not only reflects a kind of vigor, but it is also somewhat of a dig at David, with respect to his taunting me about a job. Perhaps my job, is on the planetary level, and of a higher ilk, then he, or I, for that matter imagined.

Restoring our humanity is about where I ended up out of all of this; and it is kind of a stopping point in this entire discussion. In other words, what did more than twenty years of torture produce? A man with a commitment to helping to restore our humanity; kind of neat, if I do say so myself.

Well I surely am in to humanity that is for sure. I am up in the air these days, about my eating habits, as I have changed rather dramatically in the course of a week or two, and still wondering if I must forgo nachos and the occasional beer, as in today is Sunday, albeit the Patriots do not play until tonight, and I wonder if I want to walk to this local pub to watch any football. I must say it was wonderful to sleep until 5:30 this morning, and wondering if I want to screw that up either. I used to get some joy from fun food, and now I am in Whole Foods and essentially bypassed all of my favorites.

Joel Osteen's message this morning was also kind of harsh, in terms of taking the first step out of our comfort zone and our needs will be provided from there; so I suppose it is time to start walking home, and we shall see from there. So that was Sunday; today is Tuesday, November 15, 2016, and I took a leap yesterday. I have been working on Calm

Interventions' letterhead, with an enhanced orange dove, and the estimate came in, higher than I anticipated and more than I really can do right now, and yet I took the leap. It is like this old expression: "Jump and the net will appear." That was a crucial concept I adopted ten years or so ago, at the Charles Hotel in Cambridge, and at the time it paid massive dividends in certain ways.

On some level, I am really sensing that David and Nomi really provide the energy for this familial disarray. It gets my attention; you see, it is not only my life, or even Morey and Sondra's, but my very sense of family itself, on some level a higher and broader concept. I have done unfathomable work myself, and yet the family foundation that I was given in Scranton, beginning in 1958 was also in some ways of epic proportions. I had four grandparents, living back to back on Madison and Monroe Avenues;, in Scranton the blocks are named in order after the first six or so Presidents.

My two grandfathers were Eastern European immigrants, one a doctor and one a lawyer. After my grandfathers died, my two grandmothers, both eventually moved right up near each other on Clay Avenue and lived more than 100 years each. My parents Sondra and Morey were very intense and all that; and for that matter growing up in 1960's Scranton, was a little bit like Mayberry RFD. Or Happy Days at the high school level. So, family was intensely ingrained in me.

Sure in being pushed onto football fields and chess tournaments and wrestling mats and Oberlin College and all that, I went through my undefined times; and yet at its core I had and have discovered, have an extremely intense core of family value and respect. That value would not have truly been discovered without this entire process occurring, which as I sit here writing at the larger Whole Foods, connected to my new neighborhood, I see as a deep revelation, of the moment. This revelation is a dramatic difference between David and me, for one. Through it all I virtually always had a core value underneath, that needed ALL of this to wake up that sleeping giant, if you will.

David, in how he came at me, just seemed thoroughly disconnected from any factual centered- kind of basis, and not acting with a sense of true and/or redeeming value(s). This insight at the moment is a rather astonishing occurrence, to see how on some level, all of this occurred in order to unearth my connection and legacy to the roots that were laid for me in Scranton, and acclaim that basic goodness. This takes the discussion to another level deeper, with respect to beyond a "fight;" beyond even a sense of right and not right; but even more a substantive and qualitative difference as to why this occurred.

David's energy, I see more as just David's desire to be

King, perhaps in a bloodthirsty sense, and mine is merely a legitimate expression of what is right and just for the family, starting with Sophie, Sam, and me. This is the kind of stuff that inspired my sense of the new letterhead, with qualitative improvements in terms of my assessment of the situation.

Today, November 17, 2016, God granted me a ray of brilliance in seeing this situation in consistent, and breakthrough terms I am starting to see the very basic thing of what I have stood for all of these years, as goodness, and the energy that David and others have brought as relatively speaking the opposite. I may have said these things, in disparate parts before, and yet I am not sure I have melded them together into one picture. I am starting to see myself as an influence of good, or a virtual Phoenix rising from the ashes in this situation.

In other words the virtual entire backdrop of this situation had to do with providing me with fertile ground, if not spiritually fertile soil to be born or re-born almos. I have seen generally the notion of adversity providing one with opportunity for sure; AND yet, it is seeing this, as almost one picture; in essence synthesizing the two disparate parts, the abuse against me and my commitment to growth and improvement, as one piece.

It is rather "fascinating;" one of the framed posters that survived from my time at 1110 Chestnut Street has a tiny fledgling tree, overlooked by a giant redwood or something, with the title being "Determination;" and some tag line. I was that little sapling that grew while this entire story was unfolding. The energy that David and others hit me with, on some level, ought not be survivable, and surely not encouraging thriving.

Yet that is the essence of the Science of Inner Strength. Because I had a full sense of the divine; because I had a meritorious purpose, I was able to keep my faith and positive goals, as stronger elements than the negative influences that were seeking to tear me down. It is these kind of notions that the human spirit is stronger than any of its obstacles that drive me. I mainly believe this in a general sense, and for society as a whole; yet it is rare that a human being gets to stand for something profound for more than twenty years; and take these kind of issues on, in their own life.

It is the stuff of good versus evil, in some ways, or good versus recklessness at least; and yet a person is not really supposed to be able to take these on for so long in their own life, without having to worry about financial and/or health things and the like. That is, in part the miracle of my story; that not only did I prevail on some level; it is every bit as much, if not more that I was afforded the opportunity to take this stuff on. That again, though is the theory embedded in my work, the Science of Inner Strength and all of that: There is a quote from Og Mandino something like this: "Every obstacle has the seeds of equal or greater opportunity." I see it as divine destiny too.

It was just that the avalanche was so insane and so enduring that it actually provided me with the opportunity for that much growth; and yes, ultimately: My commitment to humanity itself. That commitment to humanity is the goodness; the very essence of what I have been fighting for all of these years; if within the midst of the fray I could not always articulate it, in that manner. So, in a spiritual sense, the whole thing is a blessing if not a rebirth itself.

Yesterday, in doing some writing, I came back to the sense in a renewed sense perhaps that David's hatred is truly at root of a lot of this familial stuff. That would truly be a point of genius, to recognize David's hatred at root. What is hatred?

That is an amazing question. Hatred on some level must be fear based, right? It is so sad in David's instance that he has carried forth so much rage from childhood. For starters, different people are different; and yes, he lost a lot of boyhood contests to me. Yet wouldn't most people get over it? I can say for me as an older brother, I would have learned from it, that is the most positive instance, and yet wouldn't most people, if not relish it, at least find the positive part and/or grin and bear it? To make a life of animus out of relatively regular boyhood stuff is creepy and sad to me that a person would choose to live their life that way.

I heard a wonderful talk this morning from Joel Osteen, and I felt like I needed it, about keeping the faith during hard times even referencing thirteen-year epochs, before change took place. At times, I feel like I am hanging in by a thread. Even, me The World's Best Mediator, lol; so grave is the challenge, intense financial pressure, social isolation, cancer possibility, cut off from children who love me; it almost makes me laugh now. It cannot continue forever it will pass, maybe even soon. I mean my body seems very sore even and all that. One day at a time.

To have hung in here; this well more than twenty-year

period is unbelievable; I am "convinced"[54] that my story is one of the epic stories of human existence, to have borne this unfathomable pressure for so long, and then to found a science or at least something better out of it, is rather unbelievable. Well today, November 21, 2016 I took on Richard

S. Bishop, a bit, the Attorney from Scranton, PA, about expediting some funds to me. I could get nervous about it. Yet I suppose the best thing is, to have said that I have done my best, and let it go. The fact remains; it is those folks that remain in an abusive stance towards me; so I am in God's care and in that regard I should not worry at all. Hallelujah, that is the message above all else, when you are in God's care, do not worry.

So, I am just not going to worry about it all. If David is really at root, then it is does become an eye-opening situation. That is the billion dollar question; is it truly David that is at root here? Is David in essence, the iceberg, after more than twenty eight years of his craziness? Could David have caused all of this on some level? Clearly the situation around Morris B. Gelb's estate compounded things; AND yet was the dynamic already in place substantially, so that the iceberg had begun to form?

David's actions are David's actions; there is no way around them. The question then is: Was David created as a function of Sondra and Morey, or did David incite the hatred on his own? I surely believe that Sondra incited David somewhat, and yet, I cannot believe that Sondra could ever have known that David's animus would reach

---

[54] David once said to me that I had not "convinced" him, as if that was my aim. I have convinced myself however.

such historic levels. Case in point: David began by attacking Morey and Sondra, evidently viciously for many years, in the early 1980's, as "bad parents." I suppose in part, the answer will come too, perhaps; in how Morey and Sondra respond to the quest for some funds on my part.

It may not matter so much at the moment. The key issue is, that David will not take me down, no matter what. That is the first thing; if Sondra put him up to it, she will see, as David is defeated that she made the wrong choice. If and when David did it on his own, the family as a whole will be much the better for my victory. The enemies, either way, are hatred and animus, not necessarily people; that is a key point above all else, defeating hatred, and maybe even helping hatred to understand how misguided its actions are.

That is one of the undercurrents of this book: Can hatred be unraveled, turned back, essentially by exposing how much it comes from pain and for that matter, lack of intelligent thought? That is my unfathomable irony among ironies, to prospectively expose how the hatred that David with his high Ivy League degrees is so unintelligent, not to mention his wife with a Harvard Law Degree. Yet, it is really not my intention to ridicule or bring down, mainly to educate if at all possible, surely for society.

You know how it is, when the people who are mean, act entitled and thereby seem to act like everything is supposed to go to them, it is a function of weakness, not strength. In any event, trusting on some unfathomable, occasionally absurd level that everything is happening the way that it is supposed to be happening, is the victory of victories in this situation. Sophie called last night, and what is important, is that when she is calm, we really have a wonderful relationship; there is a part of us that really bonds. So, ALL this fight was for a reason; it was so long since I was with the two of them that I am reminded now of how close we really were and are. The closeness of that bond is what enraged everybody and made them jealous.

The more I look at it, the entire thing is a function of this massive psychological assault on me. That psychological assault is a perfect storm; a what I call a once in a millennium type of event. To have so much energy coalesced against me, for so long, for one, it takes a most unfathomable accumulation of events. Then you have the element of me rising to the occasion to meet, survive and ultimately defeat that psychological element. It is something out of Star Wars like, to have a force sustain for that long.

I wonder if I am describing it adequately; to describe what psychological/emotional abuse of such a momentous degree really is. Some people will be tempted to ascribe it all as nothing, and yet that is one of my true messages, psychological/emotional abuse is real, realer than real, as I like to say, like oxygen. Can you fathom the response of the public at large to the first guy who popped up and said there was something like oxygen; he must have been met with derision, in identifying an invisible substance just like me, at times. Lol.

What is not funny, is the intensity of the thing, and what I consider to be, its groundbreaking proportions. If I am sounding like I am leaning towards going back to court, it is because what I prospectively intend to do, as needed, is to cast a net, of evil catching, and put all of these people under it, and then see when and who leaves that tent. In other words, the anagonist will be the last one standing under the tent.

My sense is that the folks in Scranton, Morey, Sondra, even Rick Bishop may be dwarfed in their evil by David and his folks. The psychological assault was initiated by of all things, an intellectual assault, a melding of falsely superior academic perspectives, along with a weak psychological analysis, and yet wielded with shocking intensity. David was at that core of intensity, and its sheer velocity swept a lot of people into it; at this moment that is my current assessment

I am starting to feel great, and I am not sure why, more in some moments, like I am really overcoming this thing. It is just a matter of patience and perseverance; and anticipating that great things will come, in their due time.

Speaking of which, today I got an email from Rick Bishop that they were advancing me $2000, which on some level felt like a huge relief. This "advance" affords me precious time to continue to work on the true resolution. Wow, what a piece of work it is. I am still struggling with the notion as to whether David truly could have incited this entire thing, in which case, gradually extricating Rick Bishop and Morey and Sondra from the dynamic would be an awesome piece of work; if not unfathomably amazing.

I have not had a cup of coffee today, and I am feeling it. I am wondering, as to whether I should let it go, and whether I will sleep better; yet the caffeine must still be in my system. It seems possible that I could file what would amount to the first case ever for strictly emotional abuse. I am wondering if it is possible for the Morey and Sondra dynamic to collapse as far as the animus towards me. Questions like that shall remain in God's hands, as it seems that the $2000 advance was an indication of his love.

Also, at Whole Foods, I just sent an email to Sophie and Sam, and heard back from Sam in rather short order, expressing his sadness we are not together for another holiday, as well as his real love for me. I appreciate that Sam is maturing; that in and of itself is worth all of this, so not to worry, somehow, someway not to worry at all.

Quite a day as it turns out. I wish I was not financially intertwined with these folks: Well, everything happens for a reason. Maybe I should just put in one court action, and if I win I win, and if not just let it go. The fact is, that I feel due from these people. As I say, I could start to fashion a complaint based on the world's first case of emotional/psychological abuse; really establishing for the world what emotional/psychological abuse is. That I'd love in a way; perhaps that is part of, or my destiny itself. I could just in a mellow sense put out The World's Best Mediator stuff, and work on the emotional abuse stuff as well.

The question is, what is in it for Morey Myers? Why do they have this thoroughly twisted relationship with me, giving some money, and yet no relations, working to separate me from my children. They are acting abusively for the most part; that is what the world needs to know, abusers are like creatures of another dimension. Abusers thrive on emotional attachment, emotionally sadistic behavior and emotionally parasitic behavior. Profound abusers attach themselves [61] to your life, and through vast manipulations establish these chains, and based on essentially, emotional perversion; and then just feed off of this relationship over perceivably "permanent"[55] bases.

That is a breakthrough in terms of my articulation of the abusive dynamic; the parasitic facet is so "indescribable." Morey and Sondra Myers insist on no contact with me, and yet have done so much emotional and financial damage that they almost ensure come kind of relationship, through these financial chains at the moment, as well as their capacity to keep my children physically away from me. Sam however, referenced deep "love and spirit;" and those things will overcome all.

This is exciting; these seems like a wonderful breakthrough, with respect to identifying the nature of the abusive, sadistic and even parasitic relationship. Happy Thanksgiving, 2016, coming up everyone. So Thanksgiving came and went for the most part; today, November 25, 2016 is Black Friday as it is known, and I have gotten out about twenty five Calm Interventions notes and letters. The new orange is liberating; truly inspiring on many levels, and I feel inspired, in many ways.

This is also my second or third day, without caffeine. I mainly did it to see if I sleep better at night, albeit, last time I took a few days off, I noticed that I felt happier, more me. There is a guy on the internet who swears that caffeine makes us less emotionally intelligent, less in tune

---

[55] In court documents; Sondra and Morey Myers have indicated that certain things should occur "permanently;" such as my communication with them.

with other people and putting aside my love of coffee, I see some merit in the idea, so I am giving it a whirl.

Speaking of whirl, I kind of came up with the wild theory that Judy Levine, Nomi's mother really started what I now call it the Mrs. O'Leary cow[56] effect of this situation. Come to think of it; Mrs. Levine, has some similarity to Mrs. O'Leary; the prominent "L" there, lol. Actually, it is not funny, and yet because of the pardon the pun, sacred cow nature of Mrs. Levine, I am calling it that she "inadvertently" kicked over the lantern; even though she does seem to be at root of needing to demonize me for one, and perhaps this family as a whole. The rationale being, that she did not want her family to be overshadowed by ours; and/or wanted to attempt to establish a faux superiority of her family. Sorry, Mrs. Levine, not happening in this generation, this century, or most likely this millennium.

The big question at the moment, is what to do with dinner tonight? Should I continue my healthy grueling stuff, or get some take out or something like that. I just read an amazing Louise Hay affirmation that inspired me. It said: "Everything you touch is a success; and even more so was her commentary about being in the winner's circle. I am seeking to convey this sense with the new Calm Interventions letterhead; that victory is nigh and join me and the winner's circle; I put that out into the universe today. The bright orange, the lack of caffeine, who knows I am just feeling better, for sure.

In a note I wrote to family members today, I gave

---

[56] Mrs. O'Leary's cow according to legend, kicked over a lantern, which then led to a fire that burned down half of Chicago.

David and Sondra some back hand credit for inspiring me, and perhaps I am ready to soar past all of these peoples' nonsense. Today, November 27, 2016, I kind of went straight at Morey and Sondra, in a constructive way. This morning, Joel Osteen, talked about taming your tongue, and I must say, it seems to have at least for the moment brought me to another level of constructive interaction. The comments to Morey and Sondra, surely would fit with the vein of constructive criticism, and for that I am deeply thankful. So much so, that I went out and blew some money on a couple of beers and some fish tacos. I only drank half of the second beer.

So I offered some forgiveness to David, and yet, I am still feeling that something is fundamentally off in his perspective, with respect to accuracy and volatility and all of that. I am at a little coffee/ health food type of place, called Broken Grounds and I did have a wonderful Gluten-Free type of muffin. The key is, not worrying no matter what is happening. Yesterday I did have a truly intense type of dream, and it seemed to put the breaks on a certain direction and move me in another way. My dreams do that.

It moved me into a calmer realm for sure, and more cooperative, even. Every step is "fascinating" and a journey. There is a feeling in the realm of just appreciating life; beer, sets me back a bit. It is great to take a break, and yet I do not like so much to be disconnected, albeit the break from the intensity of things is welcome.

Just to show me and you God's influence; late yesterday afternoon, through some funny circumstances, some beyond my control I left my little computer bag, with this writing instrument in it, evidently at Whole Foods. I was a little panic stricken, and fortunately realized it soon, and was able to hop off a reasonably close bus stop. I hot footed back first to Walgreen's where I had made a stop, and then Whole Foods. The young man who helped me was very nice, and then found the bag on the floor at the last minute. I was relieved for sure; and felt that God's hand, was in the right person finding the bag, and returning it.

Even further, on the bus back, Richie, my pal the driver and I got into a conversation, where I referenced the bag contained a book I was working on, to help humanity. Richie agreed with me, and ended up calling the type of meanness and stuff that we confront today: "A disease." So perhaps again, there was a cosmic reason to my leaving the bag behind, only to have that conversation.

A disease is what is threatening our world in some ways, in terms of the iceberg effect, the meanness, the lack of civility and the like. Yes, there is a deep narcissism underneath it; and also some type of corporate greed, that drives the economics. The point, is we must begin teaching people that kindness and determination and that kind of stuff are the true strengths, not weaknesses.

The meanness and cruelty in our culture, is a learned behavior for most people; particularly with respect to people identifying those characteristics with intelligence and strength. These messages are what society is teaching and we are, with all due respect, off course. As I say, I am all for economic success; it is just that economic success must be integrated with a commitment to doing good. The world is at too fragile a point in some ways: The sheer number of people, the amount of nuclear and other weaponry, terrorism issues, climate issues, and our very capacity to talk and listen to one another; put us at a potentially precarious point.

I do not know everything, but I know that our capacity to set forth a different tone, bringing forth our true strength along the lines of The Science of Inner Strength, teaching people that cooperation is strength, is vital. It is not in some ways, that my ideas are all that different; it is just that I have gone through more than twenty years of relative hell to forge them, having them been forged drop by drop with figurative blood, and then sweat and tears essentially twenty-four/seven for that timeframe.

It is truly like the diamond forged as well, under unfathomable pressure from coal, of which I uniformly like to reference my Scranton, PA, old coal country background. In other words, my ideas are not merely ideas as much at this point, as a science, as parameters of societal understanding presented as steel tracks like railroad tracks. That is the Science of Inner Strength.

The Science of Inner Strength, entails recognizing and understanding our basic goodness. Then the Science entails developing and nurturing that goodness, into a sense of purpose that is true to us, and also something that society really needs at this time. Then the Science entails developing the modes and mechanisms to bring forth that inner strength, with a sense of mission and purpose. So again, the science is about our goodness and learning to develop that, as astrength to conduct our transactions with others.

The Science must demonstrate its economic strength to overcome the real meanness in our system and our

Iceberg

interactions today. It must be demonstrated to be, that goodness is indeed a strength, and that cooperation is a stronger component than cutthroat competition. I am not worried, as I trust very deeply that such things are true; the masses on some level have been given a bum steer.

Today, December 1, 2016 I got a family letter, pinning down David further, if not appropriately obliterating his position. The kicker was that I put on the outside of the envelope this reference to this wonderful GE commercial that shows the response on the part of people to new ideas; how new ideas are beaten down and scorned, pushed away, and then ultimately celebrated. The emotions that the commercial, evoked hit so close to home that it was stunning to me; Sophie later wonderfully affirmed this.

One of the very thin lines that I have chosen to walk in ALL this, because I came out of a divorce situation is that of navigating our American first amendment rights in this age of surveillance and all of that. I have been under this unfathomable bowl of pressure for more than twenty years; especially as I seek to bring positive change to our American courts and legal system. Thank God we live in America for my freedom of expression.

The other thing going on, is that I seem to be developing even further, my compassion during this rather slow time period; actually I have been working very hard. I am studying may families sense of illness. Giving up caffeine in and of itself is supposed to be enhance our emotional intelligence, make us more human; and so it has been about ten days for me, and while I do feel a little more tired at times, I have enhanced my human connections with people somewhat; so I am keeping an eye on that, as there is virtually nothing like the taste and near comfort of a great cup of coffee, as I sip my green tea at Starbuck's. The other thing I am really testing out, is how this change affects my nighttime awakening or not.

I love life; even with, if not especially, with the recent PSA test. The test has already shifted my life towards health, no matter what happens. I mean when I came into to Starbuck's today, it was a rather easy choice to select this brown rice salad, with tons of veggies. Ah, the mundane things of life that I am learning to appreciate, while working on the big stuff.

I am wondering whether I must return two keys to my old landlord to the building. I called him a day or so ago, and he did not respond. I am wondering, if I can just throw them away or something. I am reminded of a story of Abraham Lincoln who walked miles because he owed a few cents to someone or something like that. Abe maybe did not know about people with personality types of issues. We shall see what the day brings, as I need energy for my forward motion as well.

What a day, December 7, 2016, perhaps fittingly I had a dream about a big bomb going off as it is Pearl Harbor Day. I used the dream as a impetus to withdraw my Motion for a lawsuit. I equated the bombshell with Nomi, and almost in the nest breath, I decided to forgive her. Then somehow on the Prostate Possible Cancer front; I made a decision that I was just not going to fear death. The science is too all over the place; the surgeries too debilitating to rush right into that one. Just one day at a time, and this does not seem like the day that I will get the back-up PSA test, as far as I can tell.

Iceberg

I want to get totally focused on the spreading the work of Calm Interventions AND The World's Best Mediator and not worry about other stuff. One significant change that I am working on, as far as the prostate thing is the diet and exercise stuff that seems to be a real key, if not the real key, as well as living non stressfully as much as possible. I suppose not fearing death, is a wonderful step in that direction. It just seems I have come too far, not to fully commit to this work at this point.

One of the things that I am appreciating at a higher level is my capacity to work with other people. I am increasingly at peace with the notion that when I am at my best; I am in the zone of understanding, positive energy and basically getting along with others. Indeed, I came to that point with two challenging areas of my life today, and it was an affirmation of all the efforts that I have put in over the past twenty years; it does not come around so quickly. One that I choose to mention has to do with my doctor; who was pushing me on a testing angle for the prostate issue.

After reading a good amount of stuff, I have come to a few conclusions. One is that most men will get prostate issues, if not prostate cancer. Another is that in most cases, it is not clear that treating it has any overall effect on life expectancy. Third is, as with most issues in my life, attitude is all important. Another crucial element is that diet seems to make a great deal of difference to this situation. I can envision where plants and vegetables literally give the body more energy and strength, and fats in some meat and dairy, can harm the interior of the body.

The doctor agreeing to meet with me and hear my

stuff, rather than pushing straight on with testing represented a turning point, perhaps not just in prostate related stuff, but in life. I mean I stood up to the medical community and held my point. It is not at all about ego, it is as much that the medical community, in a general is not totally up to speed, even on a prostate related issue. It seems that the medical community is perhaps, randomly referring me to these radical prostate removals, virtually like lemmings going off cliffs. It is not that prostate cancer cannot hit hard, it can, but probably not to vast numbers of men.[57] I believe that number can go down.

So suffice it to say that the Jon Myers and Calm Interventions Inc. philosophy is alive and well, and making its mark in some of the most challenging areas of society. I had a great business call, too, in developing my relationship with my current printing as well. A third thing too is that I put together some court papers, which on some level seems most to lift my spirits. I finally reached the point with prospective court filings with the sense that I am a good man, and do not deserve to be treated that way. I will call it the miracle angle[58] in that I made the dividing line issue in some ways, the notion of how I define myself, based on my actions and attitude, and how my family is attempting to define me. It is kind of a "fascinating" legal argument; not totally, if much at all

---

[57] It is estimated that 3% of men, die eventually from Prostate Cancer. I am a believer that diet and lifestyle has a lot to do with it

[58] As I say, I read a wonderful article at one point about coming up with the miracle angle. My whole life has been a miracle angle and perhaps this felt like the miracle angle of miracle angles.

giving credence to the other side, but focusing on who I truly am as a person, and who I have been over the past more than thirty seven years.

So, perhaps today, December 13, 2016 it is time to start considering marketing my book. I have given my family plenty of time to make up with me; and if they rejoin me, I can always include those prospects. Today, December 14, 2016, I seem to have upped the ante with my family a tad. I mean, I got a very brief email from Sam yesterday, and I realized how outrageous it really is, that these folks have interceded in my relationship with my very own children to the degree that they have.

Any person, or surely; parent with even an iota of common sense, would know that to interfere in a parent-child relationship is something you do not do, unless you really know what you are doing, and have a great cause; neither of which these folks remotely have. What they have, is an emotionally and financially abusive family system, where they feel they can exert as much pressure as they want on the situation.

I am realizing how abhorrent abuse is to me, in any form. I just got a letter from my health plan, which I cannot access on line. If my doctor is attempting to put pressure on me, I am just going to walk away from that relationship. That is it; that is, what is necessary as it pertains to abusive people and situations, have the strength to walk away, unless such a unfathomable interest, like your children is, at stake.

Could I even contemplate backing away some with my children? They are part of that family system at this point. It is a rather unfathomable question., One must question everything sometimes. Basically, I have felt that they deserved my capacity to see through this situation. Further, I am the person most appropriately vested in the situation, and thereby should outlast others; although the system takes time to change. Still, a perfect storm of evil cannot last indefinitely.

So, today, December 15, 2016, a few twists and turns. The good old doctor, after we agreed on a meeting, as I strongly indicated prior to a follow-up PSA test, sends me a letter indicating that he wants me to have the test before our meeting, and then he "may ask" me to have follow up tests. I am representing an assertive alternative approach in some ways. Well for one, it is just basic respect and optimism in my health care outlook; and similarly a sense that perhaps the traditional medical approach to prostate issues is becoming outdated. I read, another website, and yes it was a rather random website this morning; essentially telling people on some level to ignore the PSA stuff.

I am at least in part, leaning in that direction regarding the sense it is not like men all around the country are just dying from prostate cancer. Yes, for those who have lost their lives or loved ones, it is horrific; yet there is a sense this problem is improperly represented, misleading of just plain overstated on some level. I am not saying that it is impossible, but I am leaning against the notion, that it is my prostate of all things, that will bring me down.

It is one of the things about the Science of Inner Strength Honor and how I live my life. A lot of people are somewhat trained to live in fear. For one, this is kind of learned behavior and two, people who have a spiritual center do not live so much in fear. Being able to live in a more fearless fashion gives you a real advantage in human relations; for the most part it allows you to think as a free-standing human being; which has to be the best way to think. I mean, my doctor, or doctors in general are understandably fearful of their reputation and malpractice suits.

The point of my life, AND the Science of Inner Strength Honor is that when you become a good person, you do not fear, because you base your life more on your character, than your reputation. You have confidence that you are doing the right thing; and then you do not worry about peoples' capacity to take you down. If you are strong enough to live your convictions, then a person who is right will not want to take you down, and you will be strong enough to back down the bullies, with your sheer morality.

That is how I roll, and that is how the Science of Inner Strength can move the earth to a higher level. Today is quite a day, with temperatures in Boston around 5 degrees or something. I just purchased a hat, gloves and scarf ensemble at Marshall's. This woman helped me out with gloves that were green, as the hat I got was green, and then she pointed out a grey scarf that actually had some orange trim at the bottom, so I went for it.

I heard from Rick Bishop yesterday that "something" was in the mail, and so it looks like I will make it through this round. My doctor gives me quite a challenge; there is big bill due at JTC and so on and so forth. The question is will I be able to lift this outreach to 500 honorees of the Science of Inner Strength thing up in the air, to get it off of the ground. On some level, I can envision a white jacket with an orange dove on it. When I was in high school, my junior year, we won a share of the Conference championship in football, and we got the coolest white wool jackets with stuff on them.

That jacket could be a model of what I envision. Once people earn The Science of Inner Strength Honor they deserve to live that vision. I am talking about a peaceful warrior of sorts, people who can lead and help direct the way of the world in a positive direction. It is people who have been through the trial of life, and come out the better side, and/or want to come out the better for it.

Back to my scenario, I am somewhat confused, as I took a step back, to really appropriately nail Morey and Sondra, in a letter. At times, I really believe Morey's sadistic illness is at root of this, even more than David's. I am feeling a little different, in that I really nailed them on some level, without the usual humor attached; I was not overly mean about it, just "objective"[59] and really calling out this cruel world that Morey and Sondra have created. It seems I made somewhat of a shift from hanging mostly on David, to upholding Morey and Sondra's role. It is unclear how this will play itself out.

There is a part of me, which is working with the idea of calling this, The World's Most Emotionally Abusive Family. The equal and opposite effect of that is my becoming The World's Best Mediator. This is the genius involved; the synchronicity of the universe.

Maybe these folks don't really deserve a lot of my

---

[59] Remember again, Morey saying to me he was just going to be "objective" about my life, when I went to him for some emotional support around 1998.

compassion at this point, which is a shocking notion, just treating them, even my parents, commensurate with how they are acting. There is only so much that you can do in one day, and/or one week, as it stands it is 4:44 on Friday afternoon; so I can let it rest a tad, for the moment. So, today, December 17, 2016 I began the theory again of Nomi being the instilling spark behind this landslide, not to mention this patently unreasoned and unrelenting perspective.

I thought my family had an obsession with being right, but perhaps that is it. Nomi has a virtually diabolical obsession not just to fight, but to fight to the death, and that is the quality that I am identifying. From what I know of my families' DNA, people would fight, but in the main lean towards making up; that is what is so bizarre about this situation. Somebody really wants to fight to the death it seems; and it seems like that person could "oddly" be Nomi.

The theory is that Nomi and David to some degree, essentially stung and emotionally paralyzed this family with their emotional assault. The combination of Nomi's absolutism and her mother's professed, " expertise" as a therapist; Nomi and David started making false psychological assessments of this family, eventually painfully pointing it at me. According to this theory, Morey and Sondra, were essentially emotionally blown out of the water and fell into this insane mobbing situation of me, their basically innocent first son.

The foothold that Nomi essentially has on this family is a sense of, perhaps threatening David with divorce, thereby leaving David potentially walking on egg shells for all of his adult life. On some level, I am getting ready to puncture that balloon. First of all, if and when that theory is right; then I will stand by David in the course of any prospective divorce, and Nomi will not overrun him. Second, how can I allow Nomi to step in, and even threaten to overrun this entire family this way?

The answer on some level is surely that I am not, going to allow that to happen to the best of my abilities. Therein lies the opportunity; it is to channel the realm of the infinite on some level; to channel that sense of my ancestors before me and all of that stuff. This entire thing is a divine calling remembering that it is my sacred responsibility to go through this experience and make something out of it for the world's sake.

So today, December 19, 2016 I mailed off a letter pertaining to Nomi to the family. A bit ballsy I must confess; yet it would be a wonderful occurrence for this family get to the bottom of this. I essentially threw down a gauntlet on the families' behalf, saying that if she wanted to divorce David, if David made up with me, I would be on David's side. I do not know everything, but I know that in a slippery Nomi way, she would possibly take advantage of emotional divisions and things like that

This is, really an edgy thing, but I felt the stakes were worth it. It truly is an amazing type of ride. The characteristic that I identified, is that notion of "fighting to the death" is something that seems rather inherent to Nomi. I sense that she was raised with such high academic type of pressure; that admitting she is in error is a real anathema to her. I can be compassionate to her in that manner; yet first things first, Nomi's introduction of legal tactics in this family has been a veritable atom bomb of sorts AND opportunity.

Yesterday I felt for a while, like the battle is over "oddly." I heard a talk by Joel Osteen about "dropping it." While some of Joel's talks have been inspiring to me, as I was researching other commentary about dealing with people with personality disorders, I found an on-line comment that wonderfully summed up some feelings that I had, along the lines of: "People who say drop it, when it comes to people with personality disorders, basically have no idea what they are talking about.

Even at that I watched a video of Melanie Tonia Evans, similarly saying that, do not ever attempt to persuade the narcissist of their negative qualities, as it was a losing battle. On some level, these messages were good and helped to make for a day of rest, but they did not ultimately dissuade me, it seems from working to get to the right resolution in this, although they did interject a bit of God and backing off a tad. I mean I really love trying to figure this out.

I also love the notion on some level, of demonstrating a psychological understanding, with respect to the notion that people who sought to pull me down, were ultimately the ones' with the true "illnesses and conditions." Today, December 19, 2016 a check was received for $2,000 from those folks. On some level it seems that they are insisting upon keeping the oppressive yolk in place. On another level, it may all be for the best, in some odd way.

One impression I got, is that I could fully make a commitment to my business and idea of recruiting 500 people for the Science of Inner Strength Honor. The other would be that I am, at least psychologically preparing for introducing a lawsuit strictly along the lines of emotional abuse. Can I do both? The linking element is that emotional abuse is at the root of the work and the science that I have developed. It is a tough call, I suppose I shall just lean on God. Perhaps it is best to process my emotions.

I am somewhat upset about the amount being $2,000. I could be glad that I received anything. I am, who I am. These folks have just gone too far. One day at a time. I could be flooded with money tomorrow on some level, who knows, lol. It was an extremely precarious curve that I went through in pounding Morey and Sondra recently. That could have been the end; the stumbling onto Nomi thing, could have been a saving grace, we shall see. What a battle, what a war, I will tell you. The legal profession may not let go of their stranglehold on things, without a big battle. Yet, almost everybody believes in truth; somewhere inside of them; at least most of us do.

Today, December 21, 2016 there was seemingly a terrific breakthrough in that Sophie called. Sophie said she would be in Boston next week, and we are planning to get together. One of the one or two major goals in all of this, is the restoration of great relations with my children and I have not seen Sophie in more than four years and nine months; so I am looking forward to it.

Also yesterday, I sent a whopper of a letter pertaining to Rick Bishop to the family. I ended up calling either Rick Bishop or his actions, at least, evil. It is like I just wound up and let it rip. That may be why, I am going slowly today. There also was an amazing release today, when I cancelled my doctor's appointment. I mean, I know the health issues, and yet this doctor just puts a lot of pressure on me, and a lot of other stuff opened up, once I cancelled or at least postponed that appointment.

This morning, also I sent Morey and Sondra an email indicating too, that I thought that

David's hatred was really the baseline factor in tipping the familial balance so greatly. I was getting ready to get upset at Sondra and yet Sophie's phone call mitigates that greatly. Not to mention, John Luz of JTC printing allowed me some flexibility on a bill I owed him, which I greatly appreciated. So, it seems a lot is moving in the right direction.

As far as David, something needs to reach him, because underneath his temper and rage is not only a very troubled person, but a person, in need of help on some level. That Bishop piece was something though. I felt he was mocking me about the money and acting like he was controlling something that was not his to control. So, in a slow way, suddenly it seems like a lot is prospectively happening. That letter about Bishop was something, and also talking about Morris Gelb's funds and how they were inappropriately. used and thereby influenced the family dynamic.

For the Science of Inner Strength Honor, maybe I will just go with the first 100; those in the leadership position, who will change the world for the better. 500 would take years to accomplish, so perhaps 100 or maybe 150. 100 would be wonderful! Actually over the last day or so, I moved towards 250 realizing that I could probably do that in a year.

What's the rush, maybe I should just go for the 500,

no matter how long it takes. Anyway, back to the familial thing. So I made a statement to Morey and Sondra this morning, essentially stating that I had lost my respect for Morey; which for me was a long, long, long road to travel; such is my loyalty. Then in the next breath, I did offer to help them through it. Yet, maybe it is that simple; some part of me, truly has lost my respect for him, in terms of any capacity to be in a room with him at this time.

A parent establishes a certain emotional structure or framework with a child; which has a lot of things involved. Yet in my mind, Morey just has no integrity on this stuff; ironically the thing that he is known the most for, in his enclave in Scranton. Yes, it is "integrity" stupid. Without integrity, a person cannot travel virtually anywhere in this world. To me, that on some level is what Morey and Sondra have shattered. I did send my children a quote from Thich Nhat Han pertaining to the person, who causes suffering is suffering themselves, and needs help, which is what I offered to do. Still, it also feels "oddly" pleasing to make the statement that Morey has lost integrity, as far as I am concerned. I make this statement in part inspired by stumbling across a statement unto the record of the US Senate by their friend Senator Robert P. Casey Jr. extolling their virtues, on the occasion of their sixtieth wedding anniversary.

Nobody really knows Morey and Sondra the way that I do, as their first son; and if they continue this lie they continue it. I am "strongly"[60] considering court papers that label them as The World's Most Emotionally Abusive Family and evil, even though the court system has factored into it too; perhaps I would do better to say that I went through the world's most emotionally abusive situation; as my aim might still be to preserve the family, who knows, on that last point. One of my theories is to use "evil" as an endpoint and see who runs away from it last, if at all, on their end; it does seem like Nomi would be the most recalcitrant on their side, which possibly is the appropriate legal fight that needs to happen, I am not certain; which is a clue unto itself; as Nomi is always certain.

Or could it be David, I did receive a piece of divine wisdom today, that talked about the difference between us. I am standing for my children and myself, against emotional abuse; and David, is standing for hatred. Hatred is where David comes in, although I cannot say that Morey and Sondra have been so separate from hating me themselves. Sondra, can totally have no heart it seems at times, a black hole of an emotional being. What if Sondra most represents the hatred at root. It is the eternal question as to whether it is David or Morey; and then you have the linking element being Sondra. It is kind of like Sondra may be the one inspiring it; and David and Morey are ALL too happy to carry out her antagonism.

I suppose the important thing is, to keep an even keel. It is December 24, 2016; the first night of Chanukah,

---

[60] I recall Sondra, saying she felt "strongly" about including some funds for a younger cousin of mine, after Mae Gelb's death, looking to pander on some level to her sister's family, while being willing to toss her own first son into a ditch, repeatedly.

and Christmas eve all in one. Holidays have taken on a dramatically secondary place to me over the course of the last twenty years, especially in terms of the meaning of family. Still, I will look towards a couple of quieter days, in God's spirit and trust that the answers will come to me, at the appointed hour. Still, the work at hand, is to deepen my trust in life and God.

Reminding me too, of the power of the Science of Inner Strength Honor, in identifying a word or two that will reflect your divine essence, and provide you with the confidence and divine sense of direction to move on your path, and work your way through complicated circumstances. It is believing in the illuminating facet of the Science of Inner Strength Honor. Ah well, still a couple of things to work through, over the next day or two; Sophie is due here on Tuesday, less than three days from now. Peace on earth.

I did some uncharacteristic things today, December 26, 2016. For instance, the person that I share some living space with; has really not reciprocated the sense of warmth that I have sought to convey. Instead, he seems to want to exhibit a condescending and superior attitude; needless to say I am fairly attuned to these kinds of things. So I looked at some online images last night, and one said literally ignore people who are demeaning.

The dude probably realized he went too far, and this morning offered me some fruit, and I firmly said no. Me, I am the usual total accepting soul, and all of a sudden, I find myself more committed to drawing boundaries, and just walking away from people who cannot treat me with respect. So, I am feeling a little funny, and yet it was a decision that I made.

Wow, I am enjoying a great cup of coffee this morning, at a place in Newton Highlands. That is really a good cup of coffee; three something a cup; I am wondering if I want another one, this comes in the midst of cutting down on caffeine, lol; no one's perfect. .

I just pushed too far with all of these dietary changes, in some ways too fast, with the prostate scare. I do find that this impetus in terms of prospectively shutting some people out, is fueling, as I wrote this morning, a small amount, for the next court case. I am encompassing a sense of not taking it anymore, which in some ways is what you need to prospectively enter a court battle. I was inspired somewhat by an article a guy named Steve Krasner wrote about corruption in our family courts.

I suppose doing the "impossible" is the notion of actually having a strong court victory or bringing this family back together or some combination thereof, or something that I have not considered. The angle to the court will be something along the lines that this stuff is just evil, and unless we want this country to fall down; it is time to stop it. So, I feel myself rising in that direction; which may be what I need.

The corruption in this country at the court level is vast; and maybe I am the guy to puncture it; wow, what a long and winding road. For the moment, I am wondering about another cup of coffee or just go back to business? Well, his book is business, back to other business? I am just so tired of chasing stuff around. So, I went for a decaf coffee; I suppose for prostate issues I will forgo the sugar, perhaps, lol.

Things seem good, with the direction of this court possibility. The fact that I have survived this, all of these years is a miracle unto itself. The fact that it is taking me this long to develop this case, is all the merrier. There is just no way that I could foresee doing it more quickly. For one, I am being victimized in an extremely intense manner; and but for being in the battle, and developing The Science of Inner Strength, I would have been in a puddle by the side of a curb, given the intensity of what I have experienced. I maintain the multiple aspects of being abused so intensely, developing my business, AND developing these court cases cannot be rushed.

It is a miracle that this work has occurred at all. So however long it takes, is how long it takes, and for that matter, courts cannot shoot me down, for doing something so groundbreaking and helping society. Well, they can figuratively shoot me down, but I will get back up, is how the story goes. That is the story, as I continually must remind the reader that this entire thing is like a passage through this tiny tunnel through middle earth, or something of the like. Because I am telling it, from such a ground-level first hand basis, it might get lost what I am saying.

Yet, in the best sense I am working to cut a new path for society. This is a groundbreaking journey. While to a cynical or even less attuned reader, this might seem like a path of random events, I am writing as far being inside a giant tube of emotional abuse for one; while continuing to develop three things. Those three things among others include, well perhaps four: 1) A much better, stronger and more mature person in me; 2) ongoing protection for my children; 3) The development of Calm Interventions Inc,. and The World's Best Mediator; and 4) an understanding of emotional abuse.

Ultimately too, the overarching goal through The Science of Inner Strength is to develop a more humanistic society, with the notion that goodness and kindness and that kind of stuff are our true strengths; not meanness, crassness and that kind of thing. That is the true thing, and sadly in some ways, I must fight and forage through such intensely crazy stuff to get there; and yet it is occurring in some way. I love this soft part of me, the writing and all of that.

It is such an open question as to whether my parents will fall back into supporting me. It is not that I totally need that, it would feel great to have those touches of home. Then again, there is the notion of leaving God in control, and what is to be, for me, is to be, I can appropriately fight hard, as I need to, as some people have truly discovered, perhaps my roommate, and Rick Bishop among others recently. I just want to do my thing; it is a shame, so many people fight me so much.

On the other hand, I heard a repeat of a talk by Joel Osteen recently, and it was with all the blessings, there are burdens too, and that makes a lot of sense. So while great things may be coming, as I trust that they are, there will always be burdens. The notion of wishing for life to be easy, may be a failing wish unto itself. That may have been one of the errors of Morey and Sondra early on, is the sense that they may have conveyed a false sense of security about the world.

Welcome to New England. In New England, there is little if any of that false sense of security; more of a dog eat dog mentality, which needs to calm down a tad; thus Calm Interventions, Inc, lol. That could be one of the great lessons of my life. Because yes Morey and Sondra gave me a sense of benevolence, which was basically good, and yet there were irresponsible elements on my part and theirs'. Now they have been more malicious. The more appropriate third position, would be to "restore"[61] the sense of benevolence, while reinserting the notion of an enhanced sense of responsibility. It was not that the benevolence was in error. It is more, that the benevolence without responsibility can get a tad reckless. So, the winning "position"[69] is to work towards benevolence with responsibility; not benevolence without responsibility, or not malevolence.

Today, December 28, 2016 I am recovering from a get together with Sophie yesterday. It was a pretty amazing get together. Our basic tenor seemed very good., We got some wonderful pictures. I believe I mentioned the sale of our old home in Cambridge. Well, that turned out be a miracle of some kind unto itself. My ex-wife's pasing allowed the house to be on the market. As I said, my ex-wife seemed to be moving to Oklahoma and those funds could have left with her, as she passed "peacefully" in Oklahoma. Instead the home was left to Sophie and Sam. I had no idea the house was on the market even.

---

[61] A word Sondra used with respect to relations with me, around 2005. [69] Another word introduced into the discussion by Sondra

Iceberg

I bought the house in 1990, for $172,500 or something like that. This little workers cottage sold again around October 25, 2016 for several times more than that at least. How about that for a turn of events. Sophie says they want to help out my housing situation. God seems to be doing some serious lifting at this point; I will step back in true wonder.

Although I am seriously fired up after the meeting with Sophie, I can see the ways that she has been brainwashed by others, and I get appropriately outraged about that. Still the basic parameters of our relationship are very good.

I have begun to hone in on Sondra's vulgarity as a factor in this situation and have taken that appropriate fight directly to her. Sondra, who urges fighting in others, is clueless herself about competition. Sondra has lived with a sense of entitlement in her small city environment for over eighty years. Those folks live in a strange world; it not totally strange that false, and very much at my emotional expense.

So, today December 29, 2016, Sam and I have been communicating. Sam informed me that he has been having extensive therapy. The situation continues to unfold. All of this relatively affirms that my families' actions are essentially evil. The system and these people want people to be ill, so that they can maintain a false sense of superiority. I smell Sondra and David all over this. It just sickens me on some level.

The positives are that Sam is being more forthcoming, in spite of their efforts to brainwash him. It is just another of their little booby traps, to try to get me down.

I cannot fathom a group of people so desperate to interfere in another person's life, so as to brainwash my children. Nevertheless, it is just one more obstacle to overcome.

Today, December 30, 2016 I found that I hit quite a note literally and figuratively. In the middle of the night, I relatively came to the conclusion that David was psychopathic, on some level. So I wrote a note along those lines to the family today. It seems plausible that the rational essence of the family was flipped by David's virtually perverse invasion of the family. If I am right, in this Assessment of the moment; then that it is relatively astounding: The effect that one person can have on a group.

Not that it is solely David necessarily; yet the possibility exists that one person substantially tipped the tenor of the situation so severely. It is a "fascinating" lesson to be learned for group dynamics; to see how prospectively perversely one person can affect a group as a whole. It is amazing that people can follow and/or be intimidated by an out of control personality type. Discovering this type of impact of a person with a personality disorder is a breakthrough unto itself.

That is the compassionate genius in play. David could well be the iceberg in this situation and a substantial part of the "work" is done. Time to market the book.

Well, here it is February 14, 2017, and I went one more round with respect to figuring out who is at source of this thing. After a solid stretch of pounding away at David and Nomi, appropriately, I might add; I seem face-to-face with Morey Myers again. I just sense this profound and fundamental irrationality on his part, and maybe I am really close to the answer on that.

Sophie showed up as I mentioned. Then a few days later, she identified a one bedroom condo for me in Newton, and evidently galvanized efforts to actually purchase the thing outright. The condo is due to close tomorrow. I also entered a court action, well at least to their attorney and am due a response soon. Morey's irrationality along with the outrageous mobbing of me, has caused much financial harm, as well as extraordinary emotional distress. They are also continuing to attempt to brainwash and alienate my children; and I find tht outrageous, as well as treating me like a pariah.

So, I filed the court action. It is not a great feeling; yet I made a commitment to Sophie, Sam, and me to see this through. I read a quote recently, along the lines: "If you go to take Rome; then take Rome." So here I go one more time. I have also done a lot of work to have God on my side, so I am not overly worried, I suppose. I must laugh at that last line, as it is not easy to totally not worry, and still a major element of this part of the journey is to trust God and the process along the way.

Yesterday, I had a wonderful breakthrough in that area, reading a quote or two that really inspired me. Also the notion that I am in this fight for Sophie's and Sam's sakes. Still, I cannot say that I like fighting. Perhaps I must meet the challenge head on and see what happens. Morey Myers has continually posed himself as virtually owning and controlling my life and this seems like a moment, when I appropriately confronted that issue. It is, what is, as we say in New England.

February 15, 2017 I find a little going back and forth, I am more back to Morey Myers begin a chief antagonist here. David is there as usual, and yet David's insane behavior is pretty much inspired by someone else. Everyone's insane behavior is inspired by others, for the truly psychotic, I suppose. Nonetheless, Morey and Sondra as parents and pontificators of lofty concepts, may well have a special role with respect to hatred and animus. On some level, this would be a real breakthrough in understanding, in and of itself, in identifying Morey's irrationality at root; yet something could be even deeper than Morey, in this situation.

A letter, I mailed today, referenced the notion of peeling away the layers of the onion. Perhaps Morey has such a convoluted defense system that virtually everyone is brought on board with him. The "outstanding" thing is how Morey presents such a pretense of rationality and normalcy on the outside. No one would ever guess. The absurdity and insanity on some level is of epic proportions.

Just for starters to have so much animus, jealousy and rage towards your first son, who looked up to you, in his growing years. Then to take one's marital break-up and use this as a vehicle and an avenue to inflict so much rage and animosity onto another is appalling. There is an extreme narcissism there, and yet it seems something more. I suppose it is sad on some level for a person to be so disconnected from himself. It is another reason, irrespective of the circumstances they have put me through this. I am just so delighted that I am who I am, emotionally attuned, alive and empathic. What a journey; inside another man's struggle, torment and ultimately progress.

Along with the fact that it is virtually all their creation; some people need someone to be "sick" in order for them to pretend to be well. Morey and Sondra, saw me surpassing them in some ways and created this phenomenally razor-edged system to keep me off balance and attempt to impede my progress. It is hard to say at times, who is the chicken and the egg at times, between the two of them and David and even Nomi. They can slow me down, they can hurt me, but they cannot ultimately stop me; rather the opposite they end up strengthening me.

I have been relying a lot on the sense that God knows what he (and/or she) is doing. This is all part of the process. What is amazing about this story is that I have walked the walk with ALL the spiritual things that you hear about, in this day and age. A lot of people follow affirmations and the like; but how many people actually live their lives or virtually bet their lives on the acceptance of God and goodness themselves? That kind of faith, along with hard work, is what I am betting on, with respect to my life and work. I have walked the walk with it, for twenty-one years and am believing in the return.

I am taking spiritual work, and spiritual blessing, with respect to sticking with something for so long. It is dealing with the emotional abuse of a family that is so challenging as well. It attunes me, to those abused within the Catholic Church, by their sense of a "father." It even leads me to a discussion of abuse itself. Why is it that people abuse?

To me, abuse reverts back to that spiritual emptiness of those who abuse. Those who truly have not found the light in their hearts, resort to clinging to others, and concocting AND controlling situations out of a desperate sense of longing. "Missing" is faith, in general.

Anyway, I forgot too, this morning that I took a step

forward on the forgiveness path, and pulling back yet another proposed court action. I am committing further to forgiveness today, and seeing how far that spirit and path can take me. Can forgiveness fundamentally influence others and prospectively induce them to turn over a new leaf? As I say, I am profoundly walking the walk to see how these things work. That is the only way to know for sure on some level; experience being a true teacher.

That is the unprecedented nature of my work and science. It is, at least a three step process. For one, I have been abused by these folks. Then two, I have fought back and survived. Then three, I start to discover their own weakness, and even possibly heal or at least forgive them, while still holding them accountable. Wow, that is an amazing reversal and work unto itself. Some people say what I am attempting is not possible and yet, I must play the cards that I have been dealt.

Yes, I am intrigued and testing out notions that most people can be reached in some way, and that love is an instrument that can reach people. It does take an extraordinary amount of commitment and determination. Then again, I have been presented with circumstances that require me to pursue things along these lines. Their capacity to keep my children somewhat brainwashed from me, ensures on some level that I will not give up. Not only did they create this nightmare of a challenge, but I take it, that God created this opportunity so that I can develop this science of understanding about psychopathy, emotional abuse and finding our inner strength.

It is this science of human behavior, as to how and why people function in emotionally impaired ways, and can we reach them through methods other than traditional psychoanalysis for instance. My science begins from a point of understanding the fear and pain that people experience, how these things effect them emotionally, and how we can do much better. For starters, my science centers around the notion that pain is often emotional, rather than a function of some psychological ailment.

My work points me in the direction, that it must be the pain and fear that people feel, that causes people to act in hurtful ways, more so than strictly psychological ailments. In this way, we can teach and change society in a better form. Well, here I am, at a rather miraculous juncture. Sophie and Sam led efforts to purchase and furnish a condo. I got the call this morning, after some discussion and am supposed to pick up the keys tomorrow. "Wowsie": as my late grandfather Samuel Z. Myers used to say. Similarly, in my work, I am moving towards calling this chapter the "Compassion Chronicles." The work is in, melting the iceberg, along with patience and perseverance as crucial elements.

When you are dealing with people acting in a totally irrational manner, we must draw strong boundaries, and even create penalties, as need be, and sometimes throw in some compassion, to move things forward. Once, we develop the understanding that it is really hurt people, who hurt others, then we can address them not only at the point of their actions, but at the point of their pain. Every human being desires attention and validation, for the most part; it is seemingly wired into our collective DNA. Once we start to do a better job of understanding our relatively appropriate needs for attention and nurturing; then we can develop a more emotionally intelligent, if not compassionate society.

Personally, I am beginning to address people like Nomi Stolzenberg and Morey Myers as much as I can from a position of compassion. When people are in a position of power and act the way they do, in large measure because they can get away with it, arguing with them or fighting can be fruitless. It has been a world of work on my part to start to see these people from the point of their injury, even though they have hurt me a great deal.

I have faith in Sophie and Sam. Sam seems to be somewhat vulnerable as a younger. I put a tad on his shoulders this morning, reminding him in the most gentle of ways that he made a possible error when he ran off from our home our temporarily in 2005. I just mentioned this to Sam, in a way of encouraging him to find his point of error, and work his way back. Although in fairness too; Sophie and Sam have been under unfathomable pressure in all of this, and I have been loathe to add much at all. It is all part of life and learning for Sophie, Sam and me.

So that seems to be all that I can do on that front for the moment. I am starting to feel ready to change the world for real. The preparatory work has been done for twenty-one years now.

APRIL 21, 2018

FROM CATERPILLAR TO BUTTERFLY: LESSONS FOR THE WORLD

So here, I am more than a year since I last wrote. I moved to a condo in Auburndale, MA. I have been editing for the last year, and not writing. So now I can put somethings better in perspective for you. The process I was describing, and still in some ways continue to describe is the element of having been under an indescribable emotionally abusive crucible. The combination of the forces of the divorce system, a psychopathic family system, and the leftovers of a Borderline Personality now deceased ex-wife, represent a portion of society's efforts to put the clamps on me, to bring me down, to virtually destroy me.

Not on my life. My story is an incredible one, of a person's perseverance to overcome, a certain kind of cruelty, if not evil in our world, as I say it is an assault on our mindset. It is fascinating when that assault is led by your own family of origin; they of evidently deep narcissistic, if not profound psychopathic roots.

Today, September 7, 2018, I believe I threw down with the sense that David Nathan Myers, my younger brother is the one with the deep personality disorder I will proceed on that understanding until further notice. What I am saying is that I endured, essentially a thirty year psychological, financial and social assault on epic proportions. Indeed, it made me much the better and stronger, more on that perhaps later.

What is vital for people to know at the moment, is that the great evil of our times, will in the most part be occurring through psychological and emotional assaults. Those who experience narcissistic and psychopathic assaults have experienced something from another planet. The pain caused, the assault on rationality, the senseless nature of it, to use the word of my daughter are "indescribable."

What happened in my situation is that the entire family dynamic got turned upside down, as in up equals down, and down equals up, to borrow an Alice in Wonderland reference. The heinous nature of emotional/psychological abuse is that the abuser depends on be able to function in a stealth manner, undetected, and perpetuating the abuse, while attempting to make the other person, look crazy. That simple definition of "gaslighting" I attribute to Kirsten Powers of CNN and USA Today renown, who expressed along the lines of "a crazy person, making another person look crazy…"

Due to his charm and charisma, and faux sense of victimhood as a younger brother, David for one, was able to wield and turn a whole familial situation against another, a largely imperfect and yet profoundly innocent person in me. Over the past thirty years, and especially the more than twenty two beginning in late March, 1996, I was that very caterpillar struggling and working to become a butterfly of sorts. The unfathomable pain that I was forced to endure, became the laboratory for me, to grow and change so immeasurably as a person, a swell as to develop a way to change the world for the better.

Personally, and I must begin by saying that it was the combination of the unfathomable emotional abuse AND my having a profound purpose, centered around Sophie and Sam, my life and the world that forged the crucible for this extended growing experience. Spiritually, it is the sense that the among of adversity that we encounter has the seeds for equal or greater opportunity, as earlier attributed to Og Mandino. The key element being, the discover of our inner strength; that part of us that will not quit; that will take any and all obstacles as a challenge, and thereby opportunity. Being faced with unbearable pain of emotional abuse, I chose to "dig in" to choose another phrase of Sophia and make my stand. As I say, the rewards were not merely in the outer goals, which are virtually always uncertain. The richest rewards are the things that start happening inside of you.

Characteristics such as immaturity and an inherited temper, were chiseled and melted away over the course of years and decades. Stubbornness were ironed out into determination with subtle and strong differences. Respect for myself and others landed on my shoulders in ways that would become pillars of my very being.

Maturity, wisdom, calmness, gentleness, compassion,

and vision became fruits of the many fields of pain and patience and commitment that I cultivated. It was that acceptance of things happening for a reason, along with the development of purpose that have made it all so worthwhile. In learning so much about emotional abuse and the assaults of extreme narcissism and psychopathic behavior; it became my sense over time that I had a responsibility to share such things with the world.

We are still pretty much in the dark, with the things pertaining to emotional abuse, and topics I reference. Defaming, ostracizing, mobbing, excluding, bullying and all kinds of related non-violent behaviors become "incendiary" weapons of our time, as brutal in many ways, in some even worse than a gun or knife, given the duration with which the cruelty can continue. It can be this unfathomably painful and grim situation for those who encounter emotional abuse, amounting to a form of torture, in dealing with a person with a deviant mindset.

The devastating nature of emotional abuse descends because, for one, the emotional abuser often depends on surprise and sabotage; having built a superficially trusting relationship with the target. In that way, perversion takes place, because a person falsely builds trust and then uses the pulling of the rug and then the assault to create a virtually cage like situation, where the person becomes trapped emotionally, financially or otherwise. So my journey over the course of over twenty-two years is unto itself, a message to those being abused, to not give up and keep that internal light burning; whether you consider it purpose, faith, trust or sheer doggedness.

My story is ultimately a wake-up call of massive

proportions; well beyond the admonishments of say Bob Woodward, whose focus is on President Trump and the political process. As Barack Obama even said recently: "Trump is a symptom." Unfortunately, even with the hyper fasciation on the political process these days by media, activists and candidates; I do not believe the answer resides currently in the political process.

The challenges facing America and the world right now are of a much deeper spiritual nature. Lovingly I say to our dear country we have allowed corruption and dishonesty to take roots at major levels. A society cannot thrive in the long run, if there is anything less than honesty at its core.

In the last week or so, I filed an assertive Reconsideration to a Judge's ruling on my familial situation, essentially laying out that the American court system, has traversed so far from our cherished American ideals. I had to move towards what I call my "miracle angle;" that of setting forth things ultimately in a positive and constructive way. As Gandhi said: "Everything must be done with love when speaking truth or else the messenger and the message will be rejected."

THE AMERICAN CHALLENGE: WHY MY STORY WILL CHANGE THE WORLD FOR THE BETTER

So the genius ultimately of my work is to work towards a shift in the American mindset. We may not in good measure realize it, but the combination of a corruptive spirit and the infiltration of psychopathic and extreme narcissistic thinking threatens to cripple our beloved country. My aim is to induce a shift in the mindset of our country; seeing if I can take our collective mindset all at once, with me like a shrink on a couch or even a masseuse, and see how we can restore our basic goodness at our root.

The basic message of my life and work is my survival, is my growth from caterpillar to butterfly, like diamond from coal. I do not know everything, but I know the degree of emotional abuse and hatred that I received and overcame, is of once in a millennium proportions, record-breaking and ALL that kind of thing. It is unprecedented for a family to so deceitfully and atrociously attack one of their own for so long, for so little reason.

Then mix in, the astonishing aspects of a court system, acting with impunity and recklessness; and even further an ex-wife who was used to be as vicious a tool, as could be mustered against me. I am not talking about for a year or even a decade. This very month marks thirty years since the assault materialized fully.

I will tell you a little story. At one point, in the mid 90's or so, my ex-wife had some relatives come and stay with us. At one point, I took a few of them to Fenway Park for a baseball game. We ended up in the bleachers, about four of us. Surrounding us, were a bus or two loads of really drunken guys. A stand off almost ensued with one of our guys, these guys were belligerent, virtually violent, and we were about an inch from all hell breaking loose.

I remember I sat as an intermediary for at least fifteen minutes, with my elbow in a certain position, feeling like if it moved a quarter of an inch the wrong way, a huge brawl would result, as one of our guys was not backing down from anything. Miraculously cooler heads prevailed. In the same way, on a much grander scale, I had this massive wall of pressure posed against me for thirty years.

I could not immediately overcome it; and I could not retreat. I would make incremental progress and all of that, but still the basic dynamic was very much in place; this virtual wall of animus beginning from my family for thirty years. With deep inner beliefs relating to Sophia and Samuel, my life and the world; I could not yield barely an inch. Being kept in that emotional type of prison, as I say did enormous things, to me, in terms of my emotional growth and maturity.

I chose also to take an episode of such gargantuan proportions as an opportunity, responsibility virtually to change the world for the better. While it may be harder to understand than Democrats and Republicans, I maintain what happened in my life, is a revolution for humankind to study, learn and grow from, with my loving encouragement.

Speaking of loving, I am working still on the notion of forgiveness for my family. Forgiveness is part of the miracle angle, with respect to, if anything seeking a restorative type of justice not in any way a retributive one, even encouraging an education experience, more than a punitive one.

My family took to an extreme, the very things that society is struggling with right now; in terms of being obsessed with economic success, without paying heed to the morality or surely purpose that must reside underneath our actions. We have unleashed somewhat sadistic qualities, in terms of our internet and national conversation. My loving encouragement is that we can earn as much money and more, by playing by appropriate rules, and even incorporating kindness and basic decency into our dynamic.

Fear is at that core; and our life and ways, must be much more about out trust. Look, none of us really know the ultimate answer, but trusting rather than fearing has to strengthen us for any battles we must face. Having a sense of decency and clarity of conscience gives us confidence to proceed towards our future.

Once in a millennium and the lessons that follow:

So the thing is I believe that my story is a once in a millennium type of story. Why you might ask? The perfect storm for one of courts, ex-wife and family. The last point is perhaps the most telling one. It is "indescribable" to use Sophia's word to have a situation where your own family of origin turns against you for so long, with so little substantive reason and with such intensity. It is like surviving a giant hurricane or asteroid impact.

I mean, I really never heard of such a thing. For unknown to you; for a family to essentially just haul off and start hating you one day mercilessly is like something you can never anticipate or barely understand. It has lasted for thirty years at this point more or less, more in terms of the seeds were sown before that and less in terms of the most vicious facets kicked in around March 22, 1996.

Hatred of this sort is just a phenomenon. At this point, I have emotionally removed myself enough to see it as a phenomenon unto itself, and really not anything that I am a part of; thankfully. At my best moments, I suppose that is victory, to not be hurt by it so much, and rather to be standing outside of it, describing it. Is it psychopathic? Yes, surely in part. Still, it could be more, or less.

Meaning that maybe on some level there is an illness or a rashness of thinking on my sister-in-law Nomi's part of something on David's part and somehow this tornado of a mindset just began. David needed an enemy. To the degree he struck first and viciously, I surely run the risk of people thinking that it is me, by even responding.

That is one of the challenging points that I am making: That there is such a thing as truth, at least relative truth that goes beyond mere opinions. My younger brother David Nathan Myers, thirty years ago, this month randomly jumped into my life from 3000 miles away and starting making berserk characterizations of me, with virtually no basis or connection. One part of me, could be forgiving; the competitive part of me, could work to smash his arguments.

That is a work thirty years in the making, is part of the terrain, and reflects the difference in methodology between his slash and burn tactics and my slow plodding pursuit of truth and justice. The characteristics that David exhibits have become prevalent in today's day and age, of grabbing for and searching for a headline. Set people up and attack with no rhyme or reason. So it has taken me thirty years to work through and overcome such things. All the better.

My methodology is pure and reflects an antidote to today's tactics and an illumination of psychopathic like attacks that are being put out there, aimed to destabilize mainly decent people. What is missing in society today, is truth: A sense that doing the right thing, no matter how long it takes, is the right way to go.

Not only is truth a casualty of today, but the tactics imposed blur the lines much more greatly. Gaslighting; people become sabotaged, when their sensibilities are assaulted. This is why the theme Iceberg is so important. On the surface issues, can be presented in a way to make them appear benign, when there really are wolves in sheep's clothing. That Brett Kavanaugh appears to be less than fully honest, and has engaged in behaviors that could be atrocious is reprehensible; yet the manner, in which his nomination has been sabotaged is no better.

Missing is purpose, regarding the true betterment of our great country. Each side is so beholden to winning that our basic values are assaulted. Maybe Jeff Flake was right, if he can really uphold a position of strength and decency, although it kind of seemed political.

The event itself and why it will change the world.

The amount of force that was expended to try to take me down was of other world proportions. My deep-rooted parents, a court system, lawyers and judges, an insane acting brother and his formidable wife, a highly erratic and vindictive ex-wife; ALL aligned against me for twenty-five years more or less. That is the unfathomable things, without barely a whit of reason in twenty-five plus years: No Thanksgivings, graduations, birthdays….nothing.

Hatred of this type is not passive either; it is active, not just by how cruel people will be, but by what they withhold as well, in terms of a place in the family, love, affection, you name it. That was the wall of animus irrationally and pointlessly posed against me for more than twenty-five years. So, that very pressure itself was the thing that moved me from coal to diamond capacity in my life.

It is a wall of hatred, and you cannot retreat an inch for the most part, because your children, your life, your values are seemingly on the line virtually every minute. Think about it; twenty-five years of twenty-four seven, head-to-toe pressure. As I say, for one, it was the unfathomable learning experience in my life, in the world even.

Eye-to-eye with hatred, gaining ground sometimes, not yielding. It is the "fascinating" thing of what being in such a pressurized situation will do to you. Literally, it will make or break you. So, it made me.

The personal characteristics that I describe, with respect to growth, such as patience, determination, not stubbornness, care, compassion, endurance, faith, the list goes on and on. Both the gravity of the emotional and psychological persecution that I faced AND my commitment to seeing it through produced greatness, a wisdom.

For one, as I say, it was surviving the sheer magnitude of the emotional impact. Think again of an asteroid hitting earth and the devastating impact that it would have. Ultimately the collective effect of all of it, landed at my feet. A crater created, yes; and with me standing on the brink looking towards the horizon. [62] Being able to "objectively"[63] to stand an look at what occurred is a huge victory unto itself, given the opposition. Developing an agenda to help the world is icing on the cake.

It may be my slight bias, in terms of believing in God, the spiritual and things happening for a reason, but I choose to believe "objectively" that this is one of the stories of the millennium. To the degree that it was meant to happen; it can't be just for me, it must entail my interest in sharing this story and experience with others.

---

[62] Synchronicity of sorts in that "looking towards the horizon" is a central passage of "Their Eyes Were Watching God;" the hallmark work of Zora Neale Hurston, the African American writer, who I wrote my Masters thesis at Harvard about. In enduring optimism Zora encouraged Janie, the heroine of the book, to keep looking towards the horizon.

[63] I must again note the word "objective;" as in the moment when I went to ask Morey and Sondra Myers for emotional support and Morey replied they must be "objective;" just the support one needs from ones' biological parents in the midst of a challenging divorce. Their capacity to turn against me, remains one of the staggering events of all in this. Anyway....

THE GERM OF NARCISSISM AND PSYCHOPATHIC BEHAVIOR

On some level what this entire inquiry reveals is the germ of hatred, narcissism and psychopathic behavior in our culture. Let's say it is to me, the social cancer of our time: The animus and bullying posing as strength, when it is really weakness; the corruption within American institutions including legal, political and probably financial, and most egregiously people running to their base and/or profit-point, instead of looking at the effect of their actions on society. Lovingly I would call out Chris Cuomo of CNN, who bless his heart tries on some level to bring a more elevated level of discourse. Yet, in calling out Fox News hosts this morning, Chris does not acknowledge how CNN is not being fully honest at this moment. CNN played a huge role in creating the Trump presidency, by its insatiable coverage of the Trump campaign. CNN may be a magnet for a certain political perspective, but it has moved away from its capacity of being a fair and non-partial presenter of the news at this moment.

Then again, such things are but symptoms of our larger societal illness and/or germ. Narcissism and its extreme iteration of psychopathic behavior are reflections of the germ within our culture, a cultural cancer even, that we must address. The disease is profit without purpose, stridency without empathy, and bullying weakness posing as strength.

There is a germ within us; that we must understand and purify. To me, this germ takes precedence over every other real and imagined threat. Without articulation, definition and understanding of our shared purpose, we become sharks and barracudas, ducking in an out with one another, especially in this day and age of "vetting" and investigation and virulent opinions without concern for another.

Maybe in its simplest sense this Iceberg element, is the germ of hatred. It is more complicated than solely hatred, with respect to things such as psychopathic behavior, narcissism, rage, jealousy and related cousins; yet it comes out in the form of hatred.

I am going to stop writing here, and pledge that in the main, those who read this book, in its entirety will have their lives in some way or form changed for the better. I am not certain, if I can call this book a Bible; the Bible of self-help for the twenty-first century, how about that. My story is ultimately so shocking that it represents the earth-moving, like the old Carole King song, lol; a spiritual shifting of the landscape towards bringing a more peaceful, communicative world.

On some level, while this book, is an end of a juncture for me; it is just the beginning. The beginning of a new human epoch. Let's make the journey together.

OCTOBER 30, 2018

Reclaiming Our Humanity

Compelled by events in Pittsburgh and the general rancor I our country; I must go on, for one more round at least. Our country is facing a scourge and animus; teaching ourselves and one another the wrong things about strength. This afternoon, I paused by an-line comment board; the degree of racial animus and general hatred was appalling in just a five minute perusal.

The American illness that we face has to do with superiority; and the false sense of that predominance that some people feel, masking their genuine sense of unfortunate inferiority. Rather than developing an emotionally empathic, develop from the inside society; our levels of condescension are creating wounded soul, after wounded soul, who then carries forth woundedness and animus towards the next person.

I am working on solutions, call it the Calm Revolution, the Science of Inner Strength, the campaign for decency or some combination thereof. Our greatest danger is our animus; our incapacity to relate to, and work with one another. I am having some trepidation about laying my story all out there on the table.

On the other hand, I do not know everything, but I know that I have stumbled upon a human gene of hatred and animus; which can and must be countered by a shift in mindset leading to our basic goodness. I am calling it the remedy to hatred.

The remedy entails, imposing a sense of our basic goodness. Following that we must teach ourselves and others that goodness is our path to survival, prosperity and all we cherish. We must accentuate positive ways of interacting, cooperating and all kinds of things. There is much more to say; perhaps I will continue to do so. Thank you.

With warm regards,
Jon Myers
October 30, 2018
Written from Starbucks Auburndale today

EPILOGUE (PART 2)

Why this is the book that can change the world for the better.

What is hard to understand about emotional abuse, is that it is virtually invisible on some level. Many people will be tempted to snicker and say: "Aww, toughen up." Nothing could be further from the truth. Those who have experienced deep emotional abuse, are some of the toughest survivors on this earth. Emotional abuse attacks your mindset, your sense of well-being in such irrational ways, that people tend not to believe it. Or, only see the tip of the iceberg. In this regard, my heart and prayers, as well as potentially work goes out to those who have survived the insidious emotional abuse. You are the diamonds from coal, those who have suffered the most cutting dynamics on earth. Do not give up.

What makes my story, with all due respect so extraordinary is that the emotional and psychological abuse could go on for so long, as in thirty years, so viciously and most importantly in some ways, so vacant of any rational reason for its existence. As I say, I am reminded of a story a cousin of mine told of a pit bull that attacked her, and grabbed onto her ankle, as she was walking and would just not let go, until she finally shook it off. In the same way, although much longer, this family just began attacking me. Yes, I had my human imperfections and yes, I was not perfect, yet these things fit within human parameters of things, in the main, I needed to learn.

My families' assault was decidedly nuclear, and not human scale. My family, perhaps precipitated by my younger brother by my younger brother and his wife, Nomi; just began hating me, and would not let go of it, for more than thirty years and counting. I believe other people have experienced various degrees of this type of psychopathic, extreme narcissistic, borderline, or otherwise personality-disordered attack, but what makes my so extraordinary is the confluence of events, the perfect storm if you will.

That I could have had an ex-wife, who would so buy-in and play along with my families' hatred, and that that collective energy could be coalesced within our divorce court system is so extraordinary. What is also so extraordinary is that I survived it, and in some ways thrived as a human being. The perspective I choose to bring to bear at this moment is that I am standing back, virtually outside staring at this emotional asteroid that hit the earth. It seems, like an event for historical purposes that must be recorded, as well as laying the possibility of improving the earth on the table.

As I step back and look at this historic emotional asteroid, or even tsunami in terms of its realness, I see an unfathomable storm of energy that was released at me. I am kind of starstruck, for the moment, in terms of just seen something so enormous, if not horrific. It would be almost impossible for me to have survived that, and not feel like I have some message to share with this earth. But, who knows, maybe that is it; maybe it is just for me to survive; maybe even my survival is the story, or a good part of it. It is not so much for me to predict at this moment. I did watch a talk from Joel Osteen this morning, where he emphasized our being vulnerable, in terms of not having all of the answers and that kind of thing. It does add a touch of humility at the moment, which is welcome, as true humility is a warm feeling. To go on and fight, is the fight for decency, and a better way of looking at things, and who is to say how far I will get with that, at the moment. I have believed very far, although humility tempers that to a degree.

There is so much what the past twenty-three, even thirty years has done to me, in the process. The simplest way would be to say from boy to man, but it even seems beyond that, with respect to taking on an aura of knighthood or some cherished perspective. The premise of the Science of Inner Strength is that our basic goodness, can and must be the engine for our prosperity and success. Heretofore, people have competed irrevocably, with the sense that as Donald Trump stated in the "Art of the Deal:" life was about "dog eat dog." My premise is that our goodness, can produce as much, if not more success, and keep us more sustainable as a species.

The germ of hatred that I was exposed to for so long, has a grip on our culture, and intelligence will allow us to change that. Reasonable competition sure; that is okay. Destroying ourselves and the species in the process, no way. The message is clear, people want to make money and be "prominent" and all that. By a shift in the human paradigm we can encourage cooperation as the main mode of success, rather than harm.

That is what it is, for me: A shift in the human paradigm, our very consciousness if you will. I do not want to take away peoples' rights to make tons of money, to have major advertising and all that; rather I want to see our basic premise geared towards the good and cooperation. Think about it, the same among of resources will still exist, if not more. It more that we recognize our rights to do well, and for others to do well, also.

It is as if the world needs a timeout. Maybe brief, even a few minutes although it will probably take more, but still the essence of shifting our consciousness towards goodness. More than anything we need a shift in consciousness, a slight shift towards our greater good. Inherent in that shift is a confidence, a trust that we can and will get through virtually any challenge with which we are presented. The alternative is such a fear-based perspective, which has predominated our view for centuries, if not millennia.

Update: December 1, 2018: So I filed an Appeal or am in the process of doing so, in the Commonwealth of Massachusetts pertaining to my family, emotional abuse, and the Tort for the Intentional Infliction of Emotional Distress, even referencing the word "Evil" again. I am proud that I have gotten to his point. I am clear that I am approaching things with the Commonwealth on a respectful and calm basis, which is essential to even possible success. I set forth as an endpoint in the possible appeal, as the word "decency;" with my having the possibility of real engendering a turnabout in American society towards decency. While I cannot predict what outcome will occur, a turn towards decency would be among those I consider wonderful

In this way, it is as if my personal and professional lives have merged in these kinds of turnabouts, with rough edges being turned into greatness. I am not asking anything of others that I have not done myself. I have walked the walk. Thank you for today. I will also add that in my appeal, I have appropriately called out courts towards a sense of fairness, and even in the toughest of the tough Massachusetts; I at the last moment inspired my writing to the ideal of liberty, of which Massachusetts can claim a unique history in terms of the history of this country. It is a Science of Inner Strength principle, of finding that positive strand within people.

It is true, with Lexington and Concord, the Freedom Trail, Paul Revere and on and on; Massachusetts is a bedrock of American ideals. Both in terms of my walking the walk and Massachusetts own rich history, I have a right to call upon Courts to act in the realm of high American ideals. Indeed, the Massachusetts Appeals Court is housed in a wonderfully renovated building called the John Adams Courthouse.

Perhaps the main thing is that I did not give up. Patience and perseverance have been my twin guides, no matter how tumultuous and uncharted the mission. I have wanted to give people a sense of what circumstances can be created by dealing with extreme narcissistic, even psychopathic behavior. Second, I have desired to share that methods and a commitment to overcoming such a thing.

Finally, I look to pave a way for a better society. I pose this, as the book that will change the world for the better.

It is subtle to come to that understanding. It is not always possible in black and white pages to show the depth and the extremity of a psychopathic type of assault. Still, I believe when people tome to an understanding of the enormity of the event; that a family that irrevocably poses itself as ensconced in good, functions in such a deviant way psychologically; like a true iceberg effect, people will see the psychological crater that was created by this thirty year pattern of behavior, but for my efforts to heal things.

As far, as my family itself, I continue to work on encouraging them towards goodness, as I do the courts, and inculcate some forms of forgiveness; still I do not want the basic emotional asteroid of a crater to be lost. As a phenomenon it is right up there with the Grand Canyon and the Mona Lisa, at least having seen both in my eyes. That is my task from here in some ways: Creating some three, if not four dimensional understandings of this, or at least translating it into Inner Strength, and how we ALL can grow from here.

I must confess, I am at the café at Wegman's market, having had a Irish coffee, with "deck the halls" playing in the background, so I must laugh for the moment. No matter how great the struggle the human spirit can prevail. Peace and love to our world.

THE NEW PSYCHOLOGY

What I am presenting is that there is a new psychology in our world, defined in some ways by the Iceberg effect. The Iceberg, is that psychopathic mindset that takes us away from decency, and the true spirit of what it means and it can mean to be human. Through many facets America for one, has moved far away from our American ideals. Dishonesty runs at the core of many of our systems, from educational, with the new education scandal, to financial, political and surely as I am indicating divorce and legal.

It is as if a sadistic tyranny has gripped us somewhere and promulgates this dishonesty. Hmmm... when I use the word "promulgates" I am wondering if Bill Gates, is related to any and all of this. Mr. Gates, does seem humanitarian, and yet one wonders how much Microsoft influences, if not controls things, as I sit here on a Microsoft Pro 2-in-1. As I began this memoir with a sense of pointing to the basic honesty that is "missing"[64] from American culture is a sense of honesty.

Lying is accepted and approved at so many levels of society, which then moves us away from American ideals

---

[64] I do recall, that word be used by my biological father Morey Myers, with respect to his skewed sense of my perspective.

of "life, liberty and the pursuit of happiness;" and basic "equality" itself. If people feel no requirement to be honest; then how can we relate and achieve at any acceptable level. What I am getting at, is that there is no loss ultimately in being honest; by being honest, we stand to gain.

Key is the notion of acknowledging that people are somewhat infatuated with the idea of fame and fortune. Guess what, I am all for, fame and fortune, so long as the Science of Inner Strength indicates, that fame and fortune is tied into a positive purpose. Positive purpose itself, will help to restore honesty and improve the planet. Once we are real about our aspirations, as well as connected to the improvement, if not saving of our planet, we are, as we used to say in Scranton, PA: "cooking with gas." We can and could pursue prosperity, we must tie that in to improving the human condition. The plumber becomes a person, who provides invaluable resources in a valuable home. The teacher, is educating our young, and even the financial wizard is providing wealth that others can access.

The real thing of all this, is that I truly should not have survived what happened to me, let alone being on the track to thriving. The degree of emotional pressure that was put on me; I do not know everything, but I know is of unfathomable proportions. When you take what I consider to be, a psychopathic of some sort of assault from my younger brother, and his wife, add to that parents who betrayed you, then add the Massachusetts divorce system, with an ex-wife acting vindictively, with a relatively bloodthirsty attorney; that amount of emotional pressure, would destroy most people.

I am not bragging; it is my divine destiny. Each of us,

Iceberg

is born with different skill sets and strengths. It is just that mine was geared for this specific set of circumstances. Key is the notion that I had this unwavering commitment to my children, predicated in part, from the intensity of my own familial upbringing in Scranton, four intense grandparents, two ultra-intense parents, grade school, Temple all within a six square block area.[65]. My belief that my approach to my children and my life, impelled[66] me to not give up, to swim in the roughest and murkiest of waters, to ensue my appropriate goals.

The combination of that belief system, formed a protection against the forces of emotional, legal and financial abuse that came at me in waves and waves. Like a turtle's shell, I was protected and proceeded at a turtle's pace often. I interpret it, by choice as a divine event; or at least something that was supposed to happen. The emotional asteroid that hit earth around my life was epic. It then became up to me, to survive it; combat it, and ultimately learn from it, was an extraordinary example of inner strength.

There are things then about psychopathic behavior that I would like to share, as I have done. One is to, understand the degree of manipulation that exists in facets of our society today. There are those with personality types

---

[65] The blocks in Scranton, are surely square; laid out in sequence by the Presidents Washington, Adams, Jefferson, Madison, Monroe and so on.

[66] I recall, my younger brother, after ensuing an fiasco in New York City, where he was badgered out of town, from a position, somehow using the word "impelled." The headline in the article was about David Myers quits; there is no quit I in me, that is the difference.

of disorders, who prey upon their capacity to strike at, and then abusively mock others. A person may find themselves with their life under assault, defending themselves, and being "positioned"[67] as if they are the antagonist, and acting "irrationally;" when of course, it is the other way around.

Two, our systems themselves, have an abiding dishonesty, within them at this point. The latest scandal within the educational community is but one more. Our financial, political and surely judicial systems, have deep facets of being "rigged."[68] The media loves to flaunt notions of American institutions; well our pillars cannot stand indefinitely while, we insist on faulty degrees of honesty, to keep them upright.

My life was blessed in a way, to develop a sense of decency, and a sense of science as a way forward. Part of my thriving is to develop this sense that what happened to me, all I endured, overcame and learned was all about sharing and telling the lessons learned. In that regard, a sense of decency, if not humanity are surely at the top of our list. Related are the premises of the Science of Inner Strength in the bringing together of elements of Prosperity and Purpose, along with a sense of goodness.

So, we have gotten ourselves into a cycle of poor thought; predicated perhaps on the greed of big entities.

---

[67] The heinous usage of the word "position" occurred in my life, when my biological mother, said to me, that is not our "position." Incomprehensibly, having sought out the support of parents who had supportively raised me, without a memo, they were now telling me their "position" on me.

[68] A word used from as disparate of parties, as Senator Bernie Sanders, and President Donald J. Trump.

There are things sucking the lives out of our culture, and humans are forced into thinking there is, and they have no recourse. That is also the beauty of my story. No one is supposed to survive not only emotionally, but practically what I have been through. No one, is supposed to go through, survive and then live to tell about it; let alone with a positive restorative, ultimately non-condemning sense of justice.

But for the worst of the worst; it is mainly about learning, not punishing. We are a species, we are in this together. Ultimately my life and story represents a turn towards humanity. We cannot continue on our current course, and be mindful of the very survival of the planet. As big as climate change, healthcare, immigration and all the rest are; if we cannot talk to each other, under the rubric of a civilized community then, we will waste much energy, and stand a great chance of failing.

It is a new human philosophy, a new human understanding that we need, that is within our grasp. What I am proposing is not radical in the sense that most of us, cannot understand it. It is only radical in the course of our current dynamic; where politics and news are "weaponized" in ways to defeat others and not reach our true ideals.

As highly imperfect as our human process has been; ideals of the United States of America, in the way of "liberty and justice for all," are highly noble and worth establishing. My own experience with my families' emotional/psychological attacks, and our United States court system reveals that major facets of our current culture are retributive and destructive, AND very confused. We have confused our pursuit of success and finances with a ruthless dog-eat-dog kind of economy. I am not an inherent critic of our President, I am a believer in America and our process. I will mention that Donald Trump in the "Art of the Deal' did talk about our dog eat dog way of existence.

The point is, we must delve a better way. Like our earth must become sustainable, tires on a car must last; we must develop a better way of human interaction and communication, or we will wear out, at best. Reversing the human paradigm, if even adjusting it a tad, means coming from a place of our goodness. Being more in a place of mutual support to one another will not be a luxury, our surviving and surely our thriving will be based upon those kinds of positive interactions.

We get it. People want to make money and be successful. It is out of the closet; let's embrace it, and add parameters of fair and decent engagement. Once we acknowledge that everyone, or most of us desire the benefits and rewards of society, let's continue to reward true excellence, and establish more of a supportive environment for society. This shift is not about socialism, or any crazy accusation like that; it is about building a comfort in society, where our greatest enemy is not ourselves.

How many people really actively want to die immediately? Other than heinous acts of suicide bombers and tragically those terminally ill; most of want to live long and successful lives. We get it, we do not have to outdo one another in such a cutthroat way. Surely the lives of Russian, North Korean, not to mention European, African and others peoples are as sacred as ours.

Still, it is do America that I turn again. We do bear

Iceberg

a special responsibility and possibility of true leadership in the world. In that way, our best days, are ensconced in leading by example. In order to truly lead, there are holes, ailments within America, in a loving sense I bring to the fore. Our American ailment has allowed our basic mindset to slip into intensive dishonesty. What happened to me, reveals the iceberg. What happened to me, is not merely an assault on one human being; it is a reflection of deep illness in the American psyche.

That so much intensity was directed at me, again, I choose to interpret as a divine intervention. Whether one, walks that far with me, sees it as signs from the universe, "random"[69] events or whatever; I do not know everything, but I know that it is a reflection of "Every action having an equal and opposite reaction;" as in Newton's third law and/or in a related sense, "the amount of adversity we encounter is an opportunity for equal or greater success." Og Mandino.

Having been emotionally buried in thirty years of lemons, I can make enough lemonade figuratively at least for the planet. It is the very intensity of this experience over such an extended period that allows me to bring forth such a harvest of understanding for humanity. I am walking the walk, with the expression" Everything happens for a reason." For me, it is a matter of finding the reason.

---

[69] Random, was a word David Nathan Myers directed at me, regarding some chain of events, which once again, reveals the tendency of one, with a psychopathic type personality disorder: You cause the disarray, attempt to paralyze your target, and then accuse them of the very thing, that the person with the personality disorder is doing. This book is testament to the failure of that assault, if indeed it took thirty-one years.

Finding the meaning is at the root of The Science of Inner Strength. Any adversity contains the opportunity for hidden meaning, growth and/or opportunity. Coming to terms with the extreme narcissistic, psychopathic and personality disordered undercurrents in society is a vital understanding that our community, our country, and our world needs to attain.

We must begin to end the culture of dishonesty and deceit. To do so, we must get to the very psychology and mindset of our country. Somehow, we must slow the economic pace for a moment; call a timeout, and get companies, governments and people to reconnoiter. Our realignment must fall along the lines of: 1) Embracing our sense of economic success for our country; 2) Commit to fair and meritorious competition and; 3) Uphold our pledge to positive purpose that works to improve our planet.

These principles are not too hard, and will make our dialogue and planet better and more sustainable.

At the core of ALL of this, is my message to most of us; those who will not be aimlessly trapped in personality disorder kinds of things, those exemplifying the iceberg nature of things. Adversity and challenge are sacred events. We are living in challenging times, and we cannot despair. Whether one accepts my description of adversity, being a divine event; I do not know everything, but I know adversity and challenge gives us the opportunity to remarkably remake ourselves.

I have visions of creating billions of dollars worth of ideas and programs; nevertheless, how economically successful my things become in my lifetime, the one thing that can not be taken away from me, are the changes, growth and maturity that has unfolded in my life, due to this historic event. Becoming a calm, emotionally sober, determined man is the blessing of all blessings in my life, along with my children and my work, and we shall see what else is to come.

So, if and when adversity hits, call Calm Interventions for one AND embrace it in the sense that by defining your true purpose, you will, in essence find yourself, and begin to develop strengths that you could not have ever imagined that you had. This is why, our great country America, must embrace our challenges of today; and not back down. Instead, it is our opportunity and responsibility to find our inner strength. To me, that inner strength must be encompassed in diversity, our frontier and pioneering spirit, our irrevocable commitments to liberty and justice for all.

Perhaps I could conclude this memoir, in this juncture for real this time, by identifying the ten things that I have most learned or sought to convey in this work; because I understand, to some it will seem, a sprawling rendition, with themes that are not always evident. So here goes, my ten lessons to be learned.

JON MYERS TEN LESSONS OF THIS JOURNEY

1. Do not get angry. This is my personal favorite, and became ingrained in me, at key juncture of my life. It is not to say that outrageous things do not, and are not occurring. I have fought long and hard for things, and still do. The key is anger, is ultimately a sabotaging instrument. The key is to take the outrage, the sense of justice, and channel it into enduring and effective action. The urge for anger will be there, even if, especially if, it is justified and we must learn that the most effective action will be geared to positive and just change.

2. Emotional abuse is a wicked tool of our times. Partially by attrition, by partially by what we are teaching ourselves, and partially by having unbridled access to communication through the internet, we have allowed abusive and divisive actions and rhetoric to slip into our country. The human need to denigrate on the part of some, comes across as too appealing and enticing, when we are not thinking of our better selves. The emergence of extreme narcissistic, psychopathic and borderline personality disorders, brings a

new psychology and a new reality for most of us, the good souls of society.

3. Goodness is our strength. If abuse is ultimately a deep human emotional and spiritual weakness; then the opposite our basic goodness, our desire for appropriate advancement, our can-do attitude, our sense of community, are then our true strengths. We have gotten well off-course, and it goes beyond any one political figure or party. America has ideals written down on paper; we must assert ourselves, in terms of living up to them.

4. Understanding the role of David Nathan Myers, in my situation, provides insight into how one person, can affect a group dynamic. In the course of history, and again, "if we do not learn from history, we are destined to repeated it," as the adage goes; there is a shocking role that an individual can play in bringing about dictatorships and hatred to targeted groups. While, in my situation, the damage was directly done to vast numbers of people, the sheer intensity of a thirty-one year psychopathic assault is enormous. It is shocking to see, how so many people, not necessarily inclined towards badness will fall under the spell of charismatic, dogmatic leadership. Yet another reason to train with the Science of Inner Strength as developing the true you, is the key survival and thriving skill today.

5. Each of us, does have a sacred part of us. So much, in this day and age, so much of it, has been covered up

by society. Still, we see increased realms of self-expression in our youth today. The piece that is key to me, is to invoke values and appropriateness and a sense of decency among us; along with our self-expression. The true champions will be those, who find the truly sacred parts of themselves, and then learn to bring it forward appropriately and assertively. Such an approach is the way of the Science of Inner Strength.

6. Do not let anything trump your sense of decency and common sense. We know what is right; it is a matter of developing the courage AND appropriateness to stand for ourselves.

7. As much as possible do things with love and respect. It can be a challenge in these times. Still rise above the maelstrom of opinions and be willing to speak respectfully and kindly, even, especially with those who oppose us.

8. Be appreciative for everything. As a general habit gratitude and appreciation are vital skills in these times unto themselves, and to counteract those elements of entitlement, which threaten our decency, if not sanity. Be appreciative for all your experiences, as every single one can enrich you, with the right attitude.

9. As long as you know what you are doing, go at your pace. Take your time to do things right, and to do things well. Do not be fearful.

10. Trust, trust and trust. Contrary to our way of being raised, in many cases, develop a faith, a trust in better things, a sense that you will overcome. It comes back to seeing experiences as potentially[70] sacred events that are meant to occur, or at least provide profound learning experiences in our lives.

At this moment, March 31, 2019, as I sit in Café Nero, in the Burlington Mall, I am deeply committed to the human spirit; the diamond from coal; the butterfly from caterpillar, the lemonade from lemons. Practically, we must commit to decency and our collective humanity. Spiritually, it is a matter of finding that inner strength and acting in clear, calm and appropriate, if highly imperfect ways.

With love,
Jon Myers

---

[70] On this again, I convey gratitude to my late ex-wife, who introduced me to the game of Pente, based on the move of "potentials."

www.ingramcontent.com/pod-product-compliance
Lightning Source LLC
Chambersburg PA
CBHW022054150426
43195CB00008B/131